KT-196-333

THE
COMPLETE BOOK
OF
HOUSE
PLANTS

A Step By Step Guide
To Plant Care

Text
David Squire

Photography
Neil Sutherland

Design
Michael Morey and Claire Leighton

Commissioning Editor
Andrew Preston

Publishing Assistant
Edward Doling

Editorial
Gill Waugh

Production
Ruth Arthur
David Proffit
Sally Connolly
Andrew Whitelaw

Director of Production
Gerald Hughes

Director of Publishing
David Gibbon

CLB 2421
© 1991 Colour Library Books Ltd, Godalming, Surrey, England.
Printed in Italy by Fratelli Spada SpA.
All rights reserved.
ISBN 0 86283 859 2

THE
COMPLETE BOOK
OF

HOUSE
PLANTS

A Step By Step Guide
To Plant Care

DAVID SQUIRE

CLB

COLOUR
LIBRARY
BOOKS

CONTENTS

Introduction 7

introduction

Many homes appear so packed with indoor plants that it is sometimes difficult to imagine how the family themselves can find enough space to live comfortably. Other people are not so enthusiastic about houseplants, but few homes are completely bare of them. What, then, are the qualities that make houseplants so unique as to have that near magical quality to turn a house into a home? Essentially, it is because they are alive and create an ever-changing feature in a house.

Some people may enthuse over a collection of rare figurines, a carefully chosen gallery of pictures or a library of first-edition books. All of these bring interest and fascination to a home, but unlike plants they do not need day-to-day human attention. Plants demand such a close and harmonious relationship with the human element in their existence that they become an integral part of our lives. And for many people they offer the only daily contact with something that is alive, and in need of loving, regular attention.

Wherever you live, there are plants that will thrive in your home. Shaded or sunny rooms do not present a problem, nor do those with a northerly or southerly outlook, and there are plants to suit all temperatures. Both high-rise flats and apartments in towns and cities, as well as bungalows in the country, welcome plants.

The range of houseplants increases each year, with many of them being imported from nurseries in Europe and sold through nationwide shops in high streets and out-of-town shopping centres, as well as in garden centres.

The range of sizes and shapes of houseplants is amazing, from those that happily sit on a windowsill and bask in sunshine, to those that survive sunless and cool places in the home. Some climb and form screens packed with attractive leaves or flowers, while others develop into large, eye-catching plants that live for so long that they become as much a part of a home as a dog or cat. Indeed, it is not unknown for large and long-lived plants to be given pet names!

Some plants have a trailing or pendulous nature that makes them well suited for growing in indoor hanging-baskets. In a few homes they can be suspended from beams to create eye-catching focal points; or from wall brackets, perhaps positioned over a stairwell, to introduce interest to an often otherwise barren area. They can also be positioned over a low trough of plants to create a screen that divides a room.

The opportunities to use plants in the home are nearly endless, the only limitation usually being your own imagination. This all-colour book has been created to help you get the best from houseplants, to be able to identify them easily, know how to look after them and to use them in your home.

Plant psychology has, from time to time, been a fashionable talking point among houseplant enthusiasts. Some people take it seriously, while others disregard it as being unscientific and revealing an element of quackery. However, those who do believe that plants have a rapport with humans and are able to react to harmful thoughts about them can quote examples where lie detectors have been attached to plants, with startling results. The plants became agitated when harmful thoughts were made against them, as well as reacting on the entry into a room of people who had previously harmed them. Whatever your thoughts about this, it is certain that some people – even without a great deal of knowledge about gardening – have an empathy with plants and reveal an ability to grow them to perfection. With this book we cannot enable you to read a plant's mind, but we can show you how to give it the conditions it needs for healthy growth.

For each of the plants described in Part Two of this book we have created a 'Greenfinger Guide', which, at a glance, puts the secrets for success at your fingertips. These include the optimum winter and summer temperatures, the amount of light and water needed during winter and summer, the time of year and frequency to feed it, the humidity required, compost and when to repot, as well as how to increase your plant. We also suggest the height and spread of each plant, but be aware that plants which are left with their roots cramped in small pots, unfed and neglected, will never develop into normal-sized plants.

You may totally disregard all thoughts of plants having a form of nervous system, but consider the restful, peaceful and relaxing influence of plants in the garden, perhaps a glade of trees in early summer with sunlight filtering through a canopy of fresh green leaves on to a carpet of bluebells. Or the restful foil of a newly-cut lawn framing flower beds. Or blossom-packed cherry trees in spring when framed against a blue sky. Houseplants can create a similarly tranquil atmosphere in your home.

Each year the pace of life increases, with more and more demands and pressures being placed upon us. A restful atmosphere at home therefore becomes an essential part of our lives, somewhere in which to unwind. Houseplants are superb at creating such an atmosphere. If you have yet to become addicted to growing houseplants, buy one today and join the millions of plant enthusiasts who cannot live without them.

A miniature rose (right), or a basket of mixed plants such as ivy, hyacinth, primula, daffodil and asparagus fern (facing page) makes an attractive and colourful centrepiece in any area in the home.

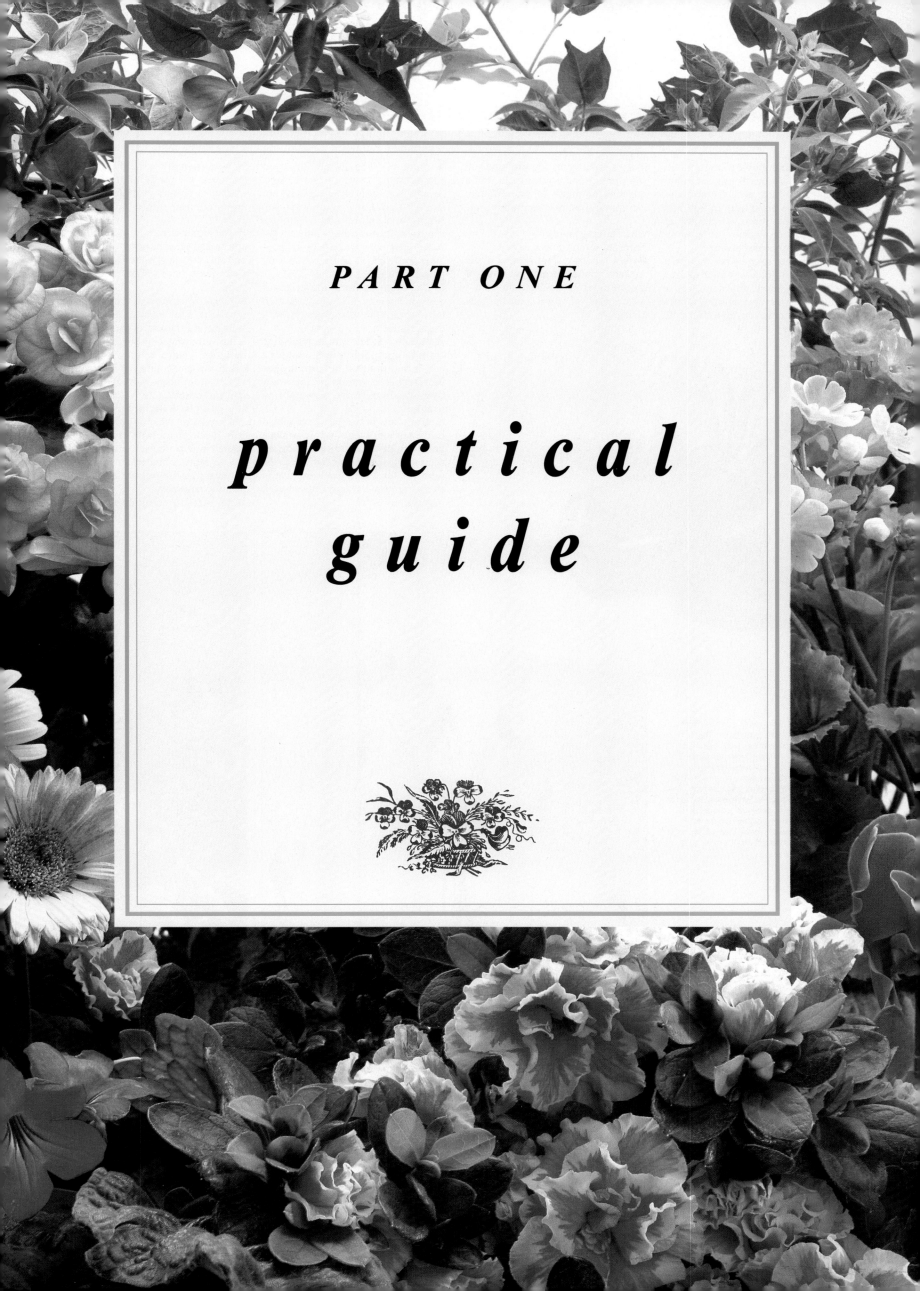

PART ONE

practical guide

choosing & buying houseplants

Choosing and buying houseplants requires just as much thought and care as when buying other items for the home. Indeed, some plants may remain with you for many years and become an integral part of a home – an essential element of the home landscape.

New plants enter homes in several ways: as a gift, because you like the look of the plant when displayed in a shop or garden centre, or from wishing to fill a space in a room and buying a plant to fill

it. If it arrived by the first two ways you will need to find a place for it, and a selection of plants to suit different locations is given elsewhere in this book.

When buying plants
There are several golden rules …
■ Always buy houseplants from reputable garden centres, nurseries or shops. Buying cheap plants from dubious sources may not be worth the financial saving.

Above: do not buy a plant that has roots growing through the pot's base. This indicates a plant that has been left in its present pot for too long, with subsequent restriction of growth. Plants severely neglected in this way seldom recover. The roots eventually become a tangled mat and even when potted into fresh compost and a new pot the plant does not grow properly. Some plants, such as chlorophytums, rapidly fill a pot with roots, then wander out of the drainage hole in a pot's base.

Right: plants that are in a 'poor' state never recover, even after receiving careful attention from the most experienced houseplant enthusiast. Do not buy plants with stems and branches bare of leaves. This Weeping Fig (*Ficus benjamina*) has been deprived of water, causing many leaves to fall off.

■ Don't buy houseplants displayed outside shops. In winter, such plants become thoroughly chilled and may not recover. Conversely, in summer they become baked by intense sunlight. It is plants with flowers or berries that chiefly suffer from extremes of temperature – these soon fall off or do not develop properly.
■ Don't buy plants that show signs of pests or diseases. Such plants seldom last long and they infect plants currently in your home.
■ Don't buy a plant with roots growing out of the drainage hole in the base of its pot. This is a symptom of a plant that has been kept in its present pot for a long time, resulting in its growth being retarded.
■ Don't buy plants with green mould on the surface of the compost, or slime on the outside of the pot. Again, these are signs that the plant has been kept in the same pot for a long time, resulting in stunted growth – a stage from which it may not recover.

■ When buying flowering plants, ensure that there are plenty of flower buds waiting to open. Avoid plants in full flower, as their display will soon be over.
■ Avoid plants with long, bare stems and an uneven appearance. They have probably been kept in the dark or where their shoots have turned towards the light.
■ Only buy those plants that are clearly labelled. For novice houseplant enthusiasts a plant which is not labelled is an unsatisfactory buy. Reputable nurseries, garden centres and shops ensure that plants are identified.
■ Do not buy plants with wilting, fallen or damaged leaves.
■ Avoid plants with a mass of stems and foliage but which are only in small pots. Such plants will have become starved and pot-bound, and may not recover when subsequently transferred to a larger pot. Conversely, avoid small plants in large pots.
■ Check that the compost is moist: avoid

plants where the compost is awash with water, as well as those where it is bone-dry. Frequently, plants are displayed on capillary watering benches, and these maintain the correct moisture content in the compost.

Getting your plants home

Getting your new plant home safely is the first step to ensuring its future well-being. Here are some guides to successful shopping for houseplants.

■ Make buying houseplants the last job on shopping expeditions. This avoids the risk of them being damaged by other purchases, or becoming exposed for a long time to cold or buffetting winds.

■ In winter, do not put plants in cold luggage areas of cars. Also, avoid these places in summer – they often become severely overheated.

■ Always put plants in shallow boxes, so that they are firmly held upright. Some garden centres and nurseries offer customers old boxes with moulded holes so that plants can be transported home safely.

■ Many nurseries when selling plants totally enclose them in a paper wrapper or polythene sleeve, and this is ideal for protecting them from knocks, as well as from cold winds in winter.

■ Avoid putting plants where young children and dogs can jump on them!

Acclimatizing plants to their new home

■ Get your new plant home rapidly and remove the wrapping. Plants left covered soon become distorted.

■ Place your plant in a moderately warm room, out of strong and direct sunlight, as well as away from cold draughts. Try not to knock the plant, as this may encourage buds to drop off.

■ Ensure that the compost is moist, but not totally saturated.

■ After about a week, move the plant into its permanent position. Flowering plants, however, are best put into their permanent positions straight away, as soon as you get them home.

■ Should a leaf of bud fall from a plant, do not worry. The plant will probably just be settling down – do not keep moving it, especially if it is delicate.

■ Keep foliage plants regularly misted. In winter, avoid soaking the leaves late in the afternoon and into evening. Preferably, the moisture should have dried before night, when the temperature usually falls.

Top: moss growing on the surface of compost and the pot indicates that the plant has been neglected, as well as watered excessively and kept in shade. Some plants, such as hydrangeas, that are placed outside during summer, often become covered with moss, but this should never be present on newly-bought plants.

Above: small plants in large pots, as well as large plants in small pots should be avoided. Large plants in small pots are deprived of nutrients and have insecure bases, while the compost in large pots with small plants is difficult to keep at the right moisture content. Additionally, the plant will look imbalanced.

Left: ensure that flowering houseplants have plenty of flower buds waiting to open, unlike this azalea, which has flowers that have opened, faded and withered.

displaying plants indoors

A few carefully chosen and thoughtfully displayed indoor plants can soon turn a house into a home and introduce a new and exciting hobby. The range of houseplants is extremely wide: many are superb when displayed on tables, others are ideal for floor-standing positions near patio windows, some are best in indoor hanging-baskets, while a few can be placed in brackets attached to walls.

The nature and size of a houseplant invariably indicates the best place to display it. Large palms require floor-standing positions, while small trailers are best in pots placed in wall brackets or grown in indoor hanging-baskets. However, for many plants there is a natural progression – first on a table or shelf and later on the floor, and for a small trailing plant first on a shelf, later in an indoor hanging-basket.

Plant containers

Clay pots have long been used for plants, their natural, baked-earth colour enabling them to blend with most plants. They have a rustic quality that does not compete for attention with plants, whatever their sizes, shapes or colours.

■ After some time in use, the outsides of clay pots often become stained with whitish salts from the compost. Also, moisture evaporating through the side of a pot keeps it moist and encourages the presence of algae. Whatever their decorative qualities when aged, clay pots are ideal containers in which to grow plants, especially when used in conjunction with loam-based composts. If, however, they become unsightly, they can be be smartened by placing them inside ornate outer containers known as cache pots.

■ Plastic pots are more modern inventions, formed of man-made materials revealing a clinical appearance that many people find more acceptable

Left: round and oval tables are enhanced by attractive containers holding either one or several low, small plants. Here are the Eyelash Begonia (*Begonia boweri*) and African Violet (*Saintpaulia ionantha*)

Far right: hanging baskets without built-in drip trays are best positioned outdoors or in conservatories, where drips of water falling on the floor do not matter. Indoor hanging baskets, however, must have drip-trays to catch surplus water.

Below: fireplaces can be brightened in summer by placing houseplants in and around them. Attractive cache pots – in a wide range of materials – bring further interest and colour. If the area is dark, occasionally give plants sojourns in bright positions.

indoors. It was in the late 1950s that plastic pots started to gain popularity, and are ideal for use with plants grown in peat-based composts.

■ Plastic pots are available in a wide colour range, as well as in different shapes – usually round but sometimes square. With their smooth surfaces, plastic pots do not reveal the presence of salts, although if placed close together and kept continually moist algae may eventually appear on them.

■ Clay and plastic pots have both advantages and disadvantages.

Cache pots and saucers

Plants – whether grown in clay or plastic pots – need to be stood in another container to prevent water seeping on to

Above: cascading houseplants, such as Spider Plants (left) and nephrolepis ferns (right), are eye-catching when displayed on

pedestals. Position in corners, where they cannot be knocked over.

polished surfaces. They can either be stood in plastic saucers or placed in ornate cache pots. These resemble ordinary pots but without drainage holes in their bases. They are usually attractive and are chosen to harmonize with a plant's leaves or flowers, as well as the room's decor.

Indoor hanging-baskets

Indoor hanging-baskets are becoming increasingly popular. They enable vertical space, perhaps under open-plan stairs, in an entrance hall or either side of a patio window, to be filled with colour.

Indoor hanging-baskets are very much like the ones used outdoors during summer to display a range of upright and trailing bedding plants, but they differ in one essential point. Outdoor hanging-baskets drip water over the area beneath them, whereas indoor types are fitted with drip trays to catch the surplus moisture. Outdoor types can be used in sunrooms and conservatories, where it may not matter if water drips on the floor. However, it is best to use an indoor type, even in a sunroom or conservatory. In winter, water splashing on plants below may encourage diseases.

Indoor types are usually ornate and visually more appealing than outdoor baskets, which rely on plants smothering the often unattractive framework. Indoor types have to be attractive, as they are visible throughout the year and may not become totally covered with foliage.

Many types of indoor baskets are available, some with a simple framework and a built-in drip tray, others formed of macrama, with plastic drip trays resting in their bases.

Hanging-baskets, whether indoors or outdoors, become very heavy, presenting a considerable strain on the basket as well as the securing point. Outdoor baskets are taken down, emptied and cleaned each autumn, when both they and their supporting brackets can be checked. Indoor hanging-baskets, however, are usually left in position for several years, and it's advisable to check these every few months.

The range of plants for use in indoor hanging-baskets is wide and includes foliage and flowering plants.

Some of these are suggested here.

Trailing flowering plants for indoor hanging-baskets:
◼ Basket Begonia
Begonia tuberhybrida pendula

◼ Christmas Cactus
◼ Easter Cactus
Rhipsalidopsis gaertneri
◼ Goldfish Plant
Columnea x banksii
◼ Goldfish Plant
Columnea gloriosa
◼ Goldfish Plant
Columnea microphylla
◼ Italian Bellflower
Campanula isophylla
◼ Ivy-leaved Geranium
Pelargonium peltatum
◼ Lipstick Vine
Aeschynanthus lobbianus
◼ Lipstick Vine
Aeschynanthus raddicans
◼ Rat's-tail Cactus
Aporocactus flagelliformis
Rhipsalidopsis rosea
Schlumbergera buckleyi
Schlumbergera russelliana
Schlumbergera truncata

Trailing foliage plants for indoor hanging-baskets:
◼ Devil's Ivy (several variegated forms)
Epipremnum pinnatum
◼ Emerald Fern
Asparagus densiflorus 'Sprengeri'
◼ Mother of Thousands
Saxifraga stolonifera
◼ Rosary Vine
Ceropegia woodii
◼ Spider Plant
Chlorophytum comosum
◼ Swedish Ivy
Plectranthus oertendahlii
◼ Swedish Ivy
Plectranthus coleoides 'Marginatus'
◼ Swedish Ivy
Plectranthus parviflorus
◼ String of Beads
Senecio rowleyanus

Many other plants have a trailing and cascading nature, but to be dramatic

Right: troughs with plants arranged in a pyramidal outline are superb when evenly positioned in the centre of a wall.

Below: displays with plants in triangular arrangements are ideal for positioning near to corners. The tall side should be the one nearest to the corner.

Below right: clinical and modernistic displays are created by using several stiff and upright plants, such as Mother-in-law's Tongue (*Sansevieria trifasciata 'Laurentii'*).

Facing page: in summer, large fireplaces packed with brightly-coloured and variegated houseplants become focal points. Both upright and cascading plants can be used.

they need to have a large amount of foliage. Those less well clad are better grown in pots and either positioned at the edge of a shelf or placed in a pot in a wall-mounted bracket.

Not all plants used in indoor hanging-baskets need to trail. If the basket framework is formed of macrama, and has a slim design, an upright plant such as a Peace Lily (*Spathiphyllum*) presents a simple yet effective display when set in it.

Because plants used in indoor hanging-baskets usually act as focal points in a room, they must always be kept in good condition. This includes keeping the compost moist to prevent flowers fading rapidly, as well as the edges of soft leaves becoming brown. As soon as a plant starts to lose its attractiveness, replace it with a fresh one. If the old plant is a long-term foliage type, place it in a position where it can recover to full health. Sunrooms, conservatories and greenhouses are excellent areas of recuperation if a suitable temperature can be maintained in winter.

Wall-mounted pot holders
These are usually formed of an ornate metal bracket which can be fixed to a wall to support a plant, as well as a saucer in which excess water can be trapped.

Wall brackets used in conservatories do not always have saucers in their bases, thereby allowing water to fall on the floor surface below. As well as creating puddles, this type sometimes allows water to run down the wall, where it soon creates an eyesore, especially on light-coloured walls.

Trailing flowering or foliage plants are the types mainly used in wall brackets. These are usually displayed singly, creating a large and dominant display. However, if the supporting bracket is large, several small plants can be set in it, each plant in its own pot. By leaving them in their own pots, different moisture needs can be met. For instance, an Umbrella Plant (*Cyperus alternifolius*) looks startlingly attractive when positioned against a white wall, with smaller plants trailing around its

sides. The Umbrella Plant likes its roots in water, whereas the others may not.

Many of the small, irregular-shaped, trailing plants are ideal in wall-brackets. These include the Wandering Jew (*Tradescantia fluminensis*), Silver Inch Plant (*Zebrina pendula*), Teddy Bear Vine (*Cynotis kewensis*), Basket Vine (*Oplismenus hirtellus*) and *Senecio sieboldii* 'Mediovariegatum'. Trailing flowering plants – again with an unbalanced outline – are wonderful when against a wall.

Plants in floor-level troughs
Some large plants have an architectural elegance that demands a solo position, perhaps near a patio window. There are many others, however, which are equally beautiful, but are small and best displayed in a group.

The size of a floor-standing trough needs to be in proportion to the position in which it is placed. For instance, a 90cm/3ft long trough positioned somewhere along an extremely long wall will look wrong. Whereas if placed by

the side of 1.2-1.5m/4-5ft long wall, and adjacent to a patio window or door, it will appear planned and be an asset to a room.

Most troughs are 0.9-1.2m/3-4ft long, 15-20cm/6-8in deep and about the same in width. Troughs longer than this become cumbersome and difficult to move when full of plants.

To prevent water from the pots seeping through the base of the trough and onto the floor or carpet, place a 5-7.5cm/2-3in deep plastic tray in its base. This should fit snugly in the base of the trough. A layer of large pebbles – or a 12-18mm/½-¾in deep carpet of shingle – in the base of the tray ensures that the bases of the pots do not rest in water if, by chance, the plants are watered excessively.

Space out the plants according to the spread of their foliage. If plants are to be left in a trough for a long period, pack moist peat between the pots. This keeps the compost moist, as well as cool in summer.

Foliage plants – both squat and upright types – look superb in floor-standing troughs. Trailing plants are not successful in low positions, as they soon trail and spread over the floor. However, those plants with a slight cascading appearance help to soften the edges of troughs. A mixture of upright and squat plants is better than a design formed of plants of a similar size. For instance, try a mixture of a Dumb Cane (*Dieffenbachia picta*), Rex Begonia (*Begonia rex*), Spider Plant (*Chlorophytum elatum*), Aluminium Plant (*Pilea cadierei*) and a small-leaved Ivy (*Hedera helix*) trained upright rather than trailing.

Floor-standing troughs which have one end near to a corner of a room are best when arranged with a tapering design, high at the corner end and tapering to the other.

Troughs can also be used to form part of a room divider, where both indoor hanging-baskets and climbing plants can be used to create a mixed screen.

Troughs on legs
These are similar to floor-standing troughs – usually 60-75cm/2-2½ft long and wide enough to take a 13-15cm/5-6in pot – but with a strong leg at each corner. Troughs on legs are invariably slightly smaller than floor-standing types; if excessively large they eventually collapse.

A plastic drip tray is needed in the bottom of the trough to prevent water dripping over floors and carpets.

The types of plants that suit troughs are those which are fairly low and with leaves and flowers that look attractive when viewed from above. Small, trailing plants are also suitable, softening the outline of the trough. A few upright plants help to create a variety of shapes, but take care that they will not cause the trough to topple over.

Similarly to floor-standing troughs, a layer of clean shingle in the bottom of the drip tray ensures excessive watering does not cause waterlogging. Also, packing moist peat between the pots keeps the compost cool and reduces the frequency of watering.

Many displays in troughs are, unfortunately, unplanned, with plants of

differing heights in a higgledy-piggledy fashion. A planned outline, however, invariably creates an eye-catching effect. If a trough is placed in a corner, taper the design with the highest point nearest a corner. Alternatively, if a trough is positioned mid-way along a wall, a pyramidal outline is attractive. For a modernistic home, with a clinical appearance, a trough filled with several Mother-in-Law's Tongue (*Sansevieria trifasciata*) presents a rectangular shape. However, troughs filled with just one species usually appeal more to devotees of room design than to those who appreciate plants as living occupants in a home.

Large floor-level displays

Many houseplants are so dominant and distinctive that they can be displayed on their own, perhaps in a corner, near a door or by the entrance to a patio. Other plants are more companionable and better displayed in groups.

To create a balanced and attractive collection, include both foliage and flowering types, some tall, others squat and bushy and able to hide the bare stems and the pots of larger plants. To protect the floor, stand each pot in a plastic saucer. A wide range of saucers is available, suiting all sizes of pots.

More formal are 'stepped' corner display units, enabling plants to be arranged at different levels. Such units are superb for displaying plants, but usually introduce too much formality for most rooms. They are best used in offices and the foyers of flats. Slightly less formal, but still creating a dominant display, are large containers – either square or corner-shaped – which enable a design just at one level to be created. When forming one of these displays, don't be frugal about the number of plants used – and be prepared for it to be expensive. These large display units look silly when adorned with just a few plants.

When plants are grouped together they create a micro-climate, producing a humid atmosphere which benefits all of them. Also, grouping plants makes misting the foliage much easier than if they were displayed individually.

Within each group of plants, use several which can be left as permanent features. These include large foliage plants – but avoid those which create dense shade for plants set around them. As small plants at the base of a display finish flowering or cease to be attractive, remove and replace them with fresh types. As well as tidying up the plants, changing the display every few weeks helps to revitalise the arrangement and to create further interest.

In addition to the containers where plants, together with their pots, are just placed inside a container, there is also a wide range of large and small self-watering containers available. In these, plants are set directly into the compost. First, a 2.5-5cm/1-2in layer of clean pea shingle is placed in the base of the container, with the plants then set in a peat-based compost. When planted, the surface of the compost can be made more attractive with a covering of shingle, expanded clay particles or, for very large containers, large granite chippings.

In the base of each container there is a water-level indicator to ensure that the plants always receive the right amount of water.

Some of the larger of these containers have small wheels built into their bases to enable plants to be easily moved around the floor.

Illuminating plants – spotlights

Light is essential to plants, but its value primarily depends on its quality. Sunlight is vital for the growth of plants. As a source of energy, it activates the chlorophyll – the green pigment in leaves and stems – and creates chemical energy that combines water and carbon dioxide to form starches and sugars. Plants obtain water from the soil and carbon dioxide from the atmosphere. The process involves the release of oxygen from water (which is formed of oxygen and hydrogen) into the atmosphere. The cycle of oxygen and carbon dioxide enables other life to exist on this planet.

Light from tungsten-filament bulbs – the type most often used indoors – is not

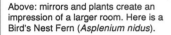

Above: mirrors and plants create an impression of a larger room. Here is a Bird's Nest Fern (*Asplenium nidus*).

Above right: two small and ornate mirrors on a corner table in the corner of a room highlight this Persian Violet (*Exacum affine*).

Facing page top: a tilting mirror brings extra interest to this Gerbera.

Below: downlighting highlights the area around a plant's base.

Below right: uplighting is best seen by people who are sitting.

within the right section of the spectrum to activate chlorophyll and subsequently to create growth. Fluorescent tubes, however, do produce the right type of light and these can be used to form growing cabinets especially suited for small houseplants such as African Violets.

A few spotlights can radically change a room and make large plants appear even more impressive. Dismal corners also benefit from additional lighting, especially during winter. These spotlights usually have tungsten-filament bulbs. They create a large amount of heat and if positioned too close to a plant damage its leaves and flowers. Also, the temperature is raised and this causes plants to respire rapidly, using stored energy at a much faster rate. This is not a problem during summer, when plants

have more natural light available to them, but in winter it may cause them to become drawn and weak.

Large plants especially benefit from spotlights, and if the background is white or light-coloured the scene is further enhanced. Large green leaves appear especially attractive when against a white background.

Experiment with spotlights – placing them above, below or to one side – to enhance plants. Dramatic shadows can be created on walls behind them, and spotlighting a plant from below produces the largest shadows.

The positioning of the lights is all important if the right effect is to be created.

Downlighting Spotlights positioned above, and set with a slight downward

angle, highlight the tops of plants but keep the lower leaves in shadow. This makes the plant appear slightly smaller than it really is. It is an ideal method of illumination if a plant is positioned where it is mainly seen from above, perhaps near the bottom of a staircase, or if the area around the base of the plant is not very exciting.

Uplighting Large plants which are usually seen by people sitting down are best highlighted from below. This creates a cosy and warm appearance. If the main light in the room is controlled by a dimmer switch, by turning down the brightness further emphasis is given to the plant. The lower leaves are highlighted more readily than the upper ones, and therefore it is essential that the area around the base of the plant is attractive and uncluttered.

Sidelighting on a glossy surface Small plants on polished surfaces are enhanced by spotlights, especially during dull winter evenings. Position the light so that shadows appear at the back of the plant and are not immediately noticeable.

The use of mirrors and lights
Just as magicians are said to remark 'it's all done with mirrors', so too can houseplant enthusiasts who wish to make rooms instantaneously appear larger. A combination of mirrors and plants creates a wonderful illusion of space and freshness. Mirrors used on their own, just to create space, often produce a clinical and eye-baffling setting, but when used with plants the eye is not so disturbed.

Try to use mirrors that are slightly larger than the plants set in front of them. If a small mirror is used, the reflection appears like a small hole in the wall. A large mirror, however, creates a surround for a plant, highlighting it and producing a framed effect.

As well as plants being placed directly in front of large mirrors, a couple of large palms positioned either side of an alcove and with a large mirror between them produces an eye-catching feature. It can be further enhanced by using spotlights directed on the plants. Position them so that their reflections do not appear in the mirrors when seen from a central and main viewing point in a room.

Spaces left in book-shelves can be effectively used by placing a small mirror at the back. Position one or two small plants in front, illuminating them with a spotlight. This gives the impression of a hole in the wall, soon capturing attention.

Plants in alcoves

Most houses have at least one room which has a recess or, if not, a bland corner that needs brightening. Large plants, such as palms, can be used to dominate and create interest in these places. These large plants, usually with a mass of green leaves, look especially effective when positioned against a white or light-coloured wall.

For extra interest, position a mirror, statue or large ornament in the centre of the recess, with two identical plants on either side. Spotlights on either side add a further touch of brightness, especially during winter.

Ornate or glass shelves fixed in an alcove offer the opportunity to display both small, upright plants as well as those which trail. Alternatively, position a wall bracket in the alcove so that the trailing plant is about eye height and the stems are able to trail freely.

Selecting plants with flowers or leaves of the right colour to blend with their background is not easy. Everyone has an opinion – often differing widely – of which colour is best with a certain background. Experiment is the essence of progress, and if you know what you like you are fortunate, but if you need guidance the following ideas may help.

■ **White walls** highlight yellows, golds, scarlets and greens.

■ **Grey walls** are admirable for showing off deep blues, pinks and reds.

■ **Light blue walls** can be blended with deep yellow, red, pink, mauve and dark blue.

■ **Light green walls** are useful for contrasting dark green, red, deep yellow, pink and orange.

Below: bright light and humidity in bathrooms encourage the growth of plants – but avoid covering them with talcum powder.

the need for light & warmth

Sunlight is essential for the growth of plants. The energy from sunlight activates a chemical process called photosynthesis, which occurs in all green parts of plants.

These green parts contain chlorophyll, and it is in these areas that a plant manufactures food. The process uses water (absorbed by roots from the soil), carbon dioxide (from the air) and energy from sunlight.

Photosynthesis can only happen in the presence of the right type of light. Obviously, sunlight is the prime source of light energy for plants. Artificial light indoors may not emit light waves within the right spectrum to initiate growth. Ordinary tungsten-filament light bulbs do not create the right light to activate chlorophyll and encourage growth. Fluorescent tubes, however, do produce the right light, and many houseplant enthusiasts use them to encourage better growth from plants, especially during winter.

Plants in gardens are acclimatized to variations in the duration and intensity of light, from day-to-day as well as throughout the year, but those grown indoors are from a wide geographical range. Some are used to diffused light on the floors of jungles, while others to bright sunshine in deserts. Also, the intensity and duration of light is less in temperate zones than in the tropics or sub-tropics.

The intensity of sunlight

■ Plants vary enormously in their need for light. Lists of plants and the light they need are given elsewhere in this book, as are the light requirements for each plant, during both winter and summer.

■ The strength of sunlight during summer is obviously much stronger than in winter. Therefore, plants which can be placed near a window and in good light during winter may need to be positioned further into a room in summer.

■ The intensity of light decreases rapidly as the distance from a window increases. For instance, at 2.4m/8ft away from a window the light intensity is 5-10% of that on a windowsill.

■ Sunlight entering a room through south or west-facing windows is far brighter than those with a north or east aspect.

■ Flowering plants need more light than foliage types. Also, those foliage plants with variegated leaves need more light than all-green types. However, even all-green foliage plants will not flourish in deep shade. Bright, but sunless, positions are usually within 1.5m/5ft of a window.

■ Full sun scorches the foliage of most houseplants except cacti and other succulents, especially in summer. Net curtains help to diffuse the light in summer, making windowsills acceptable places for more plants.

■ Rooms decorated with light colours are far brighter than those in dark shades. The former are beneficial to plants in winter, especially if the only light entering the room is from north or east-facing windows.

■ Leaves, stems and flowers soon turn towards the light source. Such plants become lop-sided, distorted and unattractive. To prevent this happening, turn the pot a quarter of a turn every few days. This will ensure even growth.

■ Plants placed close to windows in winter, to enable them to gain maximum light, may suffer from cold draughts, causing flower buds to drop.

■ Keep windows clean, especially in winter when the intensity and duration of light is at its lowest.

■ Do not suddenly move a plant from a dull position into strong light. If you feel that a plant needs more light, gradually accustom it to a brighter position. Poor light produces small, pale leaves.

■ In light that is too strong leaves become scorched, with grey or brown patches.

■ Never splash water on leaves when they are in direct and strong sunlight. Water droplets act like lenses, intensifying the light and burning the surfaces of leaves.

Matching plants with the amount of light in a room

Invariably, plants are selected to suit the light – and temperature – conditions in a room. To help with this choice, the following lists of plants is offered as guidance. However, remember that in winter plants can be placed nearer a window than in summer, when sunlight is much stronger.

Plants for bright windowsills

■ Cacti and succulents are ideal, ranging from prickly cacti such as the Hedgehog Cactus (*Echinocereus pectinatus*), Golden Barrel Cactus (*Echinocactus grusonii*) and Peanut Cactus

Bottom left: plants that are deprived of light eventually deteriorate to a point where recovery is impossible.

Bottom right: strong light is just as detrimental to some plants as shade and complete darkness.

Below: in strong sunlight, leaves can become blistered, especially if water droplets fall on them. These act like lenses and intensify the warmth of the sun.

(*Chamaecereus silvestrii*), as well as the prickly and trailing stems of the Rat's Tail Cactus (*Aporocactus flagelliformis*), to the pebble-like and smooth outlines of *Lithops salicola* and *Lithops pseudotruncatella*.

■ The Amaryllis (*Hippeastrum*) delights in good light, especially when flowering.

Plants for positions with some direct sunlight

Although they do not have to be constantly bathed in strong and direct light, these plants do need some direct sunlight. They are best positioned within 1m/3ft of a bright window – closer in winter.

■ African Violet
Saintpaulia ionantha
■ Busy Lizzie
Impatiens walleriana
■ Chrysanthemum
Chrysanthemum spp.
■ Croton
Codiaeum variegatum pictum
■ Mother-in-law's Tongue
Sansevieria trifasciata
■ Poinsettia
Euphorbia pulcherrima
■ Shrimp Plant
Beloperone guttata
(syn. *Justicia brandegeana*)
■ Silvery Inch Plant
Zebrina pendula
■ Wandering Jew
Tradescantia fluminensis

Plants for bright, but not full sunlight

These like being bathed in light, but not direct and full sun. During summer, these conditions are to be found about 1-1.8m/3-6ft from a south-facing window.

■ Aluminium Plant
Pilea cadierei
■ Bromeliads
range of genera
■ Common Ivy
Hedera helix
■ Cyclamen
Cyclamen persicum
■ Devil's Ivy
Epipremnum pinnatum 'Aureum'
(syn. *Scindapsus aureus/Pothos aureus/ Rhaphidophora aurea*)
■ Dumb Cane
Dieffenbachia picta
■ Emerald Ripple
Peperomia caperata
■ Coral Berry
Ardisia crenata
■ False Aralia
Dizygotheca elegantissima
(syn. *Aralia elegantissima*)
■ Parasol Plant
Schefflera arboricola
(syn. *Heptapleurum arboricola*)
■ Umbrella Tree
Brassaia actinophylla
(syn. *Schefflera actinophylla*)
■ Swiss Cheese Plant
Monstera deliciosa
(syn. *Philodendron pertusum*)

Plants that tolerate shade

These conditions are found about 1.8m/6ft or more in from a bright, sunny window in summer.

■ Cast Iron Plant
Aspidistra elatior
■ Chinese Evergreen
Aglaonema treubii
■ Common Ivy
Hedera helix
■ False Castor Oil Plant
Fatsia japonica
■ Ivy Tree
X Fatshedera lizei
■ Piggy-back Plant
Tolmeia menziesii
■ Sweetheart Plant
Philodendron scandens

The right light

Plants need the right type of light to encourage growth. Sunlight is the natural source of energy for activating the growth process, known as photosynthesis, in plants, but light from fluorescent tubes also provides suitable lightwaves.

Tungsten filament lights produce light within a range that does not activate the growth of plants. Also, they create hot light that can damage plants if the source is too near the foliage of flowers. Therefore, take care when using tungsten filament lights as spot ights to highlight plants. As well as burning the foliage, the additional warmth increases the transpiration rate and other growth activities, so that at night plants consume stored energy.

Influencing the flowering period

All light – whether from the sun, fluorescent tubes or tungsten filament bulbs – has an effect on a plant's flowering period. The precise effect of the light – combined with periods of darkness – depends on the type of plant, as well as the temperature.

Light influences the flowering times of plants, and their response can be classified in three ways.

■ Day Neutral Plants

The flowering periods of many plants are not influenced by relative periods of dark and light in combination with sufficient warmth. Such plants flower when they reach a certain size or stage of maturity. Most of the plants within this group are from the tropics, where the periods of light and dark are about the same throughout the year.

■ Short-day Plants

These are plants which initiate their flower buds when the period of daylight starts to decrease. In the Northern Hemisphere this happens in late summer and continues until early winter.

There are many houseplants which naturally flower from late summer to winter, including chrysanthemums and Flaming Katy (*Kalanchoe blossfeldiana*). However, specialist houseplant growers exploit these short-day plants and grow them throughout the year. By giving the plants periods of dark and light – combined with the correct temperature – they can be induced to initiate flower buds and subsequently flower at any time during the year. The well-known Poinsettia (*Euphorbia pulcherrima*) is given 'short-day' periods to ensure plants flower in winter, when there is the greatest commercial demand

for decorating homes. Growing plants in this way requires specialist equipment, and can only be satisfactorily achieved by experts.

■ Long-day Plants

These are plants which initiate flower buds when the length of light – in relation to the period of darkness – starts to increase. In nature, these are spring-flowering plants.

Growing plants under artificial light

Many houseplant enthusiasts grow plants under artificial light. It means that even houseplant enthusiasts who live in basement flats or have gloomy rooms during winter can grow plants to perfection.

Artificial light is provided by suspending fluorescent tubes above the plants. These need to be positioned 15-30cm/6-12in above flowering plants, and 30-60cm/1-2ft above those grown mainly for their foliage display. To get the right intensity of light, use two 40-watt tubes; either two Gro-Lux tubes or a combination of one 'cool white' tube and one 'daylight' tube. Aim to have about 20 watts of power to each square foot of growing surface. The two tubes need to be suspended beneath a reflector, to concentrate the light downwards and to prevent viewers receiving glare from them. The tubes usually need to be replaced every year.

Above: plants are naturally drawn towards a light source. This makes their stems and leaves bend over, creating a misshapen plant. Therefore, every few days turn plants a quarter of a turn.

Because the plants will be active in winter – when they might otherwise not be growing strongly – ensure that the compost is kept moist. This can be done by either standing the plants on capillary mats, or forming a 2.5cm/1in deep layer of pebbles in a tray and standing the pots on it. Keep the lower half of the pebbles awash with water. After watering the plants, allow excess to run into the gravel. This method also helps to maintain a humid atmosphere.

The best houseplants to grow under fluorescent tubes are compact types, such as saintpaulias, cinerarias, gloxinias, small bromeliads, begonias and peperomias. Saintpaulias are so popular for growing under lights that many houseplant enthusiasts specialize in them.

Do not leave the lights on all night. Instead, extend the day length by an hour or so every day. Use the lights for about twelve hours each day. However, remember that the length of light compared with the dark period in each day influences the initiation of flower buds in some plants.

The need for warmth

In Nature, warmth and sunlight are related: as the sun rises, both the temperature and the intensity of light increase, until early afternoon when both are at their strongest. Clouds, of course, decrease the strength of the sunlight, and they also reduce the intensity of light.

Those plants which live on the floors of tropical jungles thrive in high temperatures, but do not require strong sunlight. Mostly, however, in nature there is a balance between warmth and light, but when plants are grown indoors there is great disparity between them. In centrally-heated homes during winter, warmth and light are frequently totally out of balance, with wide temperature fluctuations between night and day.

Many plants grown indoors come from the tropics, which has encouraged the erroneous belief that exceptionally high temperatures indoors are essential. Because the amount of light is less, the temperature can also be less. Humidity is an additional factor, and in the home an adequate level is very difficult to achieve. Usually, instead of being at a level suitable for plants from humid jungles, it is often more suited to desert plants.

Warmth is essential to activate growth. As plants become more active, they both use up a proportion of their stored energy and, if sufficient light is available – as well as moisture and food materials absorbed through the roots – grow normally. But if the temperature is high and the light level low, the plant will eventually use up all its stored energy and 'burn itself out'.

It is difficult for any home to create the desired temperature for a specific plant. In winter, most families have the central-heating thermostat turned down at night. Also, families out at school or work may have the heating turned off during the major part of the day. At weekends, homes which were cool – if not cold – during the week frequently become very warm for a few days.

It is these widely fluctuating temperatures that are so harmful to plants. However, a difference between night and day is beneficial. A difference of 5-10°F is fine, but a sudden drop of 20°F causes damage. If the temperature remains high at night, when sunlight is not available to initiate growth through photosynthesis, the plant uses energy created during the day. A decrease in temperature slows up the non-productive processes such as respiration and transpiration, conserving the plant's energy.

Throughout this book, the desired ranges of temperature during both winter and summer are indicated for each plant. However, in practice the temperatures in rooms are invariably adjusted to suit the family and their goings and comings, rather than the warmth being regulated to keep plants happy. Nevertheless, the range of houseplants is so wide that there are types to suit most temperatures in a home.

Remember ...

■ Warmth needs to be in balance with the amount and intensity of light available to the plant, as well as the humidity. High temperature, little light and a dry atmosphere is a recipe for disaster.

■ Don't leave plants on cold windowsills at night, especially if they are trapped between a curtain and the cold glass. It is there that the greatest temperature drop occurs, especially if

Below: rapidly changing temperatures between night and day – and especially within the period of light – soon cause damage to plants. The first symptom is leaves falling off, especially if the compost is either too dry or too wet.

the windows are only single glazed. Double-glazing protects plants from sudden temperature drops.

■ Spotlights used to enhance plants increase the temperature without activating their growth.

■ Don't water plants in cold rooms as much as those in warm ones. They will not be able to use the excess water, which will cause the compost to become saturated and the roots eventually to rot. Many plants can survive low temperatures if the compost is kept drier than normal.

■ Don't stand plants on the tops of hot radiators.

■ Many plants need a resting period during winter, when they need a lower temperature and little water. To expose such plants to high temperatures severely damages them, especially when the temperature is being kept relatively dry.

■ High temperatures cause flowers to be short-lived. This is especially relevant to winter-flowering plants that do not need high temperatures, such as chrysanthemums and cyclamen.

■ Rapid changes of temperature will cause leaves to become yellow and eventually to fall off.

■ High temperatures and little light cause shoots to become long, soft and spindly, especially during winter and early spring.

■ Low temperatures cause leaves to curl, become brown and then fall off.

■ High temperatures, combined with dry compost and low humidity, cause leaves to wilt, their edges to become brown and eventually to fall off.

Above: plants that are grown in temperatures lower than those recommended for them suffer as much as those subjected to too much warmth. This begonia has collapsed, the flowers and leaves around the outside being the first to be affected.

Right: the combination of a high temperature, low humidity and dry compost causes plants rapidly to wilt and the foliage to shrivel.

the need for water

Like all other living things, plants are formed mainly of water. And although the need for water differs from one plant to another, as well as throughout the year, without it death soon occurs.

Water is mainly needed for internal purposes within the roots, stems, leaves and flowers. A few plants also need water for the distribution of their seeds, while many aquatic types need it to support their stems. There are, however, a few fundamental reasons why water is vital to plants:

■ Plants absorb chemicals from the soil in a solution with water. Some plants are also able to absorb food through their leaves. A solution of chemicals and water is sprayed on the foliage, and this is known as foliar feeding.

■ Once absorbed by the roots – or through leaves – the chemicals move around a plant in liquid form.

■ Moisture within a plant keeps it upright and firm. Plants without a woody structure soon wilt if not given sufficient moisture. Houseplants with soft stems, such as Busy Lizzie, rapidly wilt if not given plenty of water, whereas more firmly-structured and woody types like Rubber Plants are not so quickly affected, but nevertheless they still require a good supply of moisture.

■ The flow of water through a plant – and its evaporation into the atmosphere through special pores in leaves – acts as a way to keep plants cool. Without this mechanism, plants would soon become overheated and subsequently die, especially those in tropical regions.

■ Water is an essential ingredient in the food-building process known as photosynthesis.

Below: water is vital for the growth of plants. They absorb it through their roots and lose it into the atmosphere through their leaves.

Above: tapping the side of a clay pot is one way to judge if the compost is dry. If, when tapped, there is a ringing note, the compost needs water; if a dull note, no water is needed. This technique can only be used with clay pots, not plastic types.

Facing page top: flowering plants, such as this Cineraria, soon wilt when not given water. Flowers are irrevocably damaged and the plant seldom fully recovers.

Below: plants that are given sufficient water have leaves and stems that are firm and healthy.

Right: both too much and too little water can cause a plant to wilt. In this instance, the plant has been given too much water.

Judging if a plant needs water

Sadly, more plants die through being given too much or too little water than for any other reason. If your houseplants do not live very long, give consideration to the frequency and amount of water they receive. There are several ways to assess if a plant needs water.

■ The traditional way to judge if a plant in a clay pot needs water is to tap the side with a cotton reel spiked on the end of a small bamboo cane. If, when tapped, the pot produces a ring, then the plant needs a drink; if the sound is dull, the compost is wet. This is still a good method, but it only works on plants in clay pots.

■ The combined weight of a plant, pot and compost is another way to judge if water is needed, but it can only be used for relatively small plants – those under 30cm/12in or so high. Compost when moist is, of course, much heavier than if dry. It is relatively easy to judge when compost is completely saturated or very dry, but it is the range between these two extremes that is difficult to determine. And only experience can help to achieve this. Therefore, it is not a method for most houseplant enthusiasts.

■ Moisture meters – devices for assessing the moisture content in compost – are very accurate and clearly indicate if further water is needed. However, to use them means pushing a spike into the compost, a reading being given on a dial.

Continually pushing a spike into compost damages roots, and if you have a large number of plants it becomes a tedious job. Moisture meters, however, are ideal for gaining experience at watering plants.

■ Indicator strips – often called watering signals – are better than moisture meters as a means of judging if water is needed in pots. They are inserted into the compost and left there to indicate when moisture is needed. A change in moisture content is indicated by a certain colour appearing, or by symbols in the shapes of water droplets. This second method is the best

if you have difficulty in recognising colours

Indicator strips take the guesswork out of watering, but can visually detract from the plant. Also, if plants are displayed in small groups, it can be difficult to see the individual indicators. Nevertheless, they are ideal for helping novices to master the job of watering plants.

Relying on the feel and colour of compost is the method used by most houseplant enthusiasts. It is relatively easy to judge if compost – whether loam-based or peat-based – is moist or dry by touching it. However, repeated pressings from a thumb can eventually compact the compost.

Just looking at the compost – especially loam-based types – gives an indication if it is dry. Loam-based compost appears pale when dry, whereas when wet both loam-based and peat-based types appear dark.

Most houseplant enthusiasts rely on a combination of looking and feeling to judge if the compost needs further water. This regular checking to see if water is needed also helps early signs of pests and diseases to be noticed.

Too little or too much?

If plants in a garden are given too much water, it soon percolates downwards and disappears. And unless the area is waterlogged the roots do not become drowned and deprived of air.

Houseplants, however, if watered excessively are soon likely to have roots awash with water. Stagnant water around the roots of most houseplants is a certain recipe for disaster, for air is equally vital to the functioning of roots as an adequate supply of water.

The response of plants to the amount of water they are given is a sure indication if they are receiving too much or too little. Preferably, it is best to keep the compost evenly moist. However, remember that during winter or when plants are resting they do not need so much water. Nevertheless, there are

danger signs that plants reveal when either **excessively** or **inadequately** watered.

The whole plant wilts, with both leaves and flowers, if present, hanging limply. Plants wilt because the compost is either too wet or too dry.

Just a glance at the compost will tell you if it is totally saturated or very dry. If the plant is suffering from excessively wet compost – and has a root-ball with plenty of roots that knit the compost

together – remove the pot and use several pieces of paper towel to soak up the moisture. Leave the root-ball exposed until it starts to dry, then replace in a clean pot. If the compost is not knitted together with roots, leave the soil-ball in the pot and just withhold water until the surface of the compost becomes dry.

Plants with compost which is too dry can usually be revived if action is taken rapidly. However, there is a point at

which dehydrated plants will not revive, and once this is reached recovery is impossible, whatever the amount of water then applied. But assuming that the wilting is not too severe, stand the plant in a bowl of water so that about half of the pot's depth is submerged. Leave the pot in the water until moisture seeps through to the compost's surface. Then remove and allow excess water to drain. Mist spraying the foliage at the same time also

Saving an excessively watered plant

Knock the pot's rim on a firm surface and remove the pot, keeping the soil ball intact.

Use an absorbent kitchen towel to gently soak up excess water from the soil ball.

Leave the soil ball wrapped in absorbent paper until dry – but not bone-dry and crumbly.

Pot up the plant into fresh compost and a clean pot, and resume watering when dry.

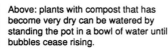

Above: plants with compost that has become very dry can be watered by standing the pot in a bowl of water until bubbles cease rising.

Left: lightly misting the leaves with clean water aids a plant's recovery. Do not mist plants with soft and hairy leaves, as it will cause unsightly marks.

Right: African Violets are best watered by placing them in a bowl shallowly filled with water. Ensure water does not splash on the soft and hairy leaves.

Far right: allow excess water to drain from pots before replacing them in a room setting.

speeds up recovery. Also, keep the plant out of direct sun rays.

In summer, and especially during very warm afternoons, plants with masses of leaves and small root-systems may wilt slightly. This is because the plant is unable to absorb enough moisture to compensate for the amount being given off by the leaves, irrespective of the water available to the roots. These plants, however, usually recover by late evening and by the following morning are healthy. If you have a plant that does this and it worries you, remove it to a position out of direct sunlight.

It is worth remembering that root-chewing pests also cause wilting. Their presence can be checked by removing the soil-ball from the pot. Most pests of compost lurk near to the young roots at the outside of the soil-ball.

Trouble shooting
■ Leaf edges become dry and brittle if the compost is dry, especially if the atmosphere is also dry.
■ Brown edges on yellow, wilting leaves also indicate compost which is being kept too dry.
■ Old leaves falling off while the upper ones are alright also suggests that the compost is too dry.
■ Flowers which fade quickly, wilt and fall off indicate dry compost. However, if the flowers are covered with a fur-like mould it is probable that the compost is too wet and the atmosphere excessively humid.

■ Leaves become soft and decayed, especially around their bases, if the compost is too wet.
■ The pot can also be a good indication if the compost is too wet: a green slime often appears on the pot, from the rim to the base, with mould on the compost's surface.

When watering, remember ...
Plants are individual in their need for water and need personalized attention. It is no good giving them all the same amount of water every Monday morning, and hoping that they will be alright. Here are a few tips to help you to give them individual attention – and the right amount of water:
■ Whenever possible, water plants from below by standing them in saucers of water and waiting until moisture percolates through to the surface. When the surface is damp, tip away water remaining in the saucer. Although watering over the rim of the pot is usually fine in summer, when a plant is growing rapidly, in winter more careful watering is needed. Also, those plants which grow from corms – such as cyclamen – can soon rot if kept constantly moist by watering over the pot's rim.
■ During winter, plants do not need as much water as they do during summer, when the duration and intensity of light is greater and the temperature higher. Winter-flowering houseplants are the exception, and when in bloom must be given adequate moisture to prevent wilting.

evaporation from their surfaces. This also acts as a cooling process and helps compost and roots to remain cool during summer. Plastic pots have non-porous sides, enabling plants to remain warmer in winter than those in clay pots.

■ Plants growing in compost formed mainly of sand need more water than those in traditional loam-based composts.

■ When compost becomes very dry, it shrinks and leaves a gap around the inside the pot. Water then runs out of the pot without soaking into the compost. Therefore, it might then take a couple of waterings to soak the compost thoroughly – the first to expand the compost to fill the gap, the second to soak into the compost.

■ Compost may not absorb water if the surface becomes caked and hard. Lightly disturb the surface and thoroughly soak the compost by standing the pot in several inches of clean water.

The type of water

When houseplants need water it seldom occurs to most gardeners to use anything but water direct from a tap. But is this the best way? Some plants are sensitive to water with a high pH figure. This is when it has a high lime content and is said to be hard. Plants such as azaleas and some ericas dislike lime and thrive in acid conditions, whereas aspidistras, campanulas and yuccas like slight alkalinity in both the compost and water. However, most plants prefer a pH between 5.5 and 6.5.

If you are unsure if your water is hard, have a look in your kettle. If there is a white deposit on the inside, this is an indication of hard water. If you see white marks on leaves after they are misted and the moisture has dried, or white scale on the outside of clay pots, this too is an indication of hard water.

There are several ways to overcome the problem of hard water if you have

sensitive plants. If the water is only slightly hard, run the tap for a few minutes and then fill a watering can each evening. By allowing the water to stand overnight, some of the lime will have settled to the bottom. Alternatively, boiling a kettle of water and then allowing it to cool produces soft water. Collecting water from a refrigerator when defrosted is another way, but this does not yield soft water on a regular basis – and allow it to warm to room temperature before using it on plants.

Don't use water from water-softeners, as most of them work on ion-exchange and do not produce soft water suitable for use with plants. If all this sounds complicated, do not worry – most plants live quite happily for many years on water from kitchen taps. It is only if you have a sensitive plant that it is worth taking the extra trouble of using soft water.

Rain water is usually soft, but collecting it in a clean state is often very difficult. Usually it trickles into a water-butt, but this can be very stagnant and the troughing and pipes may be contaminated with chemicals if you live in a city or where there is extreme atmospheric pollution. Also, it is difficult to have a constant supply of clean rain water throughout the year.

The temperature of water is important and watering tropical plants with water direct from a tap – especially in winter – can cause a chill. Preferably, stand your watering can in a warm room overnight so that the water reaches room temperature.

It is especially important to use room temperature water when filling a hydroculture unit. This is because these plants do not have the 'buffer' of compost to equal out the differences in temperature. Roots are totally submerged in water and a sudden chill damages them.

■ Large plants require more water than small ones. This may appear to be an obvious observation, but too often small plants, when trying to establish themselves, are swamped with water. This is especially so when a small plant has just been potted and there is a large amount of compost not yet filled with roots.

■ Large plants in small pots need frequent watering, as they soon absorb water held in a small amount of compost.

■ The type of compost influences the frequency and amount of water needed by a plant. Loam-based composts do not dry out so rapidly as peat-based types.

■ Don't splash water on flowers, as it soon encourages damping off, especially in winter.

■ Don't splash water on leaves – especially soft and hairy-surfaced types – as it soon marks them. Also, water droplets act like lenses in strong light.

■ Don't water plants in the evening, especially in winter when temperatures fall dramatically. Watering is best carried out early in the day, so that all moisture has evaporated by nightfall.

■ Many bromeliads absorb water through their roots and urn-like vases formed by leaves. These urns should be kept full of water. Every six or so weeks, tip out the dirty water from the vase and replace with fresh.

■ Plants growing in clay pots need more water than those in plastic types. This is because clay pots allow water to pass through their sides and escape by

humidity

The amount of moisture in the air influences the health and growth of plants. Plants living in desert areas need very little humidity to survive healthily. They usually have thick outer layers to enable them to conserve moisture. Additionally, they do not have large leaves. Indeed, any that are present are frequently modified into spines and prickles, which both further reduces the loss of water and protects the plant from animals in search of the moisture to be found in plants.

Jungle plants, however, need considerable atmospheric moisture to enable them to grow healthily. They are used to living where there is an abundance of water and a high temperature, and this means that they are adapted to living in very humid air. If grown in a dry environment they suffer, their leaves eventually becoming crisp and dry.

There are, of course, plants from temperate regions which are adapted to neither a dry nor a humid atmosphere, and which grow happily indoors without any need for extra humidity, unless the temperature is very high.

The humidity of air is very much related to its temperature. The higher the temperature, the greater the amount of moisture it can hold. It needs only a small amount of moisture for cold air to become saturated. In winter, a heated room at 15°C (59°F) has about 70% humidity. If the temperature should fall, the relative humidity would increase. Conversely, if the temperature rises the relative humidity would decrease.

In winter, when the air is generally quite dry, rooms in which the temperature is high can, as far as plants are concerned, become like deserts. This does not adversely affect cacti, but jungle plants soon suffer, both flowering and foliage types.

Some rooms, such as kitchens and bathrooms, are more humid than others, while living rooms with high temperatures are usually very dry. One solution to the problem of a dry atmosphere is to place jungle plants only in humid rooms, but of course this is not always a practical solution. Installing a humidifier is a possibility, but an expensive one. It is, therefore, better to use one of the following remedies to create a more buoyant atmosphere for your plants.

Mist spraying plants

This is the technique most widely used to increase the amount of moisture in the atmosphere. Inexpensive mist sprayers formed of a plastic bottle, nozzle and trigger mechanism can be bought from most garden centres. These create small water droplets that coat the leaves, cooling them and reducing the amount of water the plant's roots need to absorb from the compost.

A misting of water also helps to prevent red spider mites infesting plants, especially during hot and dry summers. Mist spraying is also said to remove dust from the leaves of large plants, but it is

Left and above: the leaves of many plants benefit from a light misting of clean water. Prevent moisture from getting on the flowers.

Right: aerial roots on plants such as philodendrons and the Swiss Cheese Plant (*Monstera deliciosa*) are kept soft and attractive by regularly misting them with clean water. Do not mist them when the temperature is low.

best to deal with dirty leaves as a separate job and not to confuse it with the real purpose of increasing the amount of moisture in the atmosphere. Dust-covered leaves can look much worse if covered with water droplets mixed with the dust, and then allowed to become dry.

There are a few don'ts to observe when mist spraying plants:

■ Don't mist spray plants in the evening, especially during autumn and winter. Instead, syringe them in the morning, so that moisture has the chance to dry before the onset of night. Dampness remaining on the plant in late evening, when the temperature falls, soon encourages diseases.

■ Don't mist spray flowers, as they will then soon decay and encourage other parts of the plant to rot. If necessary, place a piece of cardboard in front of the flowers before misting the leaves.

Don't mist spray leaves which are soft or covered with hairs. Such leaves soon become irreparably damaged.

Double potting

To create a humid atmosphere and to keep compost cool, plants are double potted. Use clay pots and place one inside the other.

Dribble peat between the two pots, if necessary compacting it with a small stick. Ensure the rims of both pots are level.

Use a small jug to moisten the peat between the two pots, but ensure that it is not totally saturated and waterlogged.

Left: plants displayed in groups create a humid micro-climate around themselves that is conducive to healthy growth. When a plant is displayed on its own, the circulation of air around it soon disperses moisture

■ Don't mist spray leaves when they are in strong sunlight. Small water droplets act as lenses and magnify the strength of the sun, eventually burning the leaves.

■ Don't ignore the benefit of spraying aerial roots on plants such as philodendrons. It helps to keep them soft and pliable – and far more attractive.

Grouping plants

When plants are in groups they create a micro-climate which is more humid than that obtaining when a plant is grown on its own. Moisture given off by the leaves is not so readily dispersed when plants are in a group.

There is a danger, however, that the air between the plants becomes too wet and stagnant, encouraging the presence of fungal diseases such as botrytis. Nevertheless, grouping plants does help both to create a buoyant atmosphere and to display straggly foliage plants better than when on their own.

Pebble trays

These are trays – usually plastic – filled with 2.5-5cm/1-2in of pebbles or gravel, the plants being stood on top. As well as helping to water the plants, moisture rises from the pebbles and keeps the air humid.

Pebble trays are ideal in summer, but during winter they tend to keep the compost in the pots too cool, reducing the activity of the roots. Also, low temperatures encourage the presence of some fungal diseases.

Double potting

This is when the pot containing the compost and plant is itself placed in another container and moist peat packed between the two. Moisture rises from the moist peat and creates a humid atmosphere around the plant. It also helps to keep the roots cool, which is an

advantage in summer, but a failing in winter.

Double-potting works best when both are traditional clay pots. This is because moisture passes through the sides of clay pots, but not through those made of plastic.

Signs of too little humidity

Plants soon reveal signs of being kept in an over-dry atmosphere, especially those with thin, papery leaves. The general signs of a dry atmosphere are:

■ The tips of leaves become brown, shrivelled and curled.

■ The sides of the leaves are also affected, becoming yellow.

■ The whole plant wilts if the temperature is very high, with the leaves eventually falling off.

■ Flowers invariably fade and discolour, with flower buds wilting and eventually falling off.

■ The tips of shoots wilt and then shrivel.

■ The surfaces of leaves become dull.

Signs of too much humidity

High humidity is dangerous for many plants, especially those from temperate areas which do not demand air heavily bathed in moisture. Look out for:

■ Flower petals become covered with a furry mould. Buds are also affected.

■ Plants with flowers or leaves tightly packed together will be the first to be affected by high humidity.

■ Cacti and other succulents soon develop patches of decay if kept in excessively humid conditions.

■ Soft and hairy leaves are the first to decay if too humid.

■ Those plants with leaves that clasp stems are quickly affected. Moisture tends to become trapped at the junctions of the stems and leaves.

given off through its leaves. However, when plants are in groups, rapid air circulation is restricted to the outside plants, and the inner ones are able to create a humid environment.

grooming & care

Grooming plants so that they look their best is an essential part of keeping houseplants. At some stage during their lives, all plants need attention, either to remove dead and faded flowers, to trim shoots and stems or to cut off dead leaves. Also, many plants need to be staked and supported in a firm but unobtrusive manner.

Flowers
Flowering plants need special attention. As soon as flowers start to fade they must be removed. If left, they encourage the onset of diseases, as well as reducing the development of future blooms. Also, if they are present in large numbers and fall on soft-textured leaves, this encourages the onset of decay.

Remove the flower stalks together with the flowers. If left, stalks encourage the onset of diseases, especially during winter. With plants such as hydrangeas, which have large heads of individual flowers, remove the complete head, cutting it back to just above a pair of leaves. If the plant has long flower stems, such as with cyclamen, these can be removed by both pulling and twisting a stem at the same time.

Leaves
Primarily, it is dust and dirt which are the enemies of leaves. Large, smooth-surfaced leaves can to be cleaned with a soft, damp cloth. However, don't do this when the plant is in full and direct sunlight, especially in summer. The strong light can be magnified by the small water droplets, so burning the leaf.

Proprietary ozone-friendly sprays are available, and these are ideal for large, smooth-surfaced leaves. Soft and hairy leaves need special attention. They cannot be wiped with a damp cloth and therefore are cleaned by using a small, soft brush. Cacti can also be cleaned in this way.

When using a damp cloth or a brush to clean leaves, support each leaf with one hand and do not press heavily with the other. When moistening leaf surfaces in winter, do it early in the day so that all moisture has evaporated by evening.

Many small plants with tiny, smooth-surfaced leaves can be washed, if particularly dirty, by inverting the plant and dipping all of them in bowl of tepid water. Take care that the plant and its soil-ball do not fall into the water! After immersion, allow the leaves to dry in a warm place without direct sun. If the plant is infected with small insects, add a weak liquid insecticide to the mixture – wear gloves when doing this.

Stems and shoots
Some plants have a natural sprawling, scrambling and climbing nature, and although this needs to be encouraged it invariably happens that at some time shoots need trimming. Use sharp scissors or houseplant secateurs to cut stems, severing them just above a leaf-joint. If cuts are made too high and long spurs remain above leaf-joints, this encourages diseases, as well as being unsightly. Sharp knives can be used, but unless the operator has a lot of experience it is very easy to damage the plant or to cut yourself badly.

Young foliage plants often need to have the tips of their shoots nipped out to encourage the development of side-shoots and for the plant to become bushy. This frequently applies to small trailing plants, which need to be restrained to fit their allotted position in the home. Climbing plants may also need trimming.

Some variegated plants occasionally develop shoots with all-green leaves. These shoots must be cut out cleanly at their point of origin.

Staking and supporting plants
The rule for supporting the stems and shoots of houseplants is the same as for plants in the garden – do it unobtrusively. Attractive, petite houseplants can be ruined if large and unattractive stakes are used to support them. Thin split canes are ideal for providing support. If inserted into the compost and shoots tied to it when the plant is young, it soon becomes covered with foliage.

Some climbers, such as the Pink Jasmine (*Jasminum polyanthum*), can be trained over hoops of pliable canes. The lax nature of this plant may not fully cover the canes, but because they are natural materials they harmonize with it. Man-made materials, however, are best when totally covered by foliage.

Some plants, such as philodendrons and the Swiss Cheese Plant (*Monstera deliciosa*), have aerial roots. These are roots which aid the plant in climbing, as

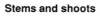

Top: use sharp scissors to trim back long and unsightly stems of slightly woody plants such as azaleas. Cut back to a pair of leaves.

Above: pinch off dead flowers on azaleas, trying not to leave a short piece of stem that will look unsightly as well as encouraging the onset of decay.

Left, above: pull off the stems of cyclamen flowers that are withered or dead. This encourages the development of further flowers, as well as preventing decayed flowers and stems from spreading infection to other parts of the plant.

Left: nipping out the tips of shoots encourages bushiness. Pinch back these tips closely to a leaf joint. If short pieces of stem remain, they will encourage decay.

well as anchoring it and absorbing nutrients. However, these roots if allowed to become dry cease absorbing nutrients and just act as supports. One way in which they can be kept pliable and soft is to provide them with damp, soft, surfaces up which to climb. This can be done by binding a stiff stake with several layers of moss, so that it is about 5cm/2in thick. The moss, which must be kept damp, can be kept in position with several spirals of green, plastic-covered wire. Alternatively, bind the stake with soft, green foam – this also needs to be kept damp, especially until the plant grows up and around it.

For those plants which only need a little support for their stems, a small loop of soft green string positioned just below a leaf-joint and tied firmly to the supporting cane will be sufficient.

The tools you will need

These are neither expensive nor extensive. The equipment normally needed to keep your plants tidy includes:

■ Sharp-pointed scissors, as well as a pair of small secateurs. The best type of secateurs for houseplants are those that function like scissors, where the cutting edges cross each another, so making a clean cut. The anvil type, where the cutting edge bites against an anvil, tends to crush tender stems. However, they are suitable for use on hard-stemmed houseplants.

■ Sharp knives can be used, but they must be very sharp and skill is needed in using them.

Soft green string is essential for tying stems to supports. Also, have a roll of green, plastic-covered wire for securing moss to poles.

■ Split canes are an essential for supporting plants, as are pliable hoops of cane.

■ A soft brush and sponge, as well as a damp cloth, are needed to keep the leaves clean.

Below: large, smooth-surfaced leaves are enhanced by wiping them with a damp cloth or proprietary leaf cleaner.

Below: immersing leaves in water removes dust. Afterwards, dry gently and position out of direct sunlight until fully dry.

Above: climbing plants need support. Here, a Pink Jasmine (*Jasminum polyanthum*) is supported by a loop of pliable canes.

propagation

Most houseplant enthusiasts want, at some time, to raise their own plants. It's an exciting part of growing plants and although occasionally it can be frustrating it is always fulfilling.

Some houseplants can be increased quite easily, special equipment not being needed. Indeed, there are many houseplants that root from cuttings inserted into pots of compost and just placed on a kitchen window. Others, however, can be temperamental and benefit from thermostatically-controlled heated propagation units.

Plastic bags, hormone rooting-powders and special composts have all helped to make raising plants much easier than it was at the turn of the century. Strangely, though, it appears that a much higher percentage of houseplant enthusiasts raised their own plants then than now. This may be because the houseplants grown then were easier to cultivate or that the pastime of growing plants in the home did not have so much competition from other hobby pursuits. Or even that the range of houseplants is much larger now and more widely available. Whatever the reason, there is no doubt that to have raised your own plants is one of the most satisfying parts of growing houseplants. And if you have a surplus of plants, these are ideal as swops with other houseplant enthusiasts. Indeed, some rare plants are not available through garden centres and if a fellow enthusiast has a spare plant it is nice to offer a few plants in exchange. Conversely, even some of the most widely grown and popular plants are not frequently offered for sale. This is because they are easily increased. Also, some of the curios of houseplant propagation are infrequently offered for sale. These include such plants as the Chandelier Plant (*Kalanchoe tubiflora*) and the Devil's Backbone (*Kalanchoe daigremontiana*) that produce small plantlets which readily produce roots when pressed into moist compost.

The ways in which plants can be increased is wide, from sowing a few seeds to taking cuttings or dividing established plants.

Raising plants from seeds

This is not a popular or widely-used method of increasing houseplants, although many flowering houseplants are raised in this way. Commercially, constantly warm temperatures can be provided, together with ways to keep the compost evenly moist. In the home this is nearly impossible, and in a greenhouse or conservatory it can be expensive, as many seed-raised plants are initially sown during winter when it is expensive to provide the correct temperature. Also, when plants are raised from seeds this usually means a large number of them are produced, when perhaps only one of two plants are eventually needed. However, if you are raising plants for friends as well as yourself, increasing plants from seeds makes sense – it also creates a wider circle of friends!

The range of houseplants that can be raised from seeds is extensive, including flowering and foliage types, as well as those grown for their attractive fruits. Seeds of insectivorous plants are also available. The houseplants listed below are some of those houseplants for which seeds are available.

Foliage
- Areca Palm
  Chrysalidocarpus lutescens
- Asparagus Fern
  Asparagus densiflorus 'Sprengeri'
- Asparagus Fern
  Asparagus setaceus
- Bird's Nest Fern
  Asplenium nidus
- Boat Lily
  Rhoeo discolor
- Button Fern
  Pellaea rotundifolia
- Cabbage Palm
  Cordyline australis
- Cabbage Palm
  Cordyline fruticosa
- Cabbage Tree
  Cordyline indivisa
- Cacti and succulents
  Wide range available
- California Fan Palm
  Washingtonia filifera
- Canary Island Palm
  Phoenix canariensis
- Castor Oil Plant
  Ricinus communis
- Century Plant
  Agave americana
- Date Palm
  Phoenix dactylifera
- Dragon Tree
  Dracaena draco
- European Fan Palm
  Chamaerops humilis
- False Aralia
  Dizygotheca elegantissima
- False Castor Oil Plant
  Fatsia japonica
- Fan Palm
  achycarpus fortunei
- Ferns
  Range of species available
- Fiddle-leaf
  Fig *Ficus lyrata*
- Flame Nettle
  Coleus blumei
- Flowering Maple
  Abutilon thompsonii
- Friendship Plant
  Pilea involucrata
- Jacaranda
  Jacaranda ovalifolia
- Kangaroo Vine
  Cissus antartica
- Kentia Palm
  Howeia forsteriana
- Madagascar Periwinkle
  Catharanthus roseus
- Maidenhair Fern
  Adiantum capillus-veneris
- Mexican Fan Palm
  Washingtonia robusta
- Parlour Palm
  Chamaedorea elegans

- Partridge-breasted Aloe
  Aloe variegata
- Plume Asparagus
  Asparagus densiflorus 'Meyeri'
- Polka Dot Plant
  Hypoestes phyllostachya
- Pony Tail Plant
  Beaucarnea recurvata
- Pygmy Date Palm
  Phoenix roebelenii
- Queen of the Agaves
  Agave victoriae-reginae
- Red Aloe
  Aloe ferox
- Reed Palm
  Chamaedorea seifrizii
- Rex Begonia
  Begonia rex
- Rubber Plant
  Ficus elastica
- Sago Palm
  Cycas revoluta
- Sensitive Plant
  Mimosa pudica
- Silky Oak
  Grevillea robusta
- Spanish Bayonet
  Yucca aloifolia
- Spider Plant
  Chlorophytum comosum
- Stag's Horn Fern
  Platycerium bifurcatum
- Swiss Cheese Plant
  Monstera deliciosa
- Tiger's Jaw
  Faucaria tigrina
- Tree Philodendron
  Philodendron bipinnatifidum
- Umbrella Grass
  Cyperus alternifolius
- Umbrella Plant
  Schefflera arboricola
- Weeping Fig
  Ficus benjamina

Flowers
- African Violet
  Sainpaulia ionantha
- Bird of Paradise Flower
  Strelitzia reginae
- Black-eyed Susan
  Thunbergia alata
- Blood Flower
  Asclepias curassavica
- Blood Lily
  Haemanthus katherinae
- Bush Violet
  Browallia speciosa
- Busy Lizzie
  Impatiens walleriana
- Butterfly Flower
  Schizanthus pinnatus
- Cape Primrose
  Streptocarpus hybridus
- Cardinal Flower
  Sinningia cardinalis
- Chilean Bell Flower
  Lapageria rosea
- Chinese Primrose
  Primula chinensis
- Chrysanthemum
  Chrysanthemum spp.
- Cigar Plant
  Cuphea ignea
- Cineraria

- *Senecio cruentus*
- Cockscombe
  Celosia cristata
- Cyclamen
  Cyclamen persicum
- Dwarf Pomegranate
  Punica granatum 'Nana'
- Fairy Primrose
  Primula malacoides
- Firecracker Flower
  Crossandra infundibuliformis
- Flaming Katy
  Kalanchoe blossfeldiana
- Glory Bush
  Tibouchina semidecandra
- Glory Lily
  Gloriosa rothschildiana
- Glory Lily
  Gloriosa superba
- Gloxinia
  Sinningia speciosa
- Hot Water Plant
  Achimenes
- Italian Bellflower
  Campanula isophylla
- Kaffir Lily
  Clivia miniata
- Lipstick Vine
  Aeschynanthus lobbianus
- Mexican Cigar Flower
  Cuphea ignea
- Persian Violet
  Exacum affine
- Plume Flower
  Celosia plumosa
- Poison Primrose
  Primula obconica
- Primula
  Primula x kewensis
- Prince of Wales' Feathers
  Celosia plumosa
- Scarborough Lily
  Vallota speciosa
- Slipper Flower
  Calceolaria herbeohybrida
- Temple Bells
  Smithiantha hybrida
- Tuberous Begonias
  Begonias
- Urn Plant
  Aechmea fasciata
- Wax Begonia
  Begonias semperflorens
- Wax Flower
  Stephanotis floribunda

Fruiting houseplants
- Christmas Pepper
  Capsicum annuum
- Coffee Plant
  Coffea arabica
- Coral Berry
  Ardisia crenata
- Winter Cherry
  Solanum capsicastrum

Insectiverous houseplants
- Hooded Pitcher Plant
  Darlingtonia californica
- Pitcher Plant
  Sarracenia purpurea
- Sundew Plant
  Drosera capensis
- Sundew Plant
  Drosera rotundifolia

Sowing seeds

To sow large numbers of seed, use a plastic seed tray rather than a pot or seed pan. Fill a clean seed tray with seed compost.

Use your fingers to firm seed compost, especially around the sides as this is where it will start to become dry.

Place more seed compost in the tray and use a straight-edged piece of wood to strike the surface level.

Use a piece of wood, with a small handle attached to it, to firm the compost, so its surface is 18mm (¾in) below the rim.

Place seeds in a V-shaped piece of paper. Gently tap the edge of the paper to spread them evenly, avoiding the tray's edges. Then label the tray.

Some seeds need light to encourage germination, but most are covered to three or four times their thickness. Use a sieve to scatter the compost.

Water the compost by standing the tray in a bowl shallowly filled with clean water. When moisture seeps to the surface, remove and allow to drain.

Sowing seeds

Because you will almost certainly be sowing only a relatively small number of seeds of each species, these are best sown in shallow pots called seed pans. Large numbers of seeds are sown in seed boxes. Resist the temptation to mix the seeds of different species in a single container. This may appear to save space, but the chances are that the seeds will germinate at varying speeds and subsequently create problems when the seedlings are pricked off into other containers.

Always use specially prepared composts, whether peat- or loam-based. Soil from the garden is not suitable as it is likely to contain pests and diseases, as well as not having the correct amounts of fertilizers. It will also be of the wrong proportions of loam, sand and peat.

Do not use potting composts instead of seed composts. They contain higher concentrations of fertilizers, which may inhibit germination. However, some peat-based composts are termed multi-purpose composts and these can be used either for seed-sowing or potting-up established plants.

When sowing seeds, the same basic method can be used, whatever the type of compost.

1 If a plastic seed pan is used, just cover the bottom of the pot with about 18mm/¾in of moist peat. When a clay seed pan is used, cover the base with broken pieces of clay pots (crocks) and then with a layer of moist peat. With both of these types of pot, ensure that they are clean. Also, if a clay pot is used, ensure that it is soaked in water for a day or so – and then allowed to dry – before use.

2 Fill the pot to the rim with compost and firm it gently with the fingers. Avoid excessively firming the compost. Then, refill the pot with compost, strike it level with the rim and use either a round soil-presser or the top of round jar to firm the surface to about 18mm/¾in below the rim.

3 Sprinkle seeds thinly over the surface of the compost, avoiding them falling in clusters. If they fall in clusters, use the point of a sharp knife to separate them. Also, do not scatter them within 12mm/½in of the edge of the seed pan, as that is the area most likely to become dry if, by chance, watering is neglected. If the seeds are very fine, first mix them with dry, fine, silver sand. This makes it easier to spread them evenly on the surface of the compost.

4 Label the seed-pans or boxes with a small plastic label as soon as seeds are sown. Unlike cuttings, it is difficult – if not impossible – to identify seeds after they are sown, even if you can see them. As well as the name of the seeds, also record the date they were sown.

5 Some seeds need complete darkness to encourage germination, others require light. The Wax Flower (*Begonia semperflorens*) is one that requires light and therefore should not have its seeds covered. Check with the instructions on the seed packet to see if the seeds you are sowing need darkness. If they do, cover them with finely sifted compost to a depth equal to three or four times their thickness.

6 The compost and seeds need to be watered by standing the seed pan in a shallow bowl with about 5cm/2in of clean water in its base. Stand the seed-pan in the water and wait until moisture percolates through to the surface. Then remove and allow excess water to drain. Don't water freshly-sown seeds by watering them with a water-can, so that water sprinkles on to the surface. This may cause the seeds to be washed around the surface, especially if they need light in which to germinate and therefore have not been covered with compost.

7 If you have a propagation case, place the seed pan in it. It is more likely, however, that you may have to germinate the seeds without such an aid. Cover the pot with a small piece of clean glass. Alternatively, place it in a polythene bag and use a plastic twist to seal the top. Ensure that the bag does not touch the compost. If a pane of glass is used, this must be removed every day, the condensation wiped from the underside and then turned upside down. If the condensation is left, it may fall on the seeds and cause the onset of disease.

Covering the glass with several sheets of newspaper helps to insulate the seed pan against fluctuations in air temperature – but don't cover if the seeds need light in which to germinate.

After sowing treatment

The temperature and moisture in a compost are the main influences on germination once seeds have been sown. Air is the other factor, but if a suitable compost has been selected this will have already been provided.

The seed packet will indicate the right temperature, but if this is not recommended about 16-21°C (61-70°F) will be suitable. Excessively high temperatures will not encourage germination.

Every day, check that the compost is moist but not saturated. If dry, water by standing the seed pan in a bowl shallowly filled with water.

As soon as the first seeds germinate, remove the newspaper (if present), as well as the glass. If left in place they encourage thin and lanky seedlings which will never recover and grow to become sturdy and healthy plants. Also, place the seed pan in good, but not strong and direct, light. Continue to keep the compost moist.

Helping seeds to germinate

A few seeds can be tricky to germinate, but there are several ways to overcome some germination problems.

Pricking off seedlings and potting up plants

When seedlings are large enough to handle, prick them off individually into boxes of potting compost. First water them, allowing excess to drain.

Use a small plastic fork to remove seedlings, taking care not to damage the roots. It is essential to keep the roots moist – place on damp newspaper.

Use a small dibber to make evenly spaced holes. Do not make the outer holes close to the sides, as this is where the compost first becomes dry.

As soon as the young plants are growing strongly, transfer them into small pots. Remove plants individually, taking care not to damage the roots.

Fill a pot's base with potting compost, so that when potted the plant will be slightly lower than before. This allows for compost settlement.

Gently hold the plant and trickle compost around the roots. Do not squeeze the roots or stem as they are easily damaged and may not recover.

■ Growth inhibitor chemicals present in some seeds can prevent rapid germination. Primulas and cyclamen, for instance, benefit from having their seeds pre-soaked in water for about twenty-four hours before sowing. Every couple of hours, replace the existing water with tepid water.

■ Hard-coated seeds resist germination. Usually these are large seeds with hard coats, and they can be helped to absorb moisture more rapidly by using a sharp knife to nick the seed coat. Alternatively, gently scrape the seeds on a piece of sandpaper.

■ Fluctuating temperatures often help difficult seeds to germinate. Most seeds germinate easily in a constant temperature, but many do better if the day temperature is about 30°C/86°F and the night about 20°C/68°F.

■ Cold periods encourage many seeds to germinate. Because most seeds naturally germinate in spring, after a cold period, giving seeds a false winter encourages germination. You can do this in your home by using your refrigerator. Place seeds on moist blotting paper or absorbent kitchen paper in a plastic container – not glass – that can be sealed. After a couple of days in a warm room, so that the moisture is readily absorbed, put the lid on the container and place just below the freezer part in a refrigerator. About four weeks later – some seeds need up to three months – remove the container and sow the seeds.

Raising plants from cuttings

Increasing plants from cuttings is a vegetative method of propagation which ensures that in every way new plants resemble the parent. This is different from increasing plants by sowing seeds, where there is a chance that the plants may be slightly different.

The range of cuttings is wide, from those formed of stems to others that are created from leaves, or a combination of stems and leaves. Some plants are suited to a particular type of cutting, the shapes and sizes of their leaves or stems dictating the method. However, they all have one thing in common: the parts taken for propagation must be healthy, free from pests and diseases and be good examples of the plant. Weak, spindly and diseased cuttings, untypical of the species, will never produce pleasing plants. Some types of cuttings soon produce roots, while those which are woody take longer. However, whatever the type of cutting there are three essential requirements:

■ adequate light
■ a suitable temperature for the species being rooted
■ well aerated yet moisture-retentive compost.

Light is essential to enable the leaves on cuttings to continue growing. Without light, the growth process known as photosynthesis cannot take place. The temperature of both the air and compost must not create a sudden change for the new cuttings. If the air temperature is too high, the cutting needs to absorb more moisture from the compost. And all this happens when the cutting has not formed roots through which moisture can be absorbed. Conversely, if the temperature is too low, the rate of chemical activity within the cutting is reduced, drastically retarding development. In general, temperatures of 13-18°C/55-64°F are needed, although when rooting cuttings from tropical plants slightly higher is better.

Moisture is needed in the compost. If dry, the compost absorbs moisture from cuttings, causing them to shrivel. Conversely, if the compost is continually saturated with water, air is excluded and the development of roots retarded. Should the compost continue to be waterlogged, the bases rot. Therefore, the compost must be both water-retentive and well aerated. This is achieved by using a mixture of equal parts moist peat and sharp sand. This has the ability to provide both moisture and air, but does not contain plant nutrients. Therefore, as soon as a cutting shows signs of having produced roots it must be transfered into a loam-based or peat-based potting compost.

Other composts for rooting cuttings can be used, and if they contain loam then the need to pot-up the cuttings immediately they have produced roots is not so vital. Such a compost is formed of equal parts of moist peat, sharp sand and loam.

Cuttings can also be rooted solely in vermiculite or perlite. These create a sterile, well-aerated and moisture-retentive rooting medium – but do not contain plant nutrients. Pot-up cuttings rooted in these immediately they show signs of having produced roots.

Helping cuttings to root

If cuttings can be encouraged to produce roots quickly, there is less chance of them rotting (if the compost is too wet and lacks air), shrivelling (if the compost

Hold each seedling by a leaf, not its stem. Position each seedling at about the same depth as before, then gently lever compost against the roots.

Gently water the seedlings from above to settle compost around the roots. Allow excess water to drain, then place in a warm position.

When the newly pricked off seedlings are established, slowly lower the temperature and increase the amount of fresh air they receive.

Use fingers gently to firm compost over and around the roots. Water plants from above, allow to drain then (right) place in slight warmth.

Left: cuttings can be encouraged to root quickly by dipping their bases in a hormone rooting powder. Rapid rooting is desirable, as cuttings that remain unrooted for a long period are likely to decay.

Below: first, however, trim each cutting's base to just below a leaf joint.

is dry) and taking up space in a propagator or greenhouse which could be used for other cuttings or plants. There are several ways to encourage rapid rooting, some easy and available to everyone, others needing specialized equipment.

■ Avoid small cuttings, as these have little reserve of food and may die before they have formed roots.

■ Water plants the day or morning before taking cuttings from them. Cuttings which are dry are more likely to shrivel and die than those which are turgid.

■ Hormone rooting powders encourage cuttings to form roots quickly, and are especially useful with difficult-to-root plants. They also help easy-rooting types to produce roots more rapidly, which is useful if they are being rooted in a propagator and where space is limited.

■ Cacti and succulent cuttings root quickly if cut surfaces are allowed to dry for about a day before they are inserted into a rooting-compost.

■ Plastic bags are an inexpensive way to increase the chances of cuttings rooting quickly. The easiest way of doing this to insert three or four split canes into the compost around the edge of the pot. Then, after inserting the cuttings and

Above: before taking cuttings, ensure that the 'mother' plant is turgid by thoroughly watering the compost. Cuttings taken from plants that are wilting are not always successful.

watering the compost, draw a plastic bag over the canes. Use a large elastic-band to secure the bag around the pot. This method can be used for many different cuttings, but not for cacti and succulents, nor geraniums.

■ Propagators create an enclosed environment for cuttings, which speeds up rooting. These are heated electrically, the temperature being controlled and set by a thermostat. Compost-warming cables are an integral part of the propagator.

Propagators are relatively inexpensive and available in a range of sizes. Propagators are sold complete with several small plastic seed trays which fit neatly into them.

These propagators enable cuttings to be rooted quickly, without the need to heat a large area – perhaps a sunroom, greenhouse or conservatory. But do remember that cuttings, when rooted and removed from the propagator, need to be slowly weaned to lower temperatures.

Unheated propagators are also available. These consist of plastic, seed-tray-like containers with domed, clear plastic lids. Small ventilators built into the lids help to control the temperature if it rises too high. This type is quite adequate for most cuttings taken in spring, but if you have delicate tropical plants which you wish to increase – especially in winter – a heated type is better.

■ Mist propagation units are now available for home gardeners. Until recently these were solely used commercially, and unless you wish to root large numbers of cuttings their use is best left to nurserymen. Their operation requires an electric and water supply, and their installation demands the services of a competent electrician.

Mist propagation units create a fine mist of water droplets which fall on the leaves of cuttings. This keeps them cool and reduces the amount of water which leaves have to absorb to counteract the effects of transpiration. The amount and timing of the periods when the unit creates 'mist' is controlled by a water-sensing leaf, positioned among the cuttings. When the top of the water-sensing leaf becomes dry an electrical relay activates a pump which sprays fine water droplets over the leaves.

Mist propagation units have compost-warming cables that keep the rooting-medium warm.

Increasing cacti

Many cacti are increased from cuttings taken between early and late summer, although not too late in the season so that they are unrooted and not established before the onset of winter. Use a sharp knife to sever each cutting from the parent plant.

Leave the cut surfaces exposed for a day before inserting the cuttings in equal parts sharp sand and moist peat.

Sprinkle sharp sand on the surface and push each cutting into the compost, firming it around the sides.

Lightly water the compost to settle it around the base of each cutting.

types of cutting

Cuttings are the main way in which houseplants are increased. The range of cuttings is extensive; some types are used for only a relatively few houseplants, others are common to many.

■ Stem-tip cuttings can be taken from many plants. These are formed of a piece of stem together with its growing tip. They are usually 7.5-13cm/3-5in long and, if possible, taken from the outer area of the parent plant, where they would have been in good light. Spindly, weak and unhealthy shoots usually occur around the base of a plant, and are not suitable as cuttings. Trailing plants, of course, have sprawling shoots, but even with these use strong and healthy shoots.

Use a sharp knife to remove cuttings from a parent plant, severing them just above leaf-joints. If the cut is made so that a short piece of stem remains and protrudes above the leaf-joint, this will decay and may encourage the onset of disease.

Each cutting needs to be prepared before it is inserted in the rooting compost. With a sharp knife, trim the base just below a leaf-joint and remove the lower leaves (or leaf). It is better to have a short, stocky and strong cutting than one that is slightly longer, weak and spindly.

These cuttings are inserted in a pot of rooting compost. If the cutting is large, perhaps a geranium, just one cutting is inserted into a small pot. But if plants such as tradescantias and zebrinas are being increased, three or five cuttings can be inserted in a 8cm/3½in wide pot. Don't insert them directly against the inside edge of the pot, as this is where the compost will dry out first if watering is neglected.

Fill a pot with rooting-compost (placing crocks in the base of a clay pot if used). Firm and level the compost to about 12mm/½in of the rim. Use a thick pencil or dibber to form a hole in the compost. Insert the cutting and firm compost around it. The lowest leaves must not be in contact with the compost, as if soft they soon rot. Dip the bases of difficult-to-root cuttings into a hormone rooting powder before inserting them in the compost.

Water the cuttings from above, so that it settles the compost around the roots. Then, either cover with a plastic bag or place in a propagator.

■ Stem cuttings resemble stem-tip cuttings, but without the tip. This type is frequently used to increase plants such as ivies, which have long, trailing or climbing stems, packed with relatively small leaves. The stems are cut into short lengths, each with one or two leaves, depending on the distance between the leaf-joints. With a sharp knife, trim just below a leaf-joint. Remove the lowest leaves (or leaf) and trim the top to just above a leaf.

To produce the maximum number of cuttings from a single ivy shoot, the stem can be cut up so that each cutting consists of a leaf, its leaf-stalk and a short piece of

Stem tip cuttings

Left: use a sharp knife to sever long, young shoots, cutting just above a leaf joint. Leaving a long piece of stem on the 'mother' plant encourages decay.

Below: trim each cutting just below a leaf joint, also severing the lower leaf or leaves. Some cuttings have two leaves at each leaf joint, others just one.

Above: dip the base of each cutting in a hormone rooting powder and use a small dibber (or thick pencil) to make a hole in the compost into which the plant can be inserted, 12-18mm½-¾in deep. Firm compost around each cutting's base and water the compost.

Right: moisture loss from cuttings can be reduced by covering with a clear plastic bag held firmly around the pot's base with an elastic band. Insert small sticks in the compost to prevent the plastic from touching the leaves.

Stem cuttings

Left: cut long, young stems from plants such as ivies. Don't use old and hard stems, as these do not develop roots quickly.

Above: cut stems into separate cuttings – sever above leaf joints, each cutting formed of a piece of stem and a leaf.

Use a small dibber (or thick pencil) to insert several cuttings into the compost. Firm and gently water the compost.

Rooting is encouraged by placing a plastic bag over the pot. Use small sticks to keep it away from the leaves.

Above: when the cuttings develop new leaves (left), pot them individually into potting compost in small containers.

Leaf petiole cuttings

Left: use a sharp knife to cut off healthy leaves close to the plant's base. Then, trim each leaf stalk 30-42mm/1½-1¾in long.

Below: use a small dibber (or thick pencil) to form a hole into which a stem can be inserted, about 25mm/1in deep. Firm compost around the stems and place in a plastic bag.

main stem, about 25-36mm/1-1½in long. The stem is inserted 18-30mm/¾-1¼in into the compost, so that the leaf is just above the surface.

Insert several of these cuttings into one pot.

■ Leaf-petiole cuttings are formed of a leaf and the small stalk which attaches it to a stem. African Violets (*Saintpaulia ionantha*) are usually increased in this way.

Select a healthy leaf and cut it off, severing it close to the base of the parent plant. Then, use a sharp knife to trim the stem to 30-42mm/1¼-1¾in. Fill a pot with a mixture of moist peat and sharp sand before inserting the stem about 25mm/1in into the compost. Firm compost around the stem. Do not allow the leaf-blade to touch the compost, as this encourages it to decay. Water the compost and place the pot in a plastic bag or a propagator.

■ Whole leaves can be used on their own to create cuttings. Many succulent plants, such as echevarias, crassulas and sedums, are increased in this way. Gently snap or cut off a whole leaf from a parent plant.

If the end is ragged, use a sharp knife

to trim off the small beards remaining on it. If the plant is a succulent, allow the leaf to dry for a day or so before pushing it 12-18mm/½-¾in into a mixture of equal parts moist peat and sharp sand, to which has been added a thin surface layer of sharp sand. As the cutting is pushed into the compost, this additional sharp sand falls in the hole and ensures that the base of the stem is well aerated and drained.

Whole leaves of plants such as large-leaved begonias, like the Rex Begonia (*Begonia rex*) and Iron Cross Begonia (*Begonia masoniana*), can be laid flat on compost in a seed-tray or large seed pan. Select a healthy leaf – not a particularly young one nor a leaf which is starting to become tough and old – and turn it upside-down. Use a razor-blade or sharp knife to slit – at right-angles – both main and secondary veins, 12-25mm/½-1in apart. Then, turn the leaf proper-way up and press it firmly on a compost of equal parts moist peat and sharp sand. Use either small stones or bent pieces of wire to hold it in firm contact with the compost. Roots and plantlets develop from the cut edges of the veins. When established, remove the plantlets and pot them up.

Whole leaf cuttings

Select a healthy leaf and sever it close to the plant's base. Short stubs of stem that remain soon decay and encourage the onset of diseases.

Cut off the leaf stalk close to the leaf. If the leaf is diseased or infested with insects, don't use it to create further plants. Use another leaf.

Use a sharp knife or razor blade to cut across the veins on the underside of the leaf, 12-25mm/½-1in apart. Sever both the main and secondary veins.

Place the leaf vein side downwards and press firmly so that it is in close contact with the compost. Hold it in position with a few stones.

Instead of using stones, small U-shaped pieces of wire can be used. Insert them so that they are astride the main veins.

Lightly water, allow to drain, then cover with a transparent lid. Occasionally remove the lid and wipe off condensation.

Left: roots eventually form from the cut veins and young shoots develop at the surface. As soon as the young plants are large enough to handle, remove them (above), and pot up individually into small pots. The old leaf deteriorates and often by the time the plants are removed it has disappeared. If not, carefully cut it from the plantlets.

Triangular leaf-cuttings

Use a sharp knife to sever a leaf stalk close to the plant's base. Do not leave short spurs, as this encourages the onset of diseases.

Turn the leaf upside down and cut off the stem. Do not propagate from leaves that are diseased or infected with pests.

Cut the leaf into triangular sections, with the narrow part taken from towards the leaf's centre. Several cuttings can be taken from one leaf.

Insert the cuttings, pointed side downwards, in compost. Firm compost around them, ensuring they are upright and not congested.

Lightly water the cuttings with a fine-rosed watering can to settle compost around their bases. Allow excess water to drain.

Right: when the surfaces of the cuttings are dry, place a transparent lid over them. Remove the lid occasionally and wipe away the condensation.

Far right: when rooted, carefully remove the cuttings from the box and pot up individually into potting compost in a small pot. The leaf will eventually rot, leaving the new plant on its own.

■ Parts of leaves also make good cuttings. Many houseplants are increased in this way, including large-leaved begonias (*Begonia rex and B. masoniana*), Cape Primrose (*Streptocarpus hybridus*) and Mother-in-Law's Tongue (*Sansevieria trifasciata*). There are slight variations with the treatment for each of these plants.

The large, long, smooth-edged and succulent leaves of Mother-in-Law's Tongue are cut laterally into sections 5-6.5cm/2-2½in deep. These are then pressed vertically to a depth of 12-18mm/½-¾in into equal parts moist peat and sharp sand. Firm the compost around the edges. Rooting is not rapid, but eventually small plantlets grow from the bases. When large enough to handle, separate these plantlets and pot up individually.

The Mother-in-Law's Tongue most commonly grown is *Sansevieria trifasciata* 'Laurentii', with creamy-yellow edges to the leaves. However, plants increased in this way will not have this attractive variegation. Only specimens of 'Laurentii' increased by division will have coloured edges.

The Cape Primrose (*Streptocarpus hybridus*) is also increased by severing the leaves laterally, into pieces about 5cm/2in deep. Use a knife to form a slit about 18mm/¾in deep in a mixture of equal parts moist peat and sharp sand. The cut surface of the Cape Primrose is then pressed into the slit and compost firmed around the edges. By cutting the leaf cross-ways, several slices can be formed from one leaf.

In addition to an entire leaf of the large-leaved begonias being laid flat on the compost, they can also be cut into squares. Use a mature – but not aged – leaf. Cut it laterally into strips about 30mm/1¼in deep. Then, cut these strips into squares. They are inserted vertically, to about one-third of their size, in equal parts moist peat and sharp sand. Firm compost around their edges. Ensure that the edge inserted into the compost is the side that was nearest to the leaf-stalk when the leaf was complete. Young plantlets develop from around the inserted edges; pot them up when large enough to handle.

■ Cane Cuttings are used to increase several thick-stemmed plants, such as Dumb Canes (*Dieffenbachia*), cordylines, dracaenas and yuccas. These are houseplants which often lose their lower leaves and become unsightly. Cutting a stem into short pieces destroys a plant, but produces several cuttings which when rooted will eventually replace the original plant.

Some cane cuttings are pressed horizontally on the surface, while others are inserted vertically into the compost. Those cane cuttings that are laid on the surface and pressed to half their thickness into the compost are usually 5-7.5cm/2-3in long. Dieffenbachias, cordylines and dracaenas are usually increased in this way. Each cutting should have at least one leaf-joint (node), and be positioned so that the leaf buds are pointing upwards. To ensure that the cutting is closely in contact with the compost, use small pieces of bent wire to secure them in position.

Cane cuttings inserted vertically into the compost are usually thicker than those positioned horizontally. Yuccas are increased in this way. Each cutting is 7.5-13cm/3-5in long and inserted one-third to half its length in compost. Firm the compost around the cutting's base. Ensure that the end of the cutting, which was the lower part, is the one inserted into the compost. Cuttings inserted upside down will fail. If possible, trim the base of the cutting just below a leaf-joint. This is not usually possible with yuccas, but thick-stemmed dieffenbachias can be trimmed in this way.

Ti-log cuttings can be bought from garden centres. Frequently, however, they are bought while you are abroad in warm countries. Those from Brazil are often known as Lucky Plants. These have usually been sealed at either end of the 7.5-13cm/3-5in long cutting with paraffin wax to reduce the rate at which they become dry. The wax must be thinly trimmed off each end of the cutting.

As well as being inserted to about one-third of their length in compost, these cuttings can also be placed in a vase with clean water covering slightly less than 2.5cm/1in of each cutting's base. Change the water every four or five days. For success, a temperature above 8°C/46°F is needed. After three weeks the dormant buds start to develop. Cuttings can be left in the water – topped up occasionally and a few drops of liquid fertilizer added every six weeks in summer – but for long-term success pot in a moisture-retentive compost is essential.

■ Heel cuttings are used to increase plants with semi-hard stems, such as hibiscus and other plants which are perennial by nature, to create a framework of shoots which will last for several years.

Heel cuttings are formed by pulling a young shoot, about 7.5cm/3in long, from a parent plant so that a small piece of older wood is attached to its base. The torn edges of the older wood at the cutting's base are lightly trimmed with a sharp knife. Leaves originating from the bottom half of the cutting are cut off. Leaving the edges of the 'heel' ragged encourages diseases to enter the cutting. Preferably, the cutting should be formed from a non-flowering shoot; if this is not possible, remove the flower buds.

Moisten the base of the cutting and dip it in a hormone rooting powder. Insert the cutting to about one-third of its length in equal parts moist peat and sharp sand, firming the compost around the base. Lightly water the compost and place in a plastic bag. Do not allow the plastic to touch the cutting. When young shoots appear, pot up into a loam-based or peat-based compost.

Square leaf cuttings

Square, as well as triangular, cuttings are created from large-leaved begonias. Cut 30mm/1¼in wide strips.

Use a sharp knife or razor blade to cut the strips into squares, ensuring each piece has several cut veins.

Insert each cutting into compost, with the edge that was nearest to the leaf stalk facing downwards.

Gently water the compost to settle it around the cuttings, and place a transparent cover over the box.

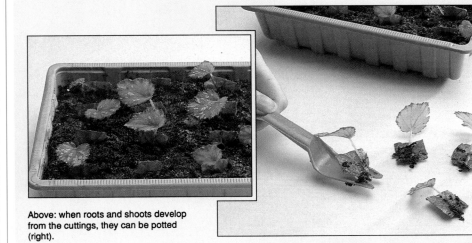

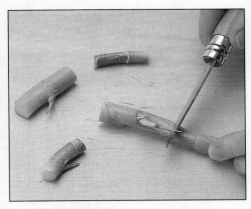

Above: when roots and shoots develop from the cuttings, they can be potted (right).

Cane cuttings

Many houseplants are easily increased from cane cuttings. Sever the stems of large Dumb Canes (*Dieffenbachia maculata*) at compost level.

Use a sharp knife to cut the stems into short lengths, 5-7.5cm/2-3in long, each having at least one strong and healthy bud.

Use small pieces of wire to secure each cutting into the compost, with the bud uppermost. Water lightly and cover with a plastic bag.

division

For many houseplants, removing them from their pots and dividing the shoots and roots is the easiest way to increase them. Plants suitable for this include the Spider Plant (*Chlorophytum comosum*), Umbrella Grasses (*Cyperus alternifolius and Cyperus diffusus*), African Violet (*Saintpaulia ionantha*), Prayer Plant (*Maranta leuconeura*), Mother-in-Law's Tongue (*Sansevieria trifasciata*) and many ferns.

In spring or early summer, when a plant is starting into growth and bursting out of its pot, remove the container and gently scrape away some of the surface compost to reveal where the stems are joined to one another. By gently pulling the stems apart – and using a sharp knife only where necessary – the original plant can be separated into several new plants. Although it may appear to be easier just to cut the entire plant into two or three pieces, this invariably results in roots and stems being damaged.

Pot up individual pieces separately into small pots. Hold a small piece of the plant in the centre of a pot and trickle soil around the roots. Ensure that the roots are well spread out. Firm the compost and water well to settle it around the roots and stems. Place the plants in a slightly shaded position until they are established. Do not pot them into large pots, where there is a vast amount of compost in comparison to the size of the plant.

Some plants, such as the Spider Plant (*Chlorophytum comosum*), have roots which swell and force the entire soil-ball out of the pot. If a plant reaches this stage before it is divided or repotted, it makes watering difficult – water runs out of the container between the soil-ball and the pot before the compost becomes saturated.

Plantlets

Some plants, such as the Spider Plant (*Chlorophytum comosum*) and Mother of Thousands (*Saxifraga stolonifera*), develop small plantlets at the ends of long stems. By pegging these into pots or boxes of compost they can be encouraged to form roots.

This is best done by standing the mother plant on another pot or piece of wood and positioning several 6-7.5cm/2.5-3in wide pots of compost in a circle around it. The plantlets can then be pegged into the compost, using small pieces of bent wire. Water the compost to settle it around the plantlets. When young shoots develop, sever the stems, both close to the plantlets and to the mother plant. Keep pots in light shade until plantlets are well established.

Alternatively, several plantlets can be pegged with small bent wires into a box of compost. When rooted, and fresh shoots develop from the plantlets, sever them from the mother plant and pot up individually into small pots of compost.

Small plantlets grow along the upper surfaces of the hairy, maple-like leaves of the Piggy-Back Plant (*Tolmiea menziesii*). Detach whole leaves bearing several young plantlets and peg them on to the surface of seed-trays of loam-based potting compost, or equal parts moist peat and sharp sand. Ensure that the bases of the young plantlets are in contact with the compost, which must be kept damp until roots form from their bases. When fresh young shoots develop from the plantlets, detach them and pot up individually into small pots of loam-based or peat-based compost.

The Hen and Chicken Fern (*Asplenium bulbiferum*) has finely-divided fronds upon which small bulbils grow, frequently weighing them down. Peg mature fronds on the surface of seed-trays of compost, ensuring that the bulbils are in close contact with the compost. When rooted and fresh shoots start to develop from their tops, transfer them individually into small pots of loam-based or peat-based compost. Alternatively, mature bulbils still on the fronds and which have developed three or four leaves can be detached and pricked off into boxes of compost. When established and growing strongly, pot them individually into small pots of the same compost.

The Mexican Hat Plant, also known as the Devil's Backbone, (*Kalanchoe daigremontiana*, but earlier and more widely known as *Bryophyllum daigremontianum*), is a succulent plant with fleshy, rather triangular leaves bearing plantlets along their edges. When mature, these plantlets fall and root into any moist, soil-like material. However, they can also be removed and lightly pricked into the surface of either a loam-

Above: many houseplants with several stems are easily increased by division when they become congested. First water the plant, allowing excess to drain.

Above right: remove the pot by tapping its rim on the edge of a firm surface – revealing congested roots and stems.

Right: gently tease apart the root ball so that each stem has an abundance of healthy roots.

based or peat-based compost. When established and growing strongly, pot up individually into small pots.

A related species, the Chandelier Plant (*Kalanchoe tubiflora*, but previously known as *Bryophyllum tubiflorum*) has fleshy, tubular leaves with plantlets at their ends. It can be increased in the same way as the Mexican Hat Plant (*Kalanchoe daigremontiana*).

Offsets

Many bromeliads, such as aechmeas and vrieseas, as well as the Mother-in-Law's Tongue (*Sansevieria trifasciata*) produce offsets. These are replicas of the parent plant which grow around the mother plant. In spring, use a sharp knife to sever them from the parent plant, then pot up individually into small pots. Cut off an offset when it is a quarter to one-third the size of the parent. Make the cut close to the main stem with, preferably, a few roots attached to it.

Pot up the offset into equal parts moist peat and sharp sand, water thoroughly and place in a temperature between 18-24°C/64-75°F. When established and growing strongly, transfer the offsets into a loam-based compost.

Right: Spider Plants (*Chlorophytum comosum*) produce plantlets at the ends of long stems. Peg these into pots of compost.

Above: select a clean pot and put a handful of potting compost in its base. Hold one of the newly divided plants so that its roots spread out over the compost and the stem is about the same depth as before. Firm compost around the roots.

When divided and potted, water each plant thoroughly.

air layering/layering

Air layering is an unusual method of increasing plants and is primarily used on thick-stemmed plants such as the Rubber Plant (*Ficus elastica*) and dracaenas. These are houseplants frequently growing 1.2m/4ft or more high and eventually reveal bare, unsightly stems. Air layering is a way of encouraging roots to form higher up on a stem – just below the lowest leaves – so that the plant can be shortened, given a new lease of life and made more attractive. Plants well-clothed with leaves but too high for a room are also candidates for air layering.

In spring or during summer, use a sharp knife to make an upward-sloping cut, about two-thirds through the stem and 7.5-10cm/3-4in below a leaf. Make the cut no more than 60cm/2ft from the top of the plant. This is because young areas towards the top of the stem produce roots quicker than older parts. Wedge the cut open with a matchstick and cover the cut surfaces with a hormone rooting powder. This is not essential, but does speed up the development of roots.

Wrap a piece of polythene film – or a plastic bag slit open – around the cut area and tie the bottom edge firmly around the stem. Then, pack moist peat or sphagnum moss around the stem so that it covers the cut and fills out the polythene. Wrap the polythene tightly around the peat and tie it firmly around the stem, above the peat and cut.

In six to eight weeks new roots usually start to form and eventually they can be seen through the polythene. When the peat appears packed with roots, remove the polythene and sever the stem just below the new roots. Pot up the new plant into loam-based potting compost, and support it with a cane until established and self-supporting.

The old plant can be kept and encouraged to develop new shoots from its base. The old stems of dracaenas can be used to form cane cuttings.

Layering

Many climbing and trailing plants are candidates for propagation by layering. This involves using pieces of bent wire to peg several shoots into a seed-box of compost, or individually into small pots.

Spring and early summer are the best times to layer shoots. Select a position on a stem, preferably 7.3-10cm/3-4in from its tip, and peg it into the compost so that it is bent. This restricts the flow of sap and encourages roots to develop at that point. Several stems from the same plant can be layered in this manner, at the same time.

Rooting is not rapid, but it is an easy way to increase a plant. When fresh growth appears from the tip of the stem – and roots can be seen at the position where the stem is pegged – sever the stem from the parent plant.

Layering an Ivy

Air layering a Rubber Plant

Rubber Plants (*Ficus elastica*) often lose leaves at their bases. Air layering converts them into attractive and leafy plants.

In spring or summer make an upward cut, two-thirds through the stem and 7.5-10cm/3-4in below the lowest leaf.

Insert a matchstick into the cut to hold it open. Take care that the top of the plant does not bend over and snap.

Use a small brush to dust the cut surfaces with a hormone rooting powder to encourage the rapid development of roots.

When full, tie the plastic sheet at the top, in the same way as that used earlier at the bottom of the plastic.

In six to eight weeks, roots develop and can be seen on the surface of the peat and under the plastic. The plant is then potted.

Hold the top of the plant securely and, with sharp secateurs, carefully sever the stem slightly below the peat.

Cut away the plastic and gently remove loose peat to reveal the roots, taking care not to damage them.

Left: many trailing houseplants, and especially small-leaved ivies (*Hedera helix*), can be increased by layering and rooting stems. Above: during spring and early summer, bend a stem 7.5-10cm/3-4in from its tip. Bending weakens a stem, restricting flow of sap and inducing root formation.

Use a small piece of U-shaped wire to hold the stem firmly in the compost.

When fresh shoots grow from the tip of the shoot, this is an indication that roots have formed and the new plant can be severed from its mother.

Use strong string to tie a piece of clear plastic sheet a few inches below the cut. Ensure that the knot is secure.

Fill up the plastic tube with moist peat or sphagnum moss, pushing it firmly but not solidly around the cut stem.

Right: within a few weeks the plant will become established and will be growing healthily – and have a more attractive appearance.

Below: instead of throwing the old plant away, cut back the stem to just above a bud. Keep the compost damp and within a few weeks shoots will start to develop from the top of the stem (right). The ensuing plant will be bushy, with several stems.

Gently but firmly pot up the roots into loam potting compost. Until established, it may be necessary to stake the plant.

hydroculture

This is a way of growing plants without the use of soil. Instead of growing houseplants in loam-based or peat-based compost, just a nutrient solution is used. It is only within relatively recent years that it has become practical to grow plants in this way indoors in ordinary homes, and the method is often known as soil-less culture or hydroponics, as well as hydroculture.

The history of growing plants without the use of soil goes back as far as Aristotle in about B.C. 350, but for the following 2000 years little attention was given to it.

In 1840, Justus von Liebig propounded a theory of growing plants without soil, but it was left to two professors, J. von Sachs in 1860 and W. Knop in 1865, to determine the relationship of mineral salts to plant growth. They developed the so-called Knoppian solution, which was used by Professor Sachs in Bonn, Germany, to grow a maize plant without the need for compost. The plant was suspended in a nutrient solution. However, it was not until 1936 that extensive crops were raised by hydroculture, at first in California. During World War II, America grew vegetable crops in this way on Ascension Island, a small island of volcanic origin in the South Atlantic, which formed an important military base.

Why grow plants by hydroculture?

If plants have grown satisfactorily for many millions of years in soil, why go to the trouble of creating a false environment for them? This is a natural question, and for most plants the cost of growing them by hydroculture is impractical, but it is an interesting and exciting way to grow houseplants. Also, it has several advantages over traditional methods of using loam- or peat-based compost.

First, it is an ideal method of growing indoor plants where they are likely to be neglected for long periods, especially in offices. Although initially they are more costly than plants grown in compost, they do not need as much regular maintenance. As long as an occasional check is made to ensure that the level is correct, there is no risk of giving your plant either too much or too little water.

Hydroponic plants have another advantage – they are always given the right amount of chemicals to keep them healthy.

Which plants suit hydroculture?

The range of plants that suit hydroculture is wide, and is certain to include a few of the houseplants you like, both flowering and foliage types, as well as cacti and succulents, along with ferns, palms and many bromeliads. Not all plants are totally successful as hydroculture subjects, and the following lists are useful as a check to ensure that your favourite plants can be grown in this manner.

Foliage houseplants
- Agave (several species)
- Aloe (several species)
- Aluminium Plant

Pilea cadieri
- Areca Palm

Chrysalidocarpus lutescens
- Artillery Plant

Pilea muscosa
- Asparagus Fern

Asparagus densiflorus 'Sprengeri'
- Bird's Nest Fern

Asplenium nidus
- Canary Date Palm

Phoenix canariensis
- Cast Iron Plant

Aspidistra elatior
- Chandelier Plant

Kalanchoe tubiflora
- Chinese Evergreen

Aglaonema (several species)
- Common Ivy

Hedera helix (several varieties)
- Croton

Codiaeum (several species)
Cryptanthus (several species)
- Devil's Backbone

Kalanchoe daigremontianum
- Dragon Tree

Dracaena (several species)
- Dumb Cane

Dieffenbachia (several species)
- Fiddle Leaf Fig

Ficus lyrata
- Fiddleleaf Philodendron

Philodendron bipennifolium
- Flowering Maple

Abutilon hybridum
- Kentia Palm

Howeia forsteriana
- Ladder Fern

Nephrolepis exaltata (several varieties)
- Maidenhair Fern

Adiantum capillus-veneris
- Mistletoe Fig

Ficus diversifolia
- Mother-in-Law's Tongue

Sansevieria trifasciata
- Parlour Palm

Chamaedorea elegans
Peperomia (several species)
- Plume Asparagus

Asparagus densiflorus 'Meyeri'
- Prayer Plant

Maranta leuconeura (several varieties)
- Purple Heart

Setcreasea purpurea
- Pygmy Date Palm

Phoenix roebelenii
- Rubber Plant

Ficus elastica (several varieties)
- Screw Pine

Pandatus veitchii
- Sentry Palm

Howeia belmoreana
- Spanish Bayonet

Yucca aloifolia
- Spineless Yucca

Yucca elephantipes
- Stags Horn Fern

Platycerium bifurcatum
- Sweetheart Plant

Philodendron scandens
- Swiss Cheese Plant

Monstera deliciosa
- Ti-log Plant

Cordyline terminalis (several varieties)
- Umbrella Tree

Schefflera actinophylla

- Wandering Jew

Tradescantia and Zebrina
- Weeping Fig

Ficus benjamina

Flowering houseplants
- African Violet

Saintpaulia ionantha
- Amaryllis

Hippeastrum
- Bloom Lily

Haemanthus albiflos
- Cape Primrose

Streptocarpus hybridus
- Christmas Cactus

Schlumbergera x buckleyi
- Easter Cactus

Rhipsalidopsis gaertneri
- Flaming Sword

Vriesea splendens
- Flamingo Flower

Anthurium scherzerianum
- Kaffir Lily

Clivia miniata
- Miniature Wax Plant

Hoya bella
- Orchid Cactus

Epiphyllum
- Painter's Palette

Anthurium andreanum
- Peace Lily

Spathiphyllum wallisii
- Poinsettia

Euphorbia pulcherrima
- Urn Plant

Aechmea fasciata
- Wax Plant

Hoya carnosa

What is involved?

If you buy a houseplant already growing as a hydroculture subject, there is little you need to do for a long time, other than topping up the water level when it falls. But it is useful to know how the system works.

There are three basic elements in growing hydroculture plants: the **container**, **aggregate** and **fertilizer**.

Growing houseplants in attractive containers and without the benefit of compost creates an interesting feature in a room. Many plants can be grown in this way, including foliage plants and flowering types.

■ The container can be any attractive, watertight pot which is large enough to hold the aggregate and a reservoir of water. There are, however, many containers specially sold for hydroculture plants, and these have water-level indicators – dip-sticks or floats, or windows in their sides. It is vital that you are able to gain an accurate idea of the water-level in the container.

Self-watering pots (which may contain a water-level indicating mechanism) can also be used. And if you have a decorative plant container which you especially like, a self-watering pot can be placed inside it.

The inner pot does not have to be decorative, its only purpose being to contain water, aggregate and the plant's roots. It is not even essential to have both an inner and outer pot, but an attractive outer container does help to create a more decorative display.

■ The aggregate, like normal soil or compost, provides support for the plant,

preventing it toppling over. Although clean gravel can be used, it is far better to buy materials sold expressly for the purpose. This consists of expanded clay granules, produced by heating small pebbles of clay to high temperatures. Each granule has a honeycomb-like structure in which pockets of air are trapped. In addition, these granules are able to absorb large amounts of water, by capillary action. This means that every clay particle is moist, even though just the lower ones are in direct contact with water in the reservoir at the base of the container.

Before using any aggregate, wash it thoroughly in running water. This is especially important, as it removes dust.

■ The fertilizer is essential for healthy growth of the plants. In normal soil and compost, even without the addition of fertilizers, it contains many basic elements. With hydroculture, however, all the fertilizers have to be provided in a balanced and readily useable form.

Plants need relatively large amounts of some fertilizers, but only traces of others. The long-term health of hydroculture plants means that these have to be 'in the right balance'.

In the early days of hydroculture, achieving the right balance of fertilizers was difficult, making it virtually impossible for the technique to be tackled by amateurs. Now, fertilizer technology enables hydroculture plants to be fed by 'fertilizer batteries' clipped to the bottom of hydroculture inner containers. Alternatively, they can be fed as granules sprinkled over the aggregate and washed down by a thorough watering.

For success and trouble-free results, use a special hydroculture fertilizer such as Lewatit HD5, which is manufactured in Germany. It is becoming increasingly available through garden centres. This fertilizer holds the key to successful hydroculture indoors. It is an ion-exchange fertilizer with the ability to exchange chemicals such as fluoride and

chlorine in tap water for chemicals which plants need for healthy growth. It is, therefore, essential that ordinary tap water is used to water hydroculture plants.

This fertilizer also has the ability to release plant foods only at the rate plants need them, which eliminates the risk of plants being given too much or too little food at one time. A single application or 'charge' of this fertiliser lasts a plant between six months and a year. Large plants will use the fertiliser 'charge' sooner than small ones. If, after six months or so, the leaves of a large plant assume lighter shades of green, or yellow, it is an indication that a further application is necessary. Always stick a small label into the pot, indicating when it was last fed, as it is easy to forget when each of your plants was last nourished.

Range of containers
The range of containers for hydroculture plants is wide, enabling them to be grown either as specimens on a table or, for

Converting a plant to hydroculture

Plants growing in compost can be converted to hydroculture. Remove the plant and root ball from the pot by knocking its rim on a firm surface.

Wash compost from the roots by gently immersing the root ball in lukewarm water and teasing out the roots. Ensure no particles of compost remain.

Use sharp scissors to trim back long roots, especially those that are damaged or brown. It may also be necessary to trim a few shoots.

larger types, on the floor. Also, some containers are large enough to enable several plants to be grouped together in a floor-standing arrangement.

There are containers to suit all rooms, whether modern or cottage-like, and there is a wide colour range. The choice of shapes is also wide – round, oval, square and oblong. Some enthusiasts for hydroculture plants have even tried glass containers, but these tend to promote the growth of algae, are difficult to clean, and allow light to reach roots which have grown through the inner pot.

Routine care

Even though watering hydroculture plants is easier than with normal plants, it is dangerous to become complacent about this vital part of plant care. The frequency of watering is less than with compost-grow plants, the critical factor being to keep the water-level indicator between the minimum and maximum points. It is best to allow the level to fall to the minimum point and then to top-up to the maximum position. Keeping the level excessively high prevents air circulating around the roots, which in time causes a plant's death. A water depth of about 20mm/¾in is about right. If it rises to 50mm/2in, the roots will suffer.

It is essential that tap-water is used, preferably at room temperature. The roots of hydroculture plants are sensitive and it is best to use water which has been left standing overnight in the same room, so that when applied it is at the same temperature as that existing.

Hydroculture plants are just as vulnerable to attack from pests and diseases as ordinary plants. Therefore, vigilance is need to ensure that infestations do not build-up to levels when they become difficult to control – when they may well infect other plants.

Converting a plant to hydroculture

Most hydroculture enthusiasts start with a ready-made hydroculture plant bought from a specialist shop or garden centre. After gaining invaluable experience looking after a hydroculture plant, some enthusiasts then like to convert existing houseplants which are growing in peat-based or loam-based compost into hydroculture plants. It is possible, but not a straightforward job.

It is not possible just to remove a traditionally-grown plant from its compost and to put it directly into a hydroculture unit. There is always a risk of the plant not adapting to its new environment. The age of the plant, health and time in its growing cycle influence its rapid and successful adaptation. Plants not more than two or three years old, healthy and not affected by pests or diseases, and growing vigorously are the ones most easily adapted to hydroculture specimens. And it is a job best tackled during late spring and early summer. Small plants transfer more easily than large ones, so do not select large, leafy specimens. Light, warmth and humidity also influence the speed at which a plant adapts to its new situation. After conversion, place the plant in a warm, but not excessively hot, place in good, but not direct sunlight. Also, mist spray the foliage regularly, especially during the first week. This helps to reduce the plant's need to absorb moisture when its roots are not established.

Transferring a plant

■ The first stage is to remove the soil ball – without damaging the roots – from the pot. If this is difficult and the compost adheres strongly to the pot, run a sharp knife around the pot's inner rim, and soak the pot and the compost in a bowl of luke-warm water.

■ When the soil-ball can be easily removed, and is thoroughly soaked, use luke-warm water to wash away the compost. Make sure that no particle of compost remains on the roots. This is not a quick job and demands care if the roots are to remain undamaged. Use clean, luke-warm running water to wash away the last of the soil. Ideally, the water should be 20-21°C/68-72°F.

■ Use sharp scissors to trim off damaged roots – those which have been torn or are brown. Because the roots are being cut back, it may also be necessary to trim off a few shoots and leaves. This ensures that the roots and foliage are in balance and that a small amount of root is not trying to support a mass of foliage.

■ Choose an inner container that will easily accommodate the roots, but also allow for their growth so that repotting is not necessary within the next year or so.

■ Fill the base of the inner container with well-washed expanded clay granules, to a depth which allows the roots to be spread out and the stem to be at the same level as before. Slowly and gently add further granules – rotating and turning the pot slowly – until they are fractionally below the level of the rim. It is not necessary to leave a 'watering space' at the top, in the same way as with traditionally-grown plants. Do not press down the granules.

Repotting a hydroculture plant

Repotting a plant when the roots are congested is a less frequent requirement than with those grown in compost. This is because the roots do not have to search for nutrients in the same way. Therefore, the root-system is generally smaller and more compact than with plants growing in compost.

Repotting is indicated when the size of the plant is out of proportion with the container. But do remember that because the root-system is compact, even a healthy plant not requiring repotting may initially appear to be out of proportion.

However, the roots may be tightly compacted, and if this is so it may be necessary to cut the inner container to release them without damage.

Select a larger inner container and place some clean aggregate in the base. Spread out the roots and top up with more aggregate – do not allow air pockets to be formed among the roots. Gently tap the side of the container, or shake it a few times, to settle the aggregate around the roots. Do not press down the granules, and there is no need to leave a gap between the top of the granules and the rim of the pot. Until the plant is established, position out of direct sunlight but in gentle warmth. Also, frequently mist-spray the leaves. Do not repot plants when they are in flower.

Fill the base of the container with thoroughly washed, expanded clay particles to a depth that enables the roots to be spread out.

Carefully dribble clay particles around the roots until they are fractionally below the rim of the container.

Large, clean pebbles can be placed on top of the clay particles. Add clean tap water at room temperature, covering the lower half of the roots.

herbs for the home

Culinary herbs are mostly hardy garden plants, some growing quite tall. It is, therefore, not surprising that only a few of them perform well indoors. Some, however, do adapt to life in small pots on windowsills and are well worth growing, not only for their novelty value but for their practical use in the kitchen.

The botanical definition of a herb is narrow and indicates a plant which does not have a permanent framework of shoots and stems, yet persists from year to year. This means a plant with a perennial root system and shoots which grow afresh each spring and die down to soil-level in autumn. In reality, however, it is clear that although some herbs are herbaceous in nature and conform exactly to the botanical definition, there are many with a woody, permanent framework. There are even some which have an annual nature, freshly raised from seed sown each year.

To most people, a culinary herb is any plant that has parts used in a kitchen to enhance the flavour of food. In much earlier times, their role was to cloak the incipient decay in food.

Buying herbs

You may be lucky and have a friend or neighbour who grows herbs and can let you have a few plants. If not, it means buying them from a garden centre or by post from a specialist nursery. When buying through the post, order plants by early spring. Specialist nurseries soon sell out and you may not learn of this until early summer, when it could be too late to buy plants from other sources. Garden centres have an advantage in that you can inspect plants before buying them, but the range they offer is usually restricted.

Don't buy plants which are:

■ Unlabelled

■ Weak and lanky, as if they were packed closely together and each plant has been making desperate attempts to gain extra light.

■ Pot bound, with roots coming out of the bottoms of the pots.

■ Yellowing and starved, with slime covering the compost or pot.

■ Wilting, especially if the pot if full of roots. Both dry and excessively wet compost can cause wilting, so check the compost.

■ Damaged by pests of diseases.

■ Neglected, and have weeds growing around them. This encourages pests such as slugs and snails to clamber over the plants.

Herbs to grow indoors

If you are restricted to growing herbs indoors, and do not have the benefit of a few pots and tubs on a patio, the range is limited. Indoors, herbs are grown individually in small pots. They can be placed directly on a windowsill, but it is better to stand them all in a shallow plastic tray. As well as preventing water and compost spilling over the windowsill, it creates an attractive surround for them

and produces a unified display.

Here are a few herbs to choose from which will not mind overwintering indoors. They include Chervil, Chives, Parsley, Pot Marjoram, Sweet Basil, Thyme, Rosemary and Savory. Both the normal cultivation through the year, as well as ways to create a winter crop, are described.

Chervil (*Anthriscus cerefolium*) is a hardy biennial, usually grown as an annual. The leaves are used in fish and egg dishes. Chervil produces bright green, fern-like leaves, resembling those of parsley. It is these leaves that are used to flavour salads, sauces, soups and omelettes.

For a succession of fresh leaves outdoors, sow seeds from spring to mid-summer in shallow drills, 30cm/12in apart. Germination usually takes ten to twenty-one days. Subsequently, thin the seedlings first to 15cm/6in apart, later to 30cm/12in.

To produce fresh leaves in winter, sow seeds in late summer or early autumn in loam-based seed compost in seedboxes or pots, placing them in 7-10°C/45-50°F. Space out the seeds in the box or pot, and prick off the seedling singly into small pots as soon as they are large enough to handle. Also, give the plants a slightly lower temperature.

Chives (*Allium schoenoprasum*) are hardy perennial herbs, 15-23cm/6-9in high and producing grass-like, tubular leaves which introduce a mild onion flavour to salads, as well as to cheese and egg dishes.

During summer it is best to grow it outside, either in pots of loam-based potting compost or planted at the edge of a well-drained border. In late summer, when plants are divided, pot up small clumps into pots of loam-based compost and place on a windowsill. These plants will produce fresh leaves during winter. Keep the compost moist and regularly trim off leaves to encourage the development of further ones.

Parsley (*Petroselinum crispum*, but also known as *P. sativum*) is a popular and well-known herb, really a hardy biennial but invariably grown as an annual and raised each year from seed. It produces branching stems, well covered with densely curled, bright green leaves which add a distinctive and spicy flavour to sauces, stuffings, savoury dishes and salads.

As well as being sown outdoors from early spring to mid-summer – 6mm/¼in deep and later the young seedlings thinned 15-23cm/6-9in apart – seeds can be sown indoors. Sow about five seeds in loam-based potting compost in a 13-15cm/5-6in pot. Germination is slow. Keep the compost moist and position the pot in good, but indirect, light. After germination, move into bright light.

Pot Marjoram (*Origanum onites*) is a hardy perennial with bright green leaves and white or mauve, tube-like flowers borne during mid-summer. It is the aromatic leaves, chopped or crushed,

that are used to flavour soups, stews, pies and stuffings.

Pot Marjoram grows to about 30cm/12in high, less than its near relative Sweet or Knotted Marjoram at 60cm/2ft high. It is a hardy perennial and raised by sowing seeds 6mm deep outdoors in mid or late spring, or 3mm deep in loam-based seed compost in 10-15°C/50-59°F in late winter or early spring. However, if you already have established plants, take 5-7.5cm/2-3in long cuttings from basal shoots in early summer, inserting them in pots of equal parts sharp sand and peat and placing in a sheltered part

of the garden – preferably in a cold frame or under a sheet of glass.

For a supply of leaves in winter, take 5-7.5cm/2-3in long cuttings from non-flowering shoots in mid-summer. Insert them in 7.5cm/3in wide pots of equal parts moist peat and sharp sand, placing them in a cold frame or in the shelter of a wall. Keep the compost moist. When the cuttings have developed roots and new growths can be seen, pot them individually into small pots of loam-based potting compost and grow on a cool windowsill. A temperature of 10°C/50°F is best.

Many culinary herbs can be grown indoors – especially on kitchen windowsills – and these include Mint, Thyme, Chives, Pot Marjoram, Parsley, Chervil, Sweet Basil, Rosemary, Summer Savory and Basil. As well as seasoning food, the herbs are attractive and bring interest to kitchen windows.

inserting them into equal parts sharp sand and moist peat. Water the compost thoroughly, allow to drain and, preferably, place the pots in a cold frame. If this is not available, place the pot in the shelter of a wall. When rooted, pot up the cuttings individually into 7.5cm/3in wide pots and overwinter on a kitchen windowsill. Leaves can be removed as needed, and in spring move the pots to a patio, or plant out into the garden. Don't remove too many leaves from a single plant.

Summer Savory (*Satureja hortensis*) is a hardy annual, while Winter Savory (*Satureja montana*) is a hardy, almost evergreen perennial. Both are grown as culinary herbs, but the flavour from the summer type is much better than the winter one, which is said to be coarse and bitter. Therefore, it is the Summer Savory which is recommended and described here.

It has dark-green leaves and lilac-coloured, tube-like flowers from mid to late summer, on bushy plants 25-30cm/10-12in high. Seeds are normally sown outdoors during late spring, 6mm deep. When large enough to handle, the seedlings are thinned to 15-20cm/6-8in apart. However, to obtain fresh leaves during winter, sow seeds in pots of loam-based seed compost in late summer and place in 7-10°C/45-50°F. Keep the compost moist but not saturated. Germination takes fourteen to twenty-one days. Lower the temperature slightly as soon as the seeds germinate, and place on a sunny windowsill.

Sweet Basil (*Ocimum basilicum*) is more popular than its near relative Bush Basil (*Ocimum minimum*). Sweet Basil is a half-hardy annual, while Bush Basil is a hardy perennial.

The shiny green, aromatic, 2.5-7.5cm/1-3in long leaves of Sweet Basil are used in tomato soup, omelettes, fish soups and egg dishes, as well as Italian tomato dishes. In France, it has been used to flavour turtle soup, and earlier was used in the once famous Fetter Lane sausages.

Sweet Basil grows to a height of 30-45cm/1-1½ft and demands well-drained compost and a sunny position. A bright windowsill suits it well indoors. It is at its best when the leaves are young, and successional sowings throughout summer are needed to produce fresh leaves. During summer it is best grown outdoors, but plants can be overwintered indoors in pots to produce a continuous supply of fresh leaves.

Plants do not like their roots to be disturbed. Therefore, sow seeds outdoors – where they are to grow – from early summer onwards, 6mm deep in drills 38-45cm/15-18in apart. Thin out the seedlings first to 13cm/5in apart, later to 38cm/15in. About mid-summer, sow seeds in pots of loam-based potting compost. When the seedlings are established, thin them to the strongest two. Seedlings, by the way, do not transplant easily and it is safer to thin out seedlings than to prick them out into pots of compost. Place in a sheltered area on a patio and in autumn move them indoors on a bright windowsill. Pinch out the tips of shoots to encourage bushiness. Bush Basil can also be grown indoors and produces smaller plants than Sweet Basil.

Common Thyme (*Thymus vulgaris*, also known as Garden Thyme), is a hardy perennial forming an evergreen mound, 10-20cm/4-8in high, of aromatic leaves which are used dried or fresh in stuffings for meat, as well as in casseroles.

During summer, grow it outdoors in well-drained border soil or in large pots on a patio. Well-established clumps are usually too large to be taken indoors. Therefore, raise fresh plants during summer – 5-7.5cm/2-3in long cuttings taken with a heel in mid-summer, or by seeds sown from late spring to mid summer – and take the young plants indoors in late summer. The number of leaves which can be safely removed from a plant will, of course, depend on its size. Usually, however, fresh leaves can be obtained from plants growing outdoors, and the only advantage of having plants on a windowsill is for their novelty value and during an exceptionally cold and damaging winter, when plants may not be accessible.

Rosemary (*Rosmarinus officinalis*) is a well-known evergreen flowering shrub from southern Europe, widely grown in gardens for its decorative value as well as for its use as a culinary herb. In gardens it frequently grows 1.5-1.8m/5-6ft high, with a spread up to 1.5m/5ft. Its size, however, need not worry you indoors, as only plants newly raised from cuttings are overwintered there.

It is the leaves, with their pungent and penetrating bouquet, that are used, mainly with pork and lamb dishes. It is also an ingredient of bouquet garni, as well as marinades for meat and fish. Bouquet garni, by the way, can be made from two or three sprigs of parsley, one sprig each of marjoram and thyme, and a bay leaf.

Take 7.5-10cm/3-4in long cuttings of half-ripe shoots in mid to late summer,

glossary

Acaricide A chemical used to kill parasitic spider mites. Houseplants, especially those in dry, warm sunrooms, conservatories and greenhouses, are likely to be attacked by red spider mites. Acid: Refers to soils and composts with a pH below 7.0. Most plants grow best in slightly acid soil or compost, one about 6.5. However, a few houseplants, such as azaleas, prefer a more acid soil.

Aerial roots These are roots which appear from a stem above soil-level, as with some Ivies (*Hedera*) and orchids. Many philodendrons, as well as the Swiss Cheese Plant, have aerial roots.

Air layering A method of increasing certain plants by encouraging roots to form on stems. The Rubber Plant (*Ficus elastica*) is a plant often increased in this way.

Alkaline Refers to soils with a pH above 7.0.

Alternate Buds or leaves that grow on opposite sides of a stem.

Annual A plant that completes its life-cycle within one year – seeds germinate, the plant grows and flowers are produced which in their turn produce seed. However, many plants that are not strictly annuals are treated as such. For instance, the Marvel of Peru (*Mirabilis jalapa*) is a perennial grown as a half-hardy annual, and Busy Lizzie (*Impatiens walleriana*) is a greenhouse perennial cultivated as a half-hardy annual.

Anther Part of a stamen, the male reproductive part of a flower. A stamen is formed of a stalk (filament) with an anther at its top. Pollen grains are contained in the anther.

Aphids Perhaps the best-known pest of plants, also known as greenfly and blackfly. They breed rapidly during spring and summer, clustering around soft parts of flowers, shoots, stems and leaves. They suck the sap, causing debilitation as well as spreading viruses between plants.

Apical The tip of a branch or shoot.

Aquatic A plant that grows partly or entirely in water.

Areole A modified sideshoot, resembling a tiny hump, unique to cacti. It bears spines, hairs, bristles or wool.

Axil The junction between a leaf and stem, from where sideshoots or flowers may develop.

Axillary A bud that grows from an axil, forming a stem and flowers, or just a stem. Some flowers – and vegetable plants – have their sideshoots removed to encourage the development of larger flowers or fruits.

Bearded A petal bearing a tuft or row of long hairs.

Biennial A plant that makes its initial growth one year and flowers the following. However, many plants, not strictly biennial by nature, are treated as such. For instance, the Common Daisy (*Bellis perennis*) and Sweet William (*Dianthus barbatus*) are perennials usually grown as a biennials.

Bigeneric hybrid A plant produced by crossing two plants from different genera.

This is indicated by a cross positioned in front of the plant's name. For instance, the Ivy Tree (*X Fatshedera lizei*) is a cross between a form of the False Castor Oil Plant (*Fatsia japonica* 'Moseri') and the Irish Ivy (*Hedera helix* 'Hiberica').

Bloom This has two meanings – either a flower or a powdery coating.

Bonsai: The art of growing dwarfed shrubs and trees in small containers. The plants are kept small by restricting and trimming their roots, and pruning leaves and shoots.

Botrytis Also known as grey mould, a fungal disease prevalent in badly ventilated, damp sunrooms, greenhouses and conservatories. Soft-tissued plants are particularly susceptible to it.

Bottle gardening Growing plants in an enclosed environment created by large glass jars, such as carboys.

Bract A modified leaf, usually associated with flowers. Some act as protection for the flower, while others appear to take the place of petals and to be the main attraction. Poinsettias (*Euphorbia pulcherrima*), for instance, have brightly coloured bracts – usually red, but also creamy-white and pink – which dominate the flowers.

Bulb A storage organ with a bud-like structure. It is formed of fleshy scales attached at their bases to a flattened stem called the basal plate. Tulips and hyacinths are examples of flowers that develop from bulbs. Erroneously, the term is often collectively used to include tubers, rhizomes and corms.

Bulbil An immature and miniature bulb, usually at the base of another bulb. However, some plants, such as the Mother Fern (*Asplenium bulbiferum*) develop plantlets on their leaves which are also known as bulbils. These can be used to increase the plant.

Cactus A succulent plant belonging to the Cactaceae family. All cactus plants are characterized by having areoles.

Calcicole A plant which likes lime in the soil or compost.

Calcifuge A plant which does not like lime in the soil or compost.

Calyx The sepals as a whole, the outer ring of a flower.

Capillary action The passage of water upwards through the soil. The finer the soil particles, the higher the rise of moisture. The same principle is used in self-watering systems for plants in pots in sunrooms, conservatories and greenhouses.

Chlorophyll The green pigment present in all plants, except for a few parasites and fungi. It absorbs energy from the sun and plays a vital role in photosynthesis, the method by which plants grow.

Chlorosis A disorder mainly of leaves, with parts becoming light-coloured or whitish. It has several causes: viruses, mutation or mineral deficiency. The variegated, speckled or mottled colouring in some plants grown specially for this sometimes attractive quality is not the result of hybridization or selection, but of a virus.

Cladode A modified, flattened stem which takes the form and function of a leaf.

Clone A plant raised vegetatively from another plant, so that it is identical in every particular to other plants raised from the same source.

Columnar A plant that rises vertically – usually used to refer to trees and conifers, but also to describe some cacti.

Compost This has two meanings. The first refers to the medium in which plants grow when in pots or containers, and is formed either of a traditional mixture of loam, sharp sand and peat, together with fertilizers, or one created mainly from peat and frequently known as a peat-based or soil-less compost. The other main meaning is the material produced after the total decay of vegetable waste. This material is applied to soil as a substitute for farmyard manure.

Compound leaf A leaf formed of two or more leaflets. Compound leaves are characterized by not having buds in the leaf-axils of the leaflets. All true leaves have buds in their leaf-axils.

Corm An underground storage organ formed of a greatly swollen stem base. An example is a gladiolus. Young corms – cormlets – form around the bases of corms, and can be removed and grown in a nursery bed for several seasons before reaching the size of a flowering corm.

Corolla The ring of petals in a flower which create the main display.

Cristate: Crested, often used to describe some ferns and cacti, as well as a few forms of houseplants. For instance, Cockscombe (*Celosia argentea cristata*) creates attractively cristate flower heads.

Cultivar A variety raised in cultivation.

Cutting A vegetative method of propagation, by which a severed piece of the parent plant is encouraged to develop roots.

Damping down A method of increasing the humidity in a sunroom, conservatory or greenhouse. Use a fine-rose watering can to dampen the floor and staging, mainly in summer. It is best carried out early enough in the day so that excess moisture dries before nightfall, when the temperature falls. Take care that the atmosphere is not damp at night.

Damping off A disease that usually attacks seedlings soon after germination, as well as older plants in greenhouses. It is encouraged by overcrowding, a stuffy atmosphere and bad drainage in the compost.

Dead heading The removal of faded and dead flowers to encourage the development of further flowers. It also helps to keep plants tidy and to prevent diseases attacking dead and decaying flowers.

Division A vegetative method of propagation, involving splitting up the roots of plants. Many houseplants can be increased in this way.

Double flowers Flowers with more than the normal number of petals in their formation.

Drawn Thin and spindly shoots, the result of crowded or dark conditions.

Epiphyte A plant that grows above ground-level, attached to trees, rocks and, sometimes, to other plants. However, it does not feed on such plants, only using them for support. Many orchids and bromeliads are epiphytes.

Etiolated Being blanched and spindly – the result of being grown in poor light.

F1 The first filial generation – the result of a cross between two pure-bred parents. F1 hybrids are large and strong plants, but their seeds will not produce replicas of the parents.

Fertilization The sexual union of the male cell (pollen) and the female cell (ovule). Fertilization may be the result of pollination, when pollen falls upon the stigma. However, not all pollen germinates after falling on a stigma.

Filament The slender stalk that supports the anthers of a flower. Collectively, the anthers and filaments are the stamen.

Fimbriated Fringed; usually applied to a flower or a petal.

Flore-pleno Refers to flowers having a larger than normal number of petals.

Floret A small flower that is part of an entire flower.

Forcing Making a plant bear flowers or come to maturity before its natural season.

Frond The leaf of a palm or fern.

Fungicide A chemical to combat fungal diseases, such as mildew.

Genus A group of plants with similar botanical characteristics. Some genera contain many species, other just one and are then said to be monotypic.

Germination The process that occurs within a seed when given adequate moisture, air and warmth. The coat of the seed ruptures and a seed leaf (or leaves) grows towards the light. A root develops at the same time. However, to most gardeners, germination is when they see shoots appearing through the surface of compost or soil.

Glaucous Greyish-green or bluish-green in colour, usually applied to the stems, leaves or fruits of ornamental plants.

Glochid A small hooked hair growing on some cacti.

Growing point The terminal part of a stem or shoot, which creates extension growth.

Half-hardy A plant that can withstand fairly low temperatures, but needs protection from frost. For example, half-hardy annuals are raised in warmth in a greenhouse early in the year and subsequently planted out into the garden as soon as all risk of frost has passed.

Hardening off The gradual accustoming of protected plants to outside conditions.

Heel A hard, corky layer of bark and stem left at the base of a sideshoot when gently pulled from a main stem. Some cuttings root quickly if this area remains. However, torn edges from around its sides must be trimmed. Cuttings taken in this way are called heel cuttings. The Rose of China (*Hibiscus rosa-sinensis*) is a plant frequently increased in this way.

Hormone A growth-regulating chemical that occurs naturally in both plant and animal tissue. Synthetic hormones are widely used to encourage cuttings to produce roots.

Hybrid The progeny from parents of distinct varieties, sub-species, species or, occasionally, genera.

Hybridization The crossing of one or more generations of plants to improve a wide range of characteristics, such as flower size, time of flowering and sturdiness.

Hydroponics The growing of plants without the aid of soil; also known as hydroculture.

Incurved The petals of some flowers which curl inwards. Some chrysanthemums, for instance, have incurved flowers.

Insecticide A chemical used to kill insects.

Insectivorous A plant that is adapted to trap, kill and digest insects. In this way a plant is able to supplement the food supply its roots are able to absorb.

Joint The junction of a shoot and stem, and a leaf and leaf-stalk. Frequently, these junctions are known as nodes.

Juvenile leaf Several plants grown as houseplants have, when young, differently shaped leaves from those on mature plants. For instance, when young the False Aralia (*Dizygotheca elegantissima*) has long, wavy-edged leaves. In mature specimens, these broaden and lose their delicate and lacy appearance.

Layering A vegetative method of increasing plants by lowering stems and slightly burying them in soil or compost. By creating a kink, twist, bend or slit in the stem, the flow of sap is restricted and roots induced to develop. This method of increasing plants is not widely used for houseplants, other than those with trailing stems.

Leggy Plants which become tall and spindly, often through being kept in dark places.

Loam A mixture of fertile soil – formed of sand, clay, silt and organic material.

Mist propagation A mechanical device which sprays fine droplets of water over

cuttings. This keeps the cuttings cool, as well as reducing their need to absorb moisture before they have formed roots. Soft-leaved cuttings are placed under the misting unit, which, because the loss of moisture from the cuttings is being controlled, can be kept at a slightly higher temperature to encourage rapid rooting.

Mutation Part of a plant – usually the flower – that differs from the plant's normal characteristics.

Neutral Neither acid nor alkaline. Chemically, neutral on the pH scale is 7.0, but horticulturally neutral is considered to be between 6.5 and 7.0.

Node A leaf joint or point where a shoot grows from a stem or main branch.

NPK A formula for the percentages of nitrogen, phosphate and potash in compound fertilizers.

Opposite Buds or leaves which are borne in pairs along shoots and stems.

Perennial Usually used when referring to herbaceous perennials, but also applied to any plant that lives for several years, including trees, shrubs and climbers. Many houseplants live for several years, especially those grown in sunrooms, conservatories and greenhouses.

Pesticide A chemical compound for killing insects and other pests.

Photosynthesis The food-building process when chlorophyll in the leaves is activated by sunlight. It reacts with moisture absorbed by the roots and carbon dioxide gained from the atmosphere to create growth.

Phototropism This is the action on a plant which makes it grow towards a light source.

pH A logarithmic scale used to define the acidity or alkalinity of a soil-water solution. Chemically, neutral is 7.0, with figures above indicating increasing alkalinity, and below increasing acidity. Most plants grow well in 6.5-7.0.

Pinching out The removal of the tip of a shoot, or a terminal bud, to encourage the development of sideshoots.

Pip This has two distinct meanings – the seed of some fruits, such as apples and

pears, as well as citrus types, and the rootstock of plants such as Lily of the Valley (*Convallaria majalis*).

Pollen The male fertilizing agent from the anthers.

Potting-on The transfer of an established plant from one pot to a larger one.

Potting-up The transfer of a young plant from a seedbox or seed-pan into a pot.

Pricking-out The transfer of seedlings from a seedbox or seed-pan into another box, where they can be given more space.

Propagation The raising of new plants.

Rhizome An underground or partly buried horizontal stem. They can be slender or fleshy.

Root ball The compost in which a houseplant grows, together with the roots. When the compost in which a houseplant is growing is full of roots, the plant is repotted into a larger pot.

Seed leaf The first leaf (sometimes two) that appears after germination.

Self-coloured Flowers which are just one colour, as opposed to bicoloured (two colours) and multicoloured flowers (several colours).

Sessile Leaves and flowers which do not have stalks or stems attaching them to the plant.

Sideshoot A shoot growing out from the side of a main shoot or stem.

Simple leaves This is when there is just one leaf attached to the leaf stalk. With such leaves there would always be a bud at the joint between the leaf stalk and the main stem.

Single flowers These have the normal number of petals present, arranged in a single row.

Softwood cutting A cutting taken from non-woody growth. Many houseplants are increased in this manner.

Species A group of plants that breed together and have the same characteristics.

Spores The reproductive cells of non-flowering plants such as ferns.

Sport A plant which reveals a marked difference from its parent. It is also known as a mutation.

Stamen The male part of a flower, formed of anthers and filaments.

Stigma The female part of flower, where pollen alights.

Stipule A leaf-like sheath at the base of some flower stalks.

Stoma Minute holes – usually on the undersides of leaves – that enable the exchange of gases between the plant and the air surrounding it. During respiration, the plant absorbs air, retaining and using oxygen and giving off carbon dioxide. However, during photosynthesis the plant absorbs air, using the carbon dioxide and giving off oxygen. (The singular of stoma is stomata.)

Stop The removal of a growing tip to encourage the development of sideshoots.

Strain Seed-raised plants from a common ancestor.

Style Part of the female reproductive organs of a flower, linking the style to the ovary.

Succulent Any plant with thick and fleshy leaves. Cacti are succulent plants, but not all succulents are cacti.

Synonym A previous botanical name for a plant. It frequently happens that a plant is better known and sold by nurseries under an earlier name.

Systemic Chemicals that penetrate a plant's tissue, killing pests which suck or bite it. The time they remain active within a plant depends on the type of plant, the temperature and the chemical.

Tender A plant which is damaged by low temperatures.

Tendril A thread-like growth that enables many climbers to cling to their supports.

Terrarium A glass container which is partly or wholly closed and used to house plants.

Terrestrial Plants which grow in soil at ground level.

Transpiration The loss of moisture from a plant.

Variegated Multi-coloured leaves.

Variety A naturally occurring variation of a species. However, the term variety is commonly used to include both true varieties and cultivars. Cultivars are plants which are variations of a species and have been raised in cultivation.

Left: crocuses create eye-catching displays in pots indoors, but cannot be forced into flower in the same way as daffodils and hyacinths. They should be given only slight and gentle warmth.

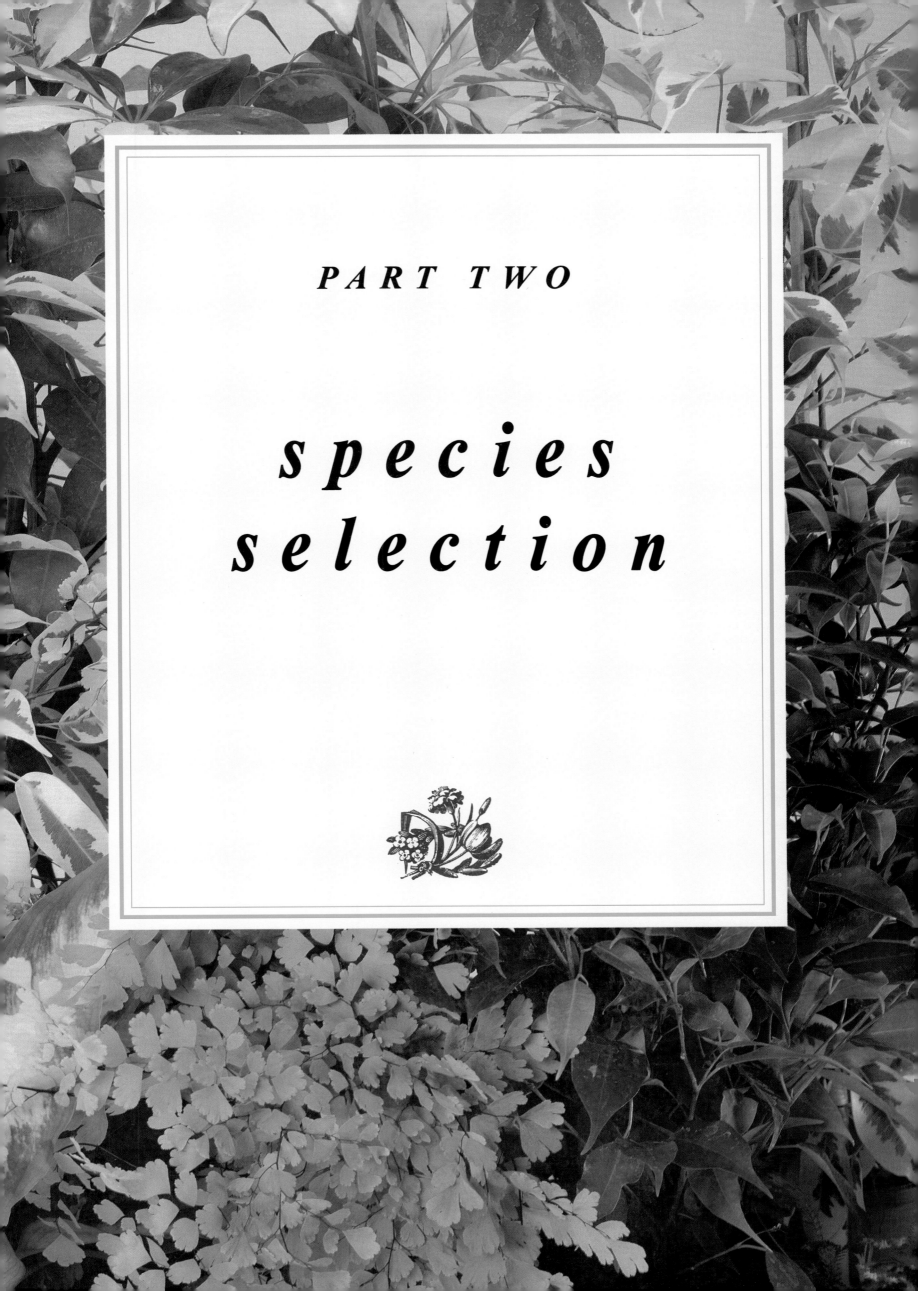

PART TWO

species selection

palms

Caryota mitis

**Burmese Fishtail Palm/Clustered Fishtail Palm/
Fishtail Palm/Tufted Fishtail Palm**

Height 1.5-2.4m/5-8ft – in a pot indoors
Spread 0.6-1m/2-3½ft – in a pot indoors
Native Burma, Malaya, Philippines, Java

Greenfinger Guide

Temperature W 13-18°C/55-64°F S 18-27°C/
64-80°F

Light W Full light. S Diffused light.

Watering W Just moist. S Water moderately, but
do not saturate the compost. And ensure good
drainage.

Feeding From mid-spring to late summer feed
every three to four weeks.

Humidity Mist spray the fronds in summer.

Compost Loam-based type.

Potting Repot in spring when roots fill the
container. However, this is a vigorous palm and to
keep it to a size that suits most rooms it is better to
constrain the roots. When it has reached the largest
pot you have, replace the top soil with fresh in
spring.

Propagation In early summer remove basal
suckers and pot into small pots. Keep warm until
established.

The Burmese Fishtail Palm grows to 12m/40ft high in
the wild. Indoors it can soon outgrow a room if
repotted too often, but in a sun-room forms a spectacular
palm. It is distinctive, with many ragged-edged, wedge-
shaped, leaflets up to 15cm/6in long and 10cm/4in
wide and borne on arching fronds.

Caryota mitis

Chamaedorea elegans

Chamaedorea elegans

Parlour Palm/Good-luck Palm

Height 0.45-1.2m/1½-4ft
Spread 45-75cm/1½-2½ft
Native Mexico and Guatemala

Greenfinger Guide

Temperature W 10-13°C/50-55°F S 13-18°C/
55-64°F

Light W Bright, lightly filtered light. S Light
shade to lightly filtered light.

Watering W Barely moist. S Evenly moist –
ensure good drainage.

Feeding From late spring to late summer feed
every four weeks.

Humidity Mist spray fronds in summer – avoid
placing in draughts.

Compost Loam-based type.

Potting In spring, but only when the roots are
congested – it dislikes root disturbance.

Propagation Sow seeds in equal parts moist peat
and sharp sand in spring. Place in 24-27°C/75-80°F.
Pot up seedlings when large enough to handle, and
keep in 18°C/64°F.

The Parlour Palm is widely grown and frequently sold
when young in a collection of houseplants in one pot.
Eventually, the other plants die and the palm can be
repotted and grown on its own, creating a superb
display on a side table or, eventually, in a grouping of
other plants or on a low table in a corner. It is not
usually suited for positioning on the floor.

Chamaedorea erumpens
Bamboo Palm

Height 1.5-3m/5-10ft
Spread 0.75-1.2m/2½-4ft
Native Guatemala/Honduras

Greenfinger Guide

Temperature W 10-13°C/50-55°F **S** 13-18°C/55-64°F

Light W Lightly filtered light. **S** Light shade.

Watering W Barely moist. **S** Evenly moist – ensure good drainage.

Feeding From late spring to late summer feed every three to four weeks.

Humidity Mist spray fronds in summer.

Compost Loam-based type.

Potting In spring, but only when the roots are congested – it dislikes root disturbance.

Propagation Sow seeds in spring in equal parts moist peat and sharp sand. Alternatively, divide congested plants in spring when being repotted.

Chamaedorea erumpens

Chamaedorea seifrizii

Chamaedorea humilis

The Bamboo Palm is, as its name suggests, a bamboo-like palm that forms a cluster of stems from compost level. Indeed, in the wild it rapidly spreads from suckers. The fronds are formed of about fifteen deep green leaves, up to 27cm/11in long and 30mm/1.25in wide.

It creates a dominant floor-standing display, superb when positioned against a white wall and with spot lights upon it.

The Reed Palm, *Chamaedorea seifrizii* , is similar to the Bamboo Palm, but with up to eighteen, longer and narrower, deep green leaflets to each frond.

Chamaerops humilis
Dwarf Fan Palm/European Fan Palm/European Palm/Mediterranean Fan Palm

Height 0.9-1.5m/3-5ft
Spread 0.9-1.5m/3-5ft
Native Southern Europe (along the Mediterranean coast) and North Africa

Greenfinger Guide

Temperature W 5-7°C/41-45°F **S** 7-16°C/45-61°F

Light W Full sun. **S** Light shade to full sun.

Watering W Moderately, keeping the compost lightly moist. **S** Water more freely, but ensure that the compost is well drained and that the compost does not become waterlogged. Remember that this palm naturally grows in dry, sandy and rocky places.

Feeding From late spring to late summer feed every three or four weeks.

Humidity Lightly mist spray the fronds in summer.

Compost Loam-based type, with extra sharp sand.

Potting In spring, when the roots fill the pot – usually every two or three years.

Propagation The easiest way is to remove and pot up suckers from around the plant in spring. Alternatively, sow seeds 2.5cm/1in deep in spring, placing the container in 24-27°C/75-80°F.

The Dwarf Fan Palm is normally a tufted plant, but occasionally produces a trunk more than 1.8m/6ft high. Indeed, in its native area plants grow to 9m/30ft or so – but usually less.

Each fan of grey-green leaves can be 45cm/1½ft long and 30cm/1ft across. These are borne at the ends of rather thorny stems, usually 23-30cm/9-12in long, but in the wild and on vigorous plants frequently 1.2m/4ft long. In addition to the normal type, there are forms with differently and attractively coloured leaves, such as *C. h. argenta* with silvery leaves and *C. h. elegans* with rather delicately-cut foliage.

Chrysalidocarpus lutescens

Chrysalidocarpus lutescens
Areca Palm/Butterfly Palm/Yellow Palm/Golden Feather Palm/Yellow Butterfly Palm/Cane Palm/ Golden Cane Palm

Height 1.5-3m/5-10ft
Spread 0.9-1.5m/3-5ft
Native Madagascar

Greenfinger Guide
Temperature W 13-16°C/55-61°F **S** 16-27°C/ 61-80°F
Light W Filtered light. **S** Indirect to dappled light.
Watering W Just moist – do not let the compost dry out. **S** Water freely, but ensure good drainage. The compost must not become soggy.
Feeding From late spring to late summer feed every three to four weeks.
Humidity Mist spray fronds in summer – it loves high humidity, especially when the weather is very hot.
Compost Loam-based type.
Potting In spring, when the roots fill the pot – usually every two or three years. However, allow the roots to become really congested before repotting. When the plant is in the largest pot you have, replace the topsoil with fresh every spring.
Propagation Divide congested plants in spring. Alternatively, remove and pot up sucker-like shoots when the plant is being repotted in spring. Seeds can be sown in spring and placed in 18-21°C/64-70°F, but it takes several years to produce reasonably sized plants.

The Areca Palm gains this common name from its former classification as *Areca lutescens*. The feather-like fronds, about 90cm/3ft long, gently arch downwards and create a spectacular palm for the home. Many stems grow from compost level, and under good conditions it grows 15-20cm/6-8in in a year.

It looks best when positioned against a white background, where the fronds can be seen unobscured by other plants.

Cycas revoluta
Sago Palm/Sago Palm/Japanese Sago Palm/ Japanese Fern Palm

Height 30-75cm/1-2½ft
Spread 38-50cm/15-20in
Native Indonesia and Japan

Greenfinger Guide
Temperature W 15-18°C/59-64°F **S** 18-27°C/ 64-80°F
Light W Bright, indirect light. **S** Light shade.
Watering W Just moist – if the temperature is low, give less water. **S** Water freely, but ensure good drainage.
Feeding From late spring to late summer feed every four to six weeks.
Humidity Mist spray in summer.
Compost Loam-based type.
Potting In spring, when the roots completely fill the pot – usually three or four years.
Propagation Sow seeds in sandy compost during early summer. Place in 24-27°C/75-80°F. Alternatively, if the plant produces offsets these are removed in spring or summer and potted into potting compost. Place in 24-27°C/75-80°F until established.

The Sago Palm is not a true palm, but a close relative that would still be recognisable to dinasaurs if they still lived. It is slow growing, usually only putting on one leaf a year. Its attractive dark green, palm-like fronds create a rosette which arises from a ball-like base.

It loves a humid and warm atmosphere and therefore is best grown in a sun-room. Indoors, the atmosphere is often too dry.

Howeia belmoreana
Sentry Palm/Belmore Sentry Palm/Curly Palm

Height 1.8-3m/6-10ft

Cycas revoluta

Howeia belmoreana

Howeia forsteriana

Spread 1.5-2.4m/5-8ft
Native Lord Howe Islands

Greenfinger Guide
Temperature W 10-12°C/50-54°F – will survive temperatures down to 7°C/45°F for short periods. **S** 15-24°C/59-75°F

Light W Full light. **S** Light shade.

Watering W Barely moist. **S** Water freely, but ensure good drainage.

Feeding From mid-spring to late summer feed every three to four weeks.

Humidity Mist spray fronds during summer.

Compost Loam-based type.

Potting In spring, when the roots fill the pot – usually every two or three years. Disturb the roots as little as possible when repotting.

Propagation Sow seeds in early spring on the surface of a peat-based compost. Place in 27-30°C/80-85°F. Pot up when the first leaf is well developed and place in 18°C/64°F until well established.

The Sentry Palm eventually creates a large and spectacular display, and is ideal for placing in spacious and empty corners or alcoves – especially if the background is white. This both contrasts with the beautiful green leaflets and reflects light during winter.

It is distinguished from the Kentia Palm by having a larger number and more erect leaflets, which are narrow and delicately pointed.

Howeia forsteriana
Kentia Palm/Sentry Palm/Thatch Leaf Palm/Thatch Palm
Height 1.8-3m/6-10ft
Spread 1.5-2.4m/5-8ft
Native Lord Howe Islands

Greenfinger Guide
Temperature W 10-12°C/50-54°F **S** 15-24°C/59-75°F

Light W Full light. **S** Light shade.

Watering W Barely moist. **S** Water freely, but ensure good drainage.

Feeding From mid-spring to late summer feed every three to four weeks.

Humidity Mist spray fronds in summer.

Compost Loam-based type.

Potting In spring, when the roots fill the pot – usually every two or three years. Disturb the roots as little as possible when repotting.

Propagation Sow seeds in early spring on the surface of a peat-based compost. Place in 27-30°C/80-85°F. Pot up when the first leaf is well developed and place in 18°C/64°F until established.

The Kentia Palm, like the Sentry Palm, eventually forms a large and distinctive foliage plant, ideal for filling large corners. It differs from the Sentry palm in having fewer and drooping leaflets, and with stems that arch over almost horizontally. It therefore needs a large area, and one which does not allow passers by to damage the foliage.

Livistonia chinensis
Chinese Fan Palm/Chinese Fountain Palm/Fan Palm
Height 1.2-3m/4-10ft
Spread 0.6-1m/2-3½ft
Native Japan/Central China

Greenfinger Guide

Temperature W 7-15°C/45-59°F – it will survive short periods down to 5°C/41°F, but is better at 7°C/45°F or slightly above. **S** 15-24°C/59-75°F

Light W Full light. **S** Indirect light, especially for young plants. However, it appears to tolerate light to medium shade.

Watering W Just moist – do not let the compost dry out at any time. **S** Water freely, but ensure good drainage.

Feeding From late spring to late summer feed every three weeks. It needs feeding more often than many other palms.

Humidity Mist spray fronds in summer.

Compost Loam-based type. It requires a rich, moisture-retentive but well-drained compost.

Potting In spring, when the roots fill the pot – usually every two or three years.

Propagation Sow ripe seeds in spring and place in 24-27°C/75-80°F. This is best left to experts.

The Chinese Fan Palm is slow-growing when in a pot indoors, but in its native country may reach 9m/30ft or more high. It forms a grey trunk, with the old leaf bases adhering to it, and bright green fan-like fronds. Older plants reveal drooping ends to the leaflets, reminiscent of icicles. It is not a widely-grown palm, but it does create a dramatic effect with its distinctive fans borne on toothed leaf stalks. Position it on the floor, and where it cannot be damaged by children or animals. This palm was very popular more than a century and a half ago, and quite large plants with long trunks were grown in Victorian rooms with high ceilings, but it was the young plants which were the easiest to grow. However, in young plants the leaves may not be so attractively segmented. It was very popular before the introduction of Howeias.

Microcoelum weddelianum
Weddel Palm

Height 23-38cm/9-15in – but eventually reaching 1.5-1.8m/5-6ft after 15-20 years
Spread 23-30cm/9-12in – but wider if kept for many years.
Native South America

Greenfinger Guide

Temperature W 16-18°C/61-64°F – do not let the temperature fall below 16°C/61°F **S** 18-24°C/64-75°F

Light W Full light. **S** Light shade.

Watering W Barely moist. **S** Water freely, but ensure good drainage.

Feeding From late spring to late summer feed every two to three weeks.

Humidity Mist spray the leaves in summer.

Compost Loam-based type.

Potting In late spring, when the roots fill the pot – usually every two or three years.

Propagation Sow seeds in early spring on the surface of a peat-based compost. Place in 24-27°C/75-80°F.

The Weddel Palm is invariably seen as a small, delicate palm with arching leaves formed of thin leaflets. It is a plant that demands high humidity and temperatures and is therefore best grown in a warm sun-room where a surfeit of water is not a problem.

To many plant enthusiasts, this is one of the most delicate and attractive of all palms. Although not easy to grow, it is well worth the expense and trouble of seeking it out and growing it.

Phoenix canariensis
Canary Date Palm/Canary Palm/Canary Island Date

Height 1.2-1.8m/4-6ft
Spread 0.9-1.5m/3-5ft
Native Canary Islands

Greenfinger Guide

Temperature W 7-13°C/45-55°F – will do best at 10°C/50°F or slightly above **S** 13-21°C/55-70°F

Light W Full light. **S** Light shade.

Watering W Barely moist – but do not let the compost dry out. **S** Water freely, but ensure good drainage.

Feeding From late spring to late summer feed every two weeks.

Humidity Mist spray leaves in summer.

Compost Loam-based type.

Potting In spring, when the roots fill the pot – every two or three years.

Propagation Sow seeds – the fleshy date stones – in a peat-based compost during early spring. Place in 18-21°C/64-70°F. Germination can take up to two months. When large enough to handle, pot up the seedlings individually into small pots.

In its native land the Canary Date Palm grows 12m/40ft or more high, with arching leaves reaching 3m/10ft. In the home and when grown in a pot it is a little more reserved in stature and creates a beautiful plant.

Microcoelum weddelianum

Livistonia chinensis

The stiffly arching stems are covered with slender, spiky leaflets.

It is ideal for positioning against a white wall, and is further enhanced with spot lights – but ensure that they do not burn the leaflets.

Phoenix canariensis

Phoenix roebelenii

The Pygmy Date Palm is usually more suitable for most homes than most of its fellow species. It is almost stemless and creates a crown of arching fronds with very narrow leaflets that hang down at their tips. It is best displayed on a low side table, but where the fronds are unhindered and cannot be damaged by animals or passers-by.

The commercial Date Palm (*Phoenix dactylifera*) is occasionally offered as a houseplant, but is not really suited for this purpose. It is fast growing, and in North Africa, its native habitat, can reach over 30m/100ft tall.

Rhapsis excelsa
Little Lady Palm/Bamboo Palm/Broad-leaved Lady Palm/Miniature Fan Palm

Height 0.9-1.5m/3-5ft
Spread 75-90cm/2½-3ft
Native China and Japan

Greenfinger Guide

Temperature W 13-15°C/55-59°F S 16-21°C/61-70°F

Light W Bright, indirect light. S Light shade to bright, indirect light.

Watering W Just moist. S Water freely, but ensure good drainage.

Feeding From late spring to late summer feed every two to three weeks.

Humidity Mist spray leaves in summer.

Compost Loam-based type.

Potting In spring, when the roots fill the pot – usually every other year. Plants do best when the roots are contained in relatively small pots.

Propagation In spring or autumn remove suckers from around the bases of plants, transferring them into small pots. Each sucker must have a root attached to it.

The Little Lady Palm creates a clump with bamboo-like stems, each with five to eight, mid to dark green, finger-like leaves radiating from their tops like a fan. Each of the leaves are up to 20cm/8in long.

It is a superb palm for a small corner indoors, or in a sun-room.

Rhapsis excelsa

Phoenix roebelenii
Pygmy Date Palm/Miniature Date Palm/Roebelin

Height 0.9-1.2m/3-4ft
Spread 60-90cm/2-3ft
Native Eastern Asia

Greenfinger Guide

Temperature W 10-13°C/50-55°F S 13-21°C/55-70°F

Light W Full light. S Light shade.

Watering W Barely moist – but do not let the compost dry out. S Water freely, but ensure good drainage.

Feeding From late spring to late summer feed every two weeks.

Humidity Mist spray leaves in summer.

Compost Loam-based type.

Potting In spring, when the roots fill the pot – every two or three years.

Propagation In early summer detach sucker-like growths from around the parent plant and pot up singly. Keep them warm and moist until established. Alternatively, sow seeds – the fleshy date stones – in a peat-based compost during early spring. Place in 18-21°C/64-70°F. Germination can take up to two months. When large enough to handle, pot up the seedlings individually into small pots.

ferns

Adiantum capillus-veneris
Maidenhair Fern/Venus's-hair/Venus-hair Fern/ DudderGrass/Southern Maidenhair Fern

Height 15-25cm/6-10in
Spread 15-25cm/6-10in
Native Temperate and sub-tropical regions

Greenfinger Guide

Temperature W 50-55°C/10-13°F **S** 13-18°C/55-64°F – it tends to become dormant in summer if the temperature falls below 13°C/55°F.

Light W Light shade. **S** Light to medium shade.

Watering W Slightly moist. **S** Water freely, but ensure that the compost is not waterlogged.

Feeding From late spring to late summer feed every two weeks with a weak, half-strength, liquid fertilizer.

Humidity Mist spray the foliage in summer. As the temperature rises, increase the humidity around the plant by more frequent mist spraying.

Compost Loam-based compost with extra peat and sharp sand.

Potting In spring, when roots fill the pot – usually every one or two years.

Propagation Divide congested plants in spring.

The Maidenhair Fern is extremely dainty, with delicate light green fronds borne on wiry black stalks. Light shade and high humidity, with a warm and constant temperature, are the keys to success with this widely-grown plant. When grown in a sun-room or greenhouse it often naturalises itself under benches and staging, so indicating the position it loves best.

It will grow outdoors, but only in extremely sheltered and warm areas.

Adiantum raddianum
Delta Maidenhair Fern

Height 30-45cm/1-1½ft
Spread 38-60cm/15-24in
Native Brazil

Greenfinger Guide

Temperature W 50-55°C/10-13°F – will survive short periods at 7°C/45°F **S** 13-18°C/55-64°F

Light W Light shade. **S** Light to medium shade.

Watering W Slightly moist. **S** Water freely, but ensure that the compost is not waterlogged.

Feeding From late spring to late summer feed every two or three weeks with a weak, half-strength, liquid fertilizer.

Humidity Mist spray the foliage in summer.

Compost Loam-based compost with extra peat and sharp sand.

Potting In spring, when the roots fill the pot – usually every one or two years.

Propagation Divide congested plants in spring. Keep the young plants moist and in shade until established.

The Delta Maidenhair Fern is larger and more robust than the Maidenhair Fern, with long blackish stalks bearing pale green, finely-divided triangular fronds. Several superb forms are grown, including 'Fritz Luthii' (often commonly known as the Fritz Luthii Maidenhair) with long and narrow fronds with overlapping, curly-edged leaflets displaying a steel-blue appearance; 'Fragrantissima' which emits a strong fragrance, especially noticeable when plants are grown

Adiantum capillus-veneris

Adiantum raddianum

Adiantum raddianum 'Brilliantissimum'

in a bold display; 'Elegans' with compact fronds first reddish-brown and then slowly becoming yellow-green. 'Brilliantissimum' is another attractive variety for decorating homes.

These plants are ideal for growing in an indoor hanging-basket in a warm, humid and shaded corner – but be prepared to mist spray them frequently in hot weather.

Asplenium bulbiferum
Hen and Chicken Fern/Mother Fern/Mother Spleenwort/King and Queen Fern/Parsley Fern
Height 45-60cm/1½-2ft
Spread 60-90cm/2-3ft
Native Australia and New Zealand

Greenfinger Guide
Temperature W 7-10°C/45-50°F S 10-18°C/50-64°F

Light W Bright, indirect light. S Light to medium shade.

Watering W Just moist. S Water freely, but ensure good drainage.

Feeding From late spring to late summer feed every three weeks with a weak liquid fertilizer.

Humidity Mist spray in summer.

Adiantum raddianum 'Fritz Luthii'

Compost Equal parts loam-based compost, peat and sharp sand.

Potting In spring, when the roots fill the pot – usually every year for small plants.

Propagation Small bulbils grow from the upper surfaces of the fronds, especially at the edges. When these have three or four leaves, remove and prick off into boxes of equal parts moist peat and sharp sand, placing in 15°C/59°F. Pot up when rooted. Alternatively, in early summer, peg a complete leaf on the surface of compost. Detach and pot up the bulbils when rooted.

The Hen and Chicken Fern creates slender, slightly

Asplenium bulbiferum

arching black stalks up to 45cm/1½ft long that bear carrot-like mid-green fronds with small bulbils that weigh them down at their edges and tips.

It is an ideal fern for creating interest in a cool, but relatively bright room during winter. Although it will withstand temperatures down to near freezing, it benefits from a slightly more hospitable environment – but not tropical.

Asplenium nidus
Bird's Nest Fern/Nest Fern

Height 45-90cm/1½-3ft
Spread 30-60cm/1-2ft
Native Tropical Asia and Pacific Islands

Greenfinger Guide

Temperature W 13-16°C/55-61°F S 16-19°C/61-66°F

Light W Bright, indirect light. S Light to medium shade.

Watering W Just moist. S Water freely, but ensure good drainage.

Feeding From late spring to late summer feed every three weeks with a weak, half-strength, liquid fertilizer.

Humidity Mist spray fronds in summer, preferably with clean rain water.

Compost Peat-based type with sharp sand added to improve drainage.

Asplenium nidus

Potting In spring, when the rots fill the pot – usually every two years for small plants.

Propagation Usually raised from spores, but as this is a tricky operation it is best left to nurserymen.

The Bird's Nest Fern is elegant and distinctive, and certainly one of the most unusual ferns. Unlike most ferns, which have finely divided fronds, this one has large, entire-edged and spoon-shaped fronds up to 90cm/3ft or more long. They arise like a shuttlecock from around the fern's base, looking rather nest-like.

It is a fern that needs an unobstructed surface on which to be displayed. A polished dining table, where the shiny apple-green coloured leaves can reflect their beauty, is ideal.

There are several attractive forms of this fern, some with crinkly-edged fronds.

It is said that the hardiest forms of this fern have very black mid-ribs, and are able to withstand low temperatures in winter. Indeed, in Victorian times, when ferns were very popular, the variety *australasicum* was grown outdoors in warm areas during summer in bedding displays. Indeed, even today this plant benefits from a sojourn outside during hot periods – but ensure that there is shade from the sun.

Blechnum gibbum
Hard Fern/Rib Fern

Height 45-75cm/1½-2½ft
Spread 45-75cm/1½-2½ft
Native New Caledonia, New Hebrides, Isle of Pines in the South Pacific

Greenfinger Guide

Temperature W 15-18°C/59-64°F S 18-24°C/64-75°F

Light W Light shade to full sun. S Medium to light shade.

Watering W Moist, but not continually saturated. S Water freely, but ensure good drainage.

Feeding From late spring to late summer feed every three weeks with a weak, half-strength liquid fertilizer.

Humidity Mist spray the foliage in summer, especially if the temperature rises dramatically.

Compost Peat-based compost.

Potting In spring, when roots fill the pot, usually every three or four years:

Propagation Spores, but this is best left to experts.

All blechnum species are known as Hard Ferns in Britain, whereas in North America they are Rib Ferns and in Australia called Water Ferns. This species is a small tree fern and eventually forms a trunk some 30cm/12in high, although in the wild it is much more than this.

It is very attractive, with deeply-cut, mid-green fronds which form a closely knit spiral at the top of an upright stem, which eventually forms a trunk.

The Brazilian Tree Fern (*Blechnum brasiliense*) is slightly larger, eventually forming a trunk 90cm/3ft long. Although it is only small versions of it which are grown in pots, the fronds can grow to a diameter of 1.5m/5ft. It loves plenty of water in summer, when the temperature is high – a reflection of its Australian common name.

Cyrtomium falcatum
Holly Fern/Japanese Holly Fern

Height 20-38cm/8-15in
Spread 38-60cm/15-24in
Native China and Japan

Blechnum gibbum

Cyrtomium falcatum

Cyrtomium falcatum 'Rochfordianum'

Davallia canariensis

Greenfinger Guide

Temperature W 10-13°C/50-55°F – it will survive quite happily at 7°C/45°F if the compost is kept dry, but it is better at 10°C/50°F or above.
S 13-18°C/55-64°F – avoid very high temperatures.

Light W Bright, indirect light. **S** Light shade.

Watering W Slightly moist. **S** Water freely, especially when growing strongly in spring and early summer.

Feeding From late spring to late summer feed every two to three weeks with a weak, half-strength, liquid fertilizer.

Humidity Mist spray foliage during summer.

Compost Peat-based type.

Potting In spring, when the roots fill the pot – usually every two or three years.

Propagation Divide large and congested plants in spring.

The Holly Fern is well described by its common name, the fronds bearing holly-like and stiff, dark green and glossy, leaflets about 7.5cm/3in long that grow from each side of an arching stem. The form 'Rochfordianum' has slightly larger leaflets, wavy and with serrated edges.

It is a fern that needs a position that allows the fronds to arch unobstructed. It is especially attractive with a white wall as a background.

Nephrolepis exaltata

Davallia canariensis
Hare's-foot Fern/Deer's-foot Fern

Height 30-45cm/12-18in
Spread 30-38m/12-15in
Native North Africa, Canary Islands and Spain

Greenfinger Guide

Temperature W 10-15°C/50-59°F – it should not fall below 10°C/50°F S 13-21°C/55-70°F

Light W Bright, indirect sunlight. S Bright, indirect sunlight or light shade.

Watering W Keep the compost moist, but not totally and continually saturated. S Keep moist at all times, but ensure good drainage.

Feeding From late spring to late summer feed every three to four weeks with a weak liquid fertilizer.

Humidity Mist spray foliage in summer.

Compost Mixture of two parts peat and one each of loam and coarse sand. If available, add a part of chopped sphagnum moss.

Potting In spring, but only when the container is totally packed with roots.

Propagation Divide congested plants in spring.

The Hare's-foot Fern gains it name from the fleshy, rhizomatous roots which are covered with pale brown scales and resemble a hare's foot. The mid-green leaves are triangular and eventually hang down.

As well as growing in a pot it is ideal for planting in an indoor hanging-basket.

Nephrolepis exaltata
Ladder Fern

Height 45-75cm/1½-2½ft
Spread 45-90cm/1½-3ft
Native Tropics

Greenfinger Guide

Temperature W 13-16°C/55-61°F – it will survive short periods at 10°C/50°F, but is better at 13°C/55°F. S 16-21°C/61-70°F

Light W Bright, indirect light. S Bright, indirect light.

Watering W Just moist – if the temperature falls dramatically, keep the compost slightly drier. S Water freely, but ensure good drainage.

Feeding From late spring to late summer feed every two to three weeks with a weak, half-strength, liquid fertilizer.

Humidity Mist spray fronds in summer.

Compost Peat-based type.

Potting In spring, every year. Remove the plant from its pot, tease away old compost and repot into the same size pot or one slightly larger.

Propagation Divide congested plants in spring.

The Ladder Fern is one of the toughest of all indoor ferns. It is also one of the most versatile and attractive. The ordinary type has long and tapering, paper-thin and bright green, stiff and arching fronds with plain edges, but it is usually the more decorative forms that are grown. The Boston Fern (*N. e.* 'Bostoniensis') has border and shorter fronds, up to 90cm/3ft long, graceful and arching; the Lace Fern (*N. e.* 'Whitmanii') has 45cm/1½ft long fronds with frilled and finely-cut edges that have a feather-like appearance; *N.e.* 'Elegantissima' has bright green fronds with finely cut and overlapping edges; *N.e.* 'Hillii' has light green, crinkled fronds; *N.e.* 'Marshallii' displays pale green, densely-crested and wide fronds; *N. e.* 'Todeoides' displays pale green, feathery and finely-divided fronds. *N.e.* 'Rooseveltii' is another well-known and attractive form.

Nephrolepis exaltata 'Bostoniensis'

Those forms that have arching fronds are ideal for growing in an indoor hanging-basket, while the other are best displayed on a table that allows the fronds to spread unhindered. The ideal support is a Victorian plant stand, narrow but firmly-based and displaying the plant 0.9-1.2m/3-4ft above the floor.

Pellaea rotundifolia
Button Fern/New Zealand Cliff Brake
Height 25-30cm/10-12in
Spread 30-38cm/12-15in

Native New Zealand

Greenfinger Guide

Temperature W 10-13°C/50-55°F – it will survive periods down to 7°C/45°F. **S** 16-21°C/61-70°F

Light W Bright, indirect light. **S** Bright, indirect light.

Watering W Just moist. **S** Water freely – never let the compost dry out but also do not let it become waterlogged.

Feeding From late spring to late summer feed

every two to three weeks with a weak liquid fertilizer.

Humidity Mist spray foliage during summer.

Compost Peat-based compost.

Potting In spring, when roots fill the pot – usually every two years.

Propagation Divide large and congested plants in spring. It may mean cutting through the fleshy rhizomatous roots. Don't divide plants into very small pieces.

The Button Fern creates a wealth of small, button-like,

Nephrolepis exaltata 'Rooseveltii'

Pellaea rotundifolia

slightly waxy, dark green and shiny leaves along wiry stems. These stems cascade and create a neat houseplant ideal for placing on tables, shelves and shaded window-sills. Placing the growing pot in a white outer container helps to highlight the beautiful fronds. It can also be grown in an indoor hanging-basket.

The Green Cliff Brake (*Pellaea viridis*) but also known as *P. hastata* is another pretty fern for the home. It has feathery, lobed, dark green fronds which give it a much more fern-like appearance than the Button Fern. The fronds grow to about 45cm/18in long and have black, shining stalks.

Phlebodium aureum
Golden Polypody/Rabbit's-foot Fern/Hare's-foot Fern

Height 60-75cm/2-2½ft -sometimes up to 1.2m/4ft
Spread 45-60cm/1½-2ft
Native Tropical South America

Greenfinger Guide

Temperature **W** 13-16°C/55-61°F – if possible, keep to the upper limit of this range. **S** 16-21°C/16-70°F

Light **W** Indirect light. **S** Light shade.

Watering **W** Barely moist **S** Water freely, but ensure good drainage.

Feeding From late spring to late summer feed every three to four weeks with a weak liquid fertilizer.

Humidity Mist spray the fronds in summer.

Compost Loam-based type with extra peat.

Potting In spring, when roots fill the pot – usually every two or three years.

Propagation Divide congested plants in spring, when being repotted.

Phlebodium aureum

The Golden Polypody eventually forms a large and somewhat spreading fern, with deeply incised, mid-green fronds sometimes 1.2m/4ft long. When young the plant has a neat appearance, but with age can become rather sprawling, although still with a relatively upright nature.

There are several glaucous forms of this fern, sometimes erroneously labelled. However, one form to look our for is *Phlebodium aureum* 'Glaucum' with blue-grey fronds. This plant is sometimes listed as *Polypodium aureum* 'Glaucum' or just *Polypodium glaucum*.

Phyllitis scolopendrium
Hart's-tongue Fern/Deer-tongue Fern

Height 30-45cm/1-1½ft – grows slightly higher when grown in a sheltered, warm and shady part of a garden.
Spread 25-50cm/10-20in
Native Widespread in the Northern Hemisphere

Growing Guide

Temperature W 5-10°C/41-50°F – it will survive temperatures down to 2°C/36°F, but the fronds may be damaged. S 10-13°C/50-55°F

Light W Indirect light. S Light shade.

Watering W Barely moist S Water freely, but ensure good drainage.

Feeding From late spring to late summer feed every three to four weeks with a weak liquid fertilizer.

Humidity Mist spraying is not necessary.

Compost Loam-based type with extra peat.

Potting In spring, when the roots fill the pot – usually every three years.

Propagation Divide congested ferns in spring.

Phyllitis scolopendrium

Phyllitis scolopendrium 'Cristatum'

The Hart's-tongue Fern is unlike most other ferns. The fronds are not divided but have an entire outline resembling a long tongue. They are bright shiny green and create an interesting plant for a cool room. Two forms are frequently grown which have even more attractive fronds. 'Crispum' has edges to the fronds which are waved and crisped, while 'Cristatum' is slightly smaller than the normal type and has fronds which are branched and crested.

This fern can also be grown outdoors in shady positions, but in cold areas the fronds will be severely damaged. The advantage of growing this plant indoors is that it always remains attractive.

Platycerium bifurcatum
Stag Horn Fern
Height 45-60cm/1½-2ft
Spread 45-75cm/1½-2½ft
Native Australia

Greenfinger Guide
Temperature **W** 7-13°C/45-55°F, but is best at 10°C/50°F or slightly above. **S** 13-24°C/55-75°F

Light **W** Bright, indirect light. **S** Light shade.

Watering **W** Just moist. **S** Water thoroughly.

Feeding From late spring to late summer feed every four weeks with a weak liquid fertilizer.

Humidity Mist spray fronds during summer, especially when the temperature rises excessively.

Compost Mixture of equal parts peat, loam and

Platycerium bifurcatum

Platycerium grande

Polystichum setiferum 'Densum'

Polystichum setiferum 'Proliferum'

sphagnum moss for plants in indoor hanging-baskets. Alternatively, plants can be wrapped in sphagnum moss, tied to a piece of bark and hung up in a greenhouse or sun-room.

Potting Young plants are usually sold growing in small pots. In spring, either secure the plant to a piece of bark and hang up, or plant it in a hanging-basket.

Propagation In spring, remove and pot up young offsets growing around the plant.

The Stag Horn Fern eventually forms a dominant plant with large, two or three-lobed mid-green fronds covered with minute whitish hairs.

The Elk Horn Fern (*Platycerium grande*) is similar, but much larger and may reach 1.5m/5ft or more wide, with deeply-lobed pale green fronds that turn upwards. It is usually much too large for growing indoors, and is best grown in a large sun-room or greenhouse. Also, it needs a slightly higher temperature in winter.

Polystichum setiferum
Soft Shield Fern/Hedge Fern/English Hedge Fern

Height 60-75cm/2-2½ft
Spread 0.75-1.2m/2½-4ft
Native Tropical and temperate regions

Greenfinger Guide

Temperature W 7-10°C/45-50°F – although it will survive temperatures down to 5°C/45°F for short periods, but the fronds will not be so attractive. S 10-15°C/50-59°F – avoid high temperatures.

Light W Full light. S Light shade.

Watering W Just moist. S Water freely, but ensure good drainage. The compost must not become waterlogged.

Feeding From late spring to late summer feed every three to four weeks.

Humidity Mist spray fronds in summer.

Compost Loam-based type with extra peat. Ensure that the compost contains chalk, and is not acid.

Pteris cretica 'Albo-lineata'

Pteris cretica 'Major'

Potting In spring, when the roots fill the pot – usually every two or three years.

Propagation Divide congested plants when being repotted in spring.

The Soft Shield Fern has dull, mid-green, finely-divided fronds that initially rise vertically and then splay out as the clump grows. This evergreen fern is hardy enough to be grown outdoors, but often does better when planted into the soil in a cool sun-room or greenhouse, where it retains its evergreen nature more readily. When grown in a pot it can be taken indoors, but avoid high temperatures.

There are several superb varieties of this fern, including 'Densum' and 'Proliferum', both illustrated here.

There are several other polystichum species grown indoors, such as the Tsusian Holly Fern (*Polystichum tsus-simense*) with small, finely-divided fronds.

Pteris cretica
Ribbon Fern/Cretan Brake Fern

Height 30-45cm/1-1½ft
Spread 23-38cm/9-15in
Native South-west Europe, India, Iran and Japan

Greenfinger Guide

Temperature W 7-10°C/45-50°F S 10-18°C/50-64°F

Light W Light, indirect sunlight. S Light shade.

Watering W Slightly moist. S Water freely, but ensure good drainage.

Feeding From late spring to late summer feed every three weeks with a weak, half-strength, liquid fertilizer.

Humidity Mist spray foliage in summer when the temperature rises excessively.

Compost Mixture of two parts peat and one each of loam and coarse sand. Alternatively, use a peat-based type.

Potting In spring, but only when the roots fill the pot – usually every three or four years. It likes to have the pot congested with roots.

Propagation Divide congested plants in spring.

The Ribbon Fern has light green fronds formed of strap-shaped pinnae which have given rise to the common name.

There are several attractive forms of this fern. Perhaps the best known and most widely grown is 'Albo-lineata', which is slightly smaller than the normal type and displays fronds with white bands along the midribs. Never position this, or any other variegated form, in direct sunlight, especially during summer, as it stunts their growth. 'Wimsettii' is well known for its attractively crested fronds, and a closely related form 'Wimsettii Multiceps' has tassled tips to its serrated leaf edges.

'Mayi' is another variegated forms, this time with attractively divided fronds, while 'Major' has unbranched fronds but with slightly serrated edges.

There are many others, including 'Childs'i', often known as the Child's Cretan Brake Fern, which has fresh green fronds with rippled and finely ruffled edges. Also, the tips of these fronds become divided when mature. 'Wilsonii', known as the Fan Table Fern, is upright, with fresh green, fan-shaped frond with crested tips. 'Magnifica' is another upright growing type, with long, narrow fronds with small, tufted tips.

Pteris ensiformis
Sword Brake

Height 38-45cm/15-18in
Spread 25-30cm/10-12in
Native Himalayas, and Ceylon to Australia

Greenfinger Guide

***Temperature* W** 13-15°C/55-59°F **S** 15-18°C/59-64°F

***Light* W** Light, indirect sunlight. **S** Light shade.

***Watering* W** Slightly moist. **S** Water freely, but ensure good drainage.

Feeding From late spring to late summer feed every three weeks with a weak, half-strength, liquid fertilizer.

Humidity Mist spray foliage in summer when the temperature rises excessively.

Compost Mixture of two parts peat and one each of loam and coarse sand. Alternatively, use a peat-based type.

Potting In spring, but only when roots fill the pot – usually every three or four years.

Propagation Divide congested plants in spring.

This fern is quite similar to the Ribbon Fern, *Pteris cretica*, but with more delicate, slender and deeper green fronds. The form most often grown is 'Victoriae, often known as the Silver Lace Fern, Victoria Brake Fern or Silver-leaf Fern, with fronds displaying white midribs. These are quite small ferns, ideal for decorating small tables in cool and slightly shaded rooms.

Pteris quadriaurita 'Argyraea'

Pteris ensiformis 'Victoriae'

Pteris quadriaurita

Height 30-60cm/1-2ft
Spread 25-60cm/10-24in
Native Tropics

Greenfinger Guide

***Temperature* W** 10-13°C/50-55°F **S** 13-20°C/55-68°F

***Light* W** Light, indirect sunlight. **S** Light shade.

***Watering* W** Slightly moist. **S** Water freely, but ensure good drainage.

Feeding From late spring to late summer feed every three or four weeks with a weak, half-strength, liquid fertilizer.

Humidity Mist spray foliage in summer when the temperature rises excessively.

Compost Mixture of two parts peat and one each of loam and coarse sand. Alternatively, use a peat-based type.

Potting In spring, but only when the roots fill the pot – usually every three or four years.

Propagation Divide congested plants in spring.

Pteris quadriaurita is usually grown in the highly attractive form *Pteris quadriaurita argyraea*, also known as *Pteris biaurita argyraea* but usually sold under the name *Pteris argyraea*. It also has several common names, such as the Silver Fern, Silver Lace Fern, Striped Brake Fern and Silver Brake. It is a beautiful variegated form, with long, grey-green fronds distinctively marked with light greenish-white bands along their centres.

While young and small it is ideal for displaying on a small side table, but with age it will need more space.

Pteris tremula
Australian Trembling Fern/Poor Man's Cibotium/Australian Bracken

Height 60-90cm/2-3ft

Spread 60-75cm/2-2½ft
Native Australia, New Zealand and Fiji

Greenfinger Guide

Temperature W 7-10°C/45-50°F S 10-18°C/
50-64°F

Light W Light, indirect sunlight. S Light shade.

Watering W Slightly moist. S Water freely, but
ensure good drainage.

Feeding From late spring to late summer feed
every three weeks with a weak, half-strength, liquid
fertilizer.

Humidity Mist spray foliage in summer when the
temperature rises excessively.

Compost Mixture of two parts peat and one each
of loam and coarse sand. Alternatively, use a peat-
based type.

Potting In spring, but only when roots fill the pot –
usually every three or four years. It likes to have the
pot congested with roots.

Propagation Divide congested plants in spring.
When grown in a cool sun-room or greenhouse it
frequently reproduces itself from seeds, without
help from man.

The Australian Trembling Fern eventually creates a
large and imposing display, and is best suited for
growing in a sun-room or a greenhouse. The slim,

Pteris vittata

Pteris tremula

arching, triangular, bright green fronds have a feathery
nature.

Pteris vittata

**Ladder Brake/Ladder Brake Fern/Chinese Brake/
Rusty Brake**
Height 45-60cm/1½-2ft – sometimes 90cm/3ft
Spread 45-60cm/1½-2ft
Native Tropics and subtropics

Greenfinger Guide

Temperature W 10-13°C/50-55°F S 13-18°C/
55-64°F

Light W Light shade. S Light shade.

Watering W Just moist. S Water freely, but ensure
good drainage.

Feeding From late spring to late summer feed
every three to four weeks with a weak, half-
strength, liquid fertilizer.

Humidity Mist spray the foliage in summer,
especially when the temperature is high.

Compost Mixture of two parts peat and one each
of loam and coarse sand. Alternatively, use a peat-
based type.

Potting In spring, when the roots fill the pot –
usually every three years.

Propagation Increase by spores.

The Ladder Brake – not to be confused with the
Ladder Fern (*Nephrolepis exaltata*) – is a fast-growing
and easily-raised graceful plant with dark green, semi-
upright fronds which do not produce crested tips.

Pteris vittata

bromeliads

Aechmea blumenavii

Aechmea fasciata

Aechmea blumenavii

Height 60-70cm/24-28in
Spread 38-50cm/15-20in
Native Brazil

Greenfinger Guide

Temperature W 13-15°C/55-59°F – will survive temperatures down to 5°C/41°F or even fractionally lower, but best at 13°C/55°F or above. **S** 15-24°C/59-75°F

Light W Indirect light. **S** Indirect light or light shade.

Watering W Just moist. Keep the rosette full of water. If the temperature falls to 5°C/41°F or below, keep the compost only barely moist. Preferably, use clean rainwater. But in hardwater areas tapwater can be softened by adding a teaspoon of vinegar to a gallon of water. **S** Water freely, but ensure good drainage. Keep the urn full of water – tip out and replenish every four weeks.

Feeding From late spring to late summer add a weak liquid – quarter to one-third strength – fertilizer to the water every three to four weeks. This can be applied to the compost, as well as to the water in the urn.

Humidity During summer mist spray the leaves several times a day, and also in winter if the atmosphere is dry and warm.

Compost Two parts peat-based compost and one of sharp sand. It is essential that the compost does not contain lime.

Potting In spring, repot the young offsets – which were previously removed from a parent – if they are in very small pots. Ensure that the bottom third of the pot is well drained – use broken pieces of clay pots.

Propagation Once a plant has flowered it is not repotted, as the rosette slowly dies and growth is

Aechmea chantinii

taken over by offsets growing around it – the main rosette being cut off at compost level.

As well as leaving offsets around your aechmea to replace the mother plant after flowering, young offsets can be removed when 15cm/6in long. Sever with a sharp knife, allow the cut surfaces to dry for about twenty-four hours and then pot up into the normal compost. Place in 21-27°C/70-80°F. Support with thin canes and mist spray until established.

Aechmea blumenavii develops ten to fifteen strap-like – slightly arching and 36mm/1½in wide – green leaves with scaly-white overtones which form a tube. At their tops they become dark violet.

During mid to late summer the plant produces yellow flowers, each about 15mm/0.125in long and in loose clusters at the tops on long and stiff stems.

Aechmea chantinii
Amazonian Zebra Plant

Height 45-75cm/1½-2½ft
Spread 45-60cm/1½-2ft
Native Northern Peru, Brazil

Greenfinger Guide
Temperature W 13-18°C/55-64°F – this bromeliad needs a relatively high temperature, preferably towards the higher end of this winter range. S 18-27°C/64-80°F

Light W Indirect light. S Indirect light or light shade.

Watering W Just moist, and keep the rosette full of water. If the temperature falls to the lower end of the range, ensure that the compost is kept only barely moist. Use soft water, preferably clean rainwater. However, tapwater can be softened by adding a teaspoon of vinegar to a gallon of water.

S Water freely, but ensure good drainage. Keep the urn full of water – tip out and replenish every four weeks.

Feeding From late spring to late summer add a weak liquid – quarter to one-third strength – fertilizer to the water every three to four weeks. This can be applied to the compost, as well as the urn.

Humidity During summer mist spray the leaves several times a day, and also in winter if the atmosphere is dry and warm. Humidity is vital for the success of this aechmea, especially when the temperature is high.

Compost Two parts peat-based compost and one of sharp sand. It is essential that the compost does not contain lime.

Potting In spring, pot up young offsets – which were previously removed from a parent – if they are in very small pots. Ensure that the bottom of the pot is well drained – fill with broken pieces of clay pots.

Propagation Once a plant has flowered it is not repotted, as the rosette slowly dies and growth is taken over by offsets growing around it – the main rosette being cut off at compost level. As well as leaving offsets around your aechmea to replace the mother plant after flowering, offsets can be removed when 15cm/6in long. Sever with a sharp knife, allow the cut surface to dry for about twenty-four hours and then pot up into the normal compost. Support with thin canes, mist spray and place in 21-27°C/70-80°F.

The Amazonian Zebra Plant is a large plant with a rosette formed of spine-edged, spine-tipped, 30-38cm/12-15in long and 5-6cm/2-2½in wide green leaves with wide grey cross bands on both sides. During late summer and into autumn it produces a 10-15cm/4-6in long oval head formed of orange to bright red flowers.

It is an aechmea that tends to spread sideways, eventually forming a large clump.

An attractive form is sometimes seen, with white cross-banding and yellowish edges to the leaves.

Aechmea fasciata
Urn Plant/Vase Plant/Silver Vase

Height 38-45cm/15-18in
Spread 38-50cm/15-20in
Native Brazil

Greenfinger Guide
Temperature W 13-15°C/55-59°F – will survive temperatures down to 5°C/41°F, or even fractionally lower. But it is best at 13°C/55°F or above. S 15-24°C/59-75°F

Light W Indirect light. S Indirect light to light shade.

Watering W Just moist, and keep the rosette full of water. If the temperature falls to 5°C/41°F or below, keep the compost barely moist. Preferably, use clean rainwater. But in hardwater areas tapwater can be softened by adding a teaspoon of vinegar to a gallon of water. S Water freely, but ensure good drainage. Keep the urn full of water – tip out and replenish every four weeks.

Feeding From late spring to late summer add a weak liquid fertilizer to the water every three to four weeks. This can be applied to the compost as well as the water in the urn.

Humidity During summer mist spray the leaves several times a day, and also in winter if the atmosphere is dry and warm.

Compost Two parts peat-based compost and one of sharp sand. It is essential that the compost does not contain lime.

Potting In spring, pot up offsets – which were previously removed from a parent – if they are in very small pots. Ensure that the base of the pot is well drained with broken pieces of pot.

Propagation Once a plant has flowered it is not repotted, as the rosette slowly dies and growth is taken over by offsets growing around the main rosette being cut off at compost level.   As well as leaving offsets around your aechmea to replace the mother plant after it flowers, offsets can be removed when 13-15cm/5-6in high. Sever with a sharp knife, allow the cut surface to dry for about twenty-four hours and then pot up into the normal compost. Support with thin canes, mist spray and place in 21-27°C/70-80°C.

The Urn Plant is probably the most widely grown aechmea, forming a large rosette of leaves up to 50cm/20in long and 6cm/2½in wide. They are greyish-green and cross-banded with silvery-white. During late summer and into autumn a flower stem emerges from the urn and creates a head up to 15cm/6in long, formed of pale blue flowers which turn rose. The light pink bracts last for several months.

A couple of very attractive forms of this plant are sometimes available: *A. f.* 'Variegata', known as the Variegated Silver Vase, has wide creamy-white stripes down the centres of the leaves, while *A. f. marginata*, the White Margined Vase Plant, displays white stripes down the edges of the leaves.

Aechmea 'Foster's Favorite'
Lacquered Wine-cup

Height 30-38cm/12-15in
Spread 30-45cm/12-18in
Native Hybrid

Greenfinger Guide
Temperature W 13-15°C/55-59°F – will survive temperatures down to 5°C/41°F, or even fractionally lower, but is best at 13°C/55°F. S 15-24°C/59-75°F

Light W Indirect light. S Indirect light or light shade.

Watering W Just moist. Keep the small cup-shaped urn full of water. If the temperature falls to 5°C/41°F or below, keep the compost barely moist. Preferably, use clean rainwater, but in hardwater areas tapwater can be softened by adding a teaspoon of vinegar to a gallon of water. S Water freely, but ensure good drainage. Keep the small urn full of water – tip out and replenish every four weeks.

Feeding From late spring to late summer add a weak – quarter to one-third strength – liquid fertilizer to the water every three to four weeks. This is best applied to the compost, as well as water in the urn.

Aechmea 'Foster's Favorite'

Aechmea fulgens

Humidity During summer mist spray the leaves several times a day, and also in winter if the atmosphere is dry and warm.

Compost Two parts peat-based compost and one of sharp sand. It is essential that the compost does not contain lime.

Potting In spring, pot up young offsets – which were previously removed from a parent plant – if they are in very small pots.

Propagation Once a plant has flowered it is not repotted, as the rosette slowly dies and growth is taken over by offsets growing around it – the main rosette being cut off at compost level.

As well as leaving offsets around your aechmea to replace the mother plant after flowering, young offsets can be removed when 13-15cm/5-6in high. Sever with a sharp knife, allow the cut surface to dry for about twenty-four hours and pot up into the normal compost. Support with thin canes, mist spray and place in 21-27°C/70-80°F.

Aechmea 'Foster's Favorite' forms a rosette of long, tapering, fairly sparse, deep wine-red leaves. It is a relatively small aechmea and forms only a small central urn. During late summer it produces a flower spike formed of coral petals tipped with blue.

The form 'Foster's Favorite Favorite', also known as the Variegated Lacquered Wine-cup, has strikingly variegated leaves. They are mainly pale yellow, with dark green and wine-red stripes along their centres. The flower stem arches and bears berry-like flowers.

Aechmea fulgens
Coral Berry
Height 25-38cm/10-15in
Spread 30-38cm/12-15in
Native Brazil

Greenfinger Guide

Temperature W 13-15°C/55-59°F – will survive temperatures down to 5°C/41°F, or even fractionally lower. But it is best at 13°C/55°F or above. **S** 15-24°C/59-75°F

Light W Indirect light. **S** Indirect light or light shade.

Watering W Just moist. Keep the rosette full of water. If the temperature falls to 5°C/41°F or below, keep the compost barely moist. Preferably, use clean rainwater, but in hardwater areas tapwater can be softened by adding a teaspoon of vinegar to a gallon of water. **S** Water freely, but ensure good drainage. Keep the urn full of water – tip out and replenish every four weeks.

Feeding From late spring to late summer add a weak – quarter to one-third strength – liquid fertilizer to the water every three to four weeks. This can be applied to the compost as well as water in the urn.

Humidity During summer mist spray the leaves several times a day, and also in the winter if the atmosphere is dry and warm.

Compost Two parts peat-based compost and one of sharp sand. It is essential that the compost does not contain lime.

Potting In spring, pot up young offsets – which were previously removed from a parent plant – if they are in very small pots. Ensure that the bottom third of the pot is well drained.

Propagation Once a plant has flowered it is not repotted, as the rosette slowly dies and growth is taken over by rosettes growing around it – the main rosette being cut off at compost level.

As well as leaving offsets around your aechmea to replace the mother plant after flowering, offsets can be removed when 13-15cm/5-6in long. Sever with a sharp knife, allow the cut surface to dry for about twenty-four hours and then pot up into the normal compost. Support with thin canes, mist spray and

place in 21-27°C/70-80°F.

Aechmea fulgens creates a rosette of broad, strap-like, finely spine-edged leaves. They are green, rounded and spine tipped. The undersides are waxy-grey. During late summer and into autumn it bears a 10-15cm/4-5in long head formed of waxy-blue flowers. These are followed by attractive red berries which persist for several months.

The form most often grown is *A. f. discolor*, which has a strong red colour to the undersides of the leaves.

Ananas comosus
Common Pineapple/Edible Pineapple
Height 45-75cm/1½-2½ft
Spread 60-75cm/2-2½ft
Native Colombia/Brazil

Greenfinger Guide

Temperature W 13-24°C/55-75°F – will tolerate 10°C/50°F for sort periods, but is much better at 13°C/55°F or above. **S** 15-24°C/59-75°F

Light W Bright light. **S** Diffused light to full sun.

Watering W Just moist. If the temperature rises and the plant becomes more active, increase the frequency of watering. If the temperature falls, keep the compost barely moist. **S** Water freely, allowing the compost to dry out slightly between waterings.

Feeding From mid spring to early autumn feed every three to four weeks. If the temperature is high during winter, and the plant is actively growing, feed every eight weeks. Always use a weak – quarter to one-third strength – mixture.

Humidity Mist spray leaves in summer; also in winter if the atmosphere is dry and the temperature high.

Compost Two parts loam-based compost and one part each of peat and sharp sand.

Potting In spring, usually every other year.

Propagation During spring cut offsets from around the base of the plant. Allow to dry for twenty-four hours and then pot up into equal parts moist peat and sharp sand and place in 21°C/70°F. When rooted and growing strongly, pot up into the normal compost.

The Common Pineapple can grow up to 1.2m/4ft or more high, but is usually seen with a much smaller stature. It forms a rosette of arching, spiny-edged, grey-green leaves. The leaves become reddish if the plant is given a sunny position. A blue-petalled flower

Aechmea fulgens discolor

Ananas comosus 'Variegatus'

Ananas sagenaria 'Striatus'

with small pink bracts is borne at the top of a short, stiff flowering stem. Fruits appear about six months after the flowers, but these seldom develop indoors. A sun room or greenhouse with a high and even temperature is needed for this.

The form *A. c. variegatus*, the Variegated Pineapple, is more attractive and through its smaller stature is better suited to cultivation indoors. It has green, white, yellow and pink in its serrated-edged leaves. Strong sunlight enhances the colours in the leaves.

Ananas sagenaria
Red Pineapple
Height 60-75cm/2-2½ft
Spread 60-75cm/2-2½ft
Native Brazil

Greenfinger Guide
Temperature W 13-24°C/55-75°F – will tolerate 10°C/50°F for short periods, but is much better at

13°C/55°F or above. **S** 15-24°C/59-75°F

Light W Bright light. **S** Diffused light to full sun.

Watering W Just moist, but if the temperature rises and the plant becomes more active, increase the frequency of watering. If the temperature falls, keep the compost barely moist. **S** Water freely, allow the compost to dry out slightly between waterings.

Feeding From mid spring to late summer feed every three to four weeks. If the temperature is high during winter, and the plant is actively growing, feed every eight weeks. Always use a weak – quarter to one-third strength – mixture.

Humidity Mist spray leaves in summer; also in winter if the atmosphere is dry and the temperature high.

Compost Two parts loam-based compost and one part each of peat and sharp sand.

Potting In spring, usually every other year.

Propagation During spring cut offsets from around the bases of the plant. Allow them to dry for twenty-four hours and then pot into equal parts of moist peat and sharp sand. Place in 21°C/70°F. When rooted and growing strongly, pot up into the normal compost.

The Red Pineapple is slow-growing, eventually reaching 1.2m/4ft in about eight years. It forms an attractive rosette similar to *A. comosus*, but with lavender coloured flowers which are followed by brownish fruits. However, it is most often grown in the form *A. s. striatus*, also known as *A. bracteatus striatus*, brightly coloured with leaves displaying green, cream and pink stripes.

Billbergia nutans
Angel's Tears/Queen's Tears/Friendship Plant
Height 38-50cm/15-20in
Spread 30-45cm/12-18in
Native Brazil, Uruguay, Paraguay and Argentina

Greenfinger Guide
Temperature W 10-13°C/50-55°F – will survive

temperatures of 2-5°C/36-41°F for short periods, but is better at 10°C/50°F or above. **S** 16-24°C/61-75°F

Light W Bright light. **S** Lightly filtered to bright light, but not direct sunlight.

Watering W Moderately, but allow the compost to become almost dry before applying further water. If the temperature is low during winter, take extra care not to water your plant excessively or to splash the leaves, as this will cause them to rot. **S** Water freely, but allow the surface compost to nearly dry out before applying further water. Preferably, use clean rainwater. In hardwater areas, add a tablespoon of vinegar to a gallon of tapwater.

Feeding From late spring to late summer feed every two to three weeks with a half-strength liquid fertilizer. The foliage also absorbs nutrients, and a

Billbergia nutans

weak liquid fertilizer can be syringed over the leaves.

Humidity Stand the pot on a tray of moist pebbles, and mist spray the foliage during summer.

Compost Lime-free, open-textured compost such as equal parts peat, coarse leafmould and sharp sand.

Potting In spring, when the roots fill the pot. However, most bromeliads will grow in quite small pots with little compost, and repotting is an infrequent operation.

Propagation During spring, remove offsets from the plant's base and pot them up separately. Mist spray them and place in 21-24°C/70-75°F.

The Angel's Tears is an outstandingly attractive bromeliad, with dark green, narrow leaves and arching stems bearing 7.5-10cm/3-4in long clusters formed of large pink bracts and long, tubular green flowers edged in blue. These are further enhanced by golden-yellow stamens.

It is one of the easiest bromeliads to grow and well worth having as a houseplant, where it is ideal for decorating a dining table.

Billbergia x 'Windii'
Billbergia x 'Windii'
Height 38-45cm/15-18in
Spread 38-45cm/15-18in
Native Hybrid

Greenfinger Guide

Temperature W 10-13°C/50-55°F – will survive temperatures of 2-5°C/36-41°F for short periods, but is better at 10°C/50°F or above. S 16-24°C/61-75°F

Light W Bright light. S Lightly filtered to bright light, but not direct and strong sunlight.

Watering W Moderately, but allow the compost to become almost dry before applying further water. S Water freely, but allow the surface compost to nearly dry out before applying further water. If the temperature is low during winter, take extra care not to water the plant excessively or to splash the

Billbergia x 'Windii'

leaves, as this will cause them to rot.

Feeding From late spring to late summer feed every two to three weeks with a weak, half-strength, liquid fertilizer.

Humidity Stand the pot on a tray of moist pebbles, and mist spray the foliage during summer.

Compost Lime-free, open-textured compost such as equal parts peat, coarse leafmould and sharp sand.

Potting In spring, when the roots fill the pot. However, most bromeliads will grow in quite small pots with little compost, and repotting is an infrequent operation.

Propagation During spring, remove offsets from the plant's base and pot them up separately. Mist spray frequently and place in 21-24°C/70-75°F.

Billbergia x 'Windii' is a hybrid between *B. nutans* and *B. decora*. Although it bears a resemblance to *B. nutans*, the leaves are more rigid and wider, as well as arching at their tips. These are grey-green, but because of a covering of grey scales they have a slight flour-like appearance. The 2.5-4cm/1-1½in long, pendant, tubular flowers are a combination of pink and bluish-green, with long pale yellow stamens.

It makes a more compact and dense plant than *B. nutans*, and if a high temperature and high humidity can be maintained it is ideal for positioning on a table.

Canistrum x 'Leopardinum'
Basket Bromeliad
Height 38-50cm/15-20in
Spread 38-50cm/15-20in
Native Hybrid

Greenfinger Guide

Temperature W 13-18°C/55-64°F – it survives temperatures down to 10°C/50°F for short periods, but is best at 13°C/55° or above. S 18-27°C/64-80°F

Canistrum 'Leopardinum'

Cryptanthus acaulis

the outer parts of a flower. *Canistrum* 'Leopardinum' is a hybrid, a cross between *Canistrum ingratum* and *C. roseum* which forms a compact and multi-leaved bromeliad. The leaves are green with irregular black spots, with spiny tips.

Cryptanthus acaulis
Green Earth Star/Starfish Plant

Height 5-7.5cm/2-3in
Spread 7.5-13cm/3-5in
Native Brazil

Greenfinger Guide

Temperature W 16-20°C/61-68°F – it is essential that the temperature does not fall below these figures as the plants will then be damaged. **S** 21-27°C/70-80°C

Light W Full sun or light shade. **S** Full sun or light shade.

Watering W Keep the compost barely moist. If the temperature rises and plants become more active, increase the amount of water. **S** Water freely, but ensure good drainage. Always use soft water, preferably clean rainwater. If your tapwater is hard, add a tablespoon of vinegar to each gallon.

Feeding From late spring to late summer feed every five to six weeks with a weak, half-strength, liquid fertilizer. This can also be added to the water used to mist spray the leaves.

Humidity Mist spray the leaves regularly in summer.

Compost Two parts peat-based compost and one of sharp sand.

Potting In early summer, when a high temperature can be maintained to encourage rapid growth.

Propagation The offsets on cryptanthus plants develop from mid-way between the rosette leaves. They eventually fall off, roll down and root around the parent plant. Therefore, the easiest way to increase this plant is to remove a congested specimen from its pot and to carefully pull away the young offsets. These are potted up and placed in 21°C/70°F until established.

The Green Earth Star forms an attractive rosette of wavy and tooth-edged, pale green leaves. The undersides are beautifully scaled with white. It has the bonus of scented, 2.5cm/1in wide, white flowers which may appear at any time of the year, but mainly in summer. However, the plant is mainly grown for its attractive shape and foliage.

The form 'Argenteus' is slightly larger, has silvery scales on both the upper and lower sides of the leaves, while 'Rubra' has a purple-brown shade over the green. 'Roseo-pictus' is another attractive form, with attractively zoned leaves.

As well as for decorating small shelves and tables, it can be planted in a bottle garden or other closed glass container.

Cryptanthus acaulis 'Roseo-pictus'

Light W Lightly filtered light. **S** Lightly filtered light to slight shade. It grows well even in poor light, the leaves assuming a bluish tinge.

Watering W Moderately, but allow the compost to become slightly dry before applying further water. Also, keep the central vase full of water. **S** Water freely, but allow the surface to become slightly dry before applying further water. Also, keep the central vase full of water – empty and refill every four to six weeks to prevent it becoming stagnant. Use soft water, such as clean rainwater. In hardwater areas, add a tablespoon of vinegar to every gallon of water.

Feeding From late spring to late summer feed every three to four weeks with a weak, half-strength, liquid fertilizer.

Humidity Stand the pot on a tray or saucer of moist pebbles. Also, mist spray the foliage in summer.

Compost Lime-free, open-textured compost such as equal parts peat and coarse leafmould.

Potting In spring, when the roots fill the pot. However, most bromeliads will grow in quite small pots with little compost, and repotting is an infrequent task.

Propagation During spring, remove offsets from the plant's base and pot them up separately. Place in 21-24°C/70-75°F. Mist spray frequently until established.

All canistrums are known as Basket Bromeliads because the flowers appear to be surrounded by a colourful basket-like arrangement of bracts, which are

Cryptanthus acaulis 'Rubra'

Cryptanthus 'Apple Blossom'

Cryptanthus 'Pink Starlight'

Cryptanthus 'It'

Cryptanthus 'Costa's Favourite'

Cryptanthus 'Apple Blossom'

Height 10-13cm/4-5in
Spread 13-18cm/5-7in
Native Hybrid

Greenfinger Guide

Temperature W 16-20°C/61-68°F – it is essential that the temperature does not fall below these figures, as the plants will then be damaged. **S** 21-27°C/70-80°F

Light W Full sun or light shade. **S** Full sun or light shade. Good light is not so important to this cryptanthus.

Watering W Keep the compost barely moist. If the temperature rises and plants become more active, increase the amount of water. **S** Water freely, but ensure good drainage. Always used soft water, preferably clean rainwater. If your tapwater is hard, add a tablespoon of vinegar to each gallon.

Feeding From late spring to late summer feed every five to six weeks with a weak, half-strength, liquid fertilizer. This can also be added to the water used to mist spray the leaves. Add the liquid feed to the water used to mist spray the foliage.

Humidity Mist spray the leaves in summer.

Compost Two parts peat-based compost and one of sharp sand.

Potting In early summer, when a high temperature can be maintained to encourage rapid growth.

Propagation The offsets on cryptanthus plants develop from mid-way between the rosette leaves. They eventually fall off, roll down and root around the parent plant. Therefore, the easiest way to increase this plant is to remove a congested specimen from its pot and to carefully pull away the young offsets. These are potted up and placed in 21°C/70°F until established.

This hybrid Earth Star creates a dominant display of spreading, smooth-edged leaves, creamy-white around their bases and mottled and edged in bright green. It is usually too large for bottle gardens, but makes a lovely plant for a shelf in a warm room. Cryptanthus look good when positioned on strongly-supported glass shelves and with a mirror in the background.

There are many other attractive hybrids, including 'Pink Starlight', 'Costa's Favourite' and the well-known 'It', which is also known as the Colour-band Cryptanthus. Others include 'Carnival del Rio', with a marbled pattern of rose and green on a plant which forms a rosette up to 45cm/1½ft across; 'Mars' with rich silvery leaves; 'Red Bird' with undulating leaves, dull green but which redden when in diffused bright light; 'Starlight' with dark green edges to its leaves, together with rose and cream stripes along them; and 'Feuerzauber' with eye-catching silver banding.

Good light is essential for the highly-coloured hybrids, when it encourages better leaf colours.

Cryptanthus bivittatus
Earth Star

Height 6-7.5cm/2½-3in
Spread 15-25cm/6-10in
Native Brazil

Greenfinger Guide

Temperature W 16-20°C/61-68°F – it is essential that the temperature does not fall below these figures as the plants will then be damaged.
S 21-27°C/70-80°F

Light W Full sun or light shade. **S** Full sun or light shade. Good light encourages better colouring in the varieties with attractively-coloured leaves.

Watering W Keep the compost barely moist. If the temperature rises and plants become more active, increase the amount of water. **S** Water freely, but ensure good drainage. Always use soft water, preferably clean rainwater. However, if your tapwater is hard, add a tablespoon of vinegar to each gallon.

Feeding From late spring to late summer feed every five to six weeks with a weak, half-strength, liquid fertilizer. This can also be added to the water used to mist spray the leaves. This can be added to the water used to mist spray the leaves.

Humidity Mist spray the leaves regularly in summer.

Compost Two parts peat-based compost and one of sharp sand.

Potting In early summer, when a high temperature can be maintained to encourage rapid growth. However, repotting is very infrequent as it will survive in very little soil.

Propagation The offsets on cryptanthus plants develop from mid-way between the rosette leaves. They eventually fall off, roll down and root around the parent plant. Therefore, the easiest way to increase this plant is to remove a congested specimen from its pot and to carefully pull away the young offsets. These are potted up and placed in 21°C/70°F until established.

This Earth Star is one of the easiest to grow, seldom

Cryptanthus bivittatus 'Tricolor'

failing to create an attractive display with its crinkle-edged, lance-shaped light green leaves with darker green stripes down the centres.

There are several attractive forms, including 'Tricolor' which has slightly larger and narrower leaves, olive green and with creamy-white edges softer shaded with salmon-pink. 'Atropurpurea' is compact and with purplish-tinged leaves. 'Minor' is smaller with olive-green leaves with reddish-brown stripes.

Cryptanthus bromelioides

Height 20-30cm/8-12in

Cryptanthus bromelioides

Spread 25-38cm/10-15in
Native Brazil

Greenfinger Guide

Temperature W 16-20°C/61-68°F – it is essential that the temperature does not fall below these figures, as the plants will then be damaged.
S 21-27°C/70-80°F

Light W Full sun or light shade. **S** Full sun or light shade. Good light is not so essential to this species, but its coloured forms require a bright position if their colorations are to be encouraged.

Watering W Keep the compost barely moist. If the temperature rises and plants become more active, increase the amount of water. **S** Water freely, but ensure good drainage. Always use soft water, preferably clean rainwater. However, if your tapwater is hard, add a tablespoon of vinegar to a gallon.

Feeding From late spring to late summer feed every five to six weeks with a weak, half-strength, liquid fertilizer. The liquid feed can also be applied when mist spraying the foliage.

Humidity Mist spray the leaves regularly in summer.

Compost Two parts peat-based compost and one of sharp sand.

Potting In early summer, when a high temperature can be maintained to encourage rapid growth.

Propagation The offsets on cryptanthus plants develop from mid-way between the rosette leaves. They eventually fall off, roll down and root around the parent plant. Therefore, the easiest way to increase this plant is to remove a congested specimen and to carefully pull away the young offsets. These are potted up and placed in 21°C/70°F until established.

It develops a large rosette formed of mid-green, slightly fleshy, finely-spined leaves up to 20cm/8in long. The undersides are white and scaly. The whole plant has a rather upright stance and if allowed soon forms a large colony.

The form 'Tricolor', often known as the Rainbow Star, has green leaves striped with creamy-white lines

Cryptanthus fosterianus

and flushed in pale pink. The whole plant has a spreading nature.

Cryptanthus fosterianus
Pheasant Leaf

Height 6-7.5cm/2½-3in
Spread 20-38cm/10-15in
Native Brazil

Greenfinger Guide

Temperature W 16-20°C/61-68°F – it is essential that the temperature does not fall below these figures, as the plants will then be damaged. S 21-27°C/70-80°F

Light W Full sun or light shade. S Full sun or light shade. Good light is vital with this species, as the colorations in the leaves are to be encouraged and highlighted.

Watering W Keep the compost barely moist. If the temperature rises and plants become more active, increase the amount of water. S Water freely, but ensure good drainage. Always use soft water, preferably clean rainwater. If your tapwater is hard, add a teaspoon of vinegar to each gallon.

Feeding From late spring to late summer feed every five to six weeks with weak, half-strength, liquid fertilizer. This can also be added to the water used to mist spray the leaves.

Humidity Mist spray the leaves regularly in summer.

Compost Two parts peat-based compost and one of sharp sand.

Potting In early summer, when a high temperature can be maintained to encourage rapid growth.

Propagation The offsets on cryptanthus plants develop from mid-way between the rosettes of leaves. They eventually fall off, roll down and root around the parent. Therefore, the easiest way to increase this plant is to remove a congested specimen from its pot and to carefully pull away the young offsets. These are potted up and placed in 21°C/70°F until established.

The Pheasant Leaf is very colourful and attractive,

with long, flat, succulent, finely spine-edged leaves coloured copper-brown with greyish cross-banding on the upper surface. The undersides are covered with grey scales.

It is a distinctive cryptanthus, ideal for brightening a modern setting.

Dyckia brevifolia

Dyckia brevifolia
Pineapple Dyckia

Height 30-45cm/1-1½ft
Spread 25-30cm/10-12in
Native Brazil

Greenfinger Guide

Temperature W 10-18°C/50-64°F – will survive temperatures down to 7°C/45°F, but is best at 10°C/50°F or above. S 18-27°C/64-80°F

Light W Full light. S Diffused light to full sun.

Watering W Just moist. If the temperature falls dramatically in winter, keep the compost drier and take care not to splash the foliage. S Water freely, but ensure good drainage and allow the compost to dry out slightly between watering.

Feeding From late spring to late summer feed every five to six weeks with a half-strength liquid fertilizer.

Humidity Mist spray leaves during summer, and also in winter if the temperature is high and the atmosphere dry. Unlike many other bromeliads, high humidity is not so essential to it for healthy growth.

Compost Equal parts sharp sand and peat or a peat-based compost. An acid compost is essential.

Potting In spring, usually every two years – but only when the plants are congested.

Propagation Detach offsets in spring and pot up into the normal compost. Keep warm and mist the leaves frequently until established. Plants that have been left to form large and congested clumps can be divided in spring. However, such plants may take several months after being divided before they have an attractive outline.

The Pineapple Dyckia is a robust plant, with shiny

green, somewhat succulent, spine-edged, tapering and pointed-tipped leaves up to 20cm/8in long and 18mm/0.75in wide. The undersides have silver lines. During late summer, tall flower stems arise from the sides – not the centres – of the leafy rosettes, bearing bright orange flowers.

This is a bromeliad that delights in hot and dry conditions, and is therefore better suited to most homes during summer than many other species.

Guzmania lingulata
Scarlet Star
Height 25-30cm/10-12in
Spread 38-45cm/15-18in
Native Central America/West Indies/Colombia/
  Bolivia/Brazil/Ecuador/Guyana

Greenfinger Guide

Temperature W 13-18°C/55-64°F – it is essential that the temperature does not fall below 13°C/55°F. Indeed, plants are better at 16°C/61°F or above. **S** 18-27°C/64-80°F

Light W Indirect light. **S** Light shade.

Watering W Keep the compost just moist, but regularly top up the urn with soft water – preferably rainwater. If the temperature falls unexpectedly, tip out the water from the urn and keep the compost drier. **S** Water freely, but ensure good drainage. And keep the urn topped up with water. If your tapwater is hard, add a tablespoon of vinegar to every gallon.

Feeding From late spring to late summer feed every four to five weeks with a weak, half-strength, liquid fertilizer.

Humidity Mist spray the leaves regularly in summer. High humidity and a good circulation of warm air are essential – avoid cold draughts.

Compost Equal parts peat-based compost and sharp sand. Alternatively, use equal parts peat, osmunda fibre and sharp sand. An acid compost is essential.

Potting After flowering, the rosette dies and growth is eventually taken over by offsets which grow around it. In late autumn, after flowering, the old plant will start to wilt and turn colour. It can then be cut down to 5cm/2in of its base, taking care not to damage young offsets growing around it. In spring, these young offsets can be removed and potted up individually into the potting compost. Keep warm and syringe frequently until established.

Propagation As above.

The Scarlet Star is stunningly attractive, with bright metallic-green, shiny, arching, spear-shaped leaved that form a stemless rosette. During summer a flower stem emerges from the rosette, displaying large red bracts which surround small, yellowish-white flowers. The flowers are short-lived, but the colourful bracts remain for several weeks.

It creates a superbly decorative plant for display on a table in a warm, draught-free room during summer. But it does need a humid atmosphere.

The Orange Star (*Guzmania lingulata minor*, but often sold as *Guzmania minor*) is a superb form, with bright and showy orange-red bracts – which remain attractive for several months – surrounding a compact cluster of white flowers. *Guzmania lingulata minor* 'Empire', also known as Guzmania minor 'Empire', has a dominant display of dark red bracts.

Guzmania monostachya
Striped Torch
Height: 30-38cm/12-15in
Spread 38-60cm/15-24in
Native Brazil, West Indies, Southern Florida

Guzmania lingulata

Guzmania monostachya

Greenfinger Guide

Temperature W 13-18°C/55-64°F – it is essential that the temperature does not fall below 13°C/55°F. Indeed, plants are better at 16°C/61°F or above. **S** 18-27°C/64-80°F

Light W Indirect light **S** Light shade

Watering W Keep the compost just moist, but regularly top up the urn with soft water – preferably rainwater. If the temperature falls suddenly, tip out the water from the urn and keep the compost drier. **S** Water freely, but ensure good drainage and keep the urn topped up with water. If your tapwater is hard, add a tablespoon of vinegar to every gallon.

Feeding From late spring to late summer feed every four to five weeks with a weak, half-strength, liquid fertilizer.

Humidity Mist spray the leaves regularly in summer. High humidity and a good circulation of air around them are essential.

Compost Equal parts peat-based compost and sharp sand, or equal parts peat, osmunda fibre and sharp sand. An acid compost is essential.

Potting After flowering, the rosette dies and growth is eventually taken over by offsets which grow around it. In late autumn, after flowering, the old plant will start to wilt and turn colour. It can then be cut down to 5cm/2in of its base, taking care not to damage young offsets growing around it. In spring, these young offsets can be removed and potted up.

Propagation As above.

The Striped Torch develops a large, poker-like flower spike during summer – white with greenish-white bracts attractively lined with purple and tipped with vermilion. Only one flower spike is produced on each plant, amid slightly arching, narrow, green leaves.

It forms a dominant position on a table, but for success it demands a humid position, which is easier to create in a sun room or greenhouse.

Guzmania sanguinea

Guzmania sanguinea 'Red Grand Prix'

Guzmania sanguinea

Height 20-25cm/8-10in
Spread 25-38cm/10-15in
Native Colombia, Ecuador, Costa Rica

Greenfinger Guide

Temperature W 13-18°C/55-64°F – it is essential
that the temperature does not fall below 13°C/55°F.
Indeed, plants are better at 16°C/61°F or above.
S 18-27°C/64-80°F.

Light W Indirect light. S Light shade.

Watering W Keep the compost just moist, but
regularly top up the urn with soft water – preferably
rainwater. If the temperature falls suddenly, tip out
the water from the urn and keep the compost drier.
S Water freely, but ensure good drainage and keep
the urn topped up with water. If your tapwater is
hard, add a tablespoon of vinegar to every gallon.

Feeding From late spring to late summer feed
every four to five weeks with a weak, half-strength,
liquid fertilizer.

Humidity Mist spray the leaves regularly in
summer. High humidity and a good circulation
around are essential.

Compost Equal parts peat-based compost and
sharp sand, or equal parts peat, osmunda fibre and
sharp sand. An acid compost is essential.

Potting After flowering, the rosette dies and
growth is eventually taken over by offsets growing
around it. In late autumn, after flowering, the old
plant wilts and turns colour. If can then be cut down
to 5cm/2in of its base, taking care not to damage
young offsets growing around it. In spring, these
young offsets can be removed and potted up
individually into the potting compost. Keep warm
and syringe frequently until established.

Propagation As above.

Guzmania sanguinea forms a broad and flattish rosette
of red-tinged leaves which curl slightly downwards
towards their tips. Towards the centre of the rosette
they become green and then yellow. During summer,
white flowers appear, but sunken into the rosette. The
redness on the leaves is intensified when the plant is
bearing flowers.

In addition to this guzmania and the other species
described previously, there are further species and
hybrids. These include *Guzmania marlabeca*, *G.*
'Ameranthe', *G.* 'Festival', *G.* 'Giselle', *G.* 'Purple
Amaranth' and *G.* 'Red Grand Prix'. Others include
the Snake Vase (*G. vittata*) with boldly banded arching
leaves, and the Variegated Ribbon Plant (*Guzmania
zahnii variegata*) with leaves contrastingly striped in
pink, white and green.

Guzmania sanguinea 'Marlabela'

Guzmania sanguinea 'Festival'

Neoregelia carolinae
Blushing Bromeliad

Height 23-30cm/9-12in
Spread 38-50cm/15-20in
Native Brazil

Greenfinger Guide

Temperature W 13-15°C/55-59°F – will survive
brief periods at 2-5°C/36-41°F, but is best at 13°C/

Guzmania sanguinea 'Ameranthe'

55°F or above. **S** 16-27°C/61-80°F

Light W Bright, indirect light. **S** Light shade to indirect light. Good light is essential to encourage the development of attractive colours in the variegated forms of this plant. However, do not subject it to long periods of intense, strong sunlight.

Watering W Keep the compost just moist, and the urn topped up with water. **S** Water the compost moderately, but keep the urn filled with water. Every four to six weeks, tip out the water from the urn and replace with fresh. Use soft water, preferably clean rainwater. If your tapwater is hard, add a teaspoon of vinegar to a gallon of water.

Feeding From late spring to late summer feed with a weak, half-strength, liquid fertilizer every three or four weeks.

Humidity Mist spray the leaves regularly in summer. Periodically, in summer, add a very weak

Guzmania sanguinea 'Giselle'

Neoregelia carolinae 'Meyendorffii'

liquid feed to the misting water.

Compost Two parts peat-based compost and one of sharp sand. Alternatively, use equal parts peat, sharp sand and loam.

Potting In spring, usually every three or four years.

Propagation In late spring or early summer, remove offsets when about 10cm/4in long. Pot up and place in 24°C/75°F until established. It may be necessary to support them with thin split canes.

The Blushing Bromeliad develops wide rosettes of glossy, bright green, strap-shaped, flat and pointed-tipped leaves. Flowering can happen at any time, when the leaves around the rosette turn purple or bright red. The flower head rises through the urn and reveals small, violet-blue flowers surrounded by glossy red bracts.

The form 'Tricolor' has glossy green leaves attractively lined with cream and rose-pink stripes. At flowering time, the entire plant turns pinkish-red, and remains so for several months. Another form with attractive variegations is 'Flandria', with green leaves clearly edged in whitish-yellow.

'Marechallii', also known as *Neoregelia marechallii*, has glossy green leaves, with the lower parts an attractive red. The flowers are violet. 'Meyendorffii', frequently known as Meyendorff's Bromeliad, is an exciting form, thought by some authorities to be the original type of this species.

Neoregelia carolinae 'Flandria'

Neoregelia carolinae 'Perfecta Tricolor'

Neoregelia carolinae 'Tricolor'

Nidularium fulgens
Blushing Bromeliad

Height 25-30cm/10-12in
Spread 25-30cm/10-12in
Native Brazil

Greenfinger Guide

Temperature **W** 13-16°C/55-61°F – will survive temperatures down to 7°C/45°F for a short period, but is better at 13°C/55°F or above. Avoid positions in cold draughts. **S** 16-24°C/61-75°F

Light **W** Light shade. **S** Shade, away from bright light.

Watering **W** Just moist. Keep the urn full of water **S** Moderately moist. Keep the urn full of water. Tip out and replenish the water every month. Use only soft water, such as clean rainwater. If your water is hard, add a tablespoon of vinegar to a gallon of water.

Nidularium fulgens

Nidularium innocentii

Feeding From late spring to late summer feed every three to four weeks with a weak, half-strength, liquid fertilizer.

Humidity Mist spray the leaves regularly in summer. Periodically add a very weak liquid fertilizer to the misting water.

Compost Equal parts loam-based compost, peat and sharp sand.

Potting This bromeliad is relatively short-lived, and once it has flowered the rosette dies and growth is continued by offsets growing around it.

Propagation Detach offshoots in late spring – use a sharp knife. Pot up into small pots and place in 24-27°C/75-80°F. Mist spray frequently until established.

The Blushing Bromeliad forms a wide rosette of arching, strap-like, saw-edged, shiny, light green leaves with dark mottling. Flowering occurs during summer, when green-tipped red bracts appear in the centre of the urn, together with three-petalled violet-tipped white flowers. The colour of the bracts has given rise to its common name.

Nidularium innocentii

Height 38-45cm/15-18in
Spread 45-60cm/18-24in
Native Brazil

Greenfinger Guide

Temperature W 13-16°C/55-6°F – will survive temperatures down to 7°C/45°F for a short period, but is better at 13°C/55°F or above. Avoid positions in cold draughts. S 16-24°C/61-75°F

Light W Light shade. S Shade, away from bright light.

Watering W Just moist. Keep the urn full of water. S Moderately moist. Keep the urn full of water. Tip out and replenish the water every month. Use only soft water, such as clean rainwater. If your water is hard, add a tablespoon of vinegar to a gallon of water.

Nidularium innocentii 'Striatum'

Nidularium innocentii 'Purpureum'

Feeding From late spring to late summer feed every three to four weeks with a weak, half-strength, liquid fertilizer.

Humidity Mist spray the leaves regularly in summer. Periodically add a very weak liquid fertilizer to the misting water.

Compost Equal parts loam-based compost, peat and sharp sand.

Potting This bromeliad is relatively short-lived, and once it has flowered the rosette dies and growth is continued by offsets growing around it.

Propagation Detach offshoots in late spring – use a sharp knife. Pot up into small pots and place in 24-27°C/75-80°F until established. Mist spray frequently until established.

Nidularium innocentii forms a large rosette of wide, strap-like, finely tooth-edged, glossy-surfaced, brownish-green leaves with metallic-purple undersides. Flowering is usually during summer, when a short stem arises from the central urn and bears six to eight red bracts which surround a few small white flowers.

Several forms are grown, including the confusingly named *Nidularium innocentii innocentii*, which is quite similar to the parent, but with pale to deep green leaves edged and finely striped with white. 'Striatum', also known as *Nidularium striatum*, displays bronzy leaves striped with creamy-yellow in varying widths. *Nidularium innocentii lineatum*, also known as *N. longiflora,* has green leaves with many narrow white stripes. *N. i.* 'Purpureum', also known as *I. purpureum*, has purplish-brown leaves.

Tillandsia circinnata
Pot-bellied Tillandsia

Height 20-45cm/8-18in
Spread 15-25cm/6-10in
Native Southern Florida, Bahamas, Cuba, Colombia and Central America

Greenfinger Guide

Temperature W 10-15°C/50-59°F – but will survive at temperatures down to 5°C/41°F if the plants are kept slightly dry (see humidity). S 16-27°C/61-80°F

Light W Indirect light. S Indirect light to slight shade.

Watering These plants normally grow without the benefit of compost, and rely on a 'misting' to keep them alive. Plants are grown attached to attractive surfaces (see compost).

Feeding From spring to late summer add a weak – a quarter to one-third the normal rate – liquid fertilizer to the misting water every three to four weeks. Stronger applications severely damage plants.

Humidity Atmospheric moisture is essential with this type of tillandsia. The higher the temperature, the more frequent the application of a mist spray. However, if the temperature falls below that recommended – especially in winter – avoid misting the leaves directly. Instead, group the plants together and stand them on trays of moist pebbles. However, if the temperature is high, a good circulation of air is vital to prevent the extra moisture in the atmosphere causing the foliage to rot. Airplants dislike chalk. Therefore, preferably use clean rainwater. Alternatively, in hard-water areas add a tablespoon of vinegar to a gallon of water.

Compost Instead of growing the plant in compost, like normal plants, this airplant can be grown and displayed attached to many surfaces and mounts, such as cork bark, fibre slabs, driftwood, pieces of rock, seashells, and even pieces of pottery.

Sometimes the plants develop roots, otherwise – and if well secured – they do not. The plants can be secured with glue to their supports and display material. Special glue – an airplant fixative – is available. These airplants can be fixed to a support at any time during the year, except when in full flower.

Potting This is not required, as once a plant is established it will continue growing in that position. However, after a rosette has flowered it starts to die and eventually will be replaced by offshoots growing around its base.

Propagation Large plants can be divided in spring and individual rosettes detached and secured with glue to a support as described.

The Pot-bellied Tillandsia gains its common name from the egg-like swelling of its base (a pseudobulb), about 15cm/6in high. The grey leaf-blades, up to 20cm/8in long, are frequently curled, twisted or spiralled in a snail-shape. The rarely-branched flowering stem bears soft-pink bracts and blue flowers.

It is occasionally confused with *T. caput*, which has a more bulbous base.

Tillandsia circinnata (back) T. ionantha (front)

Bailey's Air Plant
Tillandsia baileyi

Height 20-30cm/8-12in
Spread 20-30cm/8-12in
Native Guatemala, Mexico and Southern U.S.A.

Bailey's Air Plant is an unusual tillandsia, with a bulbous base and narrow, usually twisted, grey-scaled leaves. Eventually it forms a dense plant, with short spikes bearing pink bracts and purple flowers.

This tillandsia is best grown in a pot, rather than on a piece of wood.

Tillandsia brachycaulos

Height 7.5-18cm/3-7in – variable plant
Spread 6-10cm/2½-5in – variable plant
Native Southern Mexico and Central America

Tillandsia brachycaulos is a superb airplant, forming short, grey-green, soft rosettes which become red just before the flowers appear. These are blue, and emerge from tight buds at the rosette's centre.

Tillandsia schiedeana major

Tillandsia geminiflora

Height 15-20cm/6-8in – including the flower heads
Spread 7.5-13cm/3-5in
Native Brazil, Paraguay, Uruguay and Argentina

Tillandsia geminiflora has tapering, lime-green leaves up to 18cm/7in long and covered with short grey scales. The beautiful flower heads have rose-tinged bracts and pinkish-violet flowers. It needs a position in good light.

Blushing Bride
Tillandsia ionantha

Height 7.5-10cm/3-4in
Spread 7.5cm/3in – forming clusters
Native Guatemala, Nicaragua and South Mexico

The Blushing Bride creates an attractive plant for securing to a cork or wood base and for displaying on a table or fixed to a wall. It is also ideal for growing in a terrarium.

The stemless rosettes are formed of silvery-grey,

T. juncea (back) T. Brachycaulos (front)

Tillandsia geminiflora

Tillandsia ixioides

scale-like leaves. During summer, just before the violet-purple flowers with yellow stamen appear at the ends of short flower spikes, the centres of the leafy rosettes become flushed red.

Tillandsia ixioides

Height 10-13cm/4-5in
Spread 25-38cm/10-15in
Native Argentina, Paraguay and Bolivia

Tillandsia ixioides is an easily-grown, clump-forming species which develops stiff, tapering leaves which recurve to form an open rosette some 25-38cm/10-15in across. Each leaf is 10-13cm/4-5in long. The flowers are very attractive, forming a slender spike, with bright yellow heads.

Tillandsia ionantha

Tillandsia juncea

Height 30-38cm/12-15in
Spread 15-20cm/6-8in
Native Southern Florida, through Central America to Bolivia and Peru.

Tillandsia juncea creates a rosette of slender, stiffly upright then slightly cascading, silver-grey leaves. They have a rush-like appearance. It develops a cylindrical spike of deep red bracts and violet flowers.

Because this tillandsia is native to such a large area, it is very variable and several forms are known.

Tillandsia schiedeana major

Height 7.5-10cm/3-4in
Spread 6-10cm/2½-4in
Native From Mexico to Venezuela and Colombia

Tillandsia schiedeana major is relatively easy to grow, creating stiff, 7.5-10cm/3-4in long and tapered, silver leaves which branch away from a narrow, central stem. The flowers are particularly attractive – tubular with bright red bracts.

The form *minor* is similar, but tends to be smaller, slender, more delicate and with silvery-green leaves.

Spanish Moss/Old Man's Beard/Grey Beard
Tillandsia usneoides

Height and spread Pendulous clusters usually up to 1m/3ft long, but in nature strands of this plant up to 7.5m/25ft have been recorded.
Native South East States of the U.S.A.

Spanish Moss is often considered to be a weed in its native country, where it festoons trees in areas of high humidity. In cultivation it is more reserved and creates an unusual and interesting houseplant. However, homes are usually too dry and a conservatory or greenhouse which can be misted frequently is better for it.

It is formed of tangled wiry stems with scaly, silvery-grey leaves up to 5cm/2in long. During summer, bright yellow-green flowers are borne in the leaf joints.

Tillandsia baileyi

Tillandsia usneoides

Tillandsia cyanea

Tillandsia lindenii

Tillandsia cyanea
Pink Quill

Height 23cm/9in
Spread 30cm/12in
Native Ecuador

Greenfinger Guide

Temperature W 10-15°C/50-59°F – but will survive at temperatures down to 5°C/41°F if the compost is kept slightly dry. S 16-27°C/61-80°F

Light W Indirect light. S Light shade.

Watering W Just moist. S Water freely, but ensure good drainage. If possible use rainwater – but it must be clean. Alternatively, if the tap-water is hard, add a teaspoon of vinegar to a gallon of water.

Feeding From spring to late summer apply a weak liquid fertilizer water every three to four weeks. Also, add a weak amount of fertilizer to the misting water.

Humidity Mist spray several times a day during summer; less frequently in winter, especially if the temperature is low.

Compost Equal parts sharp sand and osmunda fibre. Alternatively, equal parts sharp sand and peat. The addition of perlite or forest bark further aids good drainage, which is vital. Also, fill the pot to one-third of its depth with clean pieces of broken clay pots.

Potting Repot in spring, but only when the plant is being divided. Once a rosette has flowered it starts to die, although they may take a year or so before the plant looks unsightly.

Propagation Divide clustered plants in spring – see potting. Also, remove offsets in spring and pot up into the normal compost. Place in 16-18°C/61-64°F until established.

The Pink Quill very much resembles *Tillandsia lindenii*, but is slightly smaller and more compact. The narrow, green leaves, reddish-brown at their bases, are about 38cm/15in long and 2.5cm/1in wide. During late summer a central flower stem, compact and only 5-7.5cm/2-3in long, bears a flower head formed of rose to red bracts tinged green with violet-blue flowers that emerge a few at a time over several months.

This is a species that can be grown in a small pot. Because it likes high humidity it is best suited for growing in a sun room or greenhouse, where it is easier to create these conditions and to maintain a high temperature. Like all tillandsias – other than the true atmospheric types which are usually referred to as airplants – these plants are relatively hardy and easy-to-grow. Indeed, they are not as sensitive as guzmanias.

Tillandsia flabellata

Height 25-45cm/10-18in
Spread 25-38cm/10-15in
Native Mexico, Guatemala and El Salvador

Tillandsia flabellata forms a spreading rosette of narrowly triangular, green or greenish-red, long and tapering leaves. The colouring of the leaves tends to be variable from plant to plant. It is relatively easy-to-grow, and during late summer and into autumn produces reddish bracts and violet-blue flowers.

Blue-flowered Torch
Tillandsia lindenii
(syn. T. lindeniana)

Height 38-50cm/15-20in
Spread 30-38cm/12-15in
Native Peru

The Blue-flowered Torch forms a dense rosette of 30-38cm/12-15in long and 12mm/½in wide dark green

Tillandsia punctulata

Tillandsia flabellata

leaves with purple undersides. During late summer, a 30cm/12in long flower stalk develops from the centre of the rosette and displays a wide, poker-like flower head formed of coral-blue or carmine bracts from which emerge royal-blue flowers with white-spotted throats. The flowers appear a few at a time, in a succession over several months.

Unlike some tillandsias, the Blue-flowered Torch can be grown in small pots. This makes it easy to display indoors, although it does require high humidity, which is easier to provide in a conservatory or greenhouse.

Mexican Black Torch
Tillandsia punctulata
(syn. T. tricolor)

Height 30-45cm/1-1½ft
Spread 25-38cm/10-15in
Native Mexico to Costa Rica, and Surinam

The Mexican Black Torch creates an attractively spreading and dense rosette of green, scaly leaves. When in flower, in late summer, it develops reddish-brown bracts and white tipped and dotted blackish-violet petals.

Tillandsia viridiflora
(At one time this species was known as *Tillandsia grandis*, but is now considered to be a separate species.)
Height 38-60cm/15-24in
Spread 38-50cm/15-20in
Native Mexico

Tillandsia viridiflora, as its names suggests, has beautiful dark green leaves, lilac-purple on their undersides. The leaves are tongue-shaped, up to 38cm/15in or so long, and with pointed ends. When in flower, in late summer and autumn, both the bracts and flowers – which are green – rise above the foliage.

Tillandsia wagneriana

Tillandsia wagneriana
Height 30-45cm/1-1½ft
Spread 30-38cm/12-15in
Native Peru

Tillandsia wagneriana displays strap-like, pointed leaves, about 36mm/1½in wide at their bases, with wavy edges and curled tips. The upper surfaces are shiny green, while the undersides are dull green and frequently slightly red. The flower bracts are green or pinkish-lavender, while the flowers are deep, dark blue.

Vriesea fenestralis

Height 45-60cm/1½-2ft
Spread 60-75cm/2-2½ft
Native Brazil

Greenfinger Guide

Temperature W 13-18°C/55-64°F – will withstand short periods as low as 7°C/45°F, but best at 13°C/55°F or above. **S** 18-27°C/64-80°F

Light W Indirect light. **S** Filtered light.

Watering W Just moist. Keep the central urn topped up. In hard water areas, use rainwater, as vrieseas dislike lime. Hard tapwater can be improved by adding a tablespoon of vinegar to a gallon of water. If the temperature is very low, keep the compost barely moist. **S** Water freely, but ensure good drainage. Also, keep the urn filled with water – tip out and replenish every month. Use soft water.

Feeding From late spring to late summer feed every three to four weeks with a weak – quarter to one-third strength – mixture. Add this to the water used to top up the the urn, as well as to the compost.

Humidity Mist spray the leaves, especially during summer, with lime-free water.

Compost Equal parts peat-based compost and sharp sand.

Potting In spring – usually every two to three years. However, as vrieseas grow quite well in small pots, this is seldom necessary. Ensure that the bottom third of the pot is full of broken pieces of clay pots.

Propagation It is increased by removing and rooting offsets, preferably when at least 13cm/5in long. However, it is sometimes difficult to cut away offsets without ruining the plant. If this is so, leave the plant until the outer leaves are dying. At that stage these outer leaves can be cut away by running

Tillandsia viridiflora

Vriesea fenestralis

a sharp knife down the centre of the leaf and gently pulling them both down and apart. This will usually expose the offset and allow it to be removed. Pot up each offset in a 7.5cm/3in wide pot in the normal compost, water and place in shade in 24°C/75°F until roots form and the plant is well established.

Vriesea fenestralis is a very distinctive and attractive plant, even when not flowering. It forms a large rosette of shiny, yellowish-green leaves, up to 45cm/18in long and 5cm/2in wide, with dark green veins. The undersides are partially spotted purplish-red. At any time from spring to autumn, but usually in mid-summer, a flower spike up to 90cm/3ft high grows from the plant's centre. It bears tubular, rich sulphur-yellow flowers surrounded by green bracts.

Vriesea fosteriana

Height 45cm/1½ft
Spread 60-75cm/1½-2ft
Native Brazil

Greenfinger Guide

Temperature **W** 15-18°C/59-64°F – will withstand short periods as low as 7°C/45°F, but best at 13°C/55°F or above. **S** 18-27°C/64-80°F

Light **W** Indirect light. **S** Filtered light to light shade.

Vriesea fosteriana 'Selecta'

Vriesea gigantea

Vriesea fosteriana

Watering **W** Just moist. Keep the central urn topped up. In hard water areas, use rainwater, as vrieseas dislike lime. Hard tapwater can be improved by adding a tablespoon of vinegar to a gallon of water. If the temperature is very low, keep the compost barely moist. **S** Water freely, but ensure good drainage. Also, keep the urn filled with water – tip out and replenish every month. Use soft water.

Feeding From late spring to late summer feed every three to four weeks with a weak – quarter to one-third strength – mixture. Add this to the water used to top up the the urn, as well as to the compost.

Humidity Mist spray the leaves, especially during summer, with lime-free water.

Compost Equal parts peat-based compost and sharp sand.

Potting In spring – usually every two to three years. However, as vrieseas grow quite well in small pots, this is seldom necessary. Ensure that the bottom third of the pot is full of broken pieces of clay pots.

Propagation It is increased by removing and rooting offsets, preferably when at least 13cm/5in long. However, it is sometimes difficult to cut away offsets without ruining the plant. If this is so, leave the plant until the outer leaves are dying. At that stage these outer leaves can be cut away by running a sharp knife down the centre of the leaf and gently pulling them both down and apart. This will usually expose the offset and allow it to be removed. Pot up each offset in a 7.5cm/3in wide pot in the normal compost. Water and place in shade in 24°C/75°F until roots form and the plant is well established.

Vriesea fosteriana forms a large rosette of long, tongue-shaped, dark bluish-green leaves, up to 60cm/2ft long and 10cm/4in wide, with maroon pencilling. The leaves are reminiscent of *Vresia hieroglyphica*. The pale yellow flowers with reddish-brown tips are borne on stems often 1.2m/4ft or more high. Because these flowers are normally pollinated by bats, they open during the evening or at night and emit the odour of putrid fruit.

Several forms are grown, often with more intensive cross-banding. *V.f.* 'Selecta' is one of the more attractive forms.

Vriesea gigantea

Height 45-60cm/1½-2ft
Spread 60-75cm/2-2½ft
Native Brazil

Greenfinger Guide

Temperature **W** 13-18°C/55-64°F – will withstand short periods as low as 7°C/45°F, but best at 13°C/55°F or above. **S** 18-27°C/64-80°F

Light **W** Indirect light. **S** Filtered light to light shade.

Watering **W** Just moist. Keep the central urn topped up. In hard water areas use rainwater, as vrieseas dislike lime. Hard tapwater can be improved by adding a tablespoon of vinegar to a gallon of water. If the temperature is very low, keep the compost barely moist. **S** Water freely, but ensure good drainage. Also, keep the urn filled with water – tip out and replenish every month. Use soft water.

Feeding From late spring to late summer feed every three to four weeks with a weak – quarter to one-third strength – mixture. Add this to the water used to top up the urn, as well as to the compost.

Humidity Mist spray the leaves, especially during summer, with lime-free water.

Compost Equal parts peat-based compost and sharp sand.

Potting In spring – usually every two years. However, as vrieseas grow quite well in small pots, this is seldom necessary. Ensure that the bottom third of the pot is full of broken pieces of clay pots.

Propagation It is increased by removing and rooting offsets, preferably when at least 13cm/5in long. However, sometimes it is difficult to cut away offsets without ruining the plant. If this is so, leave the plant until the outer leaves are dying. At that stage these outer leaves can be cut away by running a sharp knife down the centre of the leaf and gently pulling them both down and apart. This will usually expose the offset and allow it to be removed. Pot up each offset in a 7.5cm/3in wide pot in the normal compost, water and place in shade in 24°C/75°F until roots form and the plant is well established.

Vriesea gigantea creates a dominant rosette, with dark green leaves up to 50cm/20in long and 7.5cm/3in wide. These are marked in a draughtsboard pattern with yellowish-green. It is mainly grown for the decorative leaves, as the yellow-green flowers on a stem often 1.5m/5ft or more long are not distinctively attractive.

Vriesea hieroglyphica
King of the Bromeliads

Height 50-60cm/20-24in
Spread 75-90cm/2½-3ft
Native Brazil

Greenfinger Guide

Temperature W 13-18°C/55-64°F – will withstand short periods as low as 7°C/45°F, but best at 13°C/55°F or above. **S** 18-27°C/64-80°F

Light W Indirect light. **S** Filtered light to light shade.

Watering W Just moist. Keep the central urn topped up. In hard water areas use rainwater, as vrieseas dislike lime. Hard tapwater can be improved by adding a tablespoon of vinegar to a gallon of water. If the temperature is very low, keep the compost barely moist. **S** Water freely, but ensure good drainage. Also, keep the urn filled with water – tip out and replenish every month. Use soft water.

Feeding From late spring to late summer feed every three to four weeks with a weak – quarter to one-third strength – mixture. Add this to the water used to top up the urn, as well as to the compost.

Humidity Mist spray the leaves, especially during summer, with lime-free water.

Compost Equal parts peat-based compost and sharp sand.

Potting In spring – usually every two to three years. However, as vrieseas grow quite well in small pots this is seldom necessary. Ensure that the bottom third of the pot is full of broken pieces of clay pots. Good drainage is essential.

Propagation It is increased by removing and rooting offsets, preferably when at least 13cm/5in

Vriesea hieroglyphica

long. However, sometimes it is difficult to cut away offsets without ruining the plant. If this is so, leave the plant until the outer leaves are dying. At that stage these outer leaves can be cut away by running a sharp knife down the centre of the leaf and gently pulling them both down and apart. This will usually expose the offset and allow it to be removed. Pot up each offset in a 7.5cm/3in wide pot in the normal compost, water and place in shade in 24°C/75°F until roots form and the plant is well established.

The King of the Bromeliads forms a large rosette of yellowish-green leaves, often 60cm/2ft long and up to 10cm/4in wide, covered with irregular dark purple markings in an uneven cross-banding pattern. Usually during spring a flowering stem up to 75cm/2½ft long arises from the centre of the plant. The upper third of this stem bears pale green bracts and yellow, tubular flowers.

Vriesea platynema 'Variegata'

Vriesea platynema

Height 38-45cm/15-18in
Spread 45-60cm/1½-2ft
Native West Indies, Eastern part of South America

Greenfinger Guide

Temperature W 13-18°C/55-64°F – will withstand short periods as low as 7°C/45°F, but best at 13°C/55°F or above. **S** 18-27°C/64-80°F

Light W Indirect light. **S** Filtered light to light shade.

Watering W Just moist. Keep the central urn topped up. In hard water areas, use rainwater, as vrieseas dislike lime. Hard tapwater can be improved by adding a tablespoon of vinegar to a gallon of water. If the temperature is very low, keep the compost barely moist. **S** Water freely, but ensure good drainage. Also, keep the urn filled with

water – tip out and replenish every month. Use soft water.

Feeding From late spring to late summer feed every three to four weeks with a weak – quarter to one-third strength – mixture. Add this to the water used to top up the urn, as well as to the compost.

Humidity Mist spray the leaves, especially during summer, with lime-free water.

Compost Equal parts peat-based compost and sharp sand.

Potting In spring – usually every two years. However, as vrieseas grow quite well in small pots, this is seldom necessary. Ensure that the bottom third of the pot is full of broken pieces of clay pots.

Propagation It is increased by removing and rooting offsets, preferably when at least 13cm/5in long. However, sometimes it is difficult to cut away offsets without ruining the plant. If this is so, leave the plant until the outer leaves are dying. At that stage these outer leaves can be cut away by running a sharp knife down the centre of the leaf and gently pulling them both down and apart. This will usually expose the offset and allow it to be removed. Pot up each offset in a 7.5cm/3in wide pot in the normal compost. Water and place in shade in 24°C/75°F until roots form and the plant is well established.

Vriesea platynema creates a rosette formed of leaves up to 45cm/1½ft long and 6cm/2½in wide, usually dull green, and becoming dark violet towards the tip. However, it is the forms of this bromeliad which are usually grown. These include 'Striatum' with pale stripes to the leaves, 'Rosea' with leaves green to violet, and 'Variegata' with green uppersides, reddish-violet undersides, and a pale stripe towards the tip.

Vriesea splendens
Flaming Sword

Height 38-45cm/15-18in
Spread 30-38cm/12-15im
Native Guyana, Venezuela

Greenfinger Guide

Temperature W 13-18°C/55-64°F – will withstand short periods as low as 7°C/45°F, but best at 13°C/55°F or above. **S** 18-27°C/64-80°F

Light W Indirect light. **S** Filtered light to light shade.

Watering W Just moist, and keep the central urn topped up. In hard water areas, use rainwater, as vrieseas dislike lime. Hard tapwater can be improved by adding a tablespoon of vinegar to a gallon of water. If the temperature is very low, keep the compost barely moist. **S** Water freely, but ensure good drainage. Also, keep the urn filled with water – tip out and replenish every month. Use soft water.

Feeding From late spring to late summer feed every three to four weeks with a weak – quarter to one-third strength – mixture. Add this to the water used to top up the water in the urn, as well as to the compost.

Humidity Mist spray the leaves, especially during summer, with lime-free water.

Compost Equal parts peat-based compost and sharp sand.

Potting In spring – usually every two to three years. This is usually very infrequent, as vrieseas grow quite well in small pots.

Propagation It is increased by removing and rooting offsets, preferably when at least 13cm/5in long. However, sometimes it is difficult to cut away offsets without ruining the plant. If this is so, leave the plant until the outer leaves are dying. At that stage these outer leaves can be cut away by running

Vriesea splendens

a sharp knife down the centre of the leaf and gently pulling them both down and apart. This will usually expose the offset and allow it to be removed. Pot up

Vriesea splendens 'Meyer's Favourite'

Vriesea splendens (yellow form)

each offset in a 7.5cm/3in wide pot in the normal compost. Water and place in shade in 24°C/75°F until roots form and the plant is well established.

The Flaming Sword creates an attractive rosette of sword-shaped, smooth-edged, dark green leaves with eye-catching purple-black cross-bands. Usually during late summer, but often at any time from spring to autumn, a long flower stem up to 60cm/2ft high appears from the centre of the plant and at its top bears a 30cm/12in long, sword-shaped head formed of bright red bracts which surround 4-5cm/1½-2in long bright yellow flowers. Successively, the flowers appear between the bracts.

It is a superb plant for decorating a table, but it does need a high temperature.

There are several forms of the Flaming Sword, including 'Meyer's Favourite' and 'Major'.

In addition to this vriesea and the others described earlier, there are many other, including *Vriesea* 'Christine', *Vriesea* 'Rex Hybrid' with beautiful green leaves and a yellow and red flower, *Vriesea* 'Mariae' with light green leaves and a red, feather-like flower, and *Vriesea* 'Kitteliana' with arching, olive-green leaves and a loosely-clustered flower head.

Vriesea splendens 'Christine'

flowering plants

Acalypha hispida

Achimenes x hybrida

Acalypha hispida
Chenille Plant/Red-hot Cat's Tail/Foxtail/Philippine Medusa

Height 0.9-1.2m/3-4ft – up to 2.4m/8ft or more when planted in a greenhouse border.
Spread 45-75cm/1½-2½ft – up to 1.5m/5ft or more when planted in a greenhouse border.
Native New Guinea

Greenfinger Guide
Temperature **W** 15-18°C/59-64°F **S** 16-24°C/61-75°F

Light **W** Bright light. **S** Bright, indirect light.

Watering **W** Just moist. **S** Water freely, but ensure good drainage.

Feeding From late spring to late summer feed every two weeks.

Humidity Stand the pot in a tray of moist pebbles and mist spray the foliage in summer.

Compost Loam-based compost

Potting In late winter and early spring when roots fill the pot. Plants in large pots need to have the top compost – 2.5-4cm/1-1½in – removed and replaced with fresh in spring.

Propagation Take 10-13cm/4-5in long stem-tip cuttings in spring. Insert in equal parts moist peat and sharp sand. Place in 27°C/80°F.

The Chenille Plant is a fast-growing, woody shrub that grows best in border soil in a greenhouse or large sun-room, where it grows 2.4-3m/8-10ft high. However, it can also be grown in a large pot, and by pruning stems to half their size in spring plants can be grown in the home. During summer and into autumn it bears spectacular bright scarlet flowers in tassle-like and pendulous spikes up to 45cm/18in long. Remove the tassels as soon as they fade to encourage further ones to develop.

Achimenes grandiflora
Hot Water Plant/Cupid's Bower/Monkey-faced Pansy/Widow's-tears/Mother's-tears

Height 45-60cm/1½-2ft
Spread 38-45cm/15-18in
Native Mexico

Greenfinger Guide
Temperature **W** 16°C/61°F – for starting the small, tuber-like rhizomes into growth in early or mid-spring. **S** 16-25°C/61-77°F

Light **W** Diffused light. **S** Bright, indirect light.

Watering **W** Over winter plants as rhizomes stored in dry peat. In spring, start the rhizomes into growth – see potting. **S** Keep moist, increasing the amount and frequency of water as plants grow.

Feeding From when the flower buds are visible to when the last flower fades, feed every two weeks.

Humidity Place the pot on a tray of moist pebbles. Do not allow water to fall on the leaves or flowers.

Compost Loam-based compost, or a peat-based type.

Potting During early or mid-spring, pot up dormant rhizomes, about 2.5cm/1in deep and five to a 13cm/5in wide pot or eight to a 15cm/6in one. Water thoroughly with slightly warm water and place in 16°C/61°F. In autumn, when the foliage dies, cut down the plant, withhold water and when the compost is dry remove the corms and store in dry peat. Alternatively, leave the rhizomes in dry compost in the pot until spring.

Propagation During summer, each rhizome produces three to six young rhizomes which can be removed during potting-up in spring. Pot them up into a large pot, where by the end of the season they will be large enough to create good sized plants for the following year. Alternatively, in early spring, sow seeds in a soil-based compost with extra peat added. Place in 21°C/70°F.

The Hot Water Plant creates a wealth of shoots that from mid to late summer bear purplish-red flowers up to 5cm/2in wide. Plants can be kept bushy by frequently nipping out the growing tips from the shoots.

There are several other Hot Water Plants which are widely grown. These include the Guatemalan *Achimenes heterophylla*, up to 30cm/12in high and with sharply-pointed leaves and 4cm/1½in wide orange flowers. *Achimenes longiflora*, from Mexico to Peru and up to 30cm/12in high, displays 5cm/2in wide flowers with rounded petals. The flower colour ranges from pale red to lavender and on to purple-blue. The undersurfaces of the leaves are also attractive, being flushed red. There are several attractive varieties which extend the colour range further into the blues and violets – and the flowers are larger.

Achimenes x hybrida plants are usually compacter and more floriferous than the other species. They are available in many coloured and named forms, with a flower season which lasts from early summer to early autumn. Colours include white, pink, red, purple, blue, white veined in purple, and yellow. Each flower, however, is short-lived but soon replaced by others. These plants are often used in hanging-baskets.

Aeschynanthus speciosus

Potting In spring, when the roots fill the pot – usually every three years.

Propagation 7.5cm/3in-long stem-tip cuttings during mid-summer. Insert in equal parts moist peat and sharp sand, and place in 21-24°C/70-75°F.

Aeschynanthus lobbianus, one of the Lipstick Vines, is a lax and sprawling climber, but is best grown in an indoor hanging-basket where it can trail and cascade. Small, fleshy, dark green, oval to elliptic leaves are borne on stiff stems, with 36mm/1½in long, tubular and hooded bright red flowers with creamy-yellow throats mid-summer.

'Polobia' is a recently-introduced variety, with trails of oval, leathery, dark green leaves and scarlet-

Aeschynanthus lobbianus

Aeschynanthus lobbianus
Lipstick Vine

Height 45-60cm/1½-2ft
Spread 45-60cm/1½-2ft
Native Java

Greenfinger Guide

Temperature W 13-15°C/55-59°F – if the temperature falls below this, keep the compost dry. However, low temperatures are not advisable. S 15-24°C/59-75°F

Light W Full light. S Light shade during very bright sunlight.

Watering W Barely moist. S Water freely, but ensure good drainage.

Feeding From late spring to late summer feed every four weeks.

Humidity Mist spray plants during summer.

Compost Peat-based type

red flowers which appear in bunches at the ends of the long stems.

It is best grown in a sun-room or greenhouse, where it can be left to create a dominant display.

Allamanda cathartica
Golden Trumpet

Height 3-4.5m/10-15ft
Spread 1.8-3m/6-10ft
Native South America

Greenfinger Guide

Temperature W 13-15°C/55-59°F S 16-24°C/61-75°F

Light W Full light S Light shade

Watering W Barely moist, especially if the temperature falls dramatically. S Water freely.

Feeding From late spring to late summer feed every seven to ten days with a weak liquid fertilizer.

Aeschynanthus marmoratus

Humidity Mist spray foliage in summer.

Compost Loam-based compost.

Potting In late winter or early spring, when roots fill the pot – usually every year when young. Plants in large pots or tub can be topdressed every spring, removing old top-soil and replacing it with fresh.

Propagation 7.5cm/3in-long stem-tip cuttings during late spring or early summer. Insert in equal parts moist peat and sharp sand. Place in 21-24°C/70-75°F.

The Golden Trumpet is a spectacular and vigorous climber best grown in large pots or tubs and trained over a permanent framework or wires in a sun-room or greenhouse. When the stems reach the desired height, pinch out the growing tips and train sideshoots along the wires. Alternatively, it can be grown in small pots and the stem tips repeatedly nipped out when the shoots are 30-45cm/1-1½ft high to encourage bushiness.

Golden-yellow, funnel-shaped flowers are borne during mid-summer amid long, leathery, glossy green leaves. Several varieties are commonly grown, including 'Grandiflora' (sometimes sold as *Allamanda*

Allamanda cathartica

grandiflora) with pale yellow flowers, 7.5cm/3in wide, and 'Hendersonii' (may be sold as *Allamanda hendersonii*) with large, orange-yellow blooms.

Other forms of this plant occasionally offered for sale include 'Williamsii', with masses of 7.5cm/3in wide, scented, yellow flowers with brownish-maroon throats, and 'Nobilis' with magnolia-scented, yellow flowers.

Allamanda neriifolia 'Birthe' is becoming increasingly available, forming a small, bushy plant with shiny, oval leaves. From mid to late summer it bears 5cm/2in wide pale yellow flowers, with brown stripes, in large clusters at the ends of stems which are initially upright, then slightly trailing.

Anthurium andreanum
Painter's Palette/Flamingo Lily/Oilcloth Flower

Height 38-45cm/15-18in

Anthurium andreanum

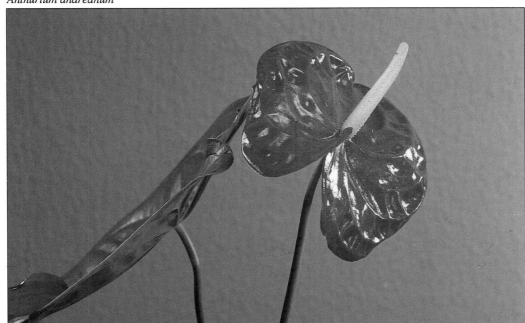

Spread 30cm/12in
Native Colombia

Greenfinger Guide

Temperature **W** 15-18°C/59-64°F – if the temperature falls to 13°C/55°F the plant will be damaged. **S** 18-27°C/64-80°F

Light **W** Indirect light. **S** Light shade.

Watering **W** Barely moist. **S** Water freely, but ensure good drainage.

Feeding From late spring to mid-summer feed every two weeks.

Humidity Mist spray leaves in summer. Also, stand pots in trays of water and pebbles.

Compost A mixture of peat-based compost and sphagnum moss, plus a little loam.

Potting In spring, when roots fill the pot – usually every two or three years.

Propagation Divide congested plants in spring. Each new plant should have a growing point and fibrous roots. Repot and place in a humid and warm position until established. Alternatively, sow seeds in spring in a mixture of peat-based compost and sphagnum moss. Place in 24°C/75°F.

The Painter's Palette gains its common name from the 10cm/4in long and 7.5cm/3in wide waxy-red, heart-shaped collars that form part of the flower. From the centres of these collars – very much resembling painter's palettes – arise 7.5cm/3in long white or yellow spires which are the real flowers. These palettes and their spires appear from late spring to late summer

It is a plant that can be displayed on a table, perhaps where the flower heads can be seen from above.

Anthurium scherzerianum
Flamingo Flower/Flamingo Plant/Pigtail Plant

Height 23-30cm/9-12in
Spread 30-38cm/12-15in
Native Guatemala

Greenfinger Guide

Anthurium scherzerianum

Astilbe x arendsii

Begonia limmingheana

Temperature W 10-13°C/50-55°F – best at the upper end of this range. **S** 13-24°C/55-75°F

Light W Indirect light. **S** Light shade.

Watering W Barely moist. **S** Water freely, but ensure good drainage.

Feeding From late spring to late summer feed every two weeks.

Humidity Mist spray leaves in summer. Also, stand pots in trays of water and pebbles.

Compost A mixture of peat-based compost and sphagnum moss, plus a little loam.

Potting In spring, when roots fill the pot – usually every two or three years.

Propagation Divide congested plants in spring. Each new plant should have a growing point and fibrous roots. Repot and place in a humid and warm position.

The Flamingo Plant is distinguished by the spiral, orange-red flower spike which arises from 7.5-10cm/ 3-4in long, brilliant scarlet, plate-like collars from mid-spring to early autumn. These heads are borne on stiff, wiry stems.

It is slightly more easy to grow as a houseplant than its near relative the Painter's Palette (*Anthurium andreanum*), surviving a lower temperature during winter.

Astilbe x arendsii
Spiraea

Height 45-60cm/1½-2ft – low-growing forms
Spread 38-45cm/15-18in – low-growing forms
Native Hybrid

Greenfinger Guide

Temperature W 10-15°C/50-59" – see text
S Placed in garden – see text

Light W Bright, but out of direct sunlight. **S** Shady position in the garden.

Watering W Keep moist, especially when flowering. **S** Moisture-retentive soil in garden.

Feeding No feeding required.

Humidity Mist spray the foliage, especially when fresh and new, but avoid saturating the flowers.

Compost Moisture-retentive, peat-based type.

Potting No repotting required – see text.

Propagation Astilbes are normally increased by division of their root-balls in spring. However, this usually does not apply to those astilbes which are forced into early flower indoors.

Frequently known as Spiraea, causing great confusion between astilbes and the well-known genus of hardy deciduous shrubs within the genus *Spiraea*. Astilbes are hardy herbaceous perennials and are really garden plants, where they create masses of colour in summer, often in herbaceous borders but more frequently around the sides of garden ponds where they create a superb display with moisture-loving primulas and water-side primulas. Some species – those which are small – are even ideal for planting in rock gardens. There are also dwarf forms of some species, especially *Astilbe x arendsii* which itself is derived from crossings between *Astilbe chinensis* 'Davidii' and other species, which can be forced into flower early in the year to decorate homes.

Most plants grown as houseplants are bought when in flower during late mid-winter. These plants are potted up – using a moisture-retentive compost such as a peat-based type – into 13cm/5in wide pots during late summer and placed in a cool place. In reality, the term 'potted-back' rather than potted is applicable, as the roots are cramped into the pot, with little extra compost being needed. The pots are covered with peat which is kept moist. During early winter, the plants are moved into a greenhouse or sun-room and given a temperature of 10-13°C/50-55°F. As soon as new growth can be seen and growing strongly, increase the temperature to 15-16°C/59-61°F. Do not give higher temperatures.

After flowering, place in a cool, frost-proof, well-ventilated position for a couple of weeks. Then plant into the garden, selecting a cool, shady, moisture-retentive position.

Don't try and force the same plants into flower for a second year.

Begonia limmingheana
Shrimp Begonia/Glaucous-leaved Begonia

Height Trailing
Spread Cascading
Native Brazil

Greenfinger Guide

Temperature W 10-13°C/50-55°F **S** 13-18°C/ 55-64°F

Light W Bright, but not direct sunlight. **S** Well-lit position, but out of direct sunlight.

Watering W Keep the compost moist, especially if the plant is in an indoor hanging-basket and does not have a large reservoir of compost which can retain moist. **S** Keep the compost moist, but not continually saturated.

Feeding From mid-spring to late summer feed every two weeks.

Humidity Mist spray the foliage in summer, especially if the temperature rises dramatically. However, do not moisten the flowers.

Compost Peat-based compost.

Potting During spring, when the container is packed with roots – usually every year when young.

Propagation From late spring to mid-summer take 10cm/4in-long stem cuttings from non-flowering shoots. Trim them below a leaf-joint and insert in equal parts moist peat and sharp sand. Place in 18-21°C/64-70°F. When rooted, pot up individually into small pots.

The Shrimp Begonia is ideal for planting in an indoor hanging basket or a pot which can be placed where the stems can trail. Although it has the appearance of a fibrous-rooted begonia, it originates from a small rhizome. One of its common names originates from its glaucous, oval leaves up to 13cm/5in long and 6cm/2½in across, which arise from rather weak, slender stems. As the leaves unfurl they are yellowish-green, but darken with age. During summer it develops large clusters of brick-red flowers.

Begonia 'Lorraine Types'
Begonia 'Lorraine Types'

Height 20-30cm/8-12in
Spread 20-30cm/8-12in
Native Hybrids

Greenfinger Guide

Begonia 'Lorraine Types'

Temperature W 7°C/45°F after the flowers fade in mid-winter, then 10-13°C/50-55°F in spring to start plants into growth, so that they will produce shoots suitable as cuttings. **S** 18°C/64°F is needed to root the cuttings, then reduce and grow at 15-20°C/59-68°F during summer, and 10-13°C/50-55°F from autumn to when the flowers fade.

Light W Bright but filtered light. **S** Bright but filtered light.

Watering W After the flowers fade, when the leaves become yellow and the shoots are subsequently cut back to 15cm/6in of the compost, gradually reduce the amount of water, but do not let the plants dry out. When warmth is given to the plants to induce fresh shoots, increase the amount and frequency of watering, but do not saturate the compost. **S** After cuttings have been taken and rooted, and when potted up, keep the compost moist but not saturated. As plants develop flowers, it is essential that the compost does not become dry.

Humidity Create a humid atmosphere by standing plants in saucers of moist pebbles, but do not mist spray the leaves and flowers.

Feeding From when plants are established in their final pots, and until the flowers fade, feed every two weeks with a weak liquid fertilizer.

Compost Peat-based compost.

Potting When cuttings are rooted and growing strongly, pot them into larger pots, as necessary, until in 13-15cm/5-6in wide. During this period it is necessary repeatedly to pinch out the growing tips of shoots to encourage plants to be bushy and compact. Also, to delay flowering and to encourage plants to produce flowers slightly later, pinch off flowers which appear before the late summer. If, however, you want some plants to flower slightly earlier, leave these early flowers on the plant.

Propagation During spring plants are started into growth to induce them to produce young shoots 5-7.5cm/2-3in long suitable as cuttings. Trim them to below leaf-joints and insert in equal parts moist peat and sharp sand and place in 18°C/64°F.

The Lorraine-type begonias are hybrids produced by crossing the now seldom-grown *Begonia socotrana* and *Begonia dregei*. The plants are rounded plants with mid-green leaves and masses of flowers from early autumn to mid-winter. There are many varieties, including the old and established ones such as 'Gloire de Lorraine' and ' Mrs Lionel de Rothschild', both with pink flowers. Newer ones include 'Astrid', 'Novo' and 'Red Virum' (red with yellow centres) and 'Snow Princess' (white with yellow centres).

Related types are the Elatior Hybrids, raised from crossings between *Begonia socotrana* and *Begonia x tuberhybrida*. These resemble the Lorraine types, but have larger flowers and come in a much wider range of colours. There is now a wide range of varieties, many with double flowers, which can be bought in flower throughout the year. There are many established varieties, but newer ones include 'Afrodite Red' (red, spring to late summer), 'Afrodite White' (white, spring to late summer), 'Aida' (pink with paler outsides, late winter to late summer) 'Christel' (orange-pink, late winter to late summer), 'Heidi' (red, late winter to late summer), 'Hollandia' (orange, late winter to late summer), 'Korona' (orange-yellow, late winter to late summer), 'Lara' (pink, late winter to late summer), 'Mandela' (yellow, late winter to early autumn), 'Nymphe' (white, late winter to late summer), 'Oleane' (red, early autumn to mid-winter), 'Schwabenland Yellow' (yellow, early autumn to mid-winter), 'Schwabenland White' (white, early autumn to mid-winter) and 'Toran' (orange, late winter to late summer). There are many other varieties, and each year further varieties become available.

Begonia x lucerna
Spotted Angel Wing Begonia

Height 0.75-1.5m/2½-5ft – or more
Spread 45-75cm/1½-2½ft
Native Hybrid

Greenfinger Guide

Temperature W 10-13°C/50-55°F **S** 13-18°C/55-64°F

Light W Bright, but not direct sunlight. **S** Well-lit position, but out of direct sunlight.

Watering **W** Keep the compost just moist. If the temperature falls, keep the compost slightly drier. **S** Keep the compost moist, but not continually saturated.

Feeding From mid-spring to late summer feed every two weeks.

Humidity Mist spray the foliage in summer, especially if the temperature rises dramatically. However, do not moisten the flowers.

Compost Loam-based compost.

Potting In spring, when roots fill the pot – usually every year when young, less frequently as the plant grows.

Propagation From late spring to mid-summer take 7.5-10cm/3-4in long stem cuttings from non-flowering shoots, trimming them immediately below a leaf-joint. Insert them in equal parts moist peat and sharp sand, and place in 18-21°C/64-70°F. When rooted, pot up individually into small pots.

The Spotted Angel Wing Begonia is one of the large cane-type begonias. This superb hybrid has large, white-and-silver spotted, olive-green leaves with red undersides. The large, pendulous clusters of pink flowers can appear at any time of the year, but chiefly in spring and summer.

Begonia semperflorens
Wax Begonia/Bedding Begonia/Wax Plant

Height 15-23cm/6-9in
Spread 15-23cm/6-9in
Native Brazil

Greenfinger Guide

Temperature **W** 20-25°C/68-77°F – when seeds are sown in spring. **S** 13-16°C/55-61°F

Light **W** After germination, place in bright, indirect light. **S** Bright, indirect light.

Watering **W** Keep the compost evenly moist, but not continually saturated. Take care when seedlings are small not to give them too much water, as at that stage the compost will remain wet for a long time. **S** Keep moist, but not saturated.

Begonia semperflorens

Begonia x lucerna

Feeding Once the plants are established in their final pots, feed every two weeks with a weak liquid fertilizer.

Humidity In summer, stand the pots in trays or saucers of moist pebbles. Do not mist spray the foliage or flowers.

Compost Peat-based compost.

Potting In spring, as soon as the seedlings are large enough to be handled, prick them off into boxes of compost, spacing them about 5cm/2in apart. When these young plants fill the box, pot them first into 7.5-8cm/3-3½in pots, and later into 13cm/5in ones.

Propagation This plant is really a greenhouse perennial, but invariably is treated as a half-hardy annual for planting out into the garden in summer-bedding displays, or for potting up and growing indoors for home decoration. During late winter and early spring, sow seeds thinly and evenly on the surface of a peat-based compost, watering them with a fine-rose watering-can. Do not cover with compost and place in 20-25°C/68-77°F. High temperatures are needed to encourage rapid germination. Also, place a sheet of glass over the seed-box to prevent the compost drying out rapidly. Germination takes two to four weeks, when the temperature can be reduced.

The Wax Begonia is superb for bringing colour indoors

in summer, although they can be encouraged to flower almost throughout the year in greenhouses and sun-rooms. They are small, bushy and compact plants, with bright green or dark purple leaves, which gives them an added attractive quality. The 18-25mm/0.75-1in wide flowers are borne from early to late summer – or even into early autumn – and appear in a colour range including red, white and pink. There are many varieties of these plants, including 'Olympia White' (pure white flowers and glossy-green leaves), 'Sheila' (vivid orange-scarlet flowers) and 'Roselyn' (deep pink flowers and glossy-green leaves). All of these are relatively dwarf (15cm/6in high) and are better than the slightly taller varieties which are best seen in summer-bedding schemes in the garden. After flowering, the plants are discarded and fresh ones bought or grown the following year.

Begonia x tuberhybrida
Tuberous Begonia

Height 30-50cm/12-20in
Spread 30-38cm/12-15in
Native Hybrid

Greenfinger Guide

Temperature **W** 18°C/64°F – starting tubers into growth during early or mid-spring. **S** 16-21°C/61-70°F

Light **W** Bright but filtered light when started into growth. **S** Bright but filtered light.

Watering **W** Store dormant tubers during winter in barely moist peat. In early or mid-spring plant

Begonia x tuberhybrida

tubers in boxes of moist peat. **S** Water moderately, increasing the amount and frequency as the foliage develops.

Feeding From when plants are in their final pots, and until the flowers fade, feed them every two weeks.

Humidity In periods of high temperature, stand the pot in a tray of moist pebbles. However, keep moisture off the flowers and leaves.

Compost Initially started into growth in moist peat, then potted up into a peat-based compost.

Potting As the foliage develops and the compost becomes full of roots, pot up first into 10-13cm/4-5in pots and later into 15-20cm/6-8in ones.

Propagation After flowering gradually reduce the amount of water – but not completely so that the tubers shrivel – and over winter the tubers in barely moist peat at 7°C/45°F. Large tubers can be cut in half when being potted in spring, ensuring each piece has at least one healthy shoot. Alternatively, in late spring or early summer, use early shoots as cuttings – 7.5cm/3in long. Insert in equal parts moist peat and sharp sand and place in 18-21°C/64-70°F.

Tuberous begonias are spectacular plants, with broadly triangular, serrated-edged, mid-green leaves 15-20cm/6-8in long. But it is the large, single or double, rose-like flowers from June to September that give the plant its beauty. Their colour range is wide, and named forms include 'Festiva' (bright yellow), 'Rosanna' (rose-pink), 'Olympia' (bright crimson), and 'Seville' (yellow, with a bright pink edge). There are many other superb varieties, and each year the range is further increased.

The ordinary forms are superb for decorating tables and shelves, but the Basket Begonia (*Begonia x tuberhybrida* 'Pendula') with a similar flowering time, displays slender shoots that bear pendulous flowers. It is ideal for growing in an indoor hanging-basket or in a pot positioned at the corner of a shelf so that the stems can trail. This plant is often sold as *Begonia pendula*.

Begonia multiflora is another tuberous-rooted begonia, smaller in statue than *Begonia x tuberhybrida*,

about 15-20cm/6-8in high, compact and very floriferous.

Beloperone guttata
Shrimp Plant/Mexican Shrimp Plant/False Hop

Height 45-60cm/1½-2ft – sometimes to 90cm/3ft
Spread 30-45cm/1-1½ft – sometimes to 75cm/2½ft
Native Mexico

Greenfinger Guide

Beloperone guttata

Temperature W 7-13°C/45-55°F – if kept at the lower end of this range the plant takes longer to come into flower in spring. **S** 13-24°C/55-75°F

Light W Full light. **S** Light shade.

Watering W Just moist – keep the compost barely moist if the temperature falls dramatically. **S** Water freely, but ensure good drainage.

Feeding From late spring to late summer feed every two weeks.

Humidity Stand pots in trays of wet pebbles. Also, mist spray foliage in summer, but avoid wetting the flowers.

Compost Loam-based type.

Potting In spring, when the roots fill the pot – usually every two or three years. When plants are too large to be repotted, topdress in spring with fresh compost.

Propagation 5-7.5cm/2-3in-long cuttings in early spring. Insert in equal parts moist peat and sharp sand. Place in 18-21°C/64-70°F.

The Shrimp Plant is a sprawling, thin but wiry-stemmed plant with distinctive, shrimp-like flowers from spring to winter. Each flower, up to 15cm/6in long, is formed of overlapping brownish-pink bracts that resemble shrimps. The true flowers are white and nearly inconspicuous, and appear to peep out from the tips of the bracts.

When young, it creates a superb plant for positioning on a dining table or on a net-curtained window-sill. However, with age it needs a floor-standing position

Bougainvillea x buttiana 'Alexandra'

and eventually is better in a greenhouse or sun-room. To encourage the development of a bushy plant, remove the growing tips from the shoots and remove all flowers during the first season.

Several varieties are occasionally available, these include 'Lutea' and 'Yellow Queen', both with yellow bracts.

Bougainvillea x buttiana
Paper Flower

Height 1.5-2.4m/5-8ft – when grown in a large pot
4.5-7.5m/15-25ft – when grown in border soil in a sun-room or greenhouse.
Spread Climber
Native Hybrid

Greenfinger Guide

Temperature W 7-10°C/45-50°F **S** 13-21°C/55-70"

Light W Full light. **S** Full light.

Watering W Just moist. **S** Water freely, but ensure good drainage.

Feeding From late spring to late summer feed every two weeks.

Humidity Mist spray leaves in summer.

Compost Loam-based compost.

Potting In late winter or early spring, when roots fill the pot – usually every year when the plant is young.

Propagation 7.5cm/3in-long stem cuttings with

Bougainvillea x buttiana

Browallia speciosa

heels in summer. Insert in a sandy compost and place in 21°C/70°F.

This Paper Flower is a hybrid between *Bougainvillea glabra* and *Bougainvillea peruviana*, a species seldom seen in cultivation. It is an eye-catching deciduous climber, best grown in a sun-room or greenhouse where it can be given a permanent framework up which to climb. In a pot indoors it needs several canes for support. During summer it creates a spectacular display of crimson or orange bracts that fade to purple or mauve. The real flowers are insignificant. The best known form of this bougainvillea is 'Mrs. Butt' (also known as 'Crimson Lake'), with cascades of rose-crimson bracts that fade to magenta. Pruning is necessary, so in late winter shorten all the main growths by about one-third. At the same time, cut back all sideshoots to the main shoots.

Another Paper Flower, with the same vigour and cultivation requirements, is *Bougainvillea glabra*. It bears 15-23cm/6-9in long clusters of insignificant white flowers surrounded by paper-like bracts in shades of purple and red during late summer and into autumn. There are several forms, including 'Alexandra'.

Bougainvillea spectabilis is another widely grown species, with a flowering season from early to late summer. It is less hardy than the previous species and needs a minimum winter temperature of 10°C/50°F. As a climber for a greenhouse or conservatory it grows to 9m/30ft or more, but in a pot it can be contained to 1.5-2.1m/5-7ft high. Its magenta bracts appear in large bunches up to 30cm/12in wide. Several named varieties are available, including 'Killi Campbell' and 'Granada', both shades of pink. There are many varieties now offered for sale, many originating from research and development carried out in California and utilized by European nurseries, including those in Denmark.

Often, these are compact, bushy and floriferous – and ideal as houseplants. The colour range is wide, and even includes a form with variegated foliage.

Browallia speciosa
Bush Violet

Height 0.9-1.2m/3-4ft – although by pinching out

growing tips it can be kept at 60cm/2ft high.
Spread 45-60cm/1½-2ft
Native Colombia

Greenfinger Guide
Temperature W 10-13°C/50-55°F S 13-65°C/55-64°F

Light W Full light. S Indirect light to full light – but not too strong.

Watering W Just moist. S Evenly moist, but not continually saturated.

Feeding From late spring to late summer feed every four to six weeks, although browallias grow quite well in poor soil.

Humidity Mist spray leaves in summer.

Compost Loam-based type.

Potting Progressively pot up young plants raised from seed early in the year until in 13cm/5in wide pots. Plants are usually discarded after flowering, although they can be overwintered.

Propagation Sow seeds 6mm/0.25in deep during late winter to early spring in a loam-based compost.

Place in 18°C/64°F. Alternatively, sow seeds in mid-summer to raise plants which flower during winter, when a temperature of 13-16°C/55-61°F is needed.

The Bush Violet is a delightful plant for indoors, a sun-room or greenhouse, creating a profusion of star-shaped and tubular, 5cm/2in wide, violet-blue flowers from early to late summer – or during winter if seeds are sown during late summer.

Dwarf varieties, 25-30cm/10-12in high, are frequently grown and are often better houseplants than the true species. Indeed, as well as creating superb pot-plants, they are often planted in indoor hanging-baskets. These dwarf varieties include 'Marine Blue' (blue), White Troll' (white), 'Blue Troll' (blue-purple with white centres) and 'Silver Bells' (white).

Brunfelsia pauciflora calycina
Yesterday, Today and Tomorrow/Morning, Noon and Night/Yesterday and Today

Height 45-60cm/1½-2ft
Spread 3-38cm/12-15in
Native Peru and Brazil

Greenfinger Guide
Temperature W 10-13°C/50-55°F – plants survive short periods down to 7°C/45°F but if this happens keep the compost relatively dry. S 13-21°C/55-70°F

Light W Full light – avoid strong sunlight in spring. S Light shade.

Watering W Barely moist. S Water freely, but ensure good drainage.

Feeding From early to late summer feed every three to four weeks.

Humidity Mist spray leaves in summer.

Compost A peat-based or loam-based type.

Potting After the flowers fade, in late summer or early autumn, when the roots fill the pot – usually every one or two years.

Propagation 7.5-10cm/3-4in-long stem-tip cuttings in late spring. Insert in equal parts moist peat and sharp sand. Place in 21°C/70°F.

Yesterday, Today and Tomorrow usually flowers from mid-spring to mid-summer, but if given a high temperature often continues to bloom throughout the year. The fragrant, violet-purple, wavy-edged flowers fade to pale white.

Although it is frequently grown indoors, it is an evergreen shrub that is at its best in a sun-room or greenhouse.

Brunfelsia pauciflora calycina

Calceolaria x herbeohybrida

Calceolaria x herbeohybrida
**Slipper Plant/Slipper Flower/Pouch Flower/
Pocketbook Flower**

Height 20-45cm/8-18in – also see text
Spread 20-38cm/8-15in
Native Hybrid

Greenfinger Guide
Temperature **W** 7-10°C/45-50°F **S** 10-15°C/
50-59°F

Light **W** Bright, indirect light. **S** Light shade.

Watering **W** Barely moist. Do not allow the
compost to dry out. **S** Keep the compost moist, but
not continually saturated as the roots may rot.

Feeding From when the plant is in its flowering
pot to when the flowers fade, feed every two weeks
with a weak liquid fertilizer.

Humidity None required – keep water off the
flowers and leaves.

Compost Loam-based type. Peat-based types are
excellent.

Potting Gradually pot on the young plants, first
into 7.5cm/3in wide ones and later into 13-15cm/5-
6in types.

Campanula isophylla

Propagation Sow seeds from late spring until mid-
summer in loam-based compost or a peat-based
type. The seeds are small, so sow them thinly and
evenly, just pressing them into the surface and not
covering with compost. Germination takes two to
three weeks. Place in 16-20°C/61-68°F and shade
them from direct light. After germination, and when
the seedlings are large enough to handle, prick them
off into small pots.

Calceolarias are greenhouse biennials and are some of
the most distinctive and attractive of summer-flowering
houseplants. Seeds sown one year produce plants in
flower during the following one. From late spring to
mid-summer they display clusters of pouch-like
flowers in shades of yellow, orange and red, some
spotted or splashed with maroon or brownish-red.
Several strains are available, in a range of colours and
sizes. Multiflora Nana types are about 20cm/8in high,
compact and with masses of small flowers in varied
and bright colours. 'Glorious Formula Mixed' hybrids
are about 30cm/12in high and display large pouched
heads in brilliant colours. 'Intermediate Special
Hybrids' are 38cm/15in high, and 'Perfection Mixed'
at 45cm/18in high displays large pouched flowers.

Calceolarias are superb for bringing colour to dining
and coffee tables during early summer.

After flowering, plants are discarded and fresh
ones bought – or raised – for the following year. It is
not worth trying to keep plants which have flowered
and to encourage them to produce flowers during the
following year. The display will not be very good.

Campanula isophylla
Italian Bellflower/Star of Bethlehem/Falling Stars

Height 10-15cm/4-6in
Spread 30-45cm/12-18in – then cascading and
trailing
Native Northern Italy

Greenfinger Guide
Temperature **W** 7-10°C/45-50°F **S** 10-16°C/
50-61°F

Light **W** Indirect light. **S** Bright, indirect light.

Watering **W** Barely moist. **S** Water freely, but
ensure good drainage.

Feeding From late spring to late summer feed
every three weeks.

Humidity Mist spray leaves in summer.

Compost Loam-based type.

Potting In early spring, when the container is
packed with roots – usually every one or two years.

Propagation Divide congested plants in spring
when being repotted. Alternatively sow seeds in

Campanula isophylla

spring in a loam-based compost, placing in 16°C/
61°F. Also, take 7.5cm long stem-tip cuttings in
spring, inserting in equal parts moist peat and sharp
sand and placing in 16°C/61°F.

The Italian Bellflower has been grown indoors for

Celosia argentea 'Cristata'

Chrysanthemum

many years, and is ideal for planting in indoor hanging-baskets as well as in pots positioned at the edges of shelves so that the stems can trail. During mid to late summer the heart-shaped, mid-green leaves become smothered with star-shaped, 2.5cm/1in wide, blue flowers. 'Alba' is a white-flowered form, while 'Mayii' has attractively variegated leaves.

Celosia argentea
Woolflower

Height 45-60cm/1½-2ft
Spread 25-30cm/10-12in
Native Tropical Asia

Greenfinger Guide

Temperature W Plants are discarded in late summer. S 16-18°C/61-64°F

Light W Plants discarded. S Bright, indirect light.

Watering W Plants discarded. S Evenly moist, not continually saturated.

Celosia argentea 'Plumosa'

Feeding From early to late summer feed every two to three weeks.

Humidity Mist spray foliage when the plants are young, but avoid wetting the flowers.

Compost Loam-based type.

Potting Progressively pot up seedlings and young plants until in 8-13cm/3½-5in wide pots.

Propagation Sow seeds 3mm/6in deep in a loam-based compost during late winter and early spring. Place in 15-20°C/59-68°F. Germination takes up to two weeks, and as soon as the seedlings are large enough to handle prick them into small pots.

Celosia argentea is a greenhouse annual mostly grown as a houseplant but occasionally for display in summer-bedding displays outdoors. From mid to late summer it bears feathery plumes, 7.5cm/3in wide, of silvery-white flowers.

Two well-known forms of this eye-catching plant are grown. *C. a. plumosa*, also known as *C. a. pyramidalis* and commonly as the Plume Flower,

Plumed Cock's Comb or Prince of Wales' Feather, has feathery flower plumes, 7.5-15cm/3-6in high, in colours including crimson, pink and yellow. These mainly are up to 60cm/2ft high, although there are several dwarf forms ideal for growing indoors.

C. a. cristata is the Cockscomb, with crested flower heads up to 13cm/5in wide and in colours including red, orange and yellow.

Chrysanthemum
Chrysanthemum

Height 20-38cm/8-15in
Spread 20-30cm/8-12in
Native China and Japan

Greenfinger Guide

Temperature W 10-16°C/50-61°F S 10-16°C/50-61°F

Light W Bright, indirect light. S Bright, indirect light.

Watering W Evenly and constantly moist. S Evenly and constantly moist.

Feeding Not necessary.

Humidity A slightly humid atmosphere is desirable, but do not mist spray the flowers.

Compost Repotting is unnecessary.

Potting Repotting is unnecessary.

Propagation Buy fresh plants (see text)

Chrysanthemums are some of the best known houseplants and can be bought throughout the year. They are sold growing in pots, with some flowers displaying colour and with buds waiting to open, creating a wealth of colour. Their colour range is wide, including yellow orange, red, ruse pink and white, and in single and or double-flowered forms.

Chrysanthemums normally flower during autumn, when the period of darkness in twenty-four hours is

Clerodendrum thomsoniae

Columnea x banksii 'Kosta'

getting long. For many years specialist nurseries have used this aspect of a chrysanthemum's nature to induce them to flower throughout the year. A strict regime of light and dark periods, combined with a certain temperature, induces the development of flower buds. Nurserymen also apply dwarfing chemicals to plants to ensure they remain small and suitable for display indoors. It is therefore best to buy fresh plants throughout the year, rather than trying to keep them.

Sometimes these chrysanthemums are sold under the name *Chrysanthemum indicum* – hybrids, and in a vast range of named varieties. These include 'Copper Hostess' (burnt orange), 'Butterball' (yellow and ball-like), 'Echo' (white with yellow centres), 'Songster' (white, quill-like, narrow petals surrounding yellow centres), 'Rofus' (deep red with yellow centres), 'Tempo' (pink), 'Maximo' (daisy like flowers with yellow petals and yellow centres) and 'Twilight' (pink petals with yellow centres). There are many other varieties, and frequently plants are sold unnamed.

Clerodendrum thomsoniae
Glory Bower/Bleeding Heart Vine/Glory Tree/ Bad-flower

Height 1.8-2.4m/6-8ft – or more
Spread Climber
Native West Africa

Greenfinger Guide

Temperature W 13-15°C/55-59°F S 15-25°C/ 59-77°F

Light W Full light. S Light shade on strongly sunny days.

Watering W Just moist. S Water freely, but ensure good drainage.

Feeding From late spring to late summer feed every two weeks.

Humidity Mist spray leaves during summer.

Compost Loam-based type.

Potting In spring, when the roots fill the pot – usually every year. When in large pots, remove the top 2.5cm/1in of compost in spring and replace with fresh.

Propagation 7.5-10cm/3-4in-long stem cuttings during spring. Insert in equal parts moist peat and sharp sand. Place in 16-18°C/61-64°F.

The Glory Bower is a sprawling climber best grown in a large tub in a sun-room or in the border soil of a greenhouse, where it creates a large and dominant display. It can also be grown in pots indoors, when it needs to be trimmed back in early autumn to encourage bushiness and to form a plant of manageable proportions indoors.

It is a climber well known for its early to late summer, white, lantern-like flowers with red tips.

Columnea x banksii 'Stavanger'

Columnea x banksii
Goldfish Plant

Trailing Stems up to 90cm/3ft long
Native Hybrid

Greenfinger Guide

Temperature W 15-16°C/59-61°F S 16-21°C/ 61-70°F

Light W Bright, diffused light. S Light shade.

Watering W Evenly moist, especially when in flower. S Water freely, but ensure good drainage.

Feeding From late spring to late summer feed every two weeks.

Humidity Mist spray in summer.

Compost Peat-based type.

Columnea x banksii 'Mercury'

Potting In late spring repot when the roots fill the container – usually every other year.

Propagation 7.5-10cm/3-4in-long cuttings from non-flowering shoots during spring and early summer. Insert in equal parts moist peat and sharp sand. Place in 18-21°C/64-70°F.

Columnea x banksii develops vermilion flowers, up to 7.5cm/3in long and with orange-yellow markings from late autumn to mid-spring. These are borne amid fleshy, dark green leaves.

It is best grown in a sun-room or greenhouse, in an indoor hanging-basket and where the stems can freely trail.

There are many other columnea offered for sale. *Columnea hirta*, often sold named as *Columnea* 'Hirta', has stiff, hairy, reddish stems and long and hairy, vermilion flowers up to 6cm/2½in long. Many columneas are sold just by their varietal name, and a range is shown here. These include 'Krakatoa', 'Stavanger', 'Mercury' (often called 'Merkur') and 'Kosta'.

Columnea gloriosa

Columnea x banksii 'Krakatoa'

Columnea x banksii 'Hirta'

Columnea gloriosa
Goldfish Plant

Trailing Stems up to 1.2m/4ft long
Native Costa Rica

Greenfinger Guide

Temperature W 15-16°C/59-61°F S 16-21°C/61-70°F

Light W Bright, diffused light. S Light shade.

Watering W Evenly moist, especially when in flower. S Water freely, but ensure good drainage.

Feeding From late spring to late summer feed every two weeks.

Humidity Mist spray in summer.

Compost Peat-based type.

Potting In late spring or early summer, repot when the roots fill the container – usually every other year.

Propagation 7.5-10cm/3-4in-long cuttings from non-flowering shoots during spring and early summer. Insert in equal parts moist peat and sharp sand. Place in 18-21°C/64-70°F.

Columnea gloriosa produces an eye-catching display of bright scarlet, 5-6cm/2-2½ in long flowers with yellow throats from early autumn to mid-spring. The pale to mid-green leaves are covered with tiny reddish hairs.

Like all other columneas it is best grown in an indoor hanging-basket, and preferably in a sun-room where the stems can trail unimpeded.

Crossandra infundibuliformis
Firecracker Plant

Height 60-90cm/2-3ft
Spread 60-75cm/2-2½ft
Native East Indies

Greenfinger Guide

Temperature W 13-15°C/55-61°F S 16-21°C/61-70°F

Light W Full light. S Light shade.

Watering W Barely moist. S Water freely, but ensure good drainage.

Feeding From early to late summer feed every two weeks.

Crossandra infundibuliformis

Humidity Mist spraying the leaves during summer is essential. Also, stand the pot in a tray of moist pebbles.

Compost Loam-based type.

Potting Pot up established plants in spring, when the roots fill the pot – usually every two or three years. Young plants need to be progressively repotted during summer.

Propagation Sow seeds in early spring in a loam-based compost. Place in 16°C/61°F. Alternatively, take 7.5cm/3in-long cuttings in spring or early summer. Insert in equal parts moist peat and sharp sand. Place in 21-24°C/70-75°F.

The Firecracker Plant is a tender evergreen shrub best suited for growing in a sun-room or greenhouse, especially if plants are to be overwintered – a constant, relatively high, winter temperature and high humidity during summer are essential. However, plants flower when very young and are often grown indoors during summer and subsequently discarded in autumn.

Flowering lasts from late mid-spring to late summer, or even into early autumn, with orange-red flowers borne in flowers spikes up to 10cm/4in high.

Cuphea ignea
Cigar Plant/Cigar Flower/Firecracker Plant/Red-whit-and-Blue-flower

Height 30-45cm/12-18in
Spread 30-38cm/12-15in
Native Mexico

Greenfinger Guide

Temperature W 7-10°C/45-50°F **S** 10-18°C/50-64°F

Light W Full light. **S** Light shade.

Watering W Barely moist. **S** Water freely, but ensure good drainage.

Feeding Feed newly-raised plants every ten days from when in their final pots until late summer.

With established plants, feed every ten days from late spring to late summer.

Humidity Mist spray leaves during summer – especially with young plants.

Compost Loam-based type.

Potting Progressively pot up young plants as they become pot-bound. Repot established plants in spring, but only when roots fill the pot – usually every two or three vears.

Cuphea ignea

Propagation Sow seeds in early spring in a loam-based seed compost. Place in 16°C/61°F. Alternatively, 5-7.5cm/2-3in-long stem-tip cuttings in late spring. Insert in equal parts moist peat and sharp sand, and place in 16-18°C/61-64°F.

The Cigar Plant is a small, rapid growing, evergreen shrub, usually cultivated as a short-lived houseplant, or for longer periods in a sun-room or greenhouse. It can also be used in summer-bedding displays in warm areas. From mid-spring to early autumn it produces tubular, 2.5cm/1in long, bright scarlet flowers. The mouth of each flower is tipped in white and purplish black.

Another cuphea sometimes grown as a houseplant is *Cuphea miniata*, a half-hardy perennial invariably grown as a half-hardy annual.

Sometimes it is grown as a summer-bedding plant, but frequently as a houseplant which is discarded after bearing its flowers. From early to late summer it reveals bright red, tubular flowers, on plants up to 30cm/12in high, amid mid-green leaves. Seeds are sown in early or mid-spring, 6mm/(in deep and placed in 15-20°C/59-70°F. Germination takes up to three weeks, and when large enough to handle the seedlings are pricked out, first into boxes and later into pots.

Cyclamen persicum
Alpine Violet/Sow Bread/Florist's Cyclamen/Persian Violet

Height 15-23cm/6-9in
Spread 15-25cm/6-10in
Native Eastern Mediterranean

Greenfinger Guide

Temperature W 13-15°C/55-59°F – when in flower 10-13°C/50-55°F – when young and still in a small pot. **S** Keep cool when plants are young and developing into flowering plants – in the region of 10-13°C/50-55°F.

Light W Full sun. **S** Light shade.

Watering W Keep the compost moist. **S** Careful watering is needed when the plants are small and in large pots. Keep the compost just moist and do not

Cyclamen persicum

Cyclamen persicum

just before Christmas. The butterfly-like flowers – some fragrant – appear above the round and marbled leaves. The plants are sold when in bud, with colour just showing on some of them.

After flowering, plants can be kept for another year. Reduce watering, stop feeding and place the pot on its side in a cool, dry, vermin-proof position. About mid-summer, repot the corm into fresh compost, burying the corm to half its depth. Water and place in bright, indirect sunlight.

Most cyclamen are bought as established plants, and the way to success with them is not to give them high temperatures or to let moisture collect around the corms. Also, as soon as a flower fades, pull off the flower stalk complete with the dead flower.

Euphorbia pulcherrima

Euphorbia pulcherrima

Euphorbia pulcherrima

continually moisten the corm.

Feeding From when the buds appear to when the flowers die, feed every two to three weeks.

Humidity Occasionally mist spray around the plant, but avoid saturating the flowers or the bases of the stems. Standing plants in saucers of moist pebbles helps to create a humid atmosphere.

Compost Loam-based type.

Potting Initially, prick off seedlings into seedtrays, then progressively into slightly larger pots.

Propagation Sow seeds thinly, 6mm/0.25in deep, placing the containers in 13-16°C/55-61°F. Germination takes three to four weeks. Seeds sown in mid or late winter will produce plants for flowering the following Christmas, but for really large plants sow seeds in late summer for flowering fifteen to eighteen months later.

This well-known flowering houseplant is sold in millions from early autumn to spring, and especially

Euphorbia pulcherrima
Poinsettia/Christmas Stars/Painted Leaf/Lobster Plant/Mexican Flameleaf

Height 30-45cm/1-1½ft – see text
Spread 30-38cm/12-15in
Native Mexico

Greenfinger Guide

Temperature W 13-61°C/55-61°F S 16-18°C/61-64°F

Light W Bright, indirect light. S Bright, indirect light.

Watering W Evenly moist. S see text.

Feeding From late spring to late summer feed every two weeks.

Humidity Do not mist spray.

Compost Loam-based type.

Potting During late spring – see text.

Propagation 7.5-10cm/3-4in long stem-tip cuttings in late spring or early summer. Insert in equal parts moist peat and sharp sand. Place in 18-21°C/64-70°F.

The Poinsettia is one of the best known flowering houseplants at Christmas, sold in millions and displaying colourful leaf-like bracts around the tips of the stems. Usually these bracts are bright crimson, but scarlet, white, pink and cream forms are widely available, as well as a slightly variegated type. Some varieties are names, such as 'Marble', others are just sold as coloured forms.

Poinsettias can be kept from one season to another, but because nurserymen often treat these plants with chemicals to keep them dwarf, during following years the plants may be larger – up to 1½ft/5ft. Cuttings taken from these plants may also develop into larger plants. After the bracts fade and the real leaves have fallen, cut back the stems to 10cm/4in high and place the plant in a frost-proof, shady position. Keep the compost almost dry. During late spring, repot the plant into the same size pot – removing old soil and replacing with fresh – or a slightly larger one. Soak the compost with water and place the plant in bright, indirect light and 13-15°C/55-59°F. Shoots will develop from the stems, are a few inches long remove all but the four or five healthiest and strongest ones. Strong shoots that are removed can be used as cuttings.

To ensure that plants develop colourful bracts during Christmas it is necessary to control the amount of light reaching the plant. Place a large black polythene back over the plant from early evening to late morning. Plants need fourteen hours of darkness for eight weeks to ensure that they flower at Christmas – start this treatment at the end of summer. After this treatment, place your plant in bright, indirect light.

Exacum affine

Exacum affine
Persian Violet/Mexican Violet/German Violet

Height 15-25cm/6-10in
Spread 15-25cm/6-10in
Native Island of Socotra

Greenfinger Guide

Temperature W 18°C/64°F for seed sowing in early spring S 13-16°C/55-61°F

Light W Light shade in spring. S Bright, but not direct light.

Watering W Plants are discarded after flowering. S Keep moist, but not continually saturated.

Feeding From early to mid-summer feed every ten to fourteen days.

Humidity Stand the pot in a tray of moist pebbles.

Compost Loam-based type.

Potting Pot up seedlings progressively until in a 7.5cm/3in wide pot.

Propagation Sow seeds 6mm/6in deep in early spring in loam-based seed compost. Place in 18°C/64°F. Germination takes between two and three weeks. Larger plants can be produced by sowing seeds in late summer and overwintering the plants at 16°C/61°F.

The Persian Violet creates a neat, rounded plant which reveal masses of violet-coloured flowers with bright yellow stamens from mid to late summer. The sweetlyscented flowers are borne above the small, glossy, oval leaves. After flowering the plants are best discarded and fresh ones raised or bought the following year. Several different varieties are available, some with double the number of petals. White forms are also available.

Tables, ledges and shelves all benefit from this plant.

Fuchsias
Lady's Eardrops

Height Wide range – see text
Spread Wide range – see text
Native Hybrids

Greenfinger Guide

Temperature W 4-7°C/39-45°F – if larger plants are desired, keep the temperature at 13°C/55°F during winter so that plants keep growing. However, this is usually impractical for a home gardener. S 10°C/50°F in spring to start the plants into growth. During summer this invariably rises to 18°C/64°F, but avoid very high temperatures.

Light W Unless the plants are being kept growing throughout winter, when they need good light, this

Fuchsia

Fuchsia

Fuchsia

Hibiscus rosa-sinensis

is not applicable. **S** Full light or slight shade.

Watering **W** If plants are kept dormant in winter, keep the compost barely moist, just damping it occasionally. However, if plants are kept growing, keep the compost moist but not continually saturated. **S** Keep the compost moist, especially when in flower.

Feeding From when the plants start to produce fresh shoots in spring, and until late summer, feed every two weeks with a weak liquid fertilizer.

Humidity Mist spray young shoots and leaves during summer, but avoid splashing the flowers unnecessarily.

Compost Loam-based type. If you have bought a new fuchsia plant, it will probably be in a peat-based compost. If this is so, repot it into a similar compost but be prepared to feed the plant more often during summer.

Potting In early spring, repot established plants. Then, in early spring prune back the shoots – up to one-third of them can safely be removed. Water the compost thoroughly and place in 10°C/50°F. Some of the young shoots which have then develop can be cut off and used as cuttings. However, don't remove too many as the plant's shape may be ruined.

Propagation In spring, use young shoots – about 7.5cm/3in long – as cuttings. Trim beneath a leaf-joint, remove the lower leaves and insert in equal parts moist peat and sharp sand. Place in 16°C/61°F.

Lady's Eardrops are some of the daintiest of all house and garden plants. The range is wide and although some true species are still grown, it is usually the hybrids which are offered for sale. Some are ideal in pots, others in hanging-baskets.

The sizes of these hybrids varies enormously, and often depends on the way they are grown.

Fuchsias grown as bushes are usually 38-50cm/15-20in high and wide, whereas those grown as standards often grow 0.9-1.4m/3-4ft high – or more – and 45-60cm/1½-2ft wide. Those suitable for growing in hanging baskets have a pendulous habit and can soon fill out a basket.

Hibiscus rosa-sinensis
Chinese Rose/Rose of China/Blocking Plant/ Hawaiian Hibiscus

Height 45-60cm/1½-2ft – in pots
Spread 38-45cm/15-18in – in pots
Native China

Greenfinger Guide

Temperature **W** 7-10°C/45-50°F **S** 13-21°C/55-70°F

Light **W** Bright, indirect light. **S** Bright, indirect light.

Watering **W** Just moist. **S** Water freely, but ensure good drainage.

Feeding From late spring to late summer feed every two weeks with a weak liquid fertilizer.

Humidity Mist spray leaves during summer, but do not allow the flowers to become wet.

Compost Loam-based type.

Potting In spring, when the roots fill the pot – usually every year when young and small.

Propagation 7.5-10cm/3-4in long cuttings of non-flowering shoots during mid-summer. Insert in equal parts moist peat and sharp sand. Place in 18°C/64°F.

The Chinese Rose can be grown in a sun-room or greenhouse border, where it grows up to 1.8m/6ft high. It can also be grown in a pot indoors, where it develops into a much smaller plant. From early to late summer it bears short-lived, deep crimson, funnel-shaped flowers up to 13cm/5in wide. The form 'Cooperi' is slightly smaller, with leaves variegated cream, green and crimson. Also, it has brilliant scarlet flowers.

Recently, many new varieties have been developed by the Danish pot plant industry, and these are widely available. They include 'Casablanca' and 'Harlekin' (both white with red centres), 'Helene' (red), 'Toronto' (pink), 'Tivoli' (red with yellow edges to the petals), 'Koeniger' (yellow), 'Holiday' (red), 'Moesiana' (burnt orange) and 'Dark Weekend' (burnt orange petals with dark red centres).

When small it is a superb plant for decorating tables

Hibiscus rosa-sinensis

Hibiscus rosa-sinensis 'Koeniger'

and large shelves, but with age its size demands more space – often an out-of-the-way corner.

Hippeastrum hybrida
Hippeastrum – although frequently called Amaryllis

Height 30-45cm/1-1½ft
Spread 15-23cm/6-9in
Native Hybrid

Hippeastrum hybrida

Greenfinger Guide
Temperature W 18°C/64°F S 13-16°C/55-61°F

Light W Bright, indirect light. S Bright, indirect light.

Watering W Water thoroughly, allowing the surface to dry between applications. S see potting.

Feeding From when the shoots appear to when they die down, feed every two weeks.

Humidity Mist spray the foliage during warm weather.

Compost Loam-based type.

Potting Early-flowering specially-prepared bulbs are potted in early autumn, while ordinary types potted in late summer or early October will flower in late winter and early spring. Pot each bulb into a 13-15cm/5-6in wide pot, so that its neck and shoulders are above the compost. Water the

compost and place the pot in a warm, dark place, such as an airing cupboard. Hippeastrums dislike repotting – usually every three years is enough. Replace the surface compost with fresh, and treat in the same way as the potted ones. When growth appears, gradually move to better light.

Propagation Buy fresh bulbs, or at potting time remove small bulbs from around the mother bulb's base and pot up into small pots. They take several years before they reach flowering size.

Hippeastrums are spectacular bulbs, producing giant, trumpet-shaped flowers mainly during late winter and spring, but also during Christmas and mid-winter if specially-prepared bulbs are used.

Many named forms are sold, in colours including orange-red, pure white, deep rose, clear orange and pale pink, some striped and tinged with other colours.

Hoya bella
Miniature Wax Plant

Height 23-30cm/9-12in
Spread 38-45cm/15-18in
Native India

Greenfinger Guide
Temperature W 10-13°C/50-55°F S 16-21°C/61-70°F

Hibiscus rosa-sinensis

Hoya bella

Light W Bright, indirect light. **S** Medium to heavy shade.

Watering W Just moist. **S** Water freely, but ensure good drainage.

Feeding From late spring to late summer feed every three to four weeks with a weak liquid fertilizer.

Humidity Mist spray leaves in summer.

Compost A loam-based or peat-based type.

Potting In late spring, but only when roots completely fill the pot – usually every two or three years.

Propagation 5-7.5cm/2-3in long stem cuttings in early summer. Insert in equal parts moist peat and sharp sand, and place in 16-18°C/61-64°F.

The Miniature Wax Plant is a small shrub with cascading branches that bear pendulous, umbrella-heads of scented, waxy-white star-like flowers with rose-crimson centres from late spring to late summer. It is at its best when grown in an indoor hanging-basket or in a pot positioned so that the stems can trail.

Hoya carnosa
Wax Plant/Honey Plant

Height 2.4-4.5m/8-15ft
Spread Climber
Native Queensland

Greenfinger Guide

Temperature W 7-10°C/45-50°F **S** 16-21°C/61-70°F

Light W Bright, indirect light. **S** Light shade.

Watering W Just moist. **S** Water freely, but ensure good drainage.

Feeding From late spring to late summer feed every three weeks.

Humidity Mist spray leaves in summer.

Compost Loam-based type.

Potting In late spring, but only when the roots completely fill the pot – usually every two or three years.

Eventually, when grown in a large pot or tub, it will be impossible to repot it. At that stage, in spring remove the top 2.5-4cm/1-1½in of compost and replace with fresh.

Propagation 7.5-10cm/3-4in long stem cuttings during early to mid-summer. Insert in equal parts moist peat and sharp sand, and place in 16-18°C/61-64°F.

The Wax Plant is a vigorous, evergreen climber best grown in a large tub in a sun-room or the border soil in a greenhouse, where it can be provided with a permanent framework up which to climb. Indoors it can be grown in a large pot, with pliable canes looped to provide a framework up which it can climb.

From late spring to late summer it bears pendulous, 7.5cm/3in wide, umbrella-like heads of fragrant, star-shaped, white to light pink flowers.

Two variegated forms are available – one has gold centres and green edges to the leaves, while the other has pink edges, slowly becoming cream. The latter one is more widely seen.

Hoya multiflora, from the Malacca Straits, can be either compact and bushy or a climber. In its bushy form – and when young – it is often grown as a houseplant. It bears large, dark green, leathery leaves and arrow-shaped white flowers – fading slightly with age – from early spring to late summer. Each flower has a brown centre and there are up to twenty-five scented flowers in each cluster.

Hyacinthus orientalis
Common Hyacinth/Dutch Hyacinth

Height 15-23cm/6-9in
Spread 7.5-13cm/3-5in
Native Eastern Europe and Western Asia

Greenfinger Guide

Temperature W When the shoot tips appear above the surface of the compost, place in 10°C/50°F, gradually increasing this to 18°C/64°F when the flower buds display colour. **S** Not applicable.

Light W Bright. **S** Not applicable.

Watering W Keep moist, especially when the bulbs are flowering.

Feeding Not necessary.

Hoya multiflora

Humidity Do not mist spray the plants.

Compost Loam-based compost, or bulb fibre.

Potting During late summer pot up fresh bulbs, leaving their necks protruding above the compost. Place in a cool position – about 5°C/50°F – and in darkness until leaf-tips appear above the compost. Keep the compost evenly moist during this period of root development.

Propagation Buy fresh bulbs each year. After flowering, allow the foliage to die down naturally, place in a frost-proof shed or greenhouse and during late spring plant the bulbs around shrubs. Do not force them again.

Hyacinths are superb for bringing colour to rooms during Christmas and until early spring. Their candle-like heads are packed with scented, wax-like flowers in a wide colour range, including white, yellow, pink, red, mauve and blue. Reliable varieties for growing indoors include 'L'Innocence' (white), 'Amethyst' (lilac-mauve), 'City of Haarlem' (creamy-yellow), 'Jan Bos' (cerise-pink), 'Delft Blue' (pale blue) and 'Pink Pearl' (pink). Hyacinths are ideal for placing in

Hyacinthus orientalis

Hydrangea macrophylla

Hydrangea macrophylla

cool rooms – high temperatures soon cause the flowers to fade and deteriorate.

When buying bulbs to flower at Christmas, choose those known as *specially-prepared bulbs*. These have been subjected to low temperatures to induce them to develop roots and to produce flowers at an early date.

Hydrangea
Common Hydrangea/French Hydrangea

Height 50-60cm/1-2ft
Spread 30-45cm/1-1½ft
Native China and Japan

Greenfinger Guide
Temperature W 7°C/45°F until mid-winter, then raise to 13°C/55°F. S 13-15°C/55-59°F – after the flowers fade reduce the temperature and eventually place outside.

Light W Bright light. S Bright, indirect light.

Watering W Barely moist. S As growth continues, apply more water, keeping the compost moist at all times.

Feeding From when the buds form and until the flowers fade, feed every seven to ten days.

Humidity Mist spray the leaves.

Compost Use a loam-based type. Omit chalk from the mixture when repotting blue varieties, as the alkalinity or acidity of the compost has an influence on the colour of the flowers. Blue varieties will not produce good blue flower colours when grown on chalky (alkaline) soils. And pink varieties are not so good when in acid compost.

Potting In late summer, as the plant loses its leaves, remove it from its pot and repot into fresh compost. Plants not yet in 15-20cm/6-8in wide pots can be given larger ones. While repotting, prune to leave a strong pair of buds on the stems produced during that year. Water the plant and place in a cool position.

Propagation 13-15cm/5-6in long stem-tip cuttings during mid or late summer. Insert in equal parts moist peat and sharp sand. Place in 15-18°C/59-64°F.

Hydrangeas are superb plants, creating dominant displays in cool rooms during late spring and early summer. There are two forms of *Hydrangea macrophylla*: the Mop-head type (sometimes called Hortensias) which has large, round, flower heads 15-20cm/6-8in wide, and the Lacecaps with flat and more open heads, 10-15cm/4-6in wide. It is the Mop-heads that are usually grown as houseplants. Their colours include white, blue, pink and red.

Impatiens walleriana
Busy Lizzie/Patience Plant/Patient Lucy/Sultana

Height 45-60cm/1½-2ft
Spread 38-45cm/15-18in
Native Africa

Greenfinger Guide
Temperature W 13°C/55°F – it can survive down to 7°C/45°F, but at this temperature the compost needs to be kept drier and there is the risk of leaves dropping off the plant. S 16-20°C/61-68°F

Light W Bright light. S Bright, indirect light.

Watering W Just moist. S Water freely, but ensure good drainage.

Feeding From late spring to late summer feed every week with a weak liquid fertilizer.

Humidity Mist spray only during summer, keeping the water off the flowers.

Compost A loam-based or peat-based type.

Potting In spring, but only when the soil-ball is congested with roots – usually every one or two years.

Propagation 7.5-10cm/3-4in long tip cuttings from

Hydrangea macrophylla

Impatiens 'New Guinea Hybrids'

Impatiens 'New Guinea Hybrids'

late spring to late summer. Insert in equal parts moist peat and sharp sand. Place in 16°C/61°F.

The Busy Lizzie is one of the best known and most widely-grown of all houseplants, displaying flat-faced, five-petalled flowers in colours including pink, red, purple, orange and white. There are also named hybrids with flowers displaying mixed colours, and forms with variegated leaves.

A sample of the hybrids includes 'Elfin Blush' (20cm/8in high, pale pink flowers with red eyes), 'Blitz Orange' (15cm/6in high, large orange-scarlet flowers amid bronze-green leaves), 'Novette Mixed' (10cm/4in high, with flowers in many bright colours) and 'Starbright' (15cm/6in high, in a range of colours including orange, red, rose and violet, each flowers having a white star). There are many other varieties to choose from.

The New Guinea Hybrids were developed from *Impatiens linearifolia* and *Impatiens hawkeri*. The plants tend to be larger than many other impatiens – 30cm/12in or more high – and include 'Sweet Sue' (deep orange flowers), 'Fanfare' (leaves yellow and green, with pink flowers) and 'Red Magic' (bronzy leaves and red flowers).

To ensure that plants do not become leggy and with bare bases during summer, nip out the growing tips to encourage the development of sideshoots.

Jasminum mesnyi
Primrose Jasmine/Japanese Jasmine/Yellow Jasmine

Height 1.8-3m/6-10ft
Spread Climber
Native China

Greenfinger Guide
Temperature W 7-10°C/45-50°F **S** 10-15°C/50-59°F

Light W Bright light. **S** Bright, but out of direct sunlight.

Watering W Moist. **S** Water freely, especially when in flower.

Feeding From when the flower buds appear to late summer, feed every two weeks with a weak liquid fertilizer.

Humidity Mist spray the leaves during summer.

Compost Loam-based type.

Potting In late summer, when roots fill the pot. If the plant is already in a large pot, topdress with fresh compost.

Propagation 7.5-10cm/3-4in long cutting in late summer. Insert in equal parts moist peat and sharp sand. Place in 16°C/61°F.

The Primrose Jasmine is an evergreen climber best suited for growing in a sun-room or greenhouse border, where from early to late spring it displays scentless, semi-double, yellow flowers up to 5cm/2in across. When grown in a sun-room or greenhouse it needs a

Jasminum mesnyi

permanent framework up which to clamber. When small and growing in a pot – with support from thin canes – it can be moved indoors from a greenhouse or sun-room when in flower. During summer it can be placed outside on a sheltered patio.

Jasminum polyanthum
Pink Jasmine/Jasmine/Poet's Jessamine

Height 90cm-1.5m/3-5ft
Spread 90cm-1.2m/3-4ft
Native China

Greenfinger Guide
Temperature W 10-13°C/50-55°F – it will survive temperatures down to 7°C/45°F, or even to 5°C/41°F, but will take much longer to come into flower. Also, water with care if the temperature falls dramatically. **S** 13-18°C/55-64°F

Light W Bright light. **S** Bright, but out of direct sunlight.

Watering W Moist, increasing the frequency as the buds develop and especially when in flower. **S** Water freely, but ensure good drainage.

Feeding From when the buds appear feed every two weeks with a weak liquid fertilizer.

Jasminum polyanthum

Humidity Mist spray the leaves in summer.

Compost Loam-based type.

PottingIn spring, when roots fill the pot. If the plant is already in a large pot, topdress with fresh compost.

Propagation 7.5-10cm/3-4in long stem-tip cuttings in late spring. Insert in equal parts moist peat and sharp sand. Place in 16-18°C/61-64°F.

The Pink Jasmine is hardy enough to be grown outside in a warm and sheltered, south or west-facing position – where it flowers from mid-spring to early summer. Indoors, it flowers from late autumn to mid-spring, creating a mass of scented, star-shaped, white or pale pink flowers in clusters up to 13cm/5in long. These are borne against a background of dark green leaves formed of five to seven leaflets.

It can be grown in a sun-room or in a greenhouse border, where it climbs and sprawls up to 3m/10ft high, but when grown in a pot and trained over a hoop of pliable canes it is a little more reserved in vigour. Plants can be stood outside in sheltered positions during summer, and this helps to ripen the wood.

Kalanchoe blossfeldiana
Flaming Katy

Height 20-30cm/8-12in
Spread 20-25cm/8-10in
Native Madagascar

Kalanchoe blossfeldiana

Kalanchoe blossfeldiana 'Tessa'

Kohleria amabilis

Greenfinger Guide

Temperature W 10-13°C/50-55°F **S** 13-18°C/55-64°F

Light W Bright, indirect light. **S** Bright, indirect light.

Watering W Slightly moist. **S** Water thoroughly, but allow the compost to dry out slightly between waterings.

Feeding From when the buds show colour, feed every two to three weeks.

Humidity No mist spraying required.

Compost Loam-based type.

Potting Plants are usually discarded after they have been potted into their final pots and have flowered.

Propagation Sow seeds in a loam-based seed compost, placing the pot in 21°C/70°F. Sow seeds in early spring to produce flowering plants from late winter to late spring of the following year. However, plants can be induced to flower during winter by controlling the ratio of darkness and light that they receive.

Flaming Katy is ideal for decorating tables, window-sills and shelves during winter and spring. Each plant remains in flower for six weeks or more, with the dark green, thick and succulent, scalloped-edged leaves surmounted by flattish flower heads of tubular flowers 6mm/0.25in across. The colour range is wide, including red, white, yellow, orange and lilac. Many are sold unnamed, but some are and these include 'Anette' and 'Bali' (both burnt-orange), 'Golden Melody' and 'Jessica' (both yellow), 'Kristina' (light purple), 'Regulus' (orange), 'Sensation' (pink), 'Singapore' (pink and red), 'Sentosa' and 'Pollux' (both red), 'Yellow Nugget' and 'Castor' (both yellow). There are also several miniature kalanchoes now available.

An interesting kalanchoe, ideal for an indoor hanging-basket, is *Kalanchoe manginii* 'Tessa'. It creates a wealth of pendulous, tubular and bell-like flowers in salmon and rose. Kalanchoes are grown throughout the year by commercial nurseries, who control the amount of light and darkness plants receive. It is, therefore, more prudent to buy plants at regular intervals throughout the year, discarding those which have borne flowers.

Kohleria amabilis
Tree Gloxinia
Height 30-50cm/12-20in
Spread 25-30cm/10-12in
Native Colombia

Greenfinger Guide

Temperature W 12°C/54°F – for storing the rhizomes 21°C/70°F – for starting the rhizomes into growth in late winter. **S** 16-18°C/61-64°F

Light W Light shade. **S** Light shade.

Watering W Store the rhizomes in a dry place. Keep rhizomes and compost moist, but not waterlogged, when starting them into growth. **S** Keep moist, but not waterlogged.

Feeding From when the plants are well established, feed every two weeks with a weak liquid fertilizer.

Humidity Mist spray the young shoots as they develop.

Compost Peat-based compost.

Potting In late winter, place the dormant rhizomes in boxes or moist peat. Position in 21°C/70°F. When shoots are 4-5cm/1½-2in high, pot up three into a 13cm/5in wide pot. Leave in 21°C/70°F. When established and growing strongly, reduce the temperature to 16-18°C/61-64°F.

Propagation Divide large rhizomes in late winter, when being potted. Also, take 6-7.5cm/2½-3in long cuttings in early and mid-summer, inserting them in equal parts moist peat and sharp sand. Place in 18°C/64°F.

Kohleria amabilis is a tender, deciduous plant with dark green, oval leaves with blackish-purple markings on the veins. From early and mid-summer it bears foxglove-like, pendent, 6cm/2½in long rose-coloured flowers spotted with purple.

Other plants in this genus which are often available include *Kohleria eriantha*, with deep red flowers speckled red and yellow from early and mid-summer.

Medinilla magnifica

Medinilla magnifica
Rose Grape

Height 60-75cm/2-2½ft – in a pot 1½-1.8m/5-6ft in a greenhouse border
Spread 38-45cm/15-18in – in a pot 0.9-1.5m/3-5ft in a greenhouse border
Native Java and the Philippines

Greenfinger Guide

Temperature W 16-21°C/61-70°F – avoid low temperatures. S 18-27°C/64-80°F

Light W Full sun. S Full light.

Watering W Just moist. S Water freely, but ensure good drainage.

Feeding From when the buds open – in mid-spring to late summer feed every two weeks with a weak liquid fertilizer.

Humidity Mist spray the foliage in summer, and if the plant is small and in a pot, stand this on a tray of moist pebbles.

Compost Loam-based type.

Potting In spring, when roots fill the pot – usually every other year. When in a large pot, remove the top 2.5-4cm/1-1½in of compost in spring and replace with fresh.

Propagation 7.5cm/3in long stem-tip cuttings in spring. Insert in equal parts moist peat and sharp sand. Place in 24-27°C/75-80°F.

The Rose Grape is a spectacular evergreen shrub, best suited to growing in a greenhouse border but when small and growing in a pot can be taken indoors when in flower. However, it is not an easy plant to grow indoors as it requires a high temperature and humidity.

It develops thick, woody stems which bear large, leathery, oval leaves heavily veined and up to 23cm/9in long. From late spring to late summer it bears pendent flower heads up to 38cm/15in long, bearing individual pink and purple flowers about 12mm/½in long. Large pink bracts develop above the pendulous flowers.

Pachystachys lutea
Lollipop Plant

Height 38-45cm/15-18in
Spread 30-38cm/12-15in
Native Peru

Greenfinger Guide

Temperature W 13°C/55°F – it will withstand temperatures around 10°C/50°F, or even lower, but if this happens the compost must be kept drier. S 13-21°C/55-70°F

Light W Full light. S Slight shade.

Watering W Barely moist. S Water freely, but ensure good drainage.

Feeding From late spring to late summer feed every two weeks with a weak liquid fertilizer.

Humidity Mist spray leaves in summer.

Compost Loam-based type.

Potting In spring, when roots fill the pot – usually every year. Plants in large pots need the top compost replacing with fresh in spring.

Propagation 10-13cm/4-5in long stem-tip cuttings in spring. Insert in equal parts moist peat and sharp sand. Place in 21°C/70°F.

The Lollipop Plant is a shrub that produces a spectacular array of golden-yellow, short, poker-like heads throughout summer and into early autumn. In can also be grown in border soil in a greenhouse, where it grows up to 60cm/2ft tall.

Indoors and when small it is ideal for decorating a low table in a cool room, throughout most of summer.

Pachystachys lutea

Pentas lanceolata
Egyptian Star Cluster/Star Cluster

Height 30-45cm/1-1½ft
Spread 30-38cm/12-15in
Native Tropical Africa

Greenfinger Guide

Temperature W 10-13°C/50-55°F S 13-18°C/55-64°F

Light W Light shade to full light. S Light shade.

Watering W Just moist. S Water freely, but ensure good drainage.

Feeding From spring to mid-summer feed every two to three weeks with a weak liquid fertilizer.

Humidity Mist spray young shoots in spring, but avoid wetting the flowers.

Compost A loam-based type or peat-based type.

Potting In spring, when roots fill the pot.

Propagation 5-7.5cm/2-3in long stem-tip cuttings from non-flowering shoots in early summer. Insert in equal parts moist peat and sharp sand, and place in 24°C/70°F.

The Egyptian Star Cluster is a tender, evergreen shrub with tubular and starry, white, pink, red or mauve flowers in umbrella-like heads up to 10cm/4in wide from mid-spring to mid-summer.

Pentas lanceolata

Pelargonium x domesticum

Pelargonium domesticum
Regal Pelargoniums/Fancy Geraniums/Pansy-flowered Geraniums

Height 30-60cm/1-2ft
Spread 23-38cm/9-15in
Native Hybrid

Greenfinger Guide

Temperature W 7-10°C/45-50°F S 18-24°C/64-75°F

Light W Full light. S Full light.

Watering W Just moist. S Water freely, but ensure good drainage.

Feeding From late spring to late summer feed every ten to fourteen days with a weak liquid fertilizer.

Humidity Mist spraying is not necessary.

Compost Loam-based type.

Potting In spring, when the roots fill the pot – usually every year when plants are small.

Propagation 7.5-10cm/3-4in long stem-tip cuttings in late summer. Insert in equal parts moist peat and sharp sand. Place in 15-18°C/59-64°F and cover with sheets of newspaper for about a week.

Regal Pelargoniums are superb in sun-rooms, greenhouses and indoors, where they create a wonderful range of flowers from late spring to early autumn. Each flower is up to 5cm/2in wide, in a range of colours including white, pink, salmon, red and purple, and frequently blotched or veined in darker shades.

There is a wide range of these hybrids, including 'Amethyst' (mauve-pink) and 'Cascade' (red). Both of these are ideal in hanging-baskets, whereas most are best when grown in pots.

Well-known varieties include 'Easter Greetings' (rose with brown blotches), 'Aztec' (white with pink blotches), 'Geronimo' (red), 'Georgia Peach' (peach), 'Sue Jarrett' (salmon-pink with maroon blotches) and 'Swabian Maid' (carmine-rose).

Pelargonium x hortorum
Zonal Pelargoniums/Horseshoe Geranium/Fish Geranium

Height 30-60cm/1-2ft – although some varieties reach 1.2m/4ft, while miniature ones are 15-30cm/6-12in high.
Spread 25-38cm/10-15in – miniature ones are 15-25cm/6-10in wide.
Native Hybrid

Greenfinger Guide

Temperature W 7-10°C/45-50°F S 18-24°C/64-75°F

Light W Full light. S Full light.

Watering W Just moist. S Water freely, but ensure good drainage.

Feeding From late spring to late summer feed every ten to fourteen days with a weak liquid fertilizer.

Humidity Mist spraying is not necessary.

Compost Loam-based type.

Potting In spring, when roots fill the pot – usually every year when plants are small.

Propagation 7.5-10cm/3-4in long stem-tip cuttings in late summer. Insert in equal parts moist peat and sharp sand. Place in 15-18°C/59-64°F and cover with sheets of newspaper for about a week.

Regal Pelargoniums are distinguished by their rounded, slightly crinkled leaves, 7.5-15cm/3-5in wide, with horseshoe-like zones of colour around their edges.

Pelargonium x hortorum

118

Primula x kewensis

These plants also produce attractive flowers, up to 2.5cm/1in wide, in umbrella-like heads from late spring to early autumn. There are many named varieties, with colours including white, pink, red and orange.

These are superb as houseplants, creating interest over a long period with their attractive flowers and leaves.

Primula x kewensis

Height 30-38cm/12-15in
Spread 25cm/10in
Native Hybrid

Greenfinger Guide

Temperature **W** 10-13°C/50-55°F **S** 10-16°C/50-61°F

Light **W** Bright, indirect sunlight. **S** Light shade.

Watering **W** Keep moist, especially when in flower. **S** Keep moist, but not waterlogged.

Feeding From when the flower buds appear, feed every ten days with a weak liquid fertilizer.

Humidity Stand the pot in a tray of moist pebbles.

Compost Loam-based type.

Potting In late summer transfer plants into their final pots, 13-15cm/5-6in wide.

Propagation During late winter and early spring sow seeds in a loam-based seed compost, placing the pot in 16°C/61°F. Prick off the seedlings when large enough to handle, slowly increasing the pot's size as the plant grows. However, sowings can also be made in late spring or early summer, but the plants will be smaller at flowering time. Nevertheless, it is an easier way in which to increase this plant.

Primula x kewensis originated at the Royal Botanic Gardens at Kew, and from early winter to mid-spring develops lax tiers of sweetly fragrant yellow flowers. The spoon-shaped, tooth-edged leaves are covered with an attractive, waxy and white powder.

It is the only yellow, indoor-flowering primula, the long-lasting flowers creating a display over a long period.

Primula malacoides
Fairy Primrose/Baby Primula

Height 30-38cm/12-15in
Spread 30-45cm/12-18in
Native China

Greenfinger Guide

Temperature **W** 10-13°C/50-55°F **S** 10-16°C/50-61°F

Light **W** Bright, indirect sunlight. **S** Light shade.

Feeding **W** Keep moist, especially when flowering. **S** Keep moist, but not waterlogged.

Feeding From when the flower buds appear, feed

Primula malacoides

every ten days with a weak liquid fertilizer.

Humidity Mist spray leaves during summer.

Compost John Innes potting compost No. 2.

Potting In late summer, transfer plants into their final pots, 13-15cm/5-6in wide.

Propagation During late winter and early spring sow seeds in loam-based seed compost, placing the pot in 16°C/61°F. Germination takes up to three weeks. Prick off the seedlings when large enough to handle, slowly increasing the pot's size as the plant grows. Sowings can also be made in late spring, but the plants will be smaller at flowering time.

The Fairy Primrose is a well-known winter-flowering houseplant, creating a beautiful array of tiered whorls of 12mm/½in wide, star-like and fragrant flowers from early winter to early spring. Flower colour ranges from pale purple to red, and includes white, with each flower having a distinctive yellow eye. The hairy, oval and tooth-edged pale green leaves create a superb foil for the flowers.

It is an ideal plant for decorating a slightly warm room during mid-winter and into spring.

Plants are usually discarded after their flowers fade.

Primula obconica
Poison Primrose/German Primrose

Height 23-38cm/9-15in
Spread 25-38cm/10-15in
Native China

Greenfinger Guide

Temperature **W** 10-13°C/50-55°F **S** 10-16°C/50-61°F

Light **W** Bright, indirect sunlight. **S** Light shade.

Watering **W** Keep moist, especially when in flower. **S** Keep moist, but not waterlogged.

Feeding From when the flower buds appear, feed every ten days with a weak liquid fertilizer.

Humidity Mist spray leaves during summer.

Compost John Innes potting compost No. 2.

Potting In late summer, transfer plants into their

final pots, 13-15cm/5-6in wide.

Propagation During late winter and early spring, sow seeds in loam-based seed compost, placing the pot in 16°C/61°F. Prick off the seedlings when large enough to handle, slowly increasing the pot's size as the plant grows. Sowings can also be made in late spring and early summer, but the plants will be smaller at flowering time.

The Poison Primrose, although a perennial, is raised from seeds each year, old plants being discarded when the flowers fade. Flowering is from early winter to late spring, with clusters of 2.5cm/1in wide flowers in pink, red, lilac or blue-purple. Many named varieties are available, in giant or large-flowered forms, with individual flowers up to 5cm/2in across.

The light green, oval to heart-shaped leaves are handsome, but they can create painful rashes on some people, usually on the insides of the wrists and arms and especially if they are damp.

Reinwardtia trigyna
Yellow Flax Flower

Height 45-60cm/1½-2ft
Spread 45-60cm/1½-2ft
Native Northern India

Greenfinger Guide

Temperature W 13°C/55°F – will survive slightly lower temperatures, but if this happens reduce the amount of water given to the plant. **S** 15-21°C/59-70°F

Light W Full sun. **S** Full sun, but with slight shading on very hot days.

Watering W Evenly moist, but not excessively wet. **S** Water freely, but ensure good drainage.

Feeding From late spring to late summer feed every ten days with a weak liquid fertilizer.

Humidity Mist spray leaves and stems in summer.

Compost Loam-based type.

Potting In spring, when roots fill the pot – usually every year.

Propagation 7.5cm/3in long basal shoots in spring. Insert in equal parts moist peat and sharp sand. Place in 16°C/61°F.

The Yellow Flax Plant is a tender, evergreen shrub that creates a mass of 25-36mm/1-1½in wide, funnel-shaped, bright yellow flowers from early autumn to early spring.

Plants are often raised each year and discarded when the flowers fade. However, plants can be kept from year to year but eventually they deteriorate and become unsightly.

Those plants growing in a greenhouse border have a much longer life. After flowering, cut shoots back to 7.5-10cm/3-4in of their bases, and during the growing season nip out the tips of young shoots several times to encourage bushiness.

Rhododendron simsii/Azalea
Indian Azalea

Height 30-45cm/12-18in
Spread 38-45cm/15-18in
Native China

Greenfinger Guide

Temperature W 10-16°C/50-61°F **S** After flowering, place in a frost-proof position, then in early summer place outdoors.

Light W Bright, indirect light. **S** Light shade – avoid direct light.

Primula obconica

Reinwardtia trigyna

Saintpaulia ionantha

Rhododendron simsii (azalea)

Watering W Water thoroughly, especially when in flower. **S** Water thoroughly.

Feeding From when the buds show colour, to when the flowers fade, feed every two weeks with a weak liquid fertilizer.

Humidity Mist spray from when the plant is moved indoors to when the buds show colour.

Compost Lime-free peaty compost such as equal parts of lime-free loam-based potting compost and peat. Alternatively, use a peat-based type.

Potting In autumn, repot large plants into the same size pot, using fresh compost. If the plant is small, use a size larger until it is in a 20-25cm/8-10in wide pot.

Propagation 7.5cm/3in long heel-cuttings in late summer. Insert in one part moist peat and two of sharp sand. Place in 10-13°C/50-55°F. However, new plants are usually bought each year, or kept from one season to another.

Azaleas are very popular houseplants around Christmas time, creating a wealth of subtle and vibrant colours in single and double-flowered forms, some with frilly edges. Colours include any shade of red, orange, pink and white, as well as multi-coloured forms. Most azaleas are given as gifts, with flower buds just starting to reveal colour, and they remain in flower for many weeks.

Some nurserymen disbud azaleas so that larger flowers are produced. If this has been done, it is no good trying to keep your plant for another year. If, however, your plant has not been disbudded, it will give you pleasure each winter – for many seasons.

Saintpaulia ionantha
African Violet

Height 7.5-13cm/3-5in – also see text
Spread 15-23cm/6-9in – also see text
Native Central Africa

Greenfinger Guide
Temperature W 13-18°C/55-64°F **S** 18-22°C/64-72°F

Light W Bright, but slightly shaded. **S** Bright, but slightly shaded.

Watering W Keep moist, but not continually saturated. **S** Keep moist, but not continually saturated.

Feeding From late spring to late summer feed every two weeks with a weak liquid fertilizer.

Humidity Do not mist spray the leaves or flowers.

Compost Peat-based type.

Potting In spring, when roots fill the pot – usually every other year.

Propagation Leaf-stem cuttings during summer. Trim the stalks to 36mm/1½in long and insert 12-18mm/)-0.75in deep in equal parts moist peat and sharp sand. Place in 18-21°C/64-70°F.

Saintpaulias are some of the most popular of all houseplants. They are tender, evergreen plants with attractive heart-shaped, velvet-textured leaves and small purple, violet-like flowers with bright, golden-yellow eyes, mainly from early summer to early autumn. Many strains and varieties have been developed and flowering can continue throughout the year if given adequate warmth, moisture and good light.

The range of these is now very wide, and includes so-called micro-miniature types which are less than 10cm/4in wide, through miniatures at 10-15cm/4-6in wide, semi-miniatures at 15-20cm/6-8in wide, standard types at 20-38cm/8-15in wide to large varieties at more than 38cm/15in wide. Also, the shapes of the leaves are varied, including those with serrated edges, spoon-shaped, variegated, lance-shaped, and the normal oval form. Additionally, the flowers can be single, semi-double, double, frill-edged, star-shaped and bicoloured. Clearly, there are saintpaulias to suit every taste.

Many enthusiasts for these plants often grow them under fluorescent tubes to supplement the poor winter light.

They are ideal plants for brightening tables, windowsill and shelves.

Saintpaulia ionantha

Schizanthus pinnatus
Butterfly Flower/Poor Man's Orchid

Height 30-75cm/1-2½ft – range of varieties
Spread 25-38cm/12-15in – range of varieties
Native Chile

Greenfinger Guide

Temperature W 16°C/61°F – for raising plants
S 8-10°C/46-50°F

Light W Bright light. **S** Full sun, with light shade
during very hot days.

Watering W Evenly moist. **S** Evenly moist.

Feeding From when the flower buds show colour
to when they fade, feed every ten days with a weak
liquid fertilizer.

Humidity Mist spray the leaves.

Compost Loam-based type.

Potting Progressively pot up young plants until in
15-20cm/6-8in wide pots. Discard plants after the
flowers fade.

Propagation Sow seeds 3mm/6in deep in a loam-
based seed compost in mid or late summer to
produce flowering plants in spring and early
summer. Place in 16-20°C/61-68°F. Germination
takes seven to fourteen days.

The Butterfly Flower is a half-hardy annual, ideal for
brightening cool rooms during spring and early
summer. Many varieties are available, in a range of
heights, all with showy orchid-like flowers and in
colours including yellow, rose, purple and red. They
are also attractively spotted.

Senecio cruentus
Cineraria

Height 30-75cm/12-30in – see text
Spread 25-45cm/10-18in – see text
Native Canary Islands

Greenfinger Guide

Temperature W 10-15°C/50-59°F **S** Propagated
during summer.

Light W Bright, indirect light. **S** Light shade.

Watering W Water freely, especially when
flowering. However, ensure good drainage as
water-saturated compost encourages the roots to rot.
S Evenly moist.

Feeding Not necessary, but larger plants can be
produced by feeding them every two weeks from
when the flower buds are formed.

Humidity None required – keep water off the
flowers and leaves.

Compost A loam-based or peat-based compost.

Potting Not necessary. Plants that have flowered
are usually discarded and fresh plants bought the
following year.

Propagation Sow seeds 3mm/6in deep from mid-
spring to early summer in a loam-based seed
compost. Place in 13°C/55°F. However, raising
plants is not easy, and unless unusual forms are
desired it is best to buy plants.

Cinerarias are very popular winter to spring flowering
plants, with masses of large, daisy-like flowers in flat
or dome-like heads from early winter to early summer
– and in a wide colour range. The true species is
seldom grown, and it is the varieties that are usually
available. The Hybrid Grandiflora strain (45cm/1½ft
high) has large, broad-petalled flowers, each 5-7.5cm/
2-3in wide.
  Double-flowered forms (30-45cm/ 1-1½ft high)
have double or semi-double flowers, each 5cm/2in
wide, while Multiflora Nana types (30-38cm/12-15in
high) have flowers 2.5-5cm/1-2in wide. The Stellata
types (38-75cm/18-30in high) bear star-like flowers
2.5-4cm/ 1-1½in wide on plants with a distinctive
branching habit.
  These plants are superb for bringing colour to cool
rooms during winter and spring, and are ideal for
decorating dining tables.

Sinningia speciosa
Gloxinia/Brazilian Gloxinia/Violet Slipper

Height 20-25cm/8-10in
Spread 23-30cm/9-12in
Native Brazil

Greenfinger Guide

Temperature W 12-14°C/54-57°F – storing the
tubers during winter 21°C/70°F – starting tubers
into growth in early spring. **S** 18°C/64°F

Light W Bright, but indirect light during spring.
S Light shade.

Watering W Moist, but not saturated in spring.

Schizanthus pinnatus

Senecio cruentus (cineraria)

S Moist, but not waterlogged.

Feeding From when the buds are visible, feed every seven to ten days.

Humidity Stand the pots in a tray of moist pebbles. Do not splash the foliage or flowers with water.

Compost A loam-based or peat-based compost.

Potting In late winter, place dormant tubers in boxes of moist peat in 21°C/70°F. When shoots are about 36mm/1½in high pot each tuber individually into 13-15cm/5-6in wide pots, using a loam-based or peat-based type.

Propagation In spring, use a sharp knife to cut up tubers, ensuring that each part has healthy shoots. Dust the cut surfaces with a fungicide to prevent infection and to seal the cut surfaces. Then pot up individually. Alternatively, sow seeds in late winter or early spring in a loam-based seed compost, placing them in 21°C/70°F. Also, take leaf-cuttings in early to mid-summer.

Gloxinias are popular summer-flowering houseplants, creating bell-shaped, foxglove-like, violet or purple flowers, 5-10cm/2-4in long, mainly from late spring

Sinningia speciosa

Sinningia speciosa

to mid-summer.

These glorious flowers are borne above almost stem-less, velvety leaves up to 20cm/8in long. The varieties usually grown are large-flowered types, probably of hybrid origin, with flowers in shades of pink, red, mauve, purple and white.

Sparmannia africana
African Hemp/African Windflower/House Lime/Indoor Linden

Height 60-90cm/2-3ft – when grown in a pot
Spread 45-60cm/1½-2ft – when grown in a pot
Native South Africa

Greenfinger Guide

Temperature W 7-10°C/45-50°F S 13-18°C/55-64°F

Light W Full sun. S Light shade.

Watering W Barely moist. S Water freely, but ensure good drainage.

Feeding From late spring to late summer feed every seven to ten days with a weak liquid fertilizer.

Humidity Mist spray leaves in summer.

Compost Loam-based type.

Potting In spring, when roots fill the pot – usually every year.

Propagation 7.5-10cm/3-4in long stem-tip cuttings from young shoots in spring or early summer. Insert in equal parts moist peat and sharp sand. Place in 16°C/61°F.

The African Hemp is a tender, shrubby evergreen shrub best grown in a greenhouse border, although

when young it can be grown indoors in a pot. When planted in a greenhouse border it may reach 1.8-2.1m/6-7ft high. Its large, bright green leaves are covered with fine, soft hairs, while during late spring and early summer 2.5cm/1in white flowers with dominant yellow stamens are borne in clusters on long stems.

Spathiphyllum wallisii
Peace Lily/Sail Plant/Spathe Flower

Height 23-30cm/9-12in
Spread 25-38cm/10-15in

Sparmannia africana

Native Colombia

Greenfinger Guide

Temperature W 10-16°C/50-61°F S 16-27°C/61-80°F

Light W Bright, indirect light. S Light shade.

Watering W Evenly moist. S Water freely.

Feeding From mid-spring to late summer feed every ten to fourteen days during the rest of the year feed with a weak liquid fertilizer at four-week intervals.

Spathiphyllum wallisii 'Mauna Loa'

Spathiphyllum wallisii

Humidity Stand the pot in a tray of moist pebbles, and mist spray the leaves during summer. Do not spray the flowers.

Compost Peat-based compost.

Potting In spring, every year.

Propagation Divide congested plants in spring, when being repotted. Keep shaded until the plants are established

The Peace Lily creates interest throughout the whole year. Its bright green, lance-shaped leaves held on long, stiff, upright stems. From mid-spring to mid-summer it produces pure-white, arum-like flowers on long stems that carry them above the leaves.

The hybrid 'Mauna Loa' is slightly larger, at 45-60cm/1½-2ft high, and during early summer it bears large white flowers. Sometimes these are produced intermittently through the whole year. This hybrid needs a slightly higher winter temperature than the ordinary Peace Lily. A minimum of 13°C/55°F is needed, and slightly brighter conditions.

It is essential to provide these plants with warmth and humidity.

Stephanotis floribunda
Madagascar Jasmine/Floradora

Height 3m/10ft or more in a sun-room or greenhouse when trailing along a permanent framework of wires. In a pot indoors, and when young, it can be trained over a large hoop of pliable canes.
Spread Climber
Native Madagascar

Greenfinger Guide

Temperature W 13-15°C/55-59°F – it can survive temperatures down to 10°C/50°F, but is better at 13°C/55°F or above. **S** 18-21°C/64-70°F

Light W Full sun. **S** Light shade.

Watering W Just moist. **S** Water freely, but ensure good drainage.

Feeding From late spring to late summer feed every two to three weeks with a weak liquid fertilizer.

Humidity Mist spray leaves in summer.

Compost Loam-based type.

Potting In spring, when roots fill the pot – initially annually but later every two or three years.

Propagation 10cm/4in long cuttings from lateral shoots in late spring or early summer. Insert in equal parts moist peat and sharp sand. Place in 21°C/70°F.

The Madagascar Jasmine is a superb evergreen climber, with sweetly-scented, waxy-white flowers borne in clusters from late spring to early autumn.

It is a climber best grown in a sun-room or greenhouse and trained along wires in the roof.

Streptocarpus x hybridus
Cape Primrose
Height 20-30cm/8-12in
Spread 23-38cm/9-15in

Native Hybrid

Greenfinger Guide

Temperature W 10-13°C/50-55°F **S** 13-15°C/55-59°F

Light W Light shade. **S** Light shade.

Watering W Just moist. **S** Water freely, but ensure good drainage.

Feeding From late spring to late summer feed every two weeks with a weak liquid fertilizer.

Humidity Stand the pot in a tray of water and pebbles. Avoid splashing the leaves with water.

Compost A loam-based or peat-based compost.

Potting In spring, when a plant fills its pot – usually every year.

Propagation Divide congested plants in spring, when being repotted. Alternatively, sow seeds 3mm/6in deep in a loam-based seed compost in late spring for flowering the following year. Place in 21°C/70°F. Leaf-cuttings can be taken in mid-summer.

The Cape Primrose is a well-known evergreen, tufted plant with long, spoon-shaped, mid-green and corrugated leaves that arise from compost level. From late spring to late summer it bears trumpet-shaped flowers on long stems, in colours which range from white through to rose and red, and also to blue and purple.

It is an ideal plant for decorating tables in cool rooms during summer.

There is now a very attractive hybrid which is a cross between a streptocarpus and a gloxinia, and known as a Strepto-gloxinia Hybrid.

Stephanotis floribunda

Streptocarpus x hybridus

Streptocarpus x hybridus

Strepto-gloxinia Hybrid

foliage plants

Aglaonema commutatum pseudobracteatum

This Chinese Evergreen creates a spectacular display of dark green, lance-shaped leaves up to 5cm/2in wide, each borne on a stem about 7.5cm/3in long. The leaves are attractively marked with thin, silvery-grey zones on either side of the lateral veins. During July, plants develop 5cm/2in long white spathes which are followed by dark red berries.

The Golden Evergreen (*Aglaonema commutatum pseudobracteatum*) is sometimes sold as *Aglaonema pseudobracteatum* and also known as the variety 'White Rajah'. Do not allow this disagreement over names to put you off buying this plant, as it is very attractive, with rich green, spear-shaped leaves which reveal creamy-gold markings.

Aglaonema costatum
Spotted Evergreen

Height 15-18cm/6-7in
Spread 23-25cm/9-10in
Native Malaya

Greenfinger Guide

***Temperature* W** 15°C/59°F **S** 16-21°C/61-70°F

***Light* W** Light shade. **S** Medium shade – avoid direct sunlight.

***Watering* W** Evenly moist – do not allow the compost to dry out. **S** Water freely, but ensure good drainage.

Feeding From late spring to late summer feed every three to four weeks with a weak liquid fertilizer.

Humidity Mist spray the leaves throughout the year. However, do not mist spray the leaves in winter if the temperature falls dramatically. Instead, stand the pot in a saucer of moist pebbles.

Compost Peat-based compost.

Potting In spring, when roots fill the pot – usually every two or three years.

Propagation The easiest way is to divide congested plants when being repotted.

Aglaonema costatum

Aglaonema commutatum
Chinese Evergreen

Height 15cm/6in
Spread 23-30cm/9-12in
Native Central Malaya and the Celebes

Greenfinger Guide

***Temperature* W** 10-15°C/50-59°F – avoid the lower end of this range. **S** 16-21°C/61-70°F

***Light* W** Light shade. **S** Medium shade – avoid direct sunlight.

***Watering* W** Evenly moist – do not allow the compost to dry out. **S** Water freely, but ensure good drainage.

Feeding From late spring to late summer feed every three to four weeks with a weak liquid fertilizer.

Humidity Mist spray the leaves throughout the year. However, do not mist spray the leaves in winter if the temperature is low. Instead, stand the pot in a saucer of moist pebbles.

Compost Peat-based compost.

Potting In spring, when roots fill the pot – usually every two or three years.

Propagation The easiest way is to divide congested plants when being repotted.

The Spotted Evergreen has leaves which differ in shape from most aglaonemas. They are more rounded, up to 20cm/8in long and about 10cm/4in wide. In colour they are a rich, glossy green with ivory midribs. It is a species, however, which is variable in colour, and some leaves may be totally green while others have white spots.

Aglaonema hospitum, now known as *Aglaonema brevispathum hospitum*, is similar to *Aglaonema costatum*, but the leaves are slightly more lance-shaped. The form 'Variegatum' has leaves irregularly marked with small, white spots.

Aglaonema crispum
Painted Drop Tongue

Height 75-90cm/2½-3ft
Spread 60-75cm/2-2½ft
Native Philippines

Greenfinger Guide

Temperature **W** 15°C/59°F **S** 16-21°C/61-70°F

Light **W** Light shade. **S** Medium shade – avoid direct light.

Watering **W** Evenly moist – but do not allow the compost to dry out. **S** Water freely, but ensure good drainage.

Feeding From late spring to late summer feed every three to four weeks with a weak liquid fertilizer.

Humidity Mist spray the leaves throughout the year. However, do not mist spray the leaves in winter if the temperature is low. Instead, stand the pot in a saucer of moist pebbles.

Compost Peat-based compost.

Potting In spring, when roots fill the pot – usually every two or three years.

Propagation The easiest way is to divide congested plants when being repotted.

The Painted Drop Tongue is not so widely grown as other aglaonemas, on account of its size. The large, leathery and somewhat oval leaves – up to 30cm/12in long and 14cm/5½in wide – are mostly silver, but in parts greenish-grey.

Aglaonema modestum
Chinese Evergreen

Height 60-75cm/2-2½ft
Spread 38-50cm/15-20in
Native Southern China to Northern Thailand

Greenfinger Guide

Aglaonema modestum 'Silver Queen'

Aglaonema crispum

Aglaonema treubii 'Silver Spear'

Anthurium crystallinum

Temperature **W** 15°C/59°F **S** 16-21°C/61-70°F

Light **W** Light shade. **S** Medium shade – avoid direct sunlight.

Watering **W** Evenly moist – never let it dry out. **S** Water freely, but ensure good drainage.

Feeding From late spring to late summer feed every three to four weeks with a weak liquid fertilizer.

Humidity Mist spray the leaves throughout the year. However, do not mist spray the leaves in winter if the temperature is low. Instead, stand the pot in a saucer of moist pebbles.

Compost Peat-based compost.

Potting In spring, when roots fill the pot – usually every two or three years.

Propagation The easiest way is to divide congested plants when being repotted.

This Chinese Evergreen is relatively slow-growing, creating a wealth of glossy, waxy-green leaves up to 23cm/9in long and 12cm/4½in wide. The mid-rib of each leaf is flecked with silvery-grey. 'Silver Queen' is a frequently-grown variety, with grey-green leaves and silvery greyish-green mottling which can dominate a leaf. Sometimes, this variety is listed as a form of *Aglaonema crispum* or even as *Aglaonema hybridum* 'Silver Queen'. Also listed under *Aglaonema hybridum* is 'Silver King', again with silvery-grey leaves. 'Marie' is another exciting variety sometimes sold as *Aglaonema hybridum* 'Marie'.

Aglaonema treubii

Height 20-23cm/8-9in
Spread 25-30cm/10-12in
Native Indonesia

Greenfinger Guide

Temperature **W** 10-15°C/50-59°F – but best towards the upper end of this range. **S** 16-21°C/61-70°F

Light **W** Light shade. **S** Medium shade – avoid direct sunlight.

Watering **W** Evenly moist – do not allow the compost to dry out. **S** Water freely, but ensure good drainage.

Feeding From late spring to late summer feed every three to four weeks with a weak liquid fertilizer.

Humidity Mist spray the leaves throughout the year. However, do not mist spray the leaves in winter if the temperature is low. Instead, stand the pot in a saucer of moist pebbles.

Compost Peat-based compost.

Potting In spring, when roots fill the pot – usually every two or three years.

Propagation The easiest way is to divide congested plants in spring when being repotted.

Aglaonema treubii is sometimes listed as being a variety of *Aglaonema commutatum*. However, it does differ slightly and has, perhaps, the narrowest leaves of all aglaenemas sold as houseplants. These are about 13cm/5in long and 36mm/1½in wide. In colour they are almost entirely pale, silvery-green, with dark green patches between the veins.

The variety *Aglaonema treubii* 'Silver Spear' (also sold as *Aglaonema commutatum* 'Silver Spear') has very attractive leaves – light creamy-green on a darker green background.

Anthurium crystallinum
Crystal Anthurium

Height 45cm/1½ft
Spread 30-38cm/12-15in
Native Colombia

Greenfinger Guide

Temperature **W** 15-18°C/59-64°F – avoid fluctuating temperatures, which if low can cause the leaves to become yellow at their edges. **S** 18-27°C/64-80°F

Light **W** Light shade. **S** Medium to deep shade.

Watering **W** Barely moist – but do not allow the compost to dry out. **S** Water freely, but ensure good drainage.

Feeding From late spring to late summer feed every two weeks with a weak liquid fertilizer.

Humidity Stand the pots in a tray of water filled with pebbles.

Compost A mixture of peat-based compost and sphagnum moss, plus a little loam.

Potting In spring, when roots fill the pot – usually every two or three years. Ensure that the pot is well drained by placing at least 2.5cm/1in of broken clay pots in its base.

Propagation Divide congested plants in spring. Each new plant should have a growing point and fibrous roots. Repot and place in a humid and warm position until established. Alternatively, sow seeds in spring in a mixture of peat-based compost and sphagnum moss. Place in 24°C/75°F.

The Crystal Anthurium is a stunningly attractive plant with large, heart-shaped leaves, up to 60cm/2ft long and 30cm/12in wide. The velvety surfaces are violet when young, maturing to deep green. They are further enhanced by the midribs and veins lined from above in ivory, and pale pink below.

It is a plant that must be given sufficient space to prevent the large leaves being damaged by children or animals.

Aphelandra squarrosa
Zebra Plant/Saffron Spike

Height 23-60cm/9-24in
Spread 30-38cm/12-15in
Native Brazil

Greenfinger Guide

Temperature **W** 13-16°C/55-61°F **S** 18-21°C/64-70°F

Light **W** Full light. **S** Very light shade.

Watering **W** Barely moist – but do not let the compost dry out. **S** Keep the compost moist – but not saturated.

Feeding From spring to late summer feed every ten to fourteen days with a weak liquid fertilizer; only feed during winter (every three weeks) if very high temperatures are maintained.

Humidity Mist spray foliage during summer, but avoid spraying the flowers.

Compost Rich, loam-based compost.

Potting In spring, when roots fill the pot – usually every year.

Propagation 7.5-10cm/3-4in long cuttings during spring and early summer. Insert in equal parts moist part and sharp sand. Place in 21°C/70°F.

Aphelandra squarrosa

Asparagus densiflorus 'Sprengeri'

Asparagus setaceus

the leaves and flowers cannot be damaged. The leaves are best appreciated when seen slightly from above.

There are several other varieties occasionally offered for sale: 'Brockfeld' is extra vigorous with crinkled-edged leaves which often grow to 23cm/9in long and reveal more ivory colouring than the normal form. 'Dania' is more compact, with smaller leaves which are borne close together. It is ideal for displaying in a small area.

Another aphelandra, *Aphelandra leopoldii* – often sold as *Aphelandra squarrosa leopoldii* – is sometimes offered for sale, but is markedly different: smaller, with thinner and shorter, light green leaves with a silvery-grey area around the midrib. The undersides are lightly flushed purple.

Asparagus densiflorus 'Meyeri'
Plume Asparagus/Foxtail Fern

Height 30-45cm/12-18in
Spread 45-75cm/1½-2½ft
Native Natal

Greenfinger Guide

Temperature W 10-13°C/50-55°F S 13-15°C/55-59°F – avoid very high temperatures.

Light W Bright, indirect sunlight. S Slight shade.

Watering W Just moist – do not allow the compost to dry out. S Water freely, but ensure good drainage.

Feeding From late spring to late summer feed every ten to fourteen days.

Asparagus densiflorus 'Meyeri'

Humidity Mist spray regularly during summer. Also during winter if the temperature is high.

Compost Loam-based type.

Potting In spring, when roots fill the pot – usually annually.

Propagation Divide congested plants in spring.

The Plume Asparagus is easily identified by its upright and arching, tapering plume-like spires packed with bright green needle-like leaves. It is ideal for growing in a pot positioned where the plumes can cascade and trail.

Asparagus densiflorus 'Sprengeri'
Emerald Fern/Asparagus Fern/Sprenger Asparagus/Emerald Feather

Height 30cm/12in
Spread 75-90cm/2½-3ft
Native Natal

Greenfinger Guide

Temperature W 10-13°C/50-55°F – it survives temperatures down to 7°C/45°F for short periods,

Few houseplants are as distinctive as the Zebra Plant, with long, dark green leaves dramatically striped with ivory veins, and the bonus of yellow, cone-shaped flower heads 7.5-10cm/3-4in long from mid to late summer. The form 'Louisae' has slightly narrower leaves, with bold white markings along the veins. Also, the yellow flowers are streaked with red.

It is an ideal plant for placing on a large table, perhaps in a dining room, or on a coffee table where

green, needle-like leaves that crowd the stems in all directions.

Asparagus setaceus
Asparagus Fern/Lace Fern
Height 38-45cm/15-18in – in its juvenile form
Spread 38-60cm/15-24in
Native South Africa

Greenfinger Guide

Temperature W 10-13°C/50-55°F – it will survive temperatures down to 7°C/45°F for short periods. **S** 13-15°C/55-59°F – avoid very high temperatures.

Light W Bright, indirect light. **S** Light shade.

Watering W Just moist – but do not let the compost dry out. **S** Water freely, but ensure good drainage.

Feeding From May to September feed every ten to fourteen days with a weak liquid fertilizer.

Humidity Mist spray regularly during summer. Also during winter if the temperature is high.

Compost Loam-based type.

Potting In spring, when the roots fill the pot – usually annually.

Propagation Divide congested plants in spring.

The Asparagus Fern is well known both as a houseplant and as the fern many florists use in the creation of a backing for button-holes. It is really a climber, often growing up to 3m/10ft high when mature. However, in its young and juvenile form it is non-climbing and creates an interesting houseplant, with main stems bearing mid-green, lace-like leaves in horizontal tiers.

Aspidistra elatior

The best form for growing as a houseplant is 'Compactus', which is non-climbing and creates a plant up to 45-60cm/1½-2ft high.

Aspidistra elatior
Parlour Palm/Cast Iron Plant/Barroom Plant/Iron Plant (syn. Aspidistra lurida)
Height 30-38cm/12-15in
Spread 38-50cm/15-20in
Native China

Greenfinger Guide

Temperature W 7-10°C/45-50°F – will survive temperatures down to 5°C/41°F for short periods. However, if this happens keep the compost slightly drier – but do not let it dry out. **S** 13-15°C/55-60°F

Light W Bright, indirect light **S** Bright, indirect light or slight shade.

Watering W Just moist **S** Water freely, but ensure good drainage.

Feeding From mid-spring to late summer feed every three to four weeks with a weak liquid fertilizer.

Humidity Mist spray the leaves in summer.

Compost Loam-based type.

Potting In late spring, when roots fill the pot – usually every two or three years. Plants too large to be repotted can be topdressed with fresh compost.

Propagation Divide congested plants in spring, when being repotted.

The Parlour Palm had a tradition of surviving the

but if this happens there is the risk of the needles falling off. **S** 13-15°C/55-59°F – avoid exceptionally high temperatures.

Light W Bright, indirect sunshine. **S** Slight shade.

Watering W Just moist. **S** Water freely, but ensure good drainage.

Feeding From late spring to late summer feed every ten to fourteen days with a weak liquid fertilizer.

Humidity Mist spray regularly during summer. Also during winter if the temperature is high.

Compost Loam-based type.

Potting In spring, when the roots fill the pot – usually annually.

Propagation Divide congested plants in spring.

The Emerald Fern is semi-arching and ideal for growing in an indoor hanging-basket or for positioning in a pot at the edge of a high shelf, where it can cascade freely. Although the common name suggests that it is a fern, it is not. It belongs to the lily family. The stems have a frothy appearance, being covered with fresh, glossy-

Aspidistra elatior 'Variegata'

worst conditions that a houseplant could be subjected to during the Victorian era – draughts, gas fumes, cigarette and cigar smoke, low temperatures and a dark, dismal corner. Although this plant is quite tolerant, it responds to good conditions, revealing glossy, fresh green leaves which with maturity become shiny and blackish-green. The variegated form, 'Variegata', in particular, with green leaves striped and banded in white to cream, especially needs good conditions if the variegations are not to be lost.

Because it will withstand relatively low temperatures it is ideal for placing in a hall or, perhaps, on a table in a little-used room.

Beaucarnea recurvata
Pony Tail Plant/Elephant Foot Tree/Bottle Ponytail

Height 38-60cm/15-24in – in a pot
Spread 20-30cm/8-12in – in a pot
Native Mexico

Greenfinger Guide

Temperature W 8-12°C/46-54°F **S** 12-18°C/54-64°F

Light W Bright light. **S** Light shade to some bright light.

Watering W Water the compost thoroughly, then leave until moderately dry. **S** Apply water in the same manner as for during winter, but this, of course, will be more frequent in summer. Always ensure – in both winter and summer – that the compost does not become continually saturated.

Feeding From late spring to mid summer feed every three to four weeks with a weak liquid fertilizer.

Humidity It is not necessary to mist spray the foliage.

Compost Loam-based type with extra sharp sand.

Potting In spring, when the plant totally fills the pot.

Propagation Remove and pot up offsets when the plant is repotted. However, this is not easy and it is best to buy young plants.

The Pony Tail Plant is grown primarily for its unusual and interesting shape. In its native country it forms a tree up to 9m/30ft high and with leaves about 1.8m/6ft long. In a pot indoors or in a conservatory it can be kept relatively small. However, leaves 0.9-1.5m/3-5ft long have been produced on pot-grown plants.

The name Elephant Foot Tree comes from its large, swollen base. This is able to store water, which helps if the plant is neglected.

Beaucarnea recurvata

Begonia boweri 'Tiger'

Begonia boweri
Eyelash Begonia

Height 15-25cm/6-10in
Spread 20-30cm/8-12in
Native Mexico

Greenfinger Guide

Temperature W 13-15°C/55-59°F **S** 15-20°C/59-68°F

Light W Bright, but out of direct sunlight. **S** Bright, but out of direct sunlight.

Watering W Just moist. Allowing the surface compost to practically dry out between waterings. **S** Keep moist, but not continually saturated.

Feeding From late spring to late summer feed every two weeks with a weak liquid fertilizer.

Humidity Stand the pot in a saucer of moist pebbles.

Compost Peat-based compost.

Potting In spring, when the roots fill the pot – usually every year.

Propagation Divide congested plants during spring when being repotted.

The Eyelash Begonia is an extremely handsome foliage houseplant, with somewhat lop-sided, heart-shaped, emerald-green leaves with brown spots along the edges which also display characteristic erect hairs.

Begonia masoniana

The 6-7.5cm/2½-3in long leaves create a bushy, somewhat domed shape. Old plants, however, are likely to become lopsided and to sprawl, especially if neglected.

It is often grown in an indoor hanging-basket, but the beautiful leaves can usually be better appreciated if the plant is displayed on a coffee table. High temperatures and lack of feeding and repotting can soon cause the leaves to bleach and become unattractive.

Begonia 'Tiger' is a hybrid of *Begonia boweri* and creates a spectacular display with its reddish-brown leaves irregularly patched in light, greenish-yellow. It has the bonus of producing small, pinkish-white flowers during winter.

Begonia masoniana
Iron Cross Begonia

Height 23cm/9in
Spread 25-30cm/10-12in
Native Southeast Asia

Greenfinger Guide

Temperature W 13-15°C/55-59°F S 15-20°C/59-68°F

Light W Bright, but out of direct sunlight.
S Bright, but out of direct sunlight.

Watering W Just moist, allowing the surface compost to practically dry out between waterings.
S Keep moist, but not continually saturated.

Feeding From late spring to late summer feed every ten to fourteen days.

Humidity Stand the pot in a saucer of moist pebbles.

Compost A loam-based or peat-based type.

Potting In spring, when roots fill the pot – usually every year.

Propagation Divide congested plants during spring, when being repotted. Alternatively, take leaf-cuttings in late spring or early summer. Whole leaves can have the veins on their undersides nicked with a sharp knife, and then be pinned with pieces of bent wire into equal parts moist peat and sharp sand. Place in 18-21°C/64-70°F.

The Iron Cross Begonia is well known for its beautiful,

lop-sided, slightly heart-shaped leaves. These have corrugated, hairy surfaces, mid-green and dominantly patterned with four or five deep bronze-purple bars that radiate from the centres.

Like the Rex Begonia, the Iron Cross Begonia is superb for decorating tables of all kinds.

Begonia rex
Rex Begonia/King Begonia/Painted-leaf Begonia

Height 20-30cm/8-12in
Spread 25-38cm/10-15in
Native Assam

Greenfinger Guide

Temperature W 13-15°C/55-59°F S 13-18°C/55-64°F

Light W Full light. S Good light, but not direct sunlight.

Watering W Just moist, allowing the surface of the compost to practically dry out between waterings.
S Water freely, but ensure good drainage.

Feeding From late spring to late summer feed every two weeks with a weak liquid fertilizer.

Humidity Stand the pot in a saucer of water filled with pebbles.

Compost Loam-based compost with extra peat. Alternatively, use a peat-based compost.

Begonia rex

Begonia rex

Begonia rex

Brassaia actinophylla

Potting In spring, when roots fill the pot – usually every year.

Propagation Divide large plants in spring – when being repotted. This destroys a plant's symmetrical outline. Alternatively, take leaf- cuttings during late spring or early summer. Cut up a mature leaf into 30mm/1.25in squares and insert them about 12mm/½in into equal parts moist peat and sharp sand. Alternatively, lay a leaf flat on the surface of compost and with small pieces of bent wire hold it in firm contact with the compost. First, however, nick the veins on the underside at 2.5cm/1in intervals. Water and place in 18-21°C/64-70°F. When young plantlets appear, pot them up individually into small pots.

The Rex Begonia brings colour to homes throughout the year, with large, highly coloured leaves in a range of patterns. The flowers are insignificant and are best removed. The true species has wrinkled, dark green leaves with silvery zones near the edges. However, this is rarely seen and it is both named and unnamed forms which are grown.

The leaves are lopsided, heart-shaped and up to 25cm/10in long, creating a dominant display of colour throughout the year. Named forms include, 'Silver Queen' with silvery-grey leaves with blue-green central veins, 'Her Majesty' with deep reddish-purple leaves with olive-green zones and silvery-white mottling, while 'Merry Christmas' displays smooth leaves with a vivid purplish-red central zone, combined with silvery-pink and deep green.

The brightness, symmetrical outline and year-round beauty of these plants makes them ideal for displaying on table tops, or on large windowsills during winter.

Brassaia actinophylla
Umbrella Tree/Umbrella Plant/Australian Umbrella Tree/Octopus Tree/Starleaf/Australian Ivy Palm/Queen's Umbrella Tree

Height 1.8-2.4m/6-8ft
Spread 60-90cm/2-3ft
Native Polynesia

Greenfinger Guide
Temperature W 3-15°C/55-59°F S 18-24°C/64-75°F

Light W Full light. S Light shade.

Watering W Keep the compost moderately moist. S Water freely, but ensure good drainage.

Feeding From late spring to late summer feed every three to four weeks.

Humidity Mist spray the leaves during summer.

Compost Loam-based type.

Potting In spring, when the roots fill the pot. Topdress with fresh compost those plants that are too large to be repotted.

Propagation 7.5-10cm/3-4in-long cuttings in spring. Insert in equal parts moist peat and sharp sand. Place in 18-24°C/64-75°F.

The Umbrella Plant is slower growing than its near relative the Parasol Plant (*Schefflera arboricola*). Unlike the Parasol Plant, which has branching stems, the Umbrella Tree is usually single stemmed, with leaves which when young bear four or five leaflets that radiate like the spokes of an umbrella.

It is an ideal plant for filling a large corner position with attractive foliage. Other plants can be positioned around its base.

Caladium x hortulanum
Angel's Wings/Elephant's Ears/Fancy-leaved Caladium

Height 23-38cm/9-15in
Spread 20-30cm/9-12in
Native Hybrid

Greenfinger Guide
Temperature W 13°C/55°F – for storing dormant tubers from late autumn to early spring. 21°C/70°F – for starting the tubers into growth in early spring. S 18-21°C/64-70°F – for growing the plants during summer.

Light W Dormant tubers are stored in a dry, vermin-proof position under greenhouse staging from late autumn to early spring. S Light shade – heavy shade will prevent the wonderful colours in the leaves developing properly.

Watering W From late autumn to early spring store the tubers in boxes of peat or a peat-based compost. Keep barely moist. After the tubers are boxed up in early spring, keep the compost lightly moist. S As the shoots and plants grow, increase the amount and frequency of water. In autumn, as the foliage dies down, slowly reduce the amount of water.

Feeding From when the pot is full of roots, and until late summer, feed every seven to ten days with a weak liquid fertilizer.

Humidity Mist spray the leaves daily during summer. High humidity is vital to the success of this plant. This is especially important when the tubers are potted up in early spring.

Compost Acid and peat-based.

Potting In early spring, box-up the tubers into shallow boxes of peat or a peat-based compost. Water the compost and place in the suggested temperature. When shoots growing from the tubers are about 5cm/2in high, pot up the tubers individually into pots ranging from 10-20cm/4-8in wide depending on the sizes of the tubers.

Caladium x hortulanum

Caladium x hortulanum

Propagation In spring, when the tubers are being repotted, detach small tubers from around them and pot up separately. These usually take up to two years before producing good-sized plants.

The Angel's Wings is a plant that dies down in mid to late autumn each year and is kept throughout winter in a dormant state. In spring, place dormant tubers in boxes of moist peat in 21°C/70°F. When they develop shoots, pot up the tubers 2.5cm/1in deep into 10-20cm/4-8in pots, depending on their size. Slowly, the tubers create beautiful plants.

Caladium x hortulanum and its many forms are derived from another widely grown Angel's Wings, *Caladium bicolor*. Forms include 'Candidum' with white leaves networked with green veins; 'Pink Cloud' with leaves mottled pink; 'Stoplight' displays leaves with narrow green edges and surfaces suffused crimson;

Calathea crocata

'John Peel' has leaves veined with metallic-red; 'Seagull' has dark green leaves with broad white veins; 'Arno Nehrling' has white leaves tinged green, with red veins; 'Lord Derby' displays pink leaves with green veins; 'Frieda Hemple' reveals red leaves framed with green; 'Rosebud' has leaves with red centres, green surrounds and red veins; 'Mrs Halderman' displays leaves with red centres, framed with green, together with green veins.

Calathea crocata

Height 20-25cm/8-10in
Spread 20-25cm/8-10in
Native Brazil

Greenfinger Guide

Temperature W 13-16°C/55-61°F – if possible, keep to the upper end of this range. S 16-20°C/61-70°F

Light W Full sun. S Light shade.

Watering W Evenly moist. S Water freely, but ensure good drainage.

Feeding From late spring to late summer feed every two weeks with a weak liquid fertilizer.

Humidity Mist spray the foliage – avoid wetting the flowers. High humidity is essential, and standing the pot in a saucer of moist pebbles helps with this.

Compost A loam-based or a peat-based type.

Potting In spring, when roots fill the pot – usually every two years.

Propagation Divide congested plants in spring.

Most calatheas are grown for their beautiful leaves. This one, however, could be grown both for its attractive foliage and beautiful flowers. The leathery leaf blades, up to 10cm/4in long and 5cm/2in wide, are maroon-purple on the undersides, while the uppersides have alternate bands of light and dark green. Each leaf is borne on a keeled, pale purple leaf-stalk about 10cm/4in long. During summer the plant bears orange flowers which emerge from pink bracts, and on stems about 23cm/9in long. Each flower head is about 5cm/2in wide.

Calathea lancifolia
Rattlesnake Plant

Height 30-45cm/12-18in
Spread 25-38cm/10-15in
Native Brazil

Greenfinger Guide

Temperature W 13-16°C/55-61°F – it survives short periods down to 10°C/50°F, but is better when given more warmth. S 16-24°C/61-75°F

Light W Light shade. S Light to medium shade.

Watering W Evenly moist. S Water freely.

Feeding From late spring to late summer feed every ten to fourteen days, with weak liquid fertilizer.

Humidity Mist spray the leaves throughout the year; more frequently in summer but also in winter, especially if a high temperature is maintained.

Compost A loam-based or peat-based type.

Potting In late spring, when roots fill the pot – usually every year if the plant is growing strongly.

Propagation In spring, when being repotted, divide congested plants.

The Rattlesnake Plant gains its name from the long, narrow, upright and splaying leaves with crinkly edges and a yellowish background. Dark green bands

Calathea lancifolia

Calathea leitzei

Calathea ornata

radiate from the mid-rib. The undersides are rich maroon.

Like other calatheas, it is excellent for decorating tables in warm rooms, and looks superb when the pot in which it is growing is placed inside a copper-coloured outer container. The reflections of the colours add a further attractive dimension.

Calathea leitzei

Height 38-60cm/15-24in
Spread 45-60cm/1½-2ft
Native Brazil

Greenfinger Guide

Temperature W 13-16°C/55-61°F – it survives short periods down to 10°C/50°F, but is better when given more warmth. **S** 16-24°C/61-75°F

Light W Light shade. **S** Light to medium shade.

Watering W Evenly moist. **S** Water freely.

Feeding From late spring to late summer feed every ten to fourteen days with a weak liquid fertilizer.

Humidity Mist spray the leaves throughout the year; more frequently in summer but also in winter, especially if a high temperature is maintained.

Compost A loam-based or a peat-based type.

Potting In late spring, when roots fill the pot – usually every year if the plant is growing strongly.

Propagation In spring, when being repotted, divide congested plants.

Calathea lietzei is an attractive species, now becoming more widely available. The 23cm/9in long, oval to lance-shaped, slightly undulating leaves tend to spread. Their upper surfaces are dark velvety-green, with olive-green stripes between the lateral veins. Underneath they are purple. Each leaf is borne on a stalk which is longer than the leaf-blade.

Calathea makoyana
Peacock Plant/Cathedral-windows/Brain Plant

Height 45-60cm/1½-2ft
Spread 30-45cm/1-1½ft
Native Brazil

Greenfinger Guide

Temperature W 13-16°C/55-61°F – it survives short periods down to 10°C/50°F, but is better when given more warmth. **S** 16-21°C/61-70°F

Light W Light shade. **S** Light to medium shade.

Watering W Evenly moist. **S** Water freely.

Calathea makoyana

Feeding From late spring to late summer feed every ten to fourteen days with a weak liquid fertilizer.

Humidity Mist spray the leaves throughout the year; more frequently in summer but also in winter, especially if a high temperature is maintained.

Compost A loam-based or peat-based type.

Potting In late spring, when roots fill the pot – usually every year if the plant is growing strongly.

Propagation In spring, when being repotted, divide congested plants.

The Peacock Plant is very beautiful, with 15cm/6in long, oval leaves, silvery-green from above and with mid-green edges irregularly marked with dark green splashes. The undersides have reddish-purple splashes. The leaves are borne on the ends of long, wiry stems which arise from the compost and create a bushy plant, ideal for decorating a dining or coffee table. Most plants are only 20cm/8in high when bought, but they soon reach the suggested size. However, plants up to 1.2m/4ft have been known.

Low temperatures, direct sunlight and a dry atmosphere can soon damage the leaves, but if the right conditions can be provided, it is a plant that soon attracts attention and admiration.

Calathea ornata

Height 38-60cm/15-24in
Spread 38-45cm/15-18in
Native Colombia

Greenfinger Guide

Temperature W 15-19°C/59-66°F – a high temperature is essential for this plant. **S** 19-25°C/66-77°F.

Light W Light Shade **S** Light to medium shade

Watering W Evenly moist **S** Water freely

Feeding From late spring to late summer feed every ten to fourteen days with a weak liquid fertilizer.

Humidity Mist spray the leaves through the year; more frequently in summer but also in winter, especially if a high temperature is maintained.

Compost A loam-based or peat-based type.

Potting In late spring, when roots fill the pot – usually every year if the plant is growing strongly.

Propagation In spring, when being repotted, divide congested plants.

Calatha ornata creates a wealth of dark green leaves, usually 15-18cm/6-7in long, with veins highlighted in light pink that slowly turn white. With age, the undersides of the thin, papery leaves become dark purple. The leaves are borne on long stalks. Two forms are frequently grown; 'Roseo-lineata' has young leaves marked with rose-coloured lines, while 'Sanderana' bears leaves slightly wider than the normal type.

It is ideal for decorating large tables in warm rooms free from cold draughts. It is also ideal for conservatories and greenhouses.

Calathea picturata

Height 23-38cm/9-15in
Spread 23-38cm/9-15in
Native Venezuela

Greenfinger Guide

Temperature **W** 13-16°C/55-61°F – it survives short periods down to 10°C/50°F, but is better when

Calathea picturata 'Argentea'

Calathea picturata 'Vandenheckei'

given more warmth. **S** 16-24°C/61-75°F

Light **W** Light shade. **S** Light to medium shade.

Watering **W** Evenly moist. **S** Water freely.

Feeding From late spring to late summer feed every ten to fourteen days with a weak liquid fertilizer.

Humidity Mist spray the leaves throughout the year; more frequently in summer but also in winter, especially if a high temperature is maintained.

Compost A loam-based or a peat-based type.

Potting In late spring, when roots fill the pot – usually every year if the plant is growing strongly.

Propagation In spring, when being repotted, divide congested plants.

Calathea picturata is very similar to *Calathea lindeniana*, but the leaves are slightly larger, up to 18cm/7in long and about 8cm/3½in wide, as well as being slightly more elliptical. The undersides of the leaves are entirely maroon, while the uppersides instead of having emerald green areas like *Calathea lindeniana*, are silvery.

There are several strikingly attractive varieties, including 'Vandenheckei', 'Argentea' and 'Freddy'. There are many others – all well worth growing.

Calathea veitchiana
Peacock Plant
Height 38-75cm/15-30in

Spread 38-60cm/15-24in
Native Venezuela

Greenfinger Guide

Temperature **W** 13-16°C/55-61°F **S** 16-24°C/61-75°F

Light **W** Light shade. **S** Light to medium shade.

Watering **W** Evenly moist. **S** Water freely.

Feeding From late spring to late summer feed every ten to fourteen days with a weak liquid fertilizer.

Humidity Mist spray the leaves throughout the year; more frequently in summer but also in winter, especially if a high temperature is maintained.

Compost A loam-based or peat-based type.

Potting In late spring, when roots fill the pot – usually every year if the plant is growing strongly.

Propagation In spring, when being repotted, divide congested plants.

In addition to *Calathea makoyana* this calathea is also

Calathea veitchiana

Calathea zebrina

Carex morrowii 'Evergold'

Chlorophytum comosum

known as the Peacock Plant. It is a very beautiful – and large – plant, said by some authorities to reach 1.2m/4ft high. Its stiff, leathery leaves are large, elongated oval in shape and often 30cm/12in long. They are patterned in shades of green, with greyish-green feather-like markings combined with brownish-green arch-shaped ones.

Calathea zebrina
Zebra Plant
Height 45-60cm/18-24in
Spread 45-60cm/18-24in
Native Brazil

Greenfinger Guide

Temperature **W** 17-19°C/63-66°F – high temperatures are essential.. **S** 9-25°C/66-77°F

Light **W** Light shade. **S** Light to medium shade.

Watering **W** Evenly moist. **S** Water freely.

Feeding From late spring to late summer feed every ten to fourteen days with a weak liquid fertilizer.

Humidity Mist spray the leaves throughout the year; more frequently in summer but also in winter, especially if a high temperature is maintained. High humidity, as well as a high temperature, is vital to this plant.

Compost A loam-based compost or a peat-based type.

Potting In late spring, when roots fill the pot – usually every year if the plant is growing strongly.

Propagation In spring, when being repotted, divide congested plants.

The Zebra Plant creates a spectacular display, with semi-erect, oblong leaves revealing a soft, emerald-green background with near horizontal dark green

Chlorophytum capense

water, especially if the temperature falls dramatically. **S** Water freely, but avoid waterlogging the compost.

Feeding From late spring to late summer feed very two to three weeks with a weak liquid fertilizer.

Humidity Mist spray leaves during winter, but only when the temperature is high.

Compost Peat-based type.

Potting In spring, when roots fill the pot – usually every two years.

Propagation In spring, when being repotted, divide congested plants.

The Japanese Sedge is a variegated form of a tufted, grassy sedge with dark reddish-brown leaf blades. This variegated form has grass-like leaves with broad, creamy-white stripes, and is ideal for brightening a cool – either sunny or shady – area in winter. It has a non-fussy nature and deserves to be more widely grown. 'Evergold' is another superb form which is sometimes available.

Another sedge-type plant often grown indoors is *Carex brunnea* 'Variegata', also known as *Carex elegantissima*. It comes from Indonesia and Australia and forms a tufted, elegant plant with small, stiff, grass-like leaves. The main attraction is white stripes near the edges of the leaves.

Chlorophytum comosum
Spider Plant/St Bernard's Lily/Spider Ivy/Ribbon Plant/Walking Anthericism

Height 15-25cm/6-10in
Spread 25-45cm/10-18in – can be more with well-grown and long established plants, which

Cissus antarctica

tend to cascade and trail long stems with plantlets at their ends.
Native South Africa

Greenfinger Guide
Temperature W 7-13°C/45-55°F **S** 13-21°C/55-70°F

Light W Full light. **S** Bright, but lightly shaded.

Watering W Barely moist – if the temperature falls dramatically, keep the compost drier. **S** Keep the compost moist.

Feeding From late spring to late summer feed every week with a weak liquid fertilizer.

Humidity Mist spray the foliage during summer.

Compost A loam-based or peat-based type.

Potting In late winter or spring, when roots fill the pot. The roots usually swell and frequently push the root-ball out of the pot, making watering and feeding the plant very difficult.

Propagation Divide congested plants when being repotted. Alternatively, peg the plantlets which grow from the long, trailing stems into small pots of compost. Sever from the parent when rooted.

The Spider Plant is quick-growing and creates a wealth of narrow, arching leaves and long, trailing stems with miniature plants at their ends. Ideally, large plants are best positioned on a waist-high pedestal, where its trailing and cascading nature can be best appreciated. Alternatively, the edge of a high shelf or an indoor hanging-basket are well suited to it.

The form most widely grown is *Chlorophytum comosum* 'Variegatum', which displays green leaves edged with white. 'Vittatum', another variegated form, has green leaves with white, central strips.

stripes radiating from the mid-rib. The undersides of the leaves are purple.

It is an ideal plant for positioning on a highly polished dining or coffee table. During dark evenings, it can be further enhanced by a spot light or a standard-lamp.

To grow the Zebra Plant successfully it must be provided with a high temperature and humidity, both in summer and during winter.

Carex morrowii 'Variegata'
Japanese Sedge/Japanese Sedge Grass

Height 20-30cm/8-12in
Spread 15-23cm/6-9in
Native Japan

Greenfinger Guide
Temperature W 2-7°C/36-45°F **S** 7-10°C/45-50°F

Light W Slight shade to full sun. **S** Medium shade to full sun.

Watering W Keep evenly moist – avoid excessive

'Mandaianum' had central yellow stripes to its green leaves, but, alas, is rarely seen.

Chlorophytum capense, also known as *Chlorophytum elatum*, is a slightly different plant and is occasionally sold in its variegated form. This has long green leaves centrally marked with broad white stripes. Unfortunately, most plants sold as *Chlorophytum capense* 'Variegatum' are really *Chlorophytum comosum* 'Variegatum'.

These complexities of nomenclature need not worry houseplant enthusiasts, as when grown well – and displayed where the plant can trail and become a focal-point in a room – it has few rivals.

Cissus antarctica
Kangaroo Vine

Height 1.8-2.4m/6-8ft – see text
Spread 60-90cm/2-3ft – see text
Native New South Wales, Australia

Greenfinger Guide

Temperature W 7-13°C/45-55°F S 13-24°C/55-75°F

Light W Full light. S Light shade.

Watering W Just moist. S Water freely, but ensure good drainage.

Feeding From late spring to late summer feed every two weeks with a weak liquid fertilizer.

Humidity Mist spray the leaves during summer.

Compost Loam-based type.

Potting In spring, when roots fill the pot – usually every one or two years.

Propagation 7.5-10cm/3-4in long cuttings formed from sideshoots during mid-summer. Insert in equal parts moist peat and sharp sand. Place in 16-18°C/61-64°F.

The Kangaroo Vine is a superb evergreen climber for clothing a large area. In a greenhouse or conservatory border it grows 4.5-5.4m/15-18ft high, but when in a 15-20cm/6-8in wide pot indoors it is less robust and more manageable. The glossy, heart-shaped and pointed dark green leaves are scalloped and spiny, about 10cm/4in long and 5cm/2in wide.

Young plants can be placed on a low table, but eventually it needs a permanent framework up which to climb. For creating a screen to separate one part of a room from another, it has few peers.

If your plant needs to be tidied, spring or early summer is the time to attend to it.

Cissus discolor
Begonia Vine/Trailing Begonia/Climbing Begonia/Rex-begonia Vine/Begonia Cissus

Height 1.2-1.8m/4-6ft – see text
Spread 38-45cm/15-18in – see text
Native Java and Cambodia

Greenfinger Guide

Temperature W 13-15°C/55-61°F – low temperatures encourage the plant to lose its leaves, especially if excessively watered at the same time. S 15-24°C/61-75°F

Light W Bright, but not direct sunlight. S Bright, but not strong and direct sunlight.

Watering W Barely, but evenly moist. S Water freely, but ensure good drainage.

Feeding From late spring to late summer feed every two to three weeks with a weak liquid fertilizer.

Humidity In summer stand the pot in a tray of moist pebbles.

Compost Loam-based compost.

Potting In spring, when the roots fill the pot –

usually every one or two years.

Propagation 7.5-10cm/3-4in-long cuttings formed from sideshoots during mid-summer. Insert in equal parts moist peat and sharp sand. Place in 16-18°C/61-64°F.

The Begonia Vine is renowned for its attractive leaves, with elongated, 10-15cm/4-6in long, heart-shaped leaves, vivid green and marbled with silvery-white and purple. The undersides are maroon-red. It is superb when grown up a moss-covered pole, which it densely clothes with leaves. The moss helps to create a humid atmosphere around the leaves.

When young it can be displayed on a small table, but eventually it needs a floor standing position. Plants which are grown in greenhouse borders, with the foliage trained up a permanent framework, will spread to 4.5m/15ft or more high and wide.

Cissus rhombifolia
Grape Ivy/Natal Vine/Venezuela Treebine

Height 1.2-1.8m/4-6ft – see text
Spread 0.6-1.2m/2-4ft – see text

Cissus rhombifolia

Native Natal
Greenfinger Guide

Temperature W 7-10°C/45-50°F S 10-16°C/50-61°F – avoid high temperatures in summer.

Light W Full light. S Light shade.

Watering W Just moist. S Water freely, but ensure good drainage.

Feeding From late spring to late summer feed every two to three weeks with a weak liquid fertilizer.

Humidity Mist spray the leaves occasionally during summer.

Compost Loam-based type.

Potting In spring, when roots fill the pot – usually every year.

Propagation 7.5cm/3in long lateral shoots during late spring and early summer. Insert in equal parts moist peat and sharp sand. Place in 16-18°C/61-64°F.

The Grape Ivy is best known by its older name *Rhoicissus rhomboidea*, and like the Kangaroo Vine it is a vigorous climber. When grown in a greenhouse or conservatory border it will climb and spread up to 6m/20ft. The dark green leaves are each formed of three diamond-shaped, scalloped and spiny-edged leaflets.

As well as the normal species, there is an attractive form with deeply-lobed leaflets, each up to 6cm/2½in

Cissus rhombifolia 'Ellen Danica'

long. This is the Mermaid Vine, 'Ellen Danica'. It tends to be more trailing than the normal type, and when young is ideal for positioning on a side table, with a few stems allowed to trail over the side.

There are several other plants in this genus which are occasionally grown as indoor plants, including the Princess Vine (*Cissus sicyoides*). It comes from South America and is less hardy than the Kangaroo Vine, therefore needing slightly more warmth in winter. The leaves are formed of four or five leaflets, each about 5cm/2in long and 2.5cm/1in wide. They are dark green, but the leaf-stalks are crimson. In a pot indoors the plant grows 1.5-2.4m/5-8ft high, but when planted in a greenhouse border 4.5-6m/15-20ft is more in order.

The Miniature Grape Ivy (*Cissus striata*) is another species sometimes available, but is more of a trailer than a vigorous climber. The leaves are about the same shape as the Princess Vine, but only 2.5cm/1in long and 12mm/½in wide. However, these leaves are produced in great numbers – dark green and with a reddish-crimson leaf-stalk. The young growth is pinkish and adds further interest to the plant.

Cissus discolor

Codiaeum variegatum pictum 'Excellent'

The Evergreen Grape Vine (*Cissus capensis*) comes from the Cape of Good Hope and has somewhat rounded leaves, up to 20cm/8in wide, with glossy, dark green surfaces and brown edges. The undersides are brown and furry. It is relatively hardy, able to withstand low temperatures and bright light. Take care not to water it excessively during winter, when dormant.

Codiaeum variegatum pictum 'Petra'

Codiaeum variegatum pictum
Joseph's Coat/Croton/Variegated Laurel
Height 45-60cm/1½-2ft
Spread 30-45cm/1-1½ft
Native Malaysia

Greenfinger Guide

Temperature W 13-15°C/55-59°F – it will survive temperatures down to 10°C/50°F, although this will check the plant's growth. However, rapidly fluctuating temperatures are worse, as they cause leaves to drop off the plant. **S** 15-18°C/59-64°F

Light W Full light. S Light shade.

Watering W Barely moist. S Water freely, but ensure good drainage.

Feeding From early to late summer feed every two to three weeks.

Humidity Mist spray leaves in summer.

Compost A loam-based or peat-based type.

Potting In spring, when roots fill the pot – usually every year.

Propagation 7.5cm/3in-long cuttings during late spring or early summer. Insert in equal parts moist peat and sharp sand. Place in 24°C/75°F.

This dazzling foliage plant has few peers, with leaves in many shapes and bright colours, creating a

Codiaeum variegatum pictum 'Iceton'

spectacular display throughout the year. In a greenhouse border plants often reach 2.4-3m/8-10ft high, but in pots in the home are less vigorous. Avoid positioning plants where they are in draughts

When young and small, codiaeums are ideal as table-top displays. With maturity, group them with other plants in a floor-standing arrangement. In summer, empty fireplaces benefit from their colour, but avoid draughts coming down the chimney.

Many distinctive colour forms are available, such as 'Carrierei' with yellow-green leaves that mature to reveal red centres; 'Reidii' has bold cream veins and laurel-like leaves; 'Disraeli' bears slender mid-green leaves blotched creamy-yellow; 'Holuffiana' has cream veining on forked leaves; 'Aucubafolia' displays green leaves spotted and flecked with yellow; 'Golden Star' has narrow, bright yellow leaves with only occasional flecks of green; 'Bravo' has large leaves with undulating edges, mainly yellow and with irregular green areas between the lateral veins; and 'Norma' reveals pear-shaped leaves, mainly yellow but with green between the lateral veins. There are many other varieties.

Coleus blumei

Coleus blumei
Flame Nettle/Painted Nettle
Height 30-45cm/12-18in
Spread 30-38cm/12-15in
Native Java

Greenfinger Guide

Temperature W 13-15°C/55-59°F, but usually fresh plants are raised each year – see propagation. **S** 15-21°C/59-70°F

Light W Bright light. S Light shade.

Watering W Just moist. S Water freely, but ensure

good drainage.

Feeding From late spring to late summer feed every two to three weeks with a weak liquid fertilizer.

Humidity Mist spray leaves in summer.

Compost Loam-based or peat-based type.

Potting In spring pot up young plants, progressively increasing the sizes of the pots.

Propagation Sow seeds in mid or late winter, 3mm/0.125in deep in loam-based seed compost. Place in 16-20°C/61-68°F. When large enough to handle, prick off into small pots. Alternatively, take 7.5-10cm/3-4in long stem-tip cuttings from mid spring to late summer – these can be taken from overwintered stock plants. Insert in loam-based compost with extra sharp sand. Place in 18-21°C/64-70°F.

The Flame Nettle creates a wealth of highly coloured nettle-like leaves, in varied shades of red, maroon, yellow and green. Blue and white tubular flowers are also produced, but these are best nipped out so that the

Cordyline australis

Cordyline australis 'Rubra'

plant directs its energy into producing attractive leaves. Pinching out growing tips throughout summer helps to keep the plant bushy.

By late summer most plants have lost some of their leaves and look rather sad. Large plants are difficult to overwinter and therefore it is usually as rooted cuttings that plants are carried over to another season. If you have a particularly attractive form, taking cuttings is the only way to ensure that similarly coloured plants are produced.

If plants are being grown on for a second year, shorten all shoots by about two-thirds in February.

Cordyline australis
Cabbage Tree/Grass Palm/Fountain Grass/Palm Lily/Giant Dracaena

Height 60-90cm/2-3ft
Spread 60-75cm/2-2½ft
Native Australia and New Zealand

Greenfinger Guide

Temperature W 4-7°C/39-45°F S 10-21°C/50-70°F

Light W Full light. S Full light.

Watering W Just moist. S Water freely.

Feeding From late spring to late summer feed every ten to fourteen days.

Humidity Mist spray leaves in summer.

Compost Loam-based or peat-based type.

Potting In early early spring, when roots fill the pot – usually every two or three years.

Propagation Detach suckers from around the plant's base in spring and pot up into a loam-based compost. Place in 10-13°C/50-55°F until rooted and established – may take a year. Alternatively, old plants with long bare bases can have the stem cut up into 7.5cm/3in long pieces in mid-summer. Insert in equal parts moist peat and sharp sand, and place in 18-21°C/64-70°F. However, by chopping up the stem the whole original plant is ruined.

The Cabbage Tree grows to 7.5m/25ft or more in its native land, with branched stems and bunched heads of arching, narrow, grey-green leaves. In the home its stature is much less, and when young has a short stem

Cordyline fruticosa 'Kiwi'

with arching leaves cascading around its sides.

There are several attractive varieties of this plant, including 'Rubra'.

During summer – in mild areas – it can be placed outside on a warm and sheltered patio. However, take care that the compost does not dry out.

Cordyline fruticosa
Ti Log/Flaming Dragon Tree/Good Luck Plant/Hawaiian Good Luck Plant/Tree of Kings

Height 45-90cm/1½-3ft
Spread 38-45cm/15-18in
Native Southeast Asia

Greenfinger Guide

Temperature W 10-13°C/50-55°F S 13-24°C/55-75°F

Light W Full light. S Light shade.

Watering W Just moist. S Water freely.

Feeding From late spring to late summer feed every ten to fourteen days.

Humidity Mist spray leaves in summer.

Compost A loam-based or peat-based type.

Potting In early spring, when roots fill the pot – usually every two or three years.

Propagation In mid-summer cut up the stems of leggy plants into 7.5cm/3in long pieces. Insert in equal parts moist peat and sharp sand, and place in 18-21°C/64-70°F.

Cordyline fruticosa 'Snow'

There are several attractive forms, including 'Tricolor' with dark green leaves variegated cream, red and pink. 'Firebrand' displays reddish leaves, while 'Red-edge' has bright reddish-purple leaves with green markings. More recent forms include 'Kiwi', 'Snow' and 'White King'.

Cordyline indivisa
Cabbage Palm/Blue Dracaena
Height 0.9-1.2m/3-4ft
Spread 0.75-1m/2½-3ft
Native New Zealand

Greenfinger Guide
Temperature W 4-7°C/39-45°F S 10-21°C/50-70°F

Light W Full light. S Full light.

Watering W Just moist. S Water freely.

Cordyline indivisa

Feeding From late spring to late summer feed every ten to fourteen days.

Humidity Mist spray leaves in summer.

Compost A loam-based or peat-based type.

Potting In early spring, when roots fill the pot – usually every two or three years.

Propagation Detach suckers from around the plant's base in spring and pot up into a loam-based compost. Place in 10-13°C/50-55°F until rooted and established – may take a year.

Cordyline indivisa grows to more than 6m/20ft in its native country, but in the home forms a more manageable plant. The short stem develops lance-shaped, long and pointed, narrow leaves, the low ones cascading outwards and downwards.

During summer – and in mild areas – it can be placed outside on a warm and sheltered patio.

Cordyline stricta
Cordyline stricta
Height 1.2-1.8m/4-6ft
Spread 38-45cm/15-18in
Native Australia

Greenfinger Guide
Temperature W 10-13°C/50-55°F S 13-24°C/55-75°F

Light W Full light. S Light shade.

Watering W Just moist. S Water freely.

Feeding From late spring to late summer feed every ten to fourteen days.

Humidity Mist spray the leaves in summer.

Compost A loam-based or peat-based type.

Potting In early spring, when roots fill the pot – usually every two or three years.

Propagation Detach suckers from around the plant base in spring and pot up into a loam-based compost. Place in 10-13°C/50-55°F until rooted and established – may take up to a year.

Cordyline fruticosa 'Lord Roberts'
A young Ti Log plant has a central stem entirely clothed with long-stemmed, narrow leaves. As the plant matures, some of the lower leaves fall off and it assumes a palm-like trunk. The normal species has attractive, lance-shaped leaves, mid-green and flushed with red, purple or cream.

When young, it can be placed on a low table, but with age needs a floor-standing position. Positioning it in a group with other plants helps to clothe bare stem bases.

Cordyline stricta

Cordyline stricta grows to 3.6m/12ft or more in its native country, creating a wealth of dull, rough-edged, sword-shaped leaves up to 60cm/2ft long and slightly more than 30mm/1.25in wide.

It forms a large and stately foliage plant.

Ctenanthe oppenheimiana
Never Never Plant

Height 45-60cm/1½-2ft
Spread 38-45cm/15-18in
Native East Brazil

Greenfinger Guide

Temperature **W** 13-16°C/55-61°F **S** 16-24°C/61-75°F

Light **W** Light shade. **S** Light to medium shade.

Watering **W** Evenly moist. **S** Water freely.

Feeding From late spring to late summer feed every two weeks with a weak liquid fertilizer.

Humidity Mist spray the leaves throughout the year; more frequently in summer but also in winter, especially if a high temperature is maintained.

Compost A loam-based or peat-based type.

Potting In late spring, when the roots fill the pot – usually every two years.

Propagation In spring, when being repotted, divided congested plants.

The Never Never Plant is clump forming, with narrow, lance-shaped leaves up to 45cm/18in long, boldly banded in contrasting light and dark green, and combined with cream and other colours. The undersides are purple.

It is an ideal houseplant when a bold display on a low table is needed, although it requires a warm and shaded position to prevent the leaves curling. Fluctuating and low temperatures are the chief hazards with this plant.

A couple of other ctenanthe species are occasionally grown as houseplants. *Ctenanthe lubbersiana*, from Brazil and earlier known as *Phrynium lubbersianum*, is vigorous and perhaps the hardiest of all the related group of ctenanthes, marantas and calatheas. Indeed, in many ways it resemble a calathea, with leaves up to 18cm/7in long and 7.5cm/3in wide. These are either light green and mottled with dark green, or light green and mottled with cream. The colouring is influenced by the age of the plant and the amount of light it is given. Older plants tend to have more cream in their leaves. Plant vary in size, but on maturity are about 45cm/18in high. Occasionally a variegated form is available.

Ctenanthe kummeriana, again from Brazil and previously known as *Maranta kummeriana*, is becoming more popular and readily available in nurseries. Growing to about 45cm/18in high, it produces large, elongated oval leaves with upper surfaces a beautiful velvet-green and undersides purplish-violet. These arise from stiff and upright stems which grow out of the compost.

Cyperus alternifolius
Umbrella Plant/Umbrella Grass/Umbrella Palm/Umbrella Sedge

Ctenanthe oppenheimiana

Cyperus alternifolius
Height 45-60cm/1½-2ft
Spread 25-38cm/10-15in
Native Africa

Greenfinger Guide

Temperature **W** 13-15°C/55-59°F **S** 18-25°C/64-77°F

Light **W** Bright light. **S** Bright but indirect light.

Watering **W** Keep the compost really moist. **S** Keep the compost really moist.

Feeding From mid-spring to late summer feed every two weeks with a weak liquid fertilizer.

Humidity Mist spray leaves in summer, and also during winter if a high temperature can be maintained.

Compost Loam-based compost plus some charcoal chippings.

Potting In late spring, when roots fill the pot – usually every two years.

Propagation Divide congested plants in spring. Alternatively, sow seeds in mid-spring in a loam-based seed compost. Place in 18-21°C/64-70°F.

Cyperus alternifolius

Watering W Keep the compost really moist.
S Keep the compost really moist.

Feeding From mid spring to late summer feed every two weeks with a weak liquid fertilizer.

Humidity Mist spray leaves in summer, and also during winter if a high temperature can be maintained.

Compost A loam-based compost plus some charcoal chippings.

Potting In late spring, when the roots fill the pot – usually every two years.

Propagation Divide congested plants in spring. Alternatively, sow seeds in mid-spring in a loam-based compost. Place in 18-21°C/64-70°F.

This is another Umbrella Plant, also liking to have its roots continually in water, together with a high temperature and a humid atmosphere. It differs from *Cyperus alternifolius* in having wider leaf-like bracts that form umbrellas at the tops of stiff stems.

Cyperus diffusus

The Umbrella Plant is an ideal houseplant for enthusiasts who tend to excessively water their plants. Cyperus plants love to have their roots continually saturated with water. Indeed, a combination of water-soaked compost, high temperature and humid atmosphere ensures success.

Long, erect and stiff stems arise from the compost and create umbrella-like heads of long, slender, green, leaf-like shoots which botanically are bracts. These may be 15-25cm/6-10in across.

The form 'Variegatus' has leaves and stems beautifully striped white.

Cyperus diffusus
Umbrella Plant/Umbrella Grass

Height 38-50cm/15-20in
Spread 38-45cm/15-18in
Native Mauritius

Greenfinger Guide
Temperature W 13-15°C/55-59°F **S** 18-25°C/64-77°F

Light W Bright light. **S** Bright but indirect light.

Several other cyperus species are occasionally available, including *Cyperus gracilis*. This plant grows 30-45cm/12-18in high and has thin, upright and round stems that terminate at their tops in umbrellas of fine, grass-like leaves.

The Egyptian Paper Rush (*Cyperus papyrus*) is a tender type best suited to a very warm conservatory or large greenhouse, where its large stance, up to 2.1m/7ft high, is not overwhelming. Its thick stems terminate in large tufts of thread-like leaves. It requires a warmer temperature than most other Umbrella Plants, in the region of 18-21°C/64-70°F.

The Umbrella Plant sold as *Cyperus* 'Sumula' is more suited to the home than the Egyptian Paper Rush. This species is much lower growing, with short stems attractively terminating in large heads of grassy leaves.

Dieffenbachia maculata
Dumb Cane/Leopard Lily/Spotted Dog Cane

Height 0.45-1.2m/1½-4ft
Spread 30-45cm/1-1½ft
Native Brazil and Colombia

Greenfinger Guide
Temperature W 15-18°C/59-64°F – do not allow the temperature to fall below 13°C/55°F.
S 18-24°C/64-75°F

Light W Full light. **S** Light shade.

Watering W Barely moist. Do not allow the compost to dry out, especially if the temperatures rises dramatically. **S** Water freely, but ensure good drainage

Feeding From mid spring to late summer feed every two weeks with a weak liquid fertilizer.

Humidity Mist spray the foliage during summer.

Compost Loam-based compost.

Potting In spring, when roots fill the pot.

Propagation In spring, cut up long, bare stems into 5-7.5cm/2-3in long pieces. Peg these horizontally into a mixture of equal parts moist peat and sharp sand. Place in 21-24°C/70-75°F.

The Dumb Cane gains its name from its sap which, if

Dieffenbachia maculata 'Jupiter'

Dieffenbachia maculata 'Neptune'

Dieffenbachia maculata 'Mars'

Dieffenbachia maculata 'Camilla'

Dieffenbachia maculata 'Katherine'

Dieffenbachia maculata 'Triumph'
Dieffenbachia maculata 'Exotica'

Dieffenbachia maculata 'Compacta'

Dieffenbachia maculata 'Bausei'

Dieffenbachia maculata 'Clementine'

in contact with the mouth causes the loss of speech for a short period. When taking cuttings, it is best to wear gloves, and avoid getting the sap in your eyes. However, despite the plant's poisonous nature, it is one that is well worth growing for the year-through attractive nature of its leaves, which are oblong and 30cm/1ft or more long.

Many varieties are widely available, including 'Splendens' which has leaves mainly rich bronze-green with irregular ivory and creamy-white splashes.

'Exotica' displays leaves almost totally creamy-yellow and with narrow, pale green edges, while 'Bausei', sometimes sold as *Dieffenbachia x bausei* and really a hybrid between *Dieffenbachia maculata* and *Dieffenbachia weirii*, has yellowish-green leaves with dark green edges. There are many other varieties, such as 'Roehrsii' with leaves up to 23cm/9in long and 12cm/4½in wide. Each leaf is mainly pale yellowish-green, with the lateral veins picked out in ivory and the edges and midrib in dark green. Others include 'Neptune', 'Jupiter', 'Camilla', 'Triumph', 'Katherine', 'Clementine' and 'Compacta'.

Dipteracanthus makoyanus

Dizygotheca elegantissima

Dipteracanthus makoyanus
Monkey Plant/Trailing Velvet Plant

Height 30-45cm/1-1½ft
Spread 30-50cm/12-20in
Native Brazil

Greenfinger Guide

Temperature W 13-15°C/55-59°F – it will survive periods down to 10°C/50°F but will not then produce flowers, although with this plant the blooms are of secondary importance. S 15-18°C/59-64°F

Light W Full light. S Light shade.

Watering W Keep moist, especially if the plant is bearing flowers. But do not waterlog the compost. S Keep moist.

Feeding From from late summer through to following mid-summer feed every two weeks with a weak liquid fertilizer.

Humidity Do not mist spray the flowers or foliage. If the temperature rises dramatically, stand the plant in a saucer of moist pebbles.

Compost A loam-based or peat-based type.

Potting In late summer, repot plants with congested roots – usually every year.

Propagation 5-7.5cm/2-3in long stem-tip cuttings in early summer, taken from plants cut back in spring. Insert them in equal parts moist peat and sharp sand, and place in 18°C/64°F.

The Monkey Plant creates attractive foliage with the bonus of trumpet-shaped, 36mm/1½in wide, reddish-purple flowers during winter. The leaves are up to 7.5cm/3in long, olive-green and marked along their veins in whitish-silver. The undersides are purple.

The rather weak stems can be left to trail. Alternatively, the growing tips can be regularly nipped out to encourage stronger stems and bushiness. There are two forms of this plant – 'White' and 'Pink'.

Dizygotheca elegantissima
False Aralia/Finger Aralia/Spider Plant

Height 0.75-1.2m/2½-4ft – in a pot
Spread 38-50cm/15-20in – in a pot
Native New Hebrides

Greenfinger Guide

Temperature W 13-15°C/55-59°F S 15-24°C/59-75°

Light W Full light. S Bright, indirect sunlight.

Watering W Barely moist. S Water moderately; avoid keeping the compost continually saturated.

Feeding From late spring to mid-summer feed every two weeks.

Humidity Mist spray the leaves frequently, especially during summer. As well as creating a moist atmosphere around the plant, the dampness helps to prevent an infestation of red spider mites.

Compost A loam-based or peat-based type.

Potting In late spring, when roots fill the pot – usually every two years.

Propagation Sow seeds in early spring in 21°C/70°F. Alternatively, take 7.5cm/3in long stem-tip cuttings in spring, placing them in 21°C/70°F.

The False Aralia is one of the most elegant of all houseplants, creating a mass of narrow, wavy-edged and notched leaflets that radiate from the tops of stems, like fingers on a hand. When young, they are deep coppery-red, but with maturity become dark green. With age, the plant loses its graceful appearance and the leaves widen. Also, some of the lower leaves fall off the plant, leaving a bare base. Such plants, if they are not too woody, can be rejuvenated in spring by cutting back the stems to just above compost level.

It is an ideal plant for filling a large space in a corner, or between two large windows.

Dracaena deremensis
Dragon Tree

Height 0.75-1.2m/2.5-4ft
Spread 38-45cm/15-18in
Native Tropical Africa

Greenfinger Guide

Temperature W 13-15°C/55-59°F S 15-27°C/59-80°F

Light W Full light S Very light shade

Watering W Barely moist S Water freely, but do not allow the compost to become waterlogged.

Dracaena deremensis

Feeding From early to late summer feed every two weeks.

Humidity Mist spray the leaves during summer.

Compost Loam-based type.

Potting In spring, when roots fill the pot – usually every one or two years.

Propagation 7.5cm/3in long tip or basal cuttings in spring. Insert in equal parts moist peat and sharp sand. Place in 21-24°C/70-75°F.

This dracaena is ideal for creating colour throughout the year. The narrow. ribbon-like but stiff leaves are up to 45cm/1.5ft long, glossy green and with two longitudinal silver stripes along them. Several forms are grown, including 'Warneckii' with white stripes, 'Souvenie de Augustus Schryer' bears glossy-green leaves with broad, creamy bands along their edges and 'Bausei' has dark green leaf edges and a white, central

Dracaena deremensis 'Warneckii'

Dracaena deremensis 'Lime'

Dracaena deremensis 'Lemon Lime'

Dracaena draco

line. Other superb varieties include 'Rhoersii' with dark green leaves which display a broad light green central strip edged with two white lines, and 'Janet Craig' with shiny-green leaves. 'Lemon Lime' and 'Lime' are two recently introduced varieties.

Young plants are ideal for placing on low tables, but with age a floor-standing position is better.

Dracaena draco
Dragon Tree

Height 1-1.2m/3½-4ft
Spread 60-75cm/2-2½ft
Native Canary Islands

Greenfinger Guide

Temperature W 7-10°C/45-50°F **S** 10-16°C/ 50-61°F

Light W Full light. **S** Very light shade.

Watering W Barely moist. **S** Water freely, but do not allow the compost to become waterlogged.

Feeding From early to late summer feed every two weeks.

Humidity Mist spray the leaves during summer.

Compost Loam-based compost.

Potting In spring, when roots fill the pot.

Propagation Sometimes shoots develop from around the base of the plant, and these can be detached in spring and potted up. Place in 16°C/ 61°F until established, and mist spray the foliage. Other methods of increasing dracaenas tend to destroy the plant.

The Dragon Plant is one of the easiest dracaenas to grow, and forms a lovely houseplant for decorating an entrance hall. It is slow growing, and in its natural environment there are specimens said to be more than 1000 years old. In the home it forms a stocky, bushy plant with tough, sword-like, bluish mid-green leaves up to 45cm/1½ft. These have red edges if the plant is positioned in good light.

149

Dracaena fragrans

Dracaena marginata

Dracaena godseffiana

This plant is one of the sources of dragon's blood, a reddish resin which exudes from the trunk and forms the basis of some varnishes.

As well as forming a superb indoor plant, in summer it can also be placed outside on a warm, sheltered patio.

Dracaena fragrans

Height 1.2m/4ft
Spread 60-75cm/2-2½ft
Native Guinea and West Africa

Greenfinger Guide
Temperature W 13-15°C/55-59°F **S** 15-27°C/59-80°F

Light W Full light. **S** Very light shade.

Watering W Barely moist. **S** Water freely, but do not allow the compost to become waterlogged.

Feeding From early to late summer feed every two weeks.

Humidity Mist spray the leaves during summer.

Compost Loam-based compost.

Potting In spring, when roots fill the pot – usually every two years.

Propagation 7.5cm/3in long tip or basal cuttings in spring. Insert in equal parts moist peat and sharp sand. Place in 21-24°C/70-75°F.

Dracaena fragrans has many similarities to *Dracaena deremensis*, but the leaves are longer, wider and less pointed. The leaves are variable in colour, but usually striped deep cream to gold. The most popular form is 'Massangeana', frequently known as the Corn Plant or Corn Palm because the leaves are striped creamy-yellow and appear like a variegated maize. The form 'Lindenii' has leaves with fine green and gold stripes

to their centres, and wide yellow edges.

Like many other dracaenas, when young it can be displayed on a low table, but with age should progress to a floor-standing position.

Dracaena godseffiana
Gold Dust Dracaena/Spotted Dracaena
Height 60-90cm/2-3ft
Spread 38-45cm/15-18in
Native Zaire

Greenfinger Guide
Temperature W 10-13°C/50-55°F **S** 13-24°C/55-75°F

Light W Full light. **S** Very light shade.

Watering W Barely moist. **S** Water freely, but do not allow the compost to become waterlogged.

Feeding From early to late summer feed every two weeks.

Humidity Mist spray the leaves in summer.

Compost Loam-based compost.

Potting In spring, when roots fill the pot – usually every one or two years.

Propagation 7.5cm/3in long tip cuttings in spring. Insert in equal parts moist peat and sharp sand. Place in 21-24°C/70-75°F.

The Gold Dust Dracaena creates an attractive, lax array of dark green leaves heavily spotted and splashed with cream. The wiry stems tend to splay outwards, and if the plant is grouped with other foliage plants it soon merges with them. When young, it can be used to decorate low tables, but with age it needs a floor-standing position. Its irregular outline is ideal for filling a corner position. Alternatively, if a low corner table is used to display a plant, positioning the Gold Dust Dracaena on the floor in front of it will hide the

Watering **W** Barely moist. **S** Water freely, but do not allow the compost to become waterlogged.

Feeding From early to late summer feed every two weeks.

Humidity Mist spray the leaves during summer.

Compost Loam-based compost.

Potting In spring, when roots fill the pot.

Propagation 7.5cm/3in long tip or basal cuttings in spring. Insert in equal parts moist peat and sharp sand. Place in 21-24°C/70-75°F.

The Madagascar Dragon Tree is much desired and grown by interior decorators, who use it as an architectural feature, perhaps in the corner of a room. The stiff, arching, narrow green leaves edged with reddish-purple are often 60cm/2ft long. These are borne in a palm-like fashion around a narrow stem, often twisted and branched. The form 'Tricolor' is even more attractive, with narrow green leaves displaying a fine cream stripe. 'Multi' and 'Colorama' are two recent introductions.

Although this plant is eventually very large, it grows slowly and is ideal for the home.

Dracaena sanderiana
Ribbon Plant/Belgian Evergreen

Height 0.6-1.2m/2-4ft
Spread 38-45cm/15-18in
Native Cameroon

Greenfinger Guide

Temperature **W** 10-13°C/50-55°F **S** 13-24°C/55-75°F

Dracaena sanderiana

Light **W** Full light. **S** Very light shade.

Watering **W** Barely moist. **S** Water freely, but do not allow the compost to become waterlogged.

Feeding From early to late summer feed every two weeks.

Humidity Mist spray the leaves in summer.

Compost Loam-based compost.

Potting In spring, when roots fill the pot – usually every two years.

Propagation 7.5cm/3in long tip or basal cuttings in spring. Insert in equal parts moist peat and sharp sand. Place in 21-24°C/70-75°F.

The Ribbon Plant is usually quite small when grown as a houseplant, but old and mature specimens grow 2.1m/7ft high. It can be kept small by keeping the roots constrained in a small pot. It gains its name Ribbon Plant from the narrow, slender, pale green leaves which have silvery or ivory edges. The leaves also have a fascinating twist to them.

It is attractive when displayed on its own on a low table or set among a group of foliage plants.

It is easily grown in a warm, centrally-heated home where the atmosphere is relatively dry.

Epipremnum pinnatum
Devil's Ivy/Golden Pothos/Pothos Vine/Golden Ceylon Creeper/Taro Vine/Hunter's Robe

Height 1.2-1.5m/4-5ft – climbing
Spread 38-45cm/15-18in
Native Solomon Islands

Greenfinger Guide

Dracaena marginata 'Tricolor'

table's legs and help to create a larger area of attractive foliage.

The form 'Florida Beauty' is less vigorous, with leaves heavily spotted in yellow and white.

Dracaena marginata
Madagascar Dragon Tree

Height 1.8-3m/6-10ft
Spread 0.9-1m/3-3½ft
Native Madagascar

Greenfinger Guide

Temperature **W** 13-15°C/55-59°F **S** 15-27°C/59-80°F

Light **W** Full light. **S** Very light shade.

Epipremnum pinnatum 'Aureum'

Temperature W 13-15°C/55-59°F – it survives temperatures of 10°C/50°F, but the compost will need to be kept slightly drier. **S** 15-24°C/59-75°F

Light W Full light. **S** Bright, but indirect sunlight.

Watering W Barely moist. **S** Water freely, but ensure that the compost is well-drained.

Feeding From late spring to late summer feed every three to four weeks with a weak liquid fertilizer.

Humidity Mist spray leaves during summer.

Compost A loam-based or peat-based type.

Potting In late spring, when roots fill the pot – usually every two or three year

Propagation 10cm/4in long tip or basal cuttings during late spring or early summer. Insert in equal parts moist peat and sharp sand. Place in 21-24°C/70-75°F.

The Devil's Ivy is best known and usually sold as *Scindapsus aureus*. Like many other houseplants, it produces both juvenile and mature leaves, which are markedly different. The juvenile ones are pointed, oval, 10cm/4in long, bright green and with yellow streaking and slight splashing. The mature leaves are up to 30cm/12in long and heart-shaped.

Several forms are available, including 'Marble Queen' with white marbling and streaking, 'Golden Queen' bearing leaves almost entirely yellow, while 'Tricolor' has leaves more densely marbled than the normal type.

It is a climber that forms aerial roots and is therefore best given a moss-covered pole up which to climb. The moss, when kept damp, helps to keep the aerial roots moist.

Episcia cupreata
Flame Violet

Height 7.5-10cm/3-4in
Spread 20-30cm/8-12in – then trailing
Native Colombia and Venezuela

Greenfinger Guide

Temperature W 13-16°C/55-61°F **S** 16-21°C/61-70°F

Episcia cupreata

X Fatshedera lizei

X Fatshedera lizei 'Variegata'

temperatures. **S** 10-18°C/50-64°F – avoid high temperatures.

Light W Full light. **S** Bright, indirect sunlight.

Watering W Just moist, but if the temperature rises be prepared to give more water. **S** Water freely, but ensure good drainage.

Feeding From mid-spring to late summer feed

X Fatshedera lizei 'Anna Michels'

every two weeks.

Humidity Mist spray leaves during summer.

Compost Loam-based compost

Potting In spring, when roots fill the pot – usually every year.

Propagation 10-13cm/4-5in long tip or sideshoot cuttings during late spring or mid-summer. Insert in equal parts moist peat and sharp sand. Place in 16°C/61°F.

The Ivy-tree is a cross between two distinct and unrelated plants, a form of the False Castor Oil Plant (*Fatsia japonica* 'Moseri') and the Irish Ivy (*Hedera helix* 'Hibernica'). The result is a plant with shiny, five-lobed, green leaves up to 21cm/7in long. When young, the plant has a central, upright stem, but with age it sprawls and climbs, and at that stage support may be necessary. It can be kept bushy by nipping out the growing tips, which encourages the development of further sideshoots.

There is an attractive variegated form, 'Variegata', with leaves displaying creamy-white blotches and edges. 'Anna Michels' is a more recently introduced variegated form, with irregular light green streaks and splashes in the centres of the leaves.

When young it can be grown in a small pot and displayed on a low table, but with age it needs a floor-standing position.

The large cross which is positioned before the plant's botanical name indicates that it is a cross between two different genera.

Light W Bright light. **S** Bright, indirect sunlight.

Watering W Barely moist – but do not let the compost dry out. **S** Water freely, but ensure good drainage.

Feeding From late spring to late summer feed every two weeks with a weak liquid fertilizer.

Humidity Create a moist atmosphere, but avoid splashing water on the leaves.

Compost Loam-based or peat-based type.

Potting In spring, when roots fill the pot – usually every year.

Propagation Layer long stems in late spring.

The Flame Violet creates a superb display with its large, oval, silvery-veined, copper-coloured leaves. Additionally, it produces orange flowers throughout summer.

It is superb when planted in an indoor hanging-basket or a pot positioned at the edge of a shelf.

X Fatshedera Lizei
**Ivy-tree/Miracle Plant/Fat-headed Lizzie/
Botanical Wonder/Aralia Ivy**

Height 1.2-1.8m/4-6ft
Spread 60-90cm/2-3ft
Native Hybrid

Greenfinger Guide

Temperature W 4-7°C/39-45°F – avoid high

Fatsia japonica

Fatsia japonica
Castor Oil Plant/False Castor Oil Plant/Japanese Fatsia/Formosa Rice Tree/Paper Plant

Height 0.9-1.2m/3-4ft
Spread 0.9-1.2m/3-4ft
Native Japan and Taiwan (Formosa)

Greenfinger Guide
Temperature W 3-7°C/37-45°F – avoid high temperatures. S 10-18°C/50-64°F – avoid high temperatures, especially above 21°C/70°F.

Light W Bright light, but avoid strong sunlight in spring. S Bright, indirect sunlight.

Fatsia japonica 'Variegata'

Watering W Just moist. S Keep the compost moist, but not continually saturated.

Feeding From mid-spring to late summer feed every two to three weeks.

Humidity Mist spray leaves in summer.

Compost Loam-based or peat-based type.

Potting In spring, when roots fill the pot – usually every year.

Propagation The easiest way to increase this plant is by removing sucker-like shoots in spring and potting them individually into a peat-based compost. Place the pot in a cold frame.
Alternatively, sow seeds in spring and place in 10-13°C/50-55°F.

The False Castor Oil Plant is hardy enough in some areas to be grown outside in a sheltered position, where it often grows up to 3m/10ft high. Indoors, it creates an ideal plant for a cool entrance or hall, producing shiny, mid to deep green leaves with seven to nine, serrated, finger-like lobes with pointed tips.
  There is an attractive variegated form, *Fatsia japonica variegata*, which is slightly smaller than the all-green type, but has attractive white tips and edges to the leaves.
  Occasionally, there is confusion between *Fatsia japonica* and *Ricinus communis*. Both are commonly known as Castor Oil Plants, but it is Ricinus communis which is the plant that produces castor oil, and therefore is the true Castor Oil Plant. Correctly, *Fatsia japonica* is the False Castor Oil Plant. Unfortunately, the distinction is not always made.

Ficus benjamina
Weeping Fig/Benjamin Tree/Java Fig/Small-leaved Rubber Plant/Tropic Laurel

Ficus benjamina

Height 1.2-1.8m/4-6ft
Spread 45-75cm/1½-2½ft
Native India

Greenfinger Guide
Temperature W 13-16°C/55-61°F S 16-24°C/61-75°F

Light W Full light. S Bright, indirect sunlight.

Watering W Just moist. S Water freely, but ensure good drainage.

Feeding From late spring to late summer feed every ten to fourteen days.

Humidity Mist spray leaves in summer.

Compost Loam-based or peat-based type.

Potting In spring, when roots fill the pot – usually every two years. When the plant is too large to be repotted, topdress with fresh compost in spring.

Propagation 5-10cm/2-4in-long cuttings from

Ficus benjamina 'Variegata'

Ficus benjamina 'Golden King'

Ficus benjamina 'Starlight'
Ficus benjamina 'Mini Golden King'

Ficus benjamina 'Mini Starlight'

sideshoots during late spring and early summer. Insert in equal parts moist peat and sharp sand. Place in 16-18°C/61-64°F.

The Weeping Fig creates a graceful, arching and freely-branching tree-like houseplant, ideal for positioning in the corner of a room. When young the leaves are soft green, but with maturity become shiny and deep green. The spear-shaped leaves, usually about 10cm/4in long, have pointed tips.

At one time only the green form was grown, but now there are many variegated forms, as well as some which have green leaves but are strikingly different from the normal species. Those with all green foliage include 'Exotica' with a wealth of shiny, deep green leaves, and 'Indica' with narrow, pointed leaves.

Variegated forms include 'Hawaii' with shiny green leaves with yellow or white edges and markings, 'Golden King', 'Gold King', 'Mini Starlight', 'Variegata', 'Starlight' and 'Golden Princess'.

Ficus benjamina 'Foliole'

Ficus benjamina 'Golden Princess'

moist peat and sharp sand. Place in 21-24°C/70-75°F. Alternatively, increase by air-layering large plants with bare stems during early and mid-summer.

The Rubber Plant is a popular houseplant, usually grown as a single-stemmed plant but eventually becoming very large and with branching stems. Many entrances to offices have large examples of this robust plant. Usually, however, it has just one main stem, with large, leathery, shiny leaves growing directly from the main stem. The form most commonly grown is 'Decora', (often called the Broad-leaved India Rubber Plant) with dark green leaves up to 30cm/12in long. 'Robusta' is a form similar to 'Decora'.

Several other forms are available, including 'Tricolor' with green leaves variegated with cream and flushed pink, 'Schryveriana' with cream patches, 'Doescheri' with pale green leaves with broad ivory edges and tinted pink, 'Variegata' with silvery-grey and white markings, and 'Belgica'.

When young it is an attractive plant for tables, but eventually it needs a floor-standing position where it cannot be damaged by children or large dogs.

Ficus deltoidea
Mistletoe Fig/Mistletree/Rubber Plant

Height 45-75cm/1½-2½ft
Spread 38-45cm/15-18in
Native Malaysia, Indonesia and India

Greenfinger Guide

Temperature W 7-10°C/45-50°F S 10-20°C/50-68°F

Light W Full light or light shade. S Light to medium shade.

Watering W Just moist. S Water freely, but ensure good drainage.

Feeding From late spring to late summer feed every ten to fourteen days.

Humidity Mist spray leaves in summer.

Compost Loam-based or peat-based type.

Potting In spring, when roots fill the pot – usually every two years. When the plant is too large to be repotted, topdress with fresh compost in spring.

Propagation 5-10cm/2-4in long cuttings from sideshoots during spring and early summer. Insert in equal parts moist peat and sharp sand. Place in 16-18°C/61-64°F.

The Mistletoe Fig when grown indoors is relatively small, compact and bushy, but in its native countries forms a large tree. It creates a mass of small, oval to pear-shaped, dark green leaves. Its common name is derived from the cluster of yellowish-grey berry-like fruits which are borne from the leaf joints.

Small specimens of this distinctive houseplant can be displayed on tables, but eventually it may need a floor-standing position where it cannot be knocked by children or large dogs.

Ficus elastica
Rubber Plant/Assam Rubber Plant/India Rubber Tree

Height 0.9-1.2m/3-4ft – see text
Spread 38-45cm/15-18in – see text
Native Tropical Asia

Greenfinger Guide

Temperature W 16-18°C/61-64°F S 18-24°C/64-75°F

Light W Full light. S Bright, indirect sunlight.

Watering W Just moist. S Water freely, but ensure good drainage.

Ficus deltoidea

Feeding From late spring to late summer feed every ten to fourteen days.

Humidity Mist spray leaves in summer.

Compost Loam-based or peat-based type.

Potting In spring, when roots fill the pot – usually every two years. When the plant is too large to be repotted, topdress with fresh compost in spring.

Propagation 10-15cm/4-6in-long cuttings during late spring and early summer. Insert in equal parts

Ficus lyrata
Fiddle-leaf Fig/Fiddle-leaf Tree

Height 1.2-1.5m/4-5ft
Spread 60-75cm/2-2½ft
Native West Africa

Greenfinger Guide

Temperature W 16-18°C/61-64°F S 18-24°C/64-75°F

Ficus elastica

Ficus eastica 'Robusta'

Ficus elastica 'Tricolor'

Light W Full light. **S** Bright, indirect light.

Watering W Just moist. **S** Water freely, but ensure good drainage.

Feeding From late spring to late summer feed every ten to fourteen days.

Ficus lyrata

Ficus elastica 'Doescheri'

Ficus pumila 'Sonny'

Humidity Mist spray leaves during summer.

Compost Loam-based or peat-based type.

Potting In spring, when roots fill the pot – usually every two years. When the plant is too large to repot, topdress with fresh compost in spring.

Propagation 10-15cm/4-6in-long cuttings during late spring and early summer. Insert in equal parts moist peat and sharp sand. Place in 21-24°C/70-75°F. Alternatively, increase by air-layering large plants with bare stems during early and mid-summer.

The Fiddle-leaf Fig has some of the most decorative and eye-catching leaves of all members of the fig family. The fiddle-shaped, glossy, dark green leaves are wavy-edged and up to 38cm/15in long, and veined in a beautiful yellowish green.

Indoors it is of great architectural value, creating a focal point perhaps in the corner of a room. Spot lights can enhance the plant during evenings, but avoid placing them too close as the heat from the bulbs may burn the leaves.

Ficus pumila
Creeping Fig/Climbing Fig/Creeping Rubber Plant

Height 45-60cm/1½-2ft – climbing or trailing
Spread 30-45cm/12-18in
Native China

Greenfinger Guide

Temperature W 7-10°C/45-50°F S 10-20°C/50-68°F

Light W Full light or light shade. S Light to medium shade.

Watering W Just moist. S Water freely, but ensure good drainage.

Feeding From late spring to late summer feed every ten to fourteen days.

Humidity Mist spray leaves in summer.

Compost Loam-based or peat-based type.

Potting In spring, when roots fill the pot, usually every two years.

Propagation 5-10cm/2-4in-long cuttings from sideshoots during spring and early summer. Insert in equal parts peat and sharp sand. Place in 18°C/64°F.

The Creeping Fig can be a rampant creeper and climber if given a screen up which to climb, soon covering an area 1.2-1.5m/4-5ft high and wide. Usually, however, it is grown in a small pot and trained up a couple of split canes or a piece of plastic trellis-work. It can also be planted in an indoor hanging-basket, where it will trail freely. Growing it in a small pot and placing the container at the edge of a high shelf is also effective.

The leaves are small, dark green and heart-shaped. Plants in the wild also develop mature and adult leaves, but these are seldom seen on houseplants.

The form 'Minima' has small leaves and a compact form, while 'Variegata' develops leaves marbled and lined in cream and green. 'Sonny' is another variegated form, with attractive white edges to the green leaves. 'Rikke' and 'Lis' are two recent all-green introductions.

Ficus radicans
Trailing Fig

Height 7.5-13cm/3-5in
Spread 30-38cm/12-15in – and trailing
Native East Indies

Greenfinger Guide

Ficus radicans 'Variegata'

Fittonia verschaffeltii

Temperature W 13-16°C/55-61°F **S** 16-24°C / 61-75°F

Light W Full light or light shade. **S** Light to medium shade.

Watering W Just moist. **S** Water freely, but ensure good drainage.

Feeding From late spring to late summer feed every ten to fourteen days.

Humidity Mist spray leaves in summer.
Compost Loam-based or peat-based type.
Potting In spring, when roots fill the pot, usually every two years.
Propagation 5-10cm/2-4in-long cuttings from sideshoots during spring and early summer. Insert in equal parts peat and sharp sand. Place in 18°C/64°F.

The Trailing Fig has wiry, trailing stems that bear leathery, lance-shaped, pointed leaves about 7.5cm/3in long. However, it is the variegated form 'Variegata' which is normally grown, with green leaves which reveal creamy-white edges.

It is best grown in an indoor hanging-basket, where it can trail freely, or in a pot positioned at the edge of a high shelf. This variegated form needs more light than the all-green type, and if placed in a dull position will lose its attractive variegations.

Fittonia verschaffeltii 'Argyroneura'

Fittonia verschaffeltii 'Mini Green'

Gynura procumbens

good drainage.

Feeding From early to late summer feed every seven days with a weak liquid fertilizer.

Humidity Mist spray leaves in summer, and stand plants in trays of water and pebbles.

Compost A loam-based or peat-based type.

Potting In spring, when roots fill the pot – usually during the second year. However, plants are usually discarded after the third year.

Propagation The stems root readily into the compost, and these can be severed during spring and early summer and potted up. Provide a high temperature and humidity until established. Alternatively, divide congested plants in spring.

The Painted Net Leaf is a somewhat sprawling plant with eye-catching, oval, dark green leaves up to 13cm/5cm long and distinctively veined in carmine. The whole plant appears to be netted.

The Silver Net Leaf, *Fittonia verschaffeltii* 'Argyroneura', although often sold as *Fittonia argyroneura*, has leaves up to 10cm/4in long and daintily but prominently veined in ivory-white.

As well as being called Silver Net Leaf, it is also known as Nerve plant and Lace Leaf.

The Snakeskin Plant, *Fittonia argyroneura nana*, is a miniature form, with 2.5cm/1in long oval leaves with white veins.

Fittonia verschaffeltii
Painted Net Leaf/Mosaic Plant/Whit-leaf Fittonia/Silver Threads

Height 7.5-13cm/3-5in
Spread Trailing and creeping
Native Colombia and Peru

Greenfinger Guide

Temperature W 16-18°C/61-64°F S 24-27°C/75-80°F

Light W Full light. S Light to medium shade.

Watering W Barely moist. Do not allow the compost to dry out. S Water freely, but ensure

Grevillea robusta
Silk OakSilky Oak

Height 0.9-1.8m/3-6ft
Spread 38-45cm/15-18in
Native Queensland and New South Wales, Australia

Greenfinger Guide

Temperature W 7-10°C/45-50°F S 18-21°C/64-70°F

Light W Full light. S Bright, but indirect sunlight.

Watering W Just moist, but do not allow the compost to dry out. S Water freely, but ensure

Grevillea robusta

good drainage.

Feeding From late spring to late summer feed every two weeks with a weak liquid fertilizer.

Humidity Mist spray during summer in very hot weather.

Compost Lime-free loam-based compost. Alternatively, use peat-based.

Potting In spring, when roots fill the pot – usually every two years.

Propagation 5-7.5cm/2-3in heel cuttings during late spring or early summer. Insert in equal parts moist peat and sharp sand. Place in 15-18°C/59-64°F. Taking heel cuttings invariably damages the plant. Therefore, it is invariably increased by sowing seeds in spring in lime-free seed compost. Place in 18-21°C/64-70°F. After germination, prick off the seedlings into individual pots. It is possible to have an attractive plant within six months of sowing the seeds.

The Silk Oak eventually forms a beautiful, floor-standing plant, with deep green, fern-like leaves

Hedera canariensis 'Variegata'

compost to dry out. **S** Water freely, but ensure good drainage.

Feeding From early to late summer feed every two weeks with a weak liquid fertilizer.

Humidity Do not mist spray the leaves, but maintain a humid atmosphere in summer. Stand the pot in a tray of moist pebbles.

Compost A loam-based or peat-based type.

Potting In spring, when roots fill the pot – usually every two years.

Propagation 7.5-10cm/3-4in long tip cuttings during spring. Insert in equal parts moist peat and sharp sand. Place in 18-21°C/65-70°F.

The Velvet Plant is a climbing and trailing plant, similar to *Gynura aurantiaca* but larger and with a twining and sprawling nature. Its leaves are smaller and covered with fine, purplish hairs. During spring it bears groundsel-like, 12mm/½in long, pale orange flowers in terminal clusters. However, they have an objectional aroma and are best nipped out.

It needs a position where it can trail freely, and this

Hedera helix 'Gold Kolibri'

is best provided by either an indoor hanging-basket or by placing the pot at the edge of a high shelf. If allowed to climb, it needs support.

Hedera canariensis 'Variegata'
Canary Island Ivy/Algerian Ivy/Gloire de Marengo Ivy/Hagenburger's Ivy
Height 1.2-3m/4-10ft
Spread Climber
Native Canary Islands and North Africa

Greenfinger Guide
Temperature W 7-10°C/45-50°F **S** 10-16°C/50-61°F

Light W Full light. **S** Light shade.

Watering W Barely moist. Excessive watering in winter will soon damage this plant, but add more water if the temperature rises dramatically, especially in early spring. **S** Keep the compost moist, but not continually saturated. Allow the compost to dry out slightly between waterings.

Feeding From mid spring to late summer feed every two to three weeks.

Humidity Mist spray leaves in summer.

Compost A loam-based or peat-based type.

Potting In spring, when roots fill the pot – usually every three years. But once the plant is in a 13cm/5in pot it usually remains there for the rest of its life.

Propagation 7.5-13cm/3-5in-long tip or stem cuttings during mid-summer. Insert in equal parts moist peat and sharp sand. Place in 59-64°C/15-18°F.

The ordinary Canary Island Ivy creates a dense canopy of large, leathery, all-green leaves. However, it is the variegated form 'Variegata' – also known as 'Gloire de Marengo' or even, erroneously, just as 'Marengo' – that is mainly grown. It has large leaves, up to 13cm/5in long, dark green and merging through silvery-grey to creamy-white at the edges.

When young and in a small pot, perhaps with a 45cm/18in long, narrow cane up which to climb, it can be positioned on a corner table, but eventually it needs a floor-standing position and a permanent trellis up

covered with silky hairs. It is ideal for a corner position, perhaps against a white wall and lit during the evening with a spot light.

During hot summers the Silk Oak becomes very susceptible to red spider infestations, which can cause leaves to fall off. Mist spraying the leaves regularly during summer helps to prevent this happening.

In Australia it forms a tree up to 24m/80ft high, the wood being highly prized in furniture making.

Gynura procumbens
Velvet Plant/Purple Passion Vine
Height 1.2-1.5m/4-5ft
Spread 38-45cm/15-18in
Native India

Greenfinger Guide
Temperature W 10-13°C/50-55°F **S** 16-21°C/61-70°F

Light W Full light. **S** Light shade.

Watering W Evenly moist – do not allow the

Hedera helix 'Golden Inge'

Hedera helix 'Glacier'

Hedera helix 'White Kolibri'

Hedera helix 'Montgomery'

Hedera helix 'New Sicilia'

which to climb.

Avoid giving it high temperatures during summer, especially if the atmosphere is dry. It is not quite so hardy as the normal ivy, *Hedera helix*, so do not expect it to survive low temperatures without some of its leaves falling off.

Hedera helix
Common Ivy/English Ivy

Height 45-90cm/1½-3ft – indoors
Spread Climbing and trailing
Native Europe

Greenfinger Guide

Temperature W 5-10°C/45-50°F – will survive temperatures down to 3°C/37°F. S 10-16°C/50-61°F

Light W Full light. S Light shade.

Watering W Barely moist – but the compost must not dry out, especially if the temperature rises dramatically in spring. S Keep the compost moist, but not continually saturated.

Feeding From mid-spring to late summer feed every two to three weeks.

Humidity Mist spray leaves in summer.

Compost Loam-based or peat-based type.

Potting In spring, when roots fill the pot – usually every two or three years.

Propagation 7.5cm/3in-long tip or stem cuttings during mid-summer. Insert in equal parts moist peat and sharp sand. Place in 59-64°C/15-18°F.

The Common Ivy, which when growing outdoors, can easily climb in excess of 15m/50ft, has many small-leaved varieties. These are excellent for growing indoors, as climbers or as trailers, from pots positioned at the corner of shelves or from indoor hanging-baskets. Most are sold in 7.5cm/3in wide pots, with three to five rooted stems in each so that a bushy and marketable plant is created rapidly, and supported by a 25cm/10in long split cane.

There are many varieties of this resilient houseplant, some old and established and others much newer. As well as providing a wide range of leaf shapes, there are many variegated forms. These plants are not expensive to buy and an interesting collection of them can soon be made. Varieties include 'Glacier' with three distinctive lobes variegated silvery-grey and with creamy-white edges; 'Sagittaefolia' with five all-green lobes, and often called the Needlepoint Ivy; 'Cristata' with green leaves displaying crisped and crinkled edges; 'Jubilee' with dark green leaves and

Hedera helix 'Stricta'

golden centres; 'Pittsburgh', a vigorous variety, with small, dark green leaves with lighter green veins; 'Chicago' with leaves about 5cm/2in long and 36mm/1½in wide, bright green when young and remaining a light green; 'Little Diamond' has very small leaves, almost without lobes, dark grey-green and with ivory edges; 'Lutzii' displays small leaves, often with three rather than five lobes, mottled in shades of pale green; 'Golden Jubilee' has small leaves, golden and with a wide dark green edge; 'Goldchild' displays beautiful

Hedera helix 'Mini Heron'

Hypoestes phyllostachya

Iresine herbstii 'Aureoreticulata'

variegated leaves, deep yellowish-green and blotched dark and light green in the centre; 'Stricta' has erect stems with dark green leaves; 'Kolibri' reveals leaves variegated green and white – there is also a golden form of this, 'Gold Kolibri'; 'Sicilia' has green leaves framed in cream; 'Eva' has leaves variegated in cream and white; 'Golden Child' reveals beautiful green leaves framed in bright yellow; 'Harald' bears leaves variegated two-tone green and cream; 'Anne Marie' has leaves variegated green and framed in cream.

Although this ivy also grows outside and can survive periods of frost, do not be tempted to place your ivy outside in winter. It will be accustomed to the warmer conditions indoors and will immediately suffer. However, during summer it can be placed outside on a patio. By the way, if ivies grown indoors are put outside in spring, after the risk of frost has passed, they will by late autumn be accustomed to outside life and will survive winter in the open. Large specimens of *Hedera helix* – as well as *Hedera canariensis* 'Variegata' – which have outgrown available space indoors can be treated in this way and converted into garden plants – but they must be given all summer and into autumn to become acclimatized to a colder life.

Hypoestes phyllostachya
Polka Dot Plant/Freckle Face/Measles Plant/Baby's-tears/Pink Dot Plant

Height 45-60cm/1½-2ft
Spread 30-45cm/1-1½ft
Native Madagascar

Greenfinger Guide

Temperature W 13-16°C/55-61°F S 16-21°C/61-70°C

Light W Full light. S Bright, but indirect sunlight.

Watering W Evenly moist – do not allow the compost to dry out, but at the same time do not keep it waterlogged. S Keep the compost moist, but not continually saturated.

Feeding From late spring to late summer feed every two to three weeks with a weak liquid fertilizer.

Humidity Stand the plant on a tray of moist pebbles.

Compost A loam-based or peat-based type.

Potting In spring, when roots fill the pot – usually annually.

Propagation 7.5cm/3in-long tip cuttings in late spring and early summer. Insert in equal parts peat and sharp sand. Place in 70°C/21°F.

The Polka Dot Plant is a highly decorative, somewhat sprawling and straggly plant. Its olive-green, oval, but sometimes spear-tipped leaves are covered with white to pinkish spots and blotches. Several varieties are now available, including 'Skjoldelev' and 'Betina'. Both are attractive and have leaves peppered with lighter markings.

To prevent it becoming too sprawling, nip out the tips of the shoots. However, when it is planted in an indoor hanging-basket this straggly and sprawling nature becomes a useful feature.

If the leaves lose their attractiveness, it is probably because the plant is in too a shady position – but avoid strong and direct sunlight in summer.

Iresine herbstii
Beef-steak Plant/Blood Leaf/Beef Plant

Maranta leuconeura 'Kerchoveana'

Maranta 'Erythroneura'

Height 38-50cm/15-20in
Spread 30-45cm/12-18in
Native South America

Greenfinger Guide

Temperature W 13-16°C/55-61°F S 16-18°C/
61-64°F

Light W Full light. S Full light, with slight shade
at midday.

Watering W Evenly moist. S Water freely, but
ensure good drainage.

Feeding From late spring to late summer feed
every two to three weeks with a weak liquid
fertilizer.

Humidity Mist spray foliage in summer.

Compost A loam-based, or peat-based compost.

Potting In spring, when roots fill the pot – usually
every year.

Propagation 10cm/4in-long stem-tip cuttings in
spring or autumn. Insert in equal parts moist peat
and sharp sand. Place in 21-75°C/70-24°F.

The Beef-steak Plant is a gloriously coloured shrubby
plant, with soft red stems that bear wine-red heart-
shaped leaves, 7.5cm/3in long, with paler red veining.
    A related plant, Iresine herbstii aureoreticulata, is
known as the Chicken Gizzard. The leaves, borne on
bright red stems, have a green misting, with broad

yellow veins.
    To keep these plants bushy, occasionally nip out
the growing tips, especially in spring.

Maranta leuconeura
Prayer Plant/Ten Commandments
Height 15-20cm/6-8in
Spread 25-30cm/10-12in
Native Brazil

Greenfinger Guide

Temperature W 10-13°C/50-55°F – do not let the
temperature fall below 10°C/50°F. S 18-24°C/
64-75°F

Light W Bright, indirect sunlight. S Light to
medium shade.

Watering W Just moist. S Water freely.

Feeding From late spring to late summer feed
every two weeks with a weak liquid fertilizer.

Humidity Mist spray leaves in summer, especially
during periods of high temperatures.

Compost Loam-based or peat-based compost.

Potting In spring, when roots fill the pot – usually
every year.

Propagation Divide congested plants in spring.

The Prayer Plant is ideal for decorating dining and
coffee tables, creating colour throughout the year. It
has a bushy and compact nature, with young leaves
displaying an emerald-green background and brown-
purple blotches between the veins. These blotches
darken as the leaves age, and the undersides are grey-
green, shot with purple. At night the leaves stand
upright and fold together, like hands in prayer. This
trait has given rise to the common name, Prayer Plant.
    Several attractive forms are available, such as
Maranta leuconeura 'Kerchoveana', erroneously
known as Maranta kerchoveana and often called
Rabbit's Foot or Rabbit's Tracks, has leaves which at
first are emerald-green with red blotches between the
main veins, but with age become dark green with
maroon blotches.
    Maranta leuconeura 'Erythrophylla', the
Herringbone Plant and also known as Maranta

Monstera deliciosa

leuconeura tricolor and Maranta erythrophylla, has
leaves with deep olive-green backgrounds, greyish-
green edges, vivid red veins and bright green irregular-
edged markings along the mid-rib.
    Maranta leuconeura massangeana, also known as
Maranta massangeana, has blackish-green leaves with
pale-green edges. The mid-rib has irregular-edged
silvery markings, with other veins lined in silver.

Monstera deliciosa
**Swiss Cheese Plant/Cheese Plant/Split Leaf
Philodendron/Breadfruit Vine/Hurricane Plant/
Window Plant/Fruit Salad Plant/Ceriman/
Mexican Breadfruit/Cut-leaf Philodendron**
Height 3.5-4.5m/12-15ft
Spread 1.5-2.1m/5-7ft
Native Guatamala and Southern Mexico

Greenfinger Guide

Temperature W 10-15°C/50-59°F – it survives
short periods down to 7°C/45°F, but if this happens
give the plant less water. S 18-24°C/64-75°F

Light W Bright, indirect light. S Bright, indirect
light.

Watering W Just moist. S Water freely, but ensure
good drainage and allow the compost to become
slightly dry between applications.

Feeding From mid-spring to late summer feed
every ten to fourteen days with a weak liquid
fertilizer. Take care not to use strong fertilizer
concentrations, as the roots may then be badly
damaged.

Humidity Mist spray the leaves frequently during
summer, especially when the temperature is high.

Compost Loam-based or peat-based type.

Potting In early spring, when roots fill the pot –
when young usually every year, then every one or
two years. When too large to be repotted, topdress

in cream and yellow.

It is thought that at one time the plant widely sold as *Monstera deliciosa* was really *Monstera deliciosa* 'Borsigiana'. This variety very much resembles the proper species, but forms a more compact plant, with mature leaves 30cm/12in long and about 25cm/10in wide. The juvenile leaves tend to be more heart-shaped and without indentations, although eventually they acquire perforations within the leaves, as well as serrations along their edges.

Ophiopogon jaburan
Jaburan Lilyturf/Snakebeard/White Lilyturf/ Jaburan Lily/White Lily/Snakebeard

Height 25-38cm/10-15in
Spread 20-25cm/8-10in
Native Japan

The Dwarf Lilyturf or Mondo Grass (*Ophiopogon japonicus*) is another species widely grown as a houseplant. It grows about 20cm/10in high, with dark green leaves.

Pandanus sanderi

Height 60-90cm/2-3ft
Spread 60-75cm/2-2½ft
Native New Guinea

Greenfinger Guide
Temperature **W** 13-16°C/55-61°F **S** 16-21°C/61-70°F

Light **W** Full light, but avoid strong sunlight in spring. **S** Bright, indirect light.

Watering **W** Barely moist. **S** Water freely, but

Ophiopogon jaburan 'Vittatus'

Greenfinger Guide
Temperature **W** 5-10°C/41-50°F **S** 0-16°C/50-61°F

Light **W** Light shade to bright light. **S** Medium to light shade – avoid direct and strong sunlight.

Watering **W** Evenly moist, but avoid excessively watering the compost. **S** Keep the compost moist at all times.

Feeding From late spring to late summer feed every two to three weeks with a weak liquid fertilizer.

Humidity Mist spray the leaves in summer, especially when the temperature rises dramatically.

Compost Peat-based compost.

Potting In spring, when roots fill the pot – usually every year.

Propagation Divide congested plants when being repotted in spring.

Jaburan Lilyturf creates a wealth of stiff, upright, 12mm/½in wide leaves. However, it is the variegated forms which are most often grown as houseplants. There are several of them, including 'Vittatus', 'Argenteo-vittatus, 'Aureo-variegatus' and 'Variegatus', all with white or yellow stripes to the leaves.

ensure good drainage.

Feeding From late spring to late summer feed every ten to fourteen days with a weak liquid fertilizer.

Humidity Stand the pot in a tray of moist pebbles. Alternatively, when the plant is young, place the pot

Pandanus sanderi

Monstera deliciosa 'Variegata'

in spring with fresh compost.

Propagation During early summer, cut off the growing tip together with one mature leaf. If this also includes an aerial root, this is all to the better. Insert in equal parts moist peat and sharp sand. Place in 24-27°C/75-80°F. Sometimes leaf-joint cuttings are taken, but these need temperatures up to 32°C/90°F to encourage rapid rooting.

The Swiss Cheese Plant creates interest throughout the year. Young leaves are heart-shaped, but as they mature they become leathery, up to 45cm/18in wide, deeply cut at their edges and perforated with round or oblong holes. Greenish-white flowers appear in summer, followed by greenish fruits. Unfortunately, these seldom appear on plants indoors. *Monstera deliciosa variegata* has leaves marbled and streaked

Pandanus veitchii

in a large one with moist peat packed between them. Mist spray in summer, but in winter take care that water does not lodge in the leaf-joints.

Compost A loam-based or peat-based type.

Potting Repot young plants in spring each year. Later, only pot on when roots fill the pot. Topdress very large plants, removing the top compost and replacing it with fresh.

Propagation In spring, remove off-shoots from around the bases of plants and pot them into small pots. Place in 24°C/75°C until established.

Pandanus sanderi creates a large rosette of long, narrow, mid-green leaves that gives the impression of the plant being stemless. The leaves have spiny edges and are attractively striped with thin, golden-yellow bands.

When young, it is ideal for growing indoors, but with age is best placed in a conservatory or greenhouse.

Pandanus veitchii
Screw Pine/Veitch Screw Pine

Height 60-75cm/2-2½ft
Spread 45-60cm/1½-2ft
Native Polynesia

Greenfinger Guide

Temperature W 13-16°C/55-61°F – it will survive temperatures down to 10°C/50°F for short periods, but is better when given a little more warmth. S 16-21°C/61-70°F

Light W Full light, but avoid strong sunlight in spring. S Bright, indirect light.

Watering W Barely moist. S Water freely, but ensure good drainage.

Feeding From late spring to late summer feed every ten to fourteen days with a weak liquid fertilizer.

Humidity Stand the pot in a tray of moist pebbles. Alternatively, place the pot in a larger pot with moist peat packed between them. Mist spray in summer, but in winter take care that water does not lodge in the leaf-joints.

Compost A loam-based or peat-based type.

Potting Repot young plants in spring each year. Later, only repot when roots fill the pot. Topdress very large plants, removing the top compost and replacing it with fresh.

Propagation In spring, remove off-shoots from around the bases of plants and pot them into small pots. Place in 24°C/75°F until established.

The Screw Pine is slow-growing, eventually having a small, palm-like stance with a central stem and long, tapering leaves which splay outwards and droop at their tips. In the home it is usually seen as a somewhat elongated, stemless rosette, although eventually it will create a stem.

It is a superb foliage plant for creating year-through colour and interest on a coffee or side table in a very warm room. Avoid positioning this plant in a draught.

Pelargonium graveolens
Rose-scented Geranium/Rose Geranium/Sweet-scented Geranium

Height 60-90cm/2-3ft
Spread 45-75cm/1½-2½ft
Native South Africa

Greenfinger Guide

Temperature W 7-10°C/45-50°F – avoid high temperatures. S 10-18°C/50-64°F

Light W Full light – avoid strong and direct sunlight in spring. S Light shade.

Watering W Just moist. S Water freely, but ensure good drainage.

Feeding From late spring to late summer feed every ten days with a weak liquid fertilizer.

Humidity Mist spraying is not necessary.

Compost Loam-based type.

Potting In spring, when roots fill the pot – usually every year.

Propagation 7.5cm/3in long stem-tip cuttings during summer. Insert in equal parts moist peat and sharp sand. Place in 16°C/61°F. When rooted, after about six weeks, transfer into small pots.

The Rose-scented Geranium has deeply-lobed and toothed green leaves which when bruised or gently crushed emit a wonderful rose-like bouquet. From early summer to early autumn it has 2.5cm/1in wide, rose-pink flowers in small terminal clusters.

Eventually, it forms a large and spreading plant, best grown in a sun room or greenhouse.

Pelargonium tomentosum
Peppermint Geranium/Herb-scented Geranium

Height 30-60cm/1-2ft
Spread 45-75cm/1½-2½ft
Native South Africa

Pelargonium graveolens

Pelargonium tomentosum

Greenfinger Guide

Temperature **W** 7-10°C/45-60°F – avoid high temperatures. **S** 10-18°C/50-64°F

Light **W** Full light – avoid strong and direct sunlight in spring. **S** Light shade.

Watering **W** Just moist. **S** Water freely, but ensure good drainage.

Feeding From late spring to late summer feed every ten days with a weak liquid fertilizer.

Humidity Mist spraying is not necessary.

Compost Loam-based type.

Potting In spring, when roots fill the pot – usually every year.

Propagation 7.5cm/3in-long stem-tip cuttings

during summer. Insert in equal parts moist peat and sharp sand. Place in 16°C/61°F. When rooted, after about six weeks, transfer into small pots.

The Peppermint Geranium has shallowly-lobed, pale green leaves which when bruised or gently crushed emit a strong peppermint fragrance. White flowers, up to 18mm/0.75in wide, are borne from early to late summer.

It is a plant with a spreading and sprawling nature, frequently with a tendency to climb and occasionally to grow 1.2m/4ft high. It is, therefore, best grown in a sun room or greenhouse, where its nature can be accommodated.

In addition to this plant – as well as the Rose-scented Geranium and the Lemon-scented Geranium – there are others which have leaves which emit superb fragrances when bruised. These include another rose-scented species, the Rose-scented Geranium (*Pelargonium capitatum*) and the Apple-scented Geranium (*Pelargonium odoratissimum*).

Pellionia repens
Trailing Watermelon Begonia/Watermelon Pellionia

Height 7.5-10cm/3-4in
Spread 20-25cm/8-10in – trailing and scrambling
Native Vietnam and the Malay Archipelago

Greenfinger Guide

Temperature **W** 13-18°C/55-64°F – it likes warmth, so do not let the temperature fall below the lower figure suggested here. **S** 18-21°C/64-70°F

Light **W** Bright light, but avoid strong and direct sunlight, especially in spring. **S** Light shade – avoid strong sunlight.

Pellionia repens

Watering W Evenly moist. **S** Water freely, but ensure good drainage. Use soft water.

Feeding From late spring to late summer feed every two weeks with a weak liquid fertilizer.

Humidity Mist spray the leaves frequently during summer.

Compost Peat-based type.

Potting In spring, when roots fill the pot – usually every two years.

Propagation Divide congested plants in spring when being repotted. Alternatively, take 5-7.5cm/3-4in-long stem-cuttings in spring. Insert in equal parts moist peat and sharp sand. Place in 18°C/64°F.

The Trailing Watermelon Begonia creates an attractive trailing and sprawling plant with succulent, pink stems up to 38cm/15in long – sometimes slightly more. These bear roundish, bronzy olive-green leaves, often 5cm/2in long, with purplish edges and broad, pale green central strips. The undersides are pinkish.

The key to success with this plant is a draught-free position, combined with warmth and humidity, especially during winter.

Peperomia caperata
Emerald Ripple/Emerald-ripple Peperomia/ Green-ripple Peperomia/Little Fantasy Peperomia

Height 10-20cm/4-8in
Spread 13-15cm/5-6in
Native Tropical America

Greenfinger Guide

Temperature W 10-13°C/50-55°FF **S** 13-18°C/55-64°F

Light W Bright, indirect light. **S** Light shade.

Watering W Barely moist. **S** Water thoroughly, but allow the compost to dry out between waterings. Continually saturated compost will soon kill peperomias.

Feeding From late spring to late summer feed

Peperomia griseoargentea

Peperomia caperata

every three to four weeks.

Humidity Mist spray leaves in summer, and also in winter if a high temperature can be maintained.

Compost Loam-based or peat-based type.

Potting In late spring, when roots fill the pot – usually every year.

Propagation Leaf-petiole (leaf and leaf-stalk) cuttings during summer. Insert each leaf-stalk half way into equal parts moist peat and sharp sand. Place in 18°C/64°F.

The Emerald Ripple is superb for decorating tables of all kinds, as well as for positioning on shelves. The heart-shaped, deep glistening-green leaves are deeply ridged, creating a ripple appearance. The lower parts of the ripples are tinged purple, while the ridges are greyish.

From spring to late autumn or Christmas it bears white flowers in spikes up to 15cm/6in high. The flower spikes are frequently branched, appearing rather antler-like.

Peperomia griseoargentea
Ivy-leaf Peperomia/Ivy Peperomia/Silver Ripple/ Platinum Peperomia/Silver-leaf Peperomia

Height 15-20cm/6-8in
Spread 15-20cm/6-8in
Native Brazil

Greenfinger Guide

Peperomia magnoliifolia

Temperature **W** 10-13°C/50-55°F **S** 13-18°C/55-64°F

Light **W** Bright, indirect light. **S** Light shade.

Watering **W** Barely moist. **S** Water thoroughly, but allow the compost to dry out between waterings. Continually saturated compost will soon kill peperomias.

Feeding From late spring to late summer feed every three to four weeks.

Humidity Mist spray leaves in summer, and also in

Peperomia argyreia

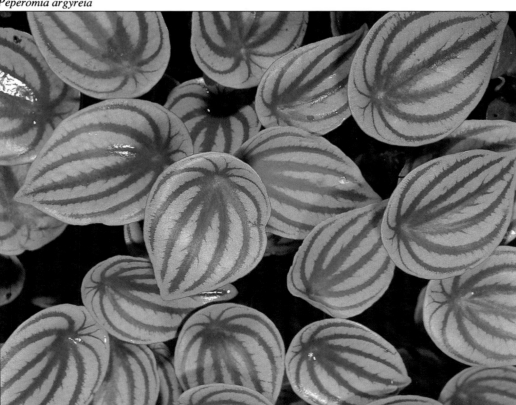

winter if a high temperature can be maintained.

Compost Loam-based or peat-based type.

Potting In late spring, when roots fill the pot – usually every year.

Propagation Leaf-petiole (leaf and leaf-stalk) cuttings during summer. Insert each leaf-stalk half way into equal parts moist peat and sharp sand. Place in 18°C/64°F.

The Ivy-leaf Peperomia is rather similar to the Emerald Ripple (*Peperomia caperata*). Leaves have a quilted

and rippled surface, and a metallic, grey-green colouring with a silvery shimmer, which has given rise to one of its common names.

Like other small, compact peperomias, it is ideal for decorating tables and shelves.

Peperomia magnoliifolia
Desert Privet

Height 20-25cm/8-10in
Spread 20-30cm/8-12in
Native Panama and the West Indies

Greenfinger Guide
Temperature **W** 10-13°C/50-55°F **S** 13-18°C/55-64°F

Light **W** Bright, indirect light. **S** Light shade.

Watering **W** Barely moist. **S** Water thoroughly, but allow the compost to dry out between waterings. Continually saturated compost will soon kill peperomias.

Feeding From late spring to late summer feed every three to four weeks.

Humidity Mist spray leaves in summer, also in winter if a high temperature can be maintained.

Compost A loam-based or peat-based type.

Propagation 7.5cm/3in-long cuttings formed of one or two leaves and a piece of stem. Alternatively, cuttings formed of stem tips can also be taken. Insert in equal parts moist peat and sharp sand. Place in 18°C/64°F.

The Desert Privet is a sturdy, bushy houseplant, ideal for bringing colour to tables and shelves throughout the year. The large, fleshy leaves are plain green, but it is invariably grown in one of its variegated forms. The variety 'Green Gold' has cream edges to light green leaves, while 'Variegata' displays cream coloured young leaves, later becoming cream and light green.

Peperomia argyreia
Water Melon Peperomia/Rugby Football Plant/Silvered Peperomia/Water-melon Peperomia

Height 15-23cm/6-9in
Spread 15-23cm/6-9in
Native Brazil

Greenfinger Guide
Temperature **W** 13-16°C/55-61°F **S** 16-24°C/61-75°F

Light **W** Bright, indirect light. **S** Light shade.

Watering **W** Barely moist. **S** Water thoroughly, but allow the compost to dry out between waterings. Continually saturated compost will soon kill peperomias.

Feeding From late spring to late summer feed every three to four weeks.

Humidity Mist spray leaves in summer, also in winter if a high temperature can be maintained.

Compost Loam-based or peat-based type.

Potting In spring, when the roots fill the pot – usually every year.

Propagation Leaf-petiole (leaf and leaf-stalk) cuttings during summer. Insert each leaf-stalk half way into equal parts moist peat and sharp sand. Place in 18°C/64°F.

The Watermelon Peperomia is a beautifully-leaved plant, ideal for decorating a dining room or coffee table, as well as low shelves and ledges. The oval to spear-shaped, thick, smooth-surfaced leaves are a waxy, bluish-green with silver bands that radiate outwards. The leaf-stalks are usually red.

During winter it needs special care when being

Peperomia scandens

Philodendron elegans

Philodendron bipinnatifidum

watered, and avoid draughts. Compost kept too moist soon encourages the stem bases to rot.

Peperomia scandens
Cupid Peperomia
Height 1.2-1.5m/4-5ft
Spread Climber or trailer
Native South America

Greenfinger Guide

Temperature W 13-16°C/55-61°F **S** 16-24°C/61-75°F

Light W Bright, indirect light. **S** Light shade.

Watering W Barely moist. **S** Water thoroughly, but allow the compost to dry out between waterings. Continually saturated compost will soon kill peperomias.

Feeding From late spring to late summer feed every three to four weeks.

Humidity Mist spray leaves in summer, also in winter if a high temperature can be maintained.

Compost Loam-based or peat-based type.

Potting In spring, when roots fill the pot – usually every year.

Propagation 7.5cm/3in-long cuttings formed of one or two leaves and a piece of stem.
Alternatively, cuttings formed of stem tips can also be taken. Insert in equal parts moist peat and sharp sand. Place in 18°C/64°F.

The Cupid Peperomia has heart-shaped, shiny green leaves, but invariably it is the variegated form *Peperomia scandens* variegata which is grown. When young, the heart-shaped leaves are almost entirely cream, but with age they become pale green with cream edges. The stems, up to 60cm/2ft long, will climb or trail, making the plant ideal for growing in an

to three weeks. Keep the compost moist during this period. A high temperature is needed to encourage germination, about 29°C/84°F. Young plants do not have incised leaves, but within two years of being raised from seed the plants have the mature leaves.

The Tree Philodendron is a non-climbing plant that creates a large, compact houseplant with leaves up to 60cm/2ft long and 45cm/1½ft wide and borne in a large, loose rosette. Young leaves are heart-shaped, while mature ones – which arise after about two years – are broadly three-lobed, slowly developing deep incisions that may extend almost to the midrib. Leaves may therefore appear to be formed of many separate leaflets.

The shape and size of the Tree Philodendron make it ideal for positioning in a corner, or perhaps along a wall and with a picture hung above it.

Philodendron elegans

Height 0.9-1.5m/3-5ft
Spread 45-75cm/1½-2½ft
Native Colombia

Greenfinger Guide

Temperature W 13-16°C/55-61°F **S** 16-24°C/61-75°F

Light W Bright, indirect sunlight. **S** Bright, but filtered sunlight or light shade.

Watering W Just moist. **S** Water freely, but ensure good drainage.

Feeding From late spring to late summer feed every two to three weeks.

Philodendron erubescens

Humidity Mist spray the leaves regularly in summer, especially if the temperature rises dramatically.

Compost Peat-based type.

Potting In spring, when roots fill the pot – usually every two or three years. Plants in large pots which cannot be repotted can be topdressed in spring, removing the top 2.5cm/1in of compost and replacing with fresh.

Propagation Divide congested plants in spring, when being repotted.

Philodendron elegans is a climber of moderate vigour, with distinctive dark-green leaves displaying narrow, finger-like lobes incised almost to the central rib. Leaves may be up to 50cm/20in long and 38cm/15in wide.

Philodendron erubescens
Blushing Philodendron/Red-leaf Philodendron

Height 1.2-1.8m/4-6ft
Spread 38-45cm/15-18in
Native Colombia

Greenfinger Guide

Temperature W 13-18°C/55-64°F **S** 18-24°C/64-75°F

Light W Bright, indirect sunlight. **S** Bright, but filtered sunlight or light shade.

Watering W Barely moist. **S** Water freely, but ensure good drainage.

Feeding From late spring to late summer feed every two to three weeks.

indoor hanging-basket as well as up a framework of small canes.

Sometimes the leaves drop off young plants, but with age this tendency diminishes.

Philodendron bipinnatifidum
Tree Philodendron

Height 0.9-1.2m/3-4ft
Spread 0.9-1m/3-3½ft
Native Brazil

Greenfinger Guide

Temperature W 13-18°C/55-64° – it can survive temperatures down to 10°C/50°F for short periods. But if this happens ensure that the compost is kept slightly drier – but still damp. **S** 18-24°C/64-75°

Light W Bright, indirect sunlight. **S** Bright, but filtered sunlight or light shade.

Watering W Just moist. **S** Water freely, but ensure good drainage. Excessive watering can lead to the roots rotting.

Feeding From late spring to late summer feed every two to three weeks.

Humidity Mist spray leaves frequently in summer, especially during hot weather.

Compost Peat-based type.

Potting In spring, when the roots fill the pot – usually every two years. However, large plants which cannot be repotted must be topdressed in spring. Take care when potting or topdressing the plant not to damage the thick, fleshy roots. If damaged they tend to smell, unpleasantly.

Propagation Divide large and congested plants in early summer. Alternatively, sow seed in spring in a seed compost. Press the seeds lightly into the compost and then lightly water it. Cover with polythene until seeds germinate, usually within two

Humidity Mist spray leaves frequently in summer, especially during hot weather.

Compost Peat-based type

Potting In spring, when the roots fill the pot – usually every two years. Plants that are too large to be repotted can be topdressed with fresh compost in spring.

Propagation Divide large and congested plants in early summer.

The Blushing Philodendron is a fairly vigorous climber, with arrow-shaped leaves up to 30cm/12in long and 18cm/7in wide and borne on long leafstalks. It is the colour of the leaves that has given rise to the common name Blushing Philodendron. When young, the leaves are rose-pink, slowly becoming dark, glossy green with a beautiful coppery tinge. The leaf-stalks are purple and very distinctive.

There are several attractive varieties, including 'Burgundy' with leaves which are initially bright coppery-red, then gradually becoming olive-green. The undersides are burgundy.

'Red Emerald' is considered to be a cross between *Philodendron erubescens* and either *Philodendron domesticum* or *P. sagittifolium*, rather than a variety of *P. erubescens*. Whatever it parentage, it is attractive and forms a compact plant with arrow-shaped leaves. When young they are pale bronze, maturing to dark olive-green with narrow purplish edges. Midribs on the undersides are also purplish.

'New Red' is another excellent variety, with long, arrow-shaped leaves, initially green, then olive-green and later becoming reddish-green.

Philodendron pedatum

Height 0.9-1.5m/3-5ft – in a pot
Spread 0.75-1.4m/3-4ft – in a pot
Native Venezuela, Brazil and Guiana

Greenfinger Guide

Temperature W 13-16°C/55-61°F – do not allow the temperature to fall below these levels. It enjoys warmth and is best when given the upper end of this range. S 16-24°F/61-75°F

Light W Bright, indirect sunlight. S Bright, but filtered sunlight or light shade.

Watering W Just moist. S Water freely, but ensure good drainage.

Feeding From late spring to late summer feed every two to three weeks.

Humidity Mist spray leaves frequently in summer, especially if the temperature rises dramatically.

Compost Peat-based type.

Potting In spring, when roots fill the pot – usually every two or three years. Plants in large pots and too large to be repotted can be topdressed in spring. Remove the top 2.5cm/1in of compost and replace with fresh.

Propagation Take stem cuttings in spring. These require a high temperature to encourage rooting – about 27°C/80°F.

Philodendron pedatum is a climber with modest vigour. Its dark green leaves are not too unlike those of *Philodendron bipinnatifidum*, but with deeper indentations. Mature leaves are about 23cm/9in long and 15cm/6in wide.

Philodendron selloum
Lacy Tree Philodendron

Height 0.75-1m/2½-3½ft – occasionally to 1.5m/5ft
Spread 60-90cm/2-3ft
Native Southern Brazil

Philodendron pedatum

Philodendron selloum

Philodendron scandens

Greenfinger Guide

Temperature **W** 13-16°C/55-61°F **S** 16-24°C/61-75°F

Light **W** Bright, indirect sunlight. **S** Bright, but filtered sunlight or light shade.

Watering **W** Just moist. **S** Water freely, but ensure good drainage.

Feeding From late spring to late summer feed every two to three weeks.

Humidity Mist spray leaves regularly during summer, especially if the temperature rises significantly.

Compost Peat-based type.

Potting In spring, when roots fill the pot – usually every two or three years. Plants in large pots can be topdressed in spring by removing the top 2.5cm/1in of compost and replacing with fresh.

Propagation In spring or early summer use shoots from the base of the stem as cuttings. Insert in equal parts moist peat and sharp sand, and place in 21-24°C/70-75°F.

The Lacy Tree Philodendron is very similar to *Philodendron bipinnatifidum*. The dark green, shiny leaves are basically triangular, with deeply-cut indentations along their edges. As plants age they produce a short tree-like trunk.

Philodendron scandens
Sweetheart Plant/Heartleaf Philodendron

Height 1-1.5m/3½-5ft – climbing
Spread 20-38cm/8-15in
Native Panama

Greenfinger Guide

Temperature **W** 13-18°C/55-64°F **S** 18-24°C/64-75°F

Light **W** Bright, indirect sunlight. **S** Bright, but filtered sunlight or light shade.

Watering **W** Barely moist. **S** Water freely, but ensure good drainage.

Feeding From late spring to late summer feed every two to three weeks.

Humidity Mist spray leaves frequently in summer, especially during hot weather.

Compost Peat-based type.

Potting In spring, when the roots fill the pot – usually every two years.

Propagation 10cm/4in-long tip cuttings during early summer. Insert in equal parts moist peat and sharp sand. Place in 21-24°C/70-75°F.

The Sweetheart Plant is one of the most popular climbers, with a dense array of mid to deep green, heart-shaped leaves, up to 10cm/4in long and 7.5cm/3in wide, that taper to long, slender points. When young, the leaves have an attractive bronze tint. It is best grown up a moss-covered pole, which as well as being decorative helps to create a humid atmosphere around the leaves.

When young it can be trained up a small support, but with maturity needs a floor-standing position and a moss-covered pole or screen up which to climb. Nipping off the growing tips of young shoots encourages bushiness.

Occasionally, a variegated form of this climber is available. It has cream blotches on the lower halves of each leaf. This variegation is thought to be the influence of a virus.

Philodendron 'Tuxla'

Height 0.6-1.2m/2-4ft – see text
Spread 45-60cm/1½-2ft
Native Mexico

Greenfinger Guide

Temperature **W** 13-16°C/55-61°F – do not allow the temperature to fall below 10°C/50°, as the plant will then be damaged. **S** 16-24°C/61-75°F

Light **W** Bright, indirect sunlight. **S** Bright, lightly filtered sunlight or light shade.

Watering **W** Just moist. **S** Water freely, but ensure good drainage.

Feeding From late spring to late summer feed every two to three weeks.

Humidity Mist spray the foliage regularly during summer, especially if the temperature is high.

Compost Peat-based compost.

Potting In spring, when roots fill the pot – usually every two years.

Propagation Divide congested plants in spring, when being repotted.

Philodendron 'Tuxla' was found in Tuxla, Mexico, and appears to be a cross between *Philodendron domesticum*, the Elephant's Ear, and *Philodendron sagittifolium*, although some authorities suggest that it is a variety of *Philodendron sagittifolium*. Whatever

Philodendron 'Tuxla'

its parentage, it is an attractive plant and when young has a bushy habit. However, it will climb and if this happens it develops aerial roots.

It has beautiful spear-shaped, shiny, dark green leaves which are borne on thick and fleshy leaf-stalks.

Pilea cadierei
Aluminium Plant/Watermelon Pilea

Height 25-30cm/10-12in
Spread 20-25cm/8-10in
Native Vietnam

Greenfinger Guide

Pilea cadierei

Temperature W 10-13°C/50-55°F **S** 16-24°C/61-75°F

Light W Bright, but indirect light. **S** Bright, but indirect light.

Watering W Barely moist. **S** Water freely, but ensure good drainage.

Feeding From late spring to late summer feed every two weeks with a weak liquid fertilizer.

Humidity Mist spray leaves in summer.

Compost Loam-based or peat-based compost.

Potting In spring, when roots fill the pot – usually every year.

Propagation 7.5-10cm/3-4in-long stem-tip cuttings in spring. Insert in equal parts moist peat and sharp sand. Place in 18-21°C/64-70°F.

The Aluminium Plant is readily identified by its oval, leathery, dark green and slightly-quilted leaves which have silvery splashes between the veins. Sometimes, plants become leggy at their bases, and if this happens they are best replaced with fresh specimens and the old one used to form cuttings. Nipping out the tips of shoots in spring helps to create a small, bushy plant.

The form 'Nana' is smaller, up to 23cm/9in high, remains compact and is ideal for growing in a carboy or other enclosed glass container.

Pilea involucrata
Friendship Plant/Panamiga/Pan-American Friendship Plant

Height 20-25cm/8-10in
Spread 20-25cm/8-10in

Native West Indies, Panama and south to the northern part of South America.

Greenfinger Guide

Temperature W 13-16°C/55-61°F **S** 16-24°C/61-75°F

Light W Indirect light to light shade. **S** Light shade – avoid strong and direct light.

Watering W Barely moist. **S** Water freely, but ensure good drainage.

Feeding From late spring to late summer feed every two weeks with a weak liquid fertilizer.

Humidity Stand the pot in a tray of water with pebbles in its base.

Compost Loam-based or peat-based type.

Potting In spring, when roots fill the pot – usually every year.

Propagation 7.5cm/3in-long stem-tip cuttings in spring. Insert in equal parts moist peat and sharp sand. Place in 18-21°C/64-70°F.

The plant usually sold as the Friendship Plant is *Pilea spruceana*. However, although *P. involucrata* and *P. spruceana* are similar, botanically they are different. The real *Pilea involucrata* is an erect and slightly trailing plant with oval to broadly pear-shaped leaves up to 36mm/1½in long. These are very attractive, dark bronzy-green above and purplish beneath. *Pilea spruceana*, however, from Peru and Bolivia, has slightly larger leaves, about 5cm/2in long – though occasionally up to 7.5cm/3in – again oval to broadly pear-shaped and with similar colouring to those of the Friendship Plant.

Further confusion is created by *Pilea* 'Norfolk' being offered for sale as both *P. involucrata* and *P. spruceana*. However, to most eyes, *P.* 'Norfolk' is far more attractive, with dark green veins on a silvery-grey base. These colours may differ if the plant is in shade, when the veins become green. The undersides of these leaves are purple. It needs a slightly higher temperature during winter, about 15°C/59°F.

There are several other attractive pileas occasionally available, including the Black Leaf Panamiga (*Pilea repens*) with nearly oval, but slightly pear-shaped, dark green or coppery, shiny, 2.5cm/1in long, leaves with purplish undersides. *Pilea* 'Bronze', commonly known as the Pilea Silver Tree, has dull bronzy-green, oval, 7.5cm/3in long leaves, with silver centres. The undersides are red.

Pilea microphylla
Artillery Plant/Gunpowder Plant/Mossy Pilea

Height 15-23cm/6-9in
Spread 15-25cm/6-10in
Native West Indies

Pilea Norfolk

Pilea involucrata

Greenfinger Guide

Temperature W 10-13°C/50-55°F **S** 16-24°C/61-75°F

Light W Bright, indirect light. **S** Bright, indirect light.

Watering W Barely moist. **S** Water freely, but ensure good drainage.

Feeding From late spring to late summer feed every two weeks with a weak liquid fertilizer.

Humidity Stand the pot in a tray of water with pebbles in it's base.

Compost Loam-based or peat-based type.

Potting In spring, when roots fill the pot – usually every year.

Propagation 7.5cm/3in-long stem-tip cuttings in spring. Insert in equal parts moist peat and sharp sand. Place in 18-21°C/64-70°F.

The Artillery Plant differs radically from most other pileas, displaying delicate, fern-like, small, pale to mid-green leaves. From late spring to late summer it produces inconspicuous, greenish-yellow flowers

Pilea microphylla

Pilea mollis (Pilea 'Moon Valley')

which, when disturbed, puff out clouds of pollen. This very much resembles smoke coming from a gun and has given rise to one of its common names.

The size and shape of the Artillery Plant make it ideal for decorating tables and shelves, where it creates year-through interest.

Pilea mollis
Moon Valley Plant

Height 20-25cm/8-10in
Spread 20-25cm/8-10in
Native Central America

Greenfinger Guide

Temperature W 13-16°C/55-61°F **S** 16-24°C/61-75°F

Light W Bright, indirect light – avoid strong sunlight in spring. **S** Light shade. It dislikes strong sunlight.

Watering W Barely moist. **S** Water freely, but ensure good drainage.

Feeding From late spring to late summer feed every two weeks with a weak liquid fertilizer.

Humidity Stand the pot in a tray of water with pebbles in its base.

Compost Loam-based or peat-based type.

Potting In spring, when roots fill the pot – usually every year.

Propagation 7.5cm/3in-long stem-tip cuttings in spring. Insert in equal parts moist peat and sharp sand. Place in 18-21°C/64-70°F. It can also be raised from seeds sown during spring.

The Moon Valley Plant, often also known as *Pilea* 'Moon Valley' or *Pilea* crassifolia, has beautifully quilted leaves, covered with minute white hairs. The spear-shaped leaves are yellowish-green with contrasting darker green veining. When young leaves are unfurling they are almost entirely maroon, with emerald-green edges.

It is one of the most attractively-leaved foliage plants, and ideal for displaying on table or shelf.

Pilea nummulariifolia
Creeping Charlie

Height 7.5-10cm/3-4in

Spread Creeping and trailing
Native West Indies, Panama and South America

Greenfinger guide

Temperature W 13-16°C/55-61°F **S** 16-24°C/61-75°F

Light W Bright, indirect light to light shade.
S Light to medium shade.

Watering W Barely moist. **S** Water freely, but ensure good drainage.

Feeding From late spring to late summer feed every two weeks with a weak liquid fertilizer.

Humidity Mist spray leaves in summer.

Compost Loam-based or peat-based type.

Potting In spring, when roots fill the pot – usually every year.

Propagation Stems root at their leaf-joints and create new plants. In spring, remove and pot them into individual pots.

Creeping Charlie is a creeping and trailing plant, ideal for planting in indoor hanging-baskets, pots positioned in wall brackets or placed at the edges of shelves. The wiry, reddish stems bear small, rounded to heart-shaped, dark green leaves, up to 18mm/0.75in wide, with quilted surfaces.

Pilea depressa is also a trailing type, with green stems bearing circular, fleshy, all-green leaves about 6mm/0.25in long. *Pilea* 'Hanne' is another all-green type, with small, round leaves on elegant, trailing stems. It is an ideal plant for an indoor hanging-basket.

Pilea nummulariifolia

Piper ornatum

Piper ornatum
Ornamental Pepper/Celebes Pepper
Height 0.9-1.5m/3-5ft
Spread 38-45cm/15-18in
Native Celebes

Greenfinger Guide

Temperature W 16°C/61°F – it will survive temperatures down to 10°C/50°F, but this encourages leaves to fall off the plant. **S** 16-21°C/61-70°F

Light W Bright to slightly indirect light. **S** Bright light, but not direct sunlight. Good light is required to bring out the beautiful colours in the leaves. However, the leaves tend to be slightly larger when the plant is grown in shade.

Watering W Evenly moist. Do not let the compost dry out. **S** Water freely, but ensure good drainage.

Feeding From late spring to late summer feed every two weeks with a weak liquid fertilizer.

Humidity Mist spray the leaves and stems – as well as aerial roots – regularly during summer, and also in winter but less frequently, especially if the temperature falls dramatically. If the plant has been given a moss-covered pole up which to climb, mist spray this as well.

Compost Peat-based type.

Potting In spring, when roots fill the pot – usually every two years. Although this plant does not produce a large root-system, it nevertheless needs repotting when congested.

Propagation 7.5-10cm/3-4in-long stem-cuttings in early spring. Insert in equal parts moist peat and sharp sand. Place in 18°C/64°F.

The Ornamental Pepper is a very attractively-leaved climber, but it can be difficult to grow if a high temperature in winter cannot be maintained. High temperatures, a damp atmosphere and light shade all help the plant to grow and produces the best colorations in the leaves – bronze and pink.

Other Ornamental Peppers grown as houseplants include *Piper crocatum.*

Plectranthus coleoides
White-edged Candle Plant/White-edged Swedish Ivy

Height 15-25cm/6-10in
Spread 25-50cm/10-20in
Native India

Greenfinger Guide

Temperature **W** 10-13°C/50-55°F **S** 13-21°C/55-70°F

Light **W** Bright sunlight – but avoid strong and direct sunlight, especially in spring. **S** Light shade.

Watering **W** Just moist. **S** Water freely, but ensure good drainage.

Feeding From late spring to late summer feed every ten days with a weak liquid fertilizer.

Humidity Mist spray foliage during summer.

Compost Loam-based or peat-based type.

Potting In spring, when roots fill the pot – usually every two or three years.

Propagation 7.5-10cm-long stem-tip cuttings during spring. Insert in equal parts moist peat and sharp sand. Place in 16-18°C/61-64°F.

The White-edged Candle Plant is erect at first, then sprawling and trailing. The scalloped-edged, hairy-surfaced, heart-shaped leaves, 5-7.5cm/2-2½in wide, are pale green and irregularly edged with white.

Like other plectranthus plants, it is ideal for planting in indoor hanging-baskets or growing in a pot positioned at the edge of a shelf, where the stems can trail freely.

Plectranthus oertendahlii
Brazilian Coleus/Swedish Ivy/Candle Plant
Height 10-15cm/4-5in
Spread Sprawling and trailing, up to 45cm/1½ft

Plectranthus oertendahlii

Plectranthus coleoides 'Marginatus'

Native South Africa

Greenfinger Guide

Temperature **W** 10-13°C/50-55°F **S** 13-21°C/55-70°F

Light **W** Bright sunlight – avoid strong and direct sunlight in spring. **S** Light shade.

Watering **W** Just moist. **S** Water freely, but ensure good drainage.

Feeding From late spring to late summer feed every ten days with a weak liquid fertilizer.

Humidity Mist spray foliage during summer.

Compost Loam-based or peat-based type.

Potting In spring, when the roots fill the pot – usually every two or three years.

Propagation Detached rooted stems from congested plants in spring and pot up individually in small pots. Alternatively, take 7.5-10cm/3-4in-long stem-tip cuttings in spring. Insert in equal parts moist peat and sharp sand. Place in 16-18°C/61-64°F.

The Swedish Ivy is a name given to several members of the Plectranthus family. This species is ideal for planting in an indoor hanging-basket. The nearly circular, 5cm/2in wide and bronze-green leaves closely clasp the sprawling, purple stems and with maturity have pronounced silvery-white veins. The undersides of the leaves become rosy-purple. Tubular, pink-white flowers are borne in upright heads from early summer to early autumn.

Rhoeo spathacea
Boat Lily/Moses in the Cradle/Purple-leaved Spiderwort/Moses-on-a-Raft/Two Men in a Boat/Oyster Plant/Three Men in a Boat
Height 30-38cm/12-15in
Spread 30cm/12in

Greenfinger Guide

Temperature **W** 10-13°C/50-55°F – it will survive temperature down to 7°C/50°F, but if this happens ensure that the compost is kept slightly drier. **S** 16-18°C/61-64°F

Light **W** Light shade. **S** Moderate shade.

Watering **W** Evenly moist. Take care not to keep the compost too wet in winter. **S** Water freely, but ensure good drainage.

Feeding From late spring to late summer feed every two weeks with a weak liquid fertilizer.

Humidity Mist spray leaves during summer.

Compost Loam-based or peat-based type.

Potting In spring, when roots fill the pot – usually every year.

Propagation 7.5-10cm/3-4in-long basal shoots in spring. Insert in equal parts moist peat and sharp sand. Place in 16-18°C/61-64°F.

The Boat Lily forms a neat, though spiky, foliage plant

Rhoeo spathacea

that creates interest throughout the year. The long, lance-shaped leaves are glossy, dark green above and rich purple beneath, forming a rosette. Short-lived flowers – which appear at any time – grow from the leaf joints. The variegated form 'Vittata' has leaves with narrow, longitudinal stripes, and is even more beautiful.

It is an ideal houseplant for decorating a dining or coffee table, and is especially attractive when displayed in a plain white porcelain pot.

Ricinus communis
Castor Oil Plant/Palma Christi/Castor Bean/ Wonder Tree

Height 0.9-1.5m/3-5ft
Spread 38-50cm/15-20in
Native Tropical Africa

Greenfinger Guide

Temperature W 7-10°C/45-50°F to overwinter plants, but usually fresh plants are raised each year. **S** 10-13°C/50-55°F

Light W Bright light. **S** Bright, slightly diffused light.

Watering W Just moist. **S** Water moderately, keeping the compost continually moist.

Feeding From early to late summer feed every three weeks.

Humidity Mist spraying is not necessary.

Compost Loam-based or peat-based type.

Potting Throughout spring and early summer repot into a larger one as the roots fill the pot.

Propagation Sow seeds in late winter or early spring in a loam-based seed compost. Place in 21°C/70°F. Prick off into small pots when large enough to handle, and reduce the temperature to 10-13°C/50-55°F.

The Castor Oil Plant is a tender, shrubby plant usually grown as a half-hardy annual, raised from seeds sown in late winter or early spring and then discarded at the end of summer. The large, greenish-purple leaves are deeply lobed and up to 30cm/12in wide.

It is often confused with the False Castor Oil Plant, *Fatsia japonica*, which is slower growing, hardier and with greener and glossy leaves.

Saxifraga stolonifera
Mother of Thousands/Strawberry Geranium/ Pedlar's Basket/Rowing Sailor

Height 20-25cm/8-10in
Spread 25-38cm/10-12in – and trailing
Native Asia

Greenfinger Guide

Temperature W 5-10°C/41-50°F **S** 10-18°C/ 50-64°F

Light W Bright, indirect light. **S** Bright, indirect light.

Watering W Barely moist. **S** Water freely, but

ensure good drainage.

Feeding From late spring to late summer feed every three to four weeks with a weak liquid fertilizer.

Humidity Mist spray occasionally during hot summers.

Compost Loam-based or peat-based compost.

Potting In spring, when roots fill the pot – usually every other year.

Propagation In spring and early summer peg down young plantlets into pot of compost. When rooted, sever the stems.

The Mother of Thousands forms a tufted plant with mid-green, rounded leaves displaying silvery veins. The undersides of the leaves are flushed with red. This plant is well known for the long, wiry runners which bear plantlets at their tips. During mid-summer graceful spikes, up to 45cm/1½ft high, bear tiny, star-like, pink or white, flowers with yellow centres. The form

Ricinus communis

'Tricolor' is widely grown, displaying leaves variegated with white, pink and green, and with red edges. However, it is less vigorous and hardy than the normal type, and does not develop so many plantlets.

Both of these plants are ideal for growing in indoor hanging-baskets or in pots secured to wall brackets or positioned at the edges of shelves.

Schefflera arboricola
Parasol Plant/Star Leaf/Umbrella Tree

Height 1.5-1.8m/5-6ft
Spread 45-75cm/1½-2½ft
Native Southeast Asia

Greenfinger Guide

Temperature W 13-15°C/55-59°F **S** 18-24°C/

Saxifraga stolonifera

Saxifraga stolonifera 'Tricolor'

Schefflera arboricola

64-75°F

Light W Full light. **S** Light shade.

Watering W Keep the compost moderately moist.
S Water freely, but ensure good drainage.

Feeding From late spring to late summer feed
every three to four weeks.

Humidity Mist spray the leaves during summer.

Compost Loam-based type.

Potting In spring, when roots fill the pot. Topdress
with fresh compost those plants that are too large to
be repotted.

Propagation 7.5-10cm/3-4in-long cuttings in
spring. Insert in equal parts moist peat and sharp
sand. Place in 18-24°C/64-75°F.

The Parasol Plant is ideal for creating interest in a
corner, or in a warm entrance hall. Eventually its size
demands a floor-standing position, but when young a
low corner table is ideal. It can also be grouped with
other foliage plants.

The form *S. a. variegata* is beautifully variegated,
with yellow splashes on glossy green leaves. Other
forms include 'Geisha Girl' with dark green leaflets
that display rounded tips, 'Hayata' with soft green
leaflets, and 'Goldcrepella'. 'Renate' is a particularly
attractive variety, with leaves slightly divided and
lobed at their ends.

Additionally, there is a form known as Schefflera

Schefflera arboricola 'Goldcrepella'

if the temperature rises dramatically.

Compost Peat-based type.

Potting Repot in spring when roots fill the pot – usually every two years.

Propagation Divide congested plants in spring, when repotting.

Stromanthe amabilis is a neat and compact foliage plant with oval to oblong leaves up to 15cm/6in long, attractively coloured in light green with broad grey bands between the lateral veins. The undersides are greyish-green.

It is an ideal plant for displaying on a coffee table, where the leaves can be seen from above.

Other stromanthes are occasionally available, such as *Stromanthe sanguinea* which grows to 90cm/3ft or more high and produces leaves over 30cm/12in long and 12cm/4½in wide. These are dark, shining green above, with undersides wine-purple or striped with green.

Stromanthe amabilis

'Kyoto', which has finger-like, deeply split leaves with slightly frilly edges.

Schefflera venulosa is a species frequently available. It is similar to *Schefflera arboricola*, but the leaves are narrower and longer, and the whole plant has a more elegant appearance. It can grow up to 3m/10ft indoors.

Stromanthe amabilis

Height 15-23cm/6-9in
Spread 20-23cm/8-9in
Native Brazil

Greenfinger Guide

Temperature W 15-18°C/59-64°F S 18-21°C/64-70°F

Light W Diffused light – avoid strong sunlight in spring. S Light shade – strong sunlight will damage the leaves.

Watering W Evenly moist. S Evenly moist.

Feeding From late spring to late summer feed every two weeks with a weak liquid fertilizer.

Humidity Mist spray leaves in summer, especially

Syngonium podophyllum
Arrowhead Vine/Goosefoot Plant/Nephthytis/African Evergreen

Height 0.9-1.8m/3-6ft – see text
Spread 38-45cm/15-18in – then climbing
Native Central America

Greenfinger Guide

Temperature W 13-18°C/55-64°F – it prefers a temperature towards the upper end of this range. S 18-24°C/64-75°F

Light W Bright, indirect sunlight. S Bright, indirect sunlight.

Watering W Just moist. S Water freely.

Feeding From mid-spring to late summer feed every ten to fourteen days with a weak liquid fertilizer.

Humidity Mist spray leaves during summer, especially during periods of high temperatures.

Compost Loam-based or peat-based type.

Potting In spring, when roots fill the pot – usually every one or two years. Thereafter, topdress large plants in spring with fresh compost.

Syngonium podophyllum

Propagation 10-13cm/4-5in-long stem cuttings during late spring and early to mid-summer. Insert in equal parts moist peat and sharp sand. Place in 18-21°C/64-70°F.

The Arrowhead Vine is a vigorous climber that soon creates a rich array of leaves. When young, the leaves are arrow-shaped, shiny and mid to dark green. With age, they develop ear-like lobes and eventually have one large central lobe and four small other ones in pairs on either side.

Plants are usually bought when 30-45cm/12-18in high, and it is not until later, as the plant ages, that it adopts a climbing attitude.

There are several attractive forms, including 'Emerald Gem' with shiny, dark green leaves, and others with variegated leaves – 'Emerald Green', 'Imperial White' and 'Green Gold'.

Like many other climbers, it likes to climb a moss-covered pole which, when kept moist, creates the humid atmosphere in which it thrives.

Several other syngoniums are occasionally

good drainage.

Feeding From late spring to late summer feed every two to three weeks with a weak liquid fertilizer.

Humidity Mist spray the foliage in summer, especially if the temperature rises dramatically.

Compost Loam-based or peat-based type.

Potting In spring, when roots fill the pot – usually every year.

Propagation 10-13cm/4-5in-long stem-tip cuttings during spring or early summer. Insert in equal parts moist peat and sharp sand. Place in 18°C/64°F.

The Chestnut Vine is a fast-growing climber which, when given the right conditions, covers a 1.5-1.8m/5-6ft wide sun room wall in one year. It is therefore not a suitable plant for small areas. Although it may begin life in a small pot – and perhaps be only 90cm/3ft high when bought – be prepared for rapid growth. In a large pot it can be grown up a tripod of bamboo canes

Tetrastigma voinierianum

inserted into the compost. When it reaches the top, long stems are encouraged to cascade and weave among other stems.

Despite its eventual size, it is a very attractively-leaved climber, with shiny-green leaves formed of one central, somewhat spear-shaped leaflet, and four others – two on each side – arising from a central position. A fully-grown leaf – formed of five leaflets – may be 20cm/8in long and up to 25cm/10in wide.

Tolmiea menziesii
Piggy-back Plant/Pig-a-back Plant/Pickaback Plant/Youth-on-Age/Thousand Mothers

Height 15cm/6in
Spread 38cm/15in

Greenfinger Guide
Temperature W 4-7°C/39-45°F S 10-18°C/50-64°F

Light W Full light to light shade. S Light to medium shade.

Watering W Just moist. S Water freely, but ensure good drainage.

Feeding From late spring to late summer feed every three weeks with a weak liquid fertilizer.

Humidity Mist spray leaves occasionally during summer.

Compost Loam-based or peat-based type.

Potting In spring, when roots fill the pot – usually every year.

Propagation Divide large and congested plants in spring. Alternatively, in late spring or summer, cut off from the parent plant leaves that bear well-developed plantlets. Peg these leaves on top of a pot or box of compost and place in 13-15°C/55-59°F. Keep moist, and when the plantlets have rooted, pot up into loam-based compost.

The Piggy-back Plant is usually of great interest to children, who invariably are amused by the small plantlets which grow from the upper surfaces of the hairy, maple-like, mid-green leaves. The weight of the plantlets tends to produce a slight cascading effect. During mid-summer it produces red-flushed greenish-white tubular flowers on stems up to 60cm/2ft long. There is also a variegated form of this plant.

Because it is a relatively hardy plant it is ideal for positioning in a cool hall or entrance.

Tradescantia albiflora
Wandering Jew

Trailing 25-38cm/10-15in
Native Central America
Greenfinger Guide
Temperature W 7-10°C/45-50°F – temperatures can fall slightly below this range, but ensure that plants are not exposed to frost. S 10-18°C/50-64°F – avoid high temperatures.

Light W Bright, indirect light. S Bright, indirect light.

Watering W Barely moist. S Water freely, but ensure good drainage.

Feeding From late spring to late summer feed every two weeks with a weak liquid fertilizer.

Humidity Mist spray leaves in summer.

Compost Loam-based or peat-based type.

Potting In spring, when roots fill the pot – usually every year.

Tolmiea menziesii

Propagation 5-7.5cm/2-3in-long tip cuttings in summer. Insert in equal parts moist peat and sharp sand. Place in 16°C/61°F. Established plants are best discarded after two years and replaced with fresh ones.

Tradescantia albiflora is a widely-grown trailing plant, with stemless, long and oval leaves slightly shorter than those on *Tradescantia fluminensis*. The true species has shiny, plain green leaves, but invariably it is variegated forms that are widely grown. These include the popular 'Tricolor' with rosy-purple leaves that reveal white stripes, 'Aurea' displaying leaves almost entirely yellow, and 'Albovittata' with green leaves striped and edged in white.

available, including *Syngonium auritum*, commonly known as Five-fingers, which develops three to five finger-like, white-marbled leaves. *Syngonium erythrophyllum* and *S. vellozianum*, are sometimes seen, but by far the most popular one is *S. podophyllum*.

Tetrastigma voinierianum
Chestnut Vine/Lizard Plant/Javan Grape

Height 3-3.6m/10-12ft – in a pot
Spread Climber
Native Vietnam

Greenfinger Guide
Temperature W 13-15°C/55-59°F – it will survive at temperatures down to 7°C/45°F. S 15-21°C/59-70°F – avoid high and fluctuating temperatures.

Light W Full light. S Light shade or good light but not direct sunlight.

Watering W Barely moist – take care not to saturate the compost. S Water freely, but ensure

Tradescantia albiflora 'Albovittata'

Tradescantia blossfeldiana
Flowering Inch Plant

Trailing and sprawling
Native Brazil and Argentina

Greenfinger Guide

Temperature **W** 7-10°C/45-50°F. **S** 10-18°F/50-64°F.

Light **W** Bright, indirect light. **S** Bright, indirect light to light shade.

Watering **W** Barely moist. **S** Water freely, but ensure good drainage.

Feeding From late spring to late summer feed every two weeks with a weak liquid fertilizer.

Humidity Mist spray leaves in summer.

Compost Loam-based or peat-based type.

Potting In spring, when roots fill the pot – usually every year.

Propagation 5-7.5cm/2-3in-long tip cuttings in summer. Insert in equal parts moist peat and sharp sand. Place in 16°C/61°F. Established plants are best discarded after two or three years and replaced with fresh ones.

The Flowering Inch Plant is a semi-erect but mainly sprawling plant with stems that eventually trail. The fleshy stems, usually purple, bear stalkless, oblong to oval, dark green leaves with purple undersides, and are covered with minute white hairs. Mature plants often produce rose-purple, white-centred flowers from early spring to mid-summer. There is an attractive variegated form, 'Variegata', which displays leaves striped with cream. It is not quite so hardy as *Tradescantia albiflora* or *T. fluminensis*, and the temperature should not fall below the range indicated. However, it tolerates more shade.

The sprawling nature of this plant makes it ideal for setting in a cluster with other plants, where it helps to merge the display. Windowsills and bright shelves are other suitable places.

Tradescantia fluminensis
Wandering Jew/Wandering Sailor/Inch Plant

Trailing 20-30cm/8-12in – often
            slightly more

Tradescantia blossfeldiana

summer. Insert in equal parts moist peat and sharp sand. Place in 16°C/61°F. Established plants are best discarded after two years and replaced with fresh ones.

Tradescantia fluminensis is a well known trailing and sprawling plant, with fleshy stems up to 30cm/12in long and bearing oval and pointed leaves about 5cm/

Tradescantia fluminensis 'Variegata'

Native Brazil and Argentina

Greenfinger Guide

Temperature **W** 7-10°C/45-50°F – it can withstand lower temperatures, but do not expose it to frost. **S** 10-18°C/50-64°F – avoid high temperatures.

Light **W** Bright, indirect light. **S** Bright, indirect light.

Watering **W** Barely moist. **S** Water freely, but ensure good drainage.

Feeding From late spring to late summer feed every two weeks with a weak liquid fertilizer.

Humidity Mist spray leaves in summer.

Compost Loam-based or peat-based type.

Potting In spring, when roots fill the pot – usually every year.

Propagation 5-7.5cm/2-3in-long tip cuttings in

2in long. These are borne on short leaf-stalks. This species can be distinguished from *Tradescantia albiflora* by these short leaf-stalks. This latter species has leaves which arise directly from the stems.

The true species has leaves which are dark green or bluish-green, with purple undersides, but invariably it is the variegated forms that are grown: 'Variegata' has bright, fresh-green leaves with irregular white or pink-tinged stripes, while 'Quicksilver' reveals leaves striped with silver.

These plants are ideal for growing in an indoor hanging-basket or for positioning at the corner of a shelf where the stems can trail freely.

Yucca elephantipes
Spineless Yucca/Palm Lily

Height 0.9-1.8m/3-6ft
Spread 30-60cm/1-2ft
Native Mexico and Guatemala

Greenfinger Guide

Temperature W 7-10°C/45-50°F – avoid high temperatures in winter. **S** 10-18°C/50-64°F

Light W Full light. **S** Full light.

Watering W Barely moist, just enough to prevent the compost drying out. **S** Water freely, but ensure good drainage.

Feeding From late spring to late summer feed every three weeks.

Humidity Mist spray leaves in summer, especially if the temperature rises dramatically.

Compost Loam-based compost.

Potting In spring, when roots fill the pot – usually every two years. However, if the size of the plant far exceeds that of the pot, it may be necessary to repot just to create a more stable base for the plant. When the plant is in a large pot, topdress in spring, replacing the surface compost.

Propagation Sow seeds in early to mid-spring in seed compost with a little extra sharp sand. Place in 21°C/70°F. Alternatively, 10cm/4in-long stem cuttings can be taken in spring or summer, but this does mean that the original plant is ruined – although if a 154cm/6cm-high stump is left it will eventually produce shoots. Insert the 'log' cuttings about 5cm/2in into equal parts moist peat and sharp sand.

In the wild, the Spineless Yucca can reach 12m/40ft, but in a pot indoors it is more reserved and creates an interesting feature throughout the year. The long leaves have rough edges and are up to 90cm/3ft long.

It gains its common name Palm Lily from the habit of old plants of producing a cluster of leaves at the top of a bare stem.

Zebrina pendula
Silvery Inch Plant/Inch Plant/Wandering Jew

Trailing 15-30cm/6-12in
Native Mexico

Greenfinger Guide

Temperature W 7-10°C/45-50°F – it can survive temperatures down to 4°C/39°F for short periods. **S** 10-21°C/50-70°F – avoid high temperatures.

Light W Full light – avoid strong and direct sunlight, especially in spring. **S** Bright, indirect light.

Watering W Just moist. **S** Water freely, but ensure good drainage.

Feeding W From late spring to late summer feed every two weeks with a weak liquid fertilizer.

Humidity Mist spray the leaves occasionally in summer.

Compost A loam-based or peat-based type.

Potting In spring, when the roots fill the pot – usually every one or two years.

Propagation 7.5cm/3in-long stem-tip cuttings during summer. Insert in equal parts moist peat and sharp sand. Place in 16-18°C/61-64°F.

The Silvery Inch Plant is a beautiful trailing plant, with stems displaying leaves up to 7.5cm/3in long, but usually 2.5-5cm/1-2in. They are mid-green, with silvery bands along the edges and glistening surfaces.

The form 'Quadricolor' has purple-tinged green leaves, banded with creamy-white and often with pinkish stripes edged in purple. However, it does need a slightly higher winter temperature – minimum of 13°C/55°F. Pinch out the growing tips several times when plants are young to encourage bushiness.

It is best grown in an indoor hanging-basket or a pot positioned at the edge of a high shelf.

Yucca elephantipes

Zebrina pendula

cacti & succulents

Agave americana 'Variegata'

Agave americana
Century Plant/Maguey/American Aloe
Height 45-75cm/1½-2½ft
Spread 38-45cm/15-18in
Native Mexico

Greenfinger Guide

***Temperature* W** 7-10°C/45-50°F – it survives temperatures down to 5°C/41°F, but avoid exposing it to frost. **S** 10-16°C/50-61°F

***Light* W** Full light **S** Full light

***Watering* W** Just moist **S** Water freely, but ensure good drainage

Feeding From mid-spring to the onset of late summer feed every week with a weak liquid fertilizer.

Humidity Mist spraying is not necessary.

Compost Four parts loam-based potting compost No. 2, two or moist peat and three of sharp grit. Alternatively, use two parts peat-based compost and one of sharp grit.

Potting In spring, when roots fill the pot – usually every year, especially when young.

Propagation Remove offsets in spring, allow to dry for several days and then pot up into small pots. Place in 15°C/59°F and slight shade until established.

The Century Plant is a fast-growing succulent plant that is ideal for cool rooms. During summer it can be placed outside on a sheltered patio. It forms a rosette of thick, sword-shaped and saw-edged, grey-green leaves, each tipped with a sharp, black spike.
This plant gains its common name from the fallacy that it would not flower until one-hundred years old. In fact, it will flower within fifteen years, but by then the plant will be far too large for growing indoors. After flowering the rosette dies.
Several attractive forms are grown, the most common one being 'Marginata' with yellow edges to the leaves. *Agave americana striata* is similar, with

***Temperature* W** 7-10°C/45-50°F – it survives temperatures down to 5°C/41°F, but avoid exposing it to frost. **S** 10-16°C/50-61°F

***Light* W** Full light **S** Full light

***Watering* W** Barely moist **S** Water freely, but ensure good drainage and do not keep the compost continually moist.

Feeding From mid-spring to the onset of late summer feed every week with a weak liquid fertilizer.

Humidity Mist spraying is not necessary.

Compost Four parts loam-based potting compost No. 2, two of moist peat and three of sharp sand. Alternatively, use two parts peat-based compost and one of sharp grit.

Potting In spring, when roots fill the pot – usually every year.

Propagation Remove offsets in spring, allow to dry for several days and then pot up into small pots. Place in 15°C/59°F and slight shade until roots form.

The Thread Agave derives its common name from the white threads which grow along the edges of the dark green, leathery leaves. Each leaf has two or three white lines on the top surface, and a sharp spine at its tip. Eventually, the rosette of leaves develops a stem about 2.4m/8ft long, bearing a flower spike some 1.5m/5ft

Agave filifera

white and yellow stripes, while *A. a. mediopicta* has cream leaves edged in green.

Agave filifera
Thread Agave
Height 23-38cm/9-15in
Spread 15-23cm/6-9in
Native Mexico

Greenfinger Guide

long and formed of purple and green bell-like flowers. However, the plant is mainly grown for the attractive rosette of leaves.
Avoid high temperatures in winter. A sunny patio or verandah creates an ideal summer home for this agave.

Agave victoriae-reginae
Height 13-23cm/5-9in

Agave victoriae-reginae

Spread 13-20cm/5-8in
Native Mexico

Greenfinger Guide
Temperature W 10°C/50°F – it survives
temperatures down to 5°C/41°F, but avoid lower
ones. **S** 10-18°C/50-64°F

Light W Full light **S** Full light

Watering W Barely moist **S** Water freely, but
ensure good drainage and do not keep the compost
continually moist.

Feeding From mid-spring to the onset of late
summer feed every week with a weak liquid
fertilizer.

Humidity Mist spraying is not necessary.

Compost Four parts loam-based potting compost
No. 2, two of moist peat and three of sharp grit.
Alternatively, use two parts peat-based compost and
one of sharp grit.

Potting In spring, when roots fill the pot – usually
every year.

Propagation This species does not produce offsets
and so cannot be increased in the same manner.
Instead, sow seeds in spring and place them in 24-
27°C/75-80°F.

Agave victoriae-reginae is perhaps the most popular
of all agaves. It forms a neat rosette of 15cm/6in long,
dark green leaves with beautiful, irregular, white
markings. Each leaf is keeled, with a spine at its tip.
Plants do not generally flower until at least ten years
old, then developing cream flowers on stems over 3m/
10ft long. The rosette then dies.

Aloe variegata
**Partridge-breasted Aloe/Tiger Aloe/Pheasant's
Wings/Kanniedood Aloe**

Height 10-15cm/4-6in
Spread 10-13cm/4-5in
Native Cape Province

Greenfinger Guide
Temperature W 5-7°C/41-45°F **S** 7-13°C/45-55°F

Light W Full light **S** Full light and sunny

Watering W Just damp **S** Water regularly, but
allow the compost to practically dry out between
applications.

Feeding From mid-spring to the onset of late
summer feed every week with a weak liquid
fertilizer.

Humidity No mist spraying required.

Compost Four parts loam-based potting compost,
two of moist peat and three of sharp sand.
Alternatively, use two parts peat-based compost and
one of sharp grit.

Potting In spring, when roots fill the pot – usually
every year.

Propagation Remove offsets during late spring,
leave to dry for a couple of days and then repot to
exactly the same depth as before. Alternatively, sow
seeds in early spring. Place in 24-27°C/75-80°F.

The Partridge-breasted Aloe is ideal for creating year-
through colour and interest on window-sills. It has
distinctively shaped, dark green leaves with irregular
cross-banding and blotching in white. The somewhat
triangular, stiff, leaves are keeled and arise in
overlapping ranks. During spring it develops orange
flowers on stems about 25cm/10in long.

Aporocactus flagelliformis
Rat's Tail Cactus/Rattail Cactos

Height 5-7.5cm/2-3in
Spread Stems trailing to 90cm/3ft
Native Mexico

Greenfinger Guide
Temperature W 7-10°C/45-50°F **S** 10-18°C/
50-64°F

Aloe variegata

Light W Full sun **S** Bright, indirect light

Watering W Keep barely moist **S** Water freely,
but ensure good drainage.

Feeding From when the buds reveal colour to the
onset of late summer feed with a high potash
fertilizer every week.

Humidity Mist spraying is not necessary.

Compost Four parts loam-based potting compost,
two of moist peat and three of sharp grit.
Alternatively, use two parts peat-based compost and
one of sharp grit.

Potting In spring, when roots fill the container –
usually every year.

Propagation 7.5cm/3in long stem cuttings during
early and mid-summer. Allow the cuttings to dry
for several days and insert them 2.5cm/1in deep in a
mixture of one part moist peat and two parts sharp
sand. Place in 21°C/70°F. Alternatively, in late
winter or early spring sow seeds in the same
compost, and place in 24-27°C/75-80°F.

The Rat's Tail Cactus is a spectacular cactus for an
indoor hanging-basket or in a pot positioned at the
edge of a high shelf so that the long, 12mm/½in wide
stems can trail freely and reveal their funnel-shaped,
magenta flowers during mid and late spring. Individual
flowers only last for a few days, but are soon replaced
by other ones.

Growing this cactus in an indoor hanging-basket

Aporocactus flagelliformis

has the advantage of enabling excess water to rapidly drain from the container – but ensure that it is fitted with a drip-tray. Plants are soon killed if water rests around their roots.

Aporocactus mallisonii, properly but infrequently called X *Heliaporus smithii*, is a cross between the Rat's Tail Cactus and *Heliocereus speciosus*. During spring it bears masses of fiery-red, funnel-shaped flowers up to 7.5cm/3in long. Twenty or more flowers may appear on each stem, which is shorter and stiffer than those produced by the Rat's Tail Cactus.

Astrophytum asterias
Sea Urchin Cactus/Sand Dollar Cactus/Silver Dollar/Sand Dollar

Height 25-30mm/1-1.25in
Spread 6-8cm/2½-3½in
Native Mexico

Greenfinger Guide

Temperature W 5-10°C/41-50°F – do not allow the temperature to fall below the minimum recommended figure. **S** 10-21°C/50-70°F

Light W Full light **S** Full light

Watering W Keep the compost completely dry. **S** Water thoroughly, whenever the compost becomes dry. And ensure good drainage.

Feeding From when the buds reveal colour to the onset of late summer, feed every week with a weak liquid fertilizer.

Humidity Mist spraying is not necessary.

Compost Four parts loam-based potting compost, two of moist peat and three of sharp grit. Alternatively, use two parts peat-based compost and one of sharp grit.

Potting In spring, when roots fill the pot – usually every two or three years.

Propagation Sow seeds in spring in a sandy compost and place in 24-27°C/75-80°F. This species does not produce offsets, and therefore is normally increased from seeds.

The Sea Urchin Cactus is very distinctive, forming a grey-green, flattened hemisphere covered with white spots and revealing eight spineless ribs. From early to mid summer it produces pale, shiny yellow, sweetly-scented flowers, up to 30mm/1½in wide, with red throats.

It is ideal for growing on a warm, sunny windowsill, which encourages the development of flowers.

Astrophytum capricorne
Goat's Horn Cactus

Height 15-25cm/6-10in
Spread 7.5-13cm/3-5in
Native Mexico

Greenfinger Guide

Temperature W 5-10°C/45-50°F **S** 10-21°C/50-70°F

Light W Full light **S** Full light

Watering W Keep the compost completely dry. **S** Water thoroughly, whenever the compost becomes dry. And ensure good drainage.

Feeding From when the buds reveal colour to the onset of late summer, feed every week with a weak liquid fertilizer.

Humidity Mist spraying is not necessary.

Compost Four parts loam-based potting compost, two of moist peat and three of sharp grit. Alternatively, use two parts peat-based compost and and one of sharp grit.

Potting In spring, when the roots fill the pot – usually every two years.

Propagation Sow seeds in spring in a sandy compost and place in 24-27°C/75-80°F. Alternatively, remove offsets in early summer and insert in a sandy compost.

The Goat's Horn Cactus is initially globular but with age becomes cylindrical. The body is light green with seven or eight prominent ribs from which develop curved, brownish-black spines that have gained the plant its common name. The body of the plant is also dappled with white, flaky scales. From early to mid summer it displays 5cm/2in wide yellow flowers with reddish centres.

Like all other plants in this genus it needs a warm, sunny windowsill, and has the advantage of even young plants producing flowers.

Astrophytum asterias

Arophytum myriostigma
Bishop's Cap Cactus/Bishop's Hood/ Monkshood

Height 15-20cm/6-8in
Spread 15-20cm/6-8in
Native Mexico

Greenfinger Guide

Temperature W 5-10°C/45-50°F – do not allow the temperature to fall below the minimum recommended figure. S 10-21°C/50-70°F

Light W Full light S Full light

Watering W Keep the compost completely dry. S Water thoroughly, whenever the compost becomes dry. And ensure good drainage.

Feeding From when the buds reveal colour to the onset of late summer, feed every week with a weak liquid fertilizer.

Humidity Mist spraying is not necessary.

Compost Four part loam-based potting compost,two of moist peat and three of sharp grit. Alternatively, use two parts peat-based compost and one of sharp grit.

Potting In spring, when roots fill the pot – usually every two years.

Propagation Sow seeds in spring in a sandy compost and place in 24-27°C/75-80°F. Old plants sometimes produce offsets. Removethese in early summer and pot up into a sandy compost. When

Astrophytum capricorne

Astrophytum myriostigma

rooted, after about two months, pot up into the normal compost.

The Bishop's Cap Cactus when young is globular, but with age becomes cylindrical. The dark green, almost grey, surface is covered with silvery scales, with five or six prominent ribs running up its body. From early to mid-summer it bears sweetly scented yellow flowers, up to 36mm/1½in wide, with reddish throats.

The Bishop's Mitre Cactus (*A. m. quadricostatum*) is similar, but distinguished by having only four ribs running up its body.

These are two highly attractive cacti for displaying on windowsills, and have the advantage of flowering at an early age.

There are several other forms of this popular cactus, including 'Nudum', which is illustrated here.

Cephalocereus senilis
Old Man Cactus

Height 20-60cm/8-24in
Spread 7.5-15cm/3-6in
Native Mexico

Greenfinger Guide

Temperature W 7-10°C/45-50°F S 10-24°C/ 50-75°F

Light W Full light S Full light

Watering W Keep the compost dry S Water thoroughly whenever the compost dries out, but do not keep continually wet. And ensure good drainage.

Feeding From late spring to the onset of late summer, feed every week with a weak liquid fertilizer.

Cephalocereus senilis

Humidity Mist spraying is not necessary.

Compost Four parts loam-based potting compost, two of moist peat and three of sharp grit. Alternatively, use two parts peat-based compost and one of sharp grit.

Potting In spring, when roots fill the pot – usually every one or two years when young but less frequently with age.

Propagation As the plant ages, the attractiveness of the lower part decreases. Cut off the top of an unsightly plant and after allowing it to dry for a few days pot up in sandy compost.

The Old Man Cactus grows to about 12m/40ft high and 45cm/1½ft wide and lives for up to 200 years in its native country. As a houseplant, however, it is a little less vigorous and when young forms an attractive plant. It is grown for its pale green stem and yellow spines which become completely hidden by long white hairs which have the appearance of an old man's beard.

The flowers are white, but these do not usually appear on plants under 6m/20ft high.

Cereus peruvianus
Column Cactus/Peruvian Apple/Apple Cactus/ Peruvian Apple Cactus

Height 60-90cm/2-3ft
Spread 7.5-15cm/3-6in
Native Brazil and Argentina

Greenfinger Guide
Temperature W 5-7°C/41-45°F S 10-24°C/

50-75°F

Light W Full light S Full light

Watering W Keep dry S Water freely whenever the compost dries out, and ensure good drainage.

Feeding From late spring to the onset of late summer feed every week with a weak liquid fertilizer.

Humidity Mist spraying is not necessary.

Compost Four parts loam-based potting compost, two of moist peat and three of sharp grit. Alternatively, use two parts peat-based compost and one of sharp grit.

Potting In early spring, when roots fill the pot – usually every year.

Propagation Plants grow rapidly and often become too large for homes. They can either be placed in a conservatory or decapitated to produce a more manageable plant. In early summer, cut off the top 25-38m/10-15in, allow it to dry for a week and then pot up into a sandy compost. Alternatively, sow seeds in spring in a sandy compost and place in 24-27°C/75-80°F.

The Column Cactus is a rapidly-growing, columnar cactus that soon grows 1.8m/6ft high – in the wild it reaches 9m/30ft or more. It forms a bluish-green column, ribbed and with stout, brown spines. Eventually it bears large, white, funnel-shaped, 5-7.5cm/2-3in wide, scented flowers that open at night.

When young it is ideal for growing on a windowsill, but eventually it needs a floor-standing position, preferably near a patio window, or a sunny area in a sun-room.

An unusual form of this species has large and distorted branched stems with irregular ribs, and is known as *C. peruvianus monstrosus*.

There are several other cacti in this genus which are widely grown indoors. These include *Cereus jamacaru*, 60-90cm/2-3ft high, deeply ribbed and bearing a similarity to *Cereus peruvianus*. The spines are yellow and white.

Cereus chalybaeus, from Argentina where it grows up to 3m/10ft tall, bears white flowers. *Cereus coerulescens*, again from Argentina, grows 60-90cm/ 2-3ft high in cultivation, with deep bluish-green stems which eventually become green. As a bonus it produces 20cm/8in long, rose or white flowers.

Ceropegia woodii
Rosary Vine/String of Hearts/Chinese Lantern Plant/Hearts Entangled/Hearts on a String/Heart Vine

Height 2.5-5cm/1-2in
Spread Trailing stems up to 90cm/3ft long
Native Natal

Greenfinger Guide
Temperature W 10-13°C/50-55°F S 13-20°C/ 55-68°F

Light W Full light S Indirect light to full light

Watering W Just moist S Water freely, but ensure good drainage and avoid keeping the compost constantly saturated.

Feeding From mid spring to the onset of late

Cereus peruvianus

summer feed every week with a weak liquid fertilizer.

Humidity Mist spraying is not necessary.

Compost Four parts loam-based potting compost, two of moist peat and three of sharp grit. Alternatively, use two parts peat-based compost and one of sharp grit.

Potting In spring, when roots fill the container – usually every two years.

Propagation Plants develop large tubers which frequently have tiny tubers at their ends. Remove these in spring, complete with a segment of stem, and pot up.

The Rosary Vine is usually grown in an indoor hanging-basket, so that the stems can trail freely. Alternatively, grow in a pot positioned at the edge of a high shelf. Dark green, heart-shaped leaves, about 18mm/½in long and marbled with silvery blotches, sparsely cluster along the purple, wire-like trailing stems.

Chamaecereus silvestrii
Peanut Cactus

Height 10-15cm/4-6in
Spread 13-15cm/5-6in – then slightly spreading
Native Argentina

Greenfinger Guide

Temperature W 2-7°C/36-45°F – it survives low temperatures, but if given the lower temperature suggested here (if even slightly lower) the compost must be kept dry. Avoid high temperatures in winter, as these discourage the formation of flower buds. **S** 10-27°C/50-80°F.

Light W Full sun **S** Full sun

Watering W Keep dry, especially if the temperature falls dramatically. **S** Water freely, but ensure good drainage.

Feeding From late spring to the onset of late summer feed every week with a weak liquid fertilizer.

Humidity Mist spraying is not necessary.

Compost Four parts loam-based potting compost, two of moist peat and three of sharp grit. Alternatively, use two parts peat-based compost and one of sharp grit.

Potting In spring, when roots fill the pot.

Propagation The plant is formed of short pieces of stem which can be easily removed and inserted into a sandy compost, where they readily root.

The Peanut Cactus is one of the most widely grown cactus – and one of the hardiest of all cacti. The finger-like green stems eventually create a sprawling plant which produces a profusion of brilliant scarlet flowers,

Ceropegia woodii

Chamaecereus silvestrii

Cotyledon orbiculata

often more than 3.6cm/1½in wide, during spring and summer.

If you tend to neglect watering plants in winter, and have a cool windowsill, then this cactus will suit you well.

There has been a great deal of cross-pollination between lobivias and chamaecereus, resulting in several superb plants, many small but with superb flowers.

Cotyledon orbiculata
Pig's Ears

Height 60-90cm/2-3ft
Spread 38-60cm/15-24in
Native Natal, Namibia and South Africa

Greenfinger Guide

Temperature W 10-13°C/50-55°F – it will quite happily survive temperatures down to 5°C/41°F if the compost is kept dry. S 13-21°C/55-70°F.

Light W Full light S Full light

Watering W Slightly moist – if the temperature is towards the lower end of that recommended, keep the compost barely moist. S Water freely, but ensure good drainage and allow the compost to become dry between waterings.

Feeding From late spring to the onset of late summer feed every week with a weak liquid fertilizer.

Humidity Mist spraying is not necessary.

Compost Four parts loam-based potting compost, two of moist peat and three of sharp grit.
Alternatively, use two parts peat-based compost and one of sharp grit.

Potting In spring, when roots fill the pot – usually every two or three years.

Propagation Remove one or two fleshy leaves in spring or early summer, allow the cut surfaces to dry and insert in sandy compost. Place in 16°C/61°F. Alternatively, sow seeds in spring in equal parts loam-based seed compost and sharp sand, and place in 24-27°C/75-80°F.

The Pig's Ears is an evergreen, shrubby and well-branched succulent plant with large, silvery-grey and red-edged, 13cm/5in long and 5-7.5cm/2-3in wide leaves, mainly towards the tips of the branches. During mid-summer it produces yellow and red tubular flowers. When young, this succulent plant can be grown in a pot indoors, but eventually it needs a large pot in a sun-room or greenhouse.

Several forms of the plant are grown, including the diminutive *C. o. dinteri* with almost cylindrical leaves up to 15cm/6in tall and with a 20-30cm/8-12in spread. Its rounded, 2.5-5cm/1-2in long leaves have blunt, tooth-shaped indentations at their tips. They are dark green, fleshy, slightly sticky and covered with tiny white hairs. *Cotyledon teretifolia*, from Southern Africa, is 10-15cm/4-6in high and wide, with glaucous-green leaves displaying a groove on the upper surface. Tubular, yellow flowers appear during winter.

There are a few deciduous species which are occasionally available, including *Cotyledon paniculata*

with 2.5cm/1in long, narrowly spoon-shaped, light green leaves.

Crassula falcata
Airplane Propeller Plant/Propeller Plant/Scarlet Paint Brushes/Sickle Plant/Airplane Plant

Height 38-60cm/15-24in
Spread 23-30cm/9-12in
Native Cape Province

Greenfinger Guide

Temperature W 7-13°C/45-55°F – it survives temperatures down to 5°C/41°F, but keep the compost drier. S 13-21°C/55-70°F

Light W Full light S Full light

Watering W Barely moist, but do not allow the compost to dry out. S Water freely, but ensure good drainage.

Feeding From late spring to the onset of late summer feed every week with a weak liquid fertilizer.

Humidity Mist spraying is not necessary.

Compost Four parts loam-based potting compost, two of moist peat and three of sharp grit.
Alternatively, use two parts peat-based compost and one of sharp grit.

Potting In spring, when the roots fill the pot – usually every two years.

Propagation Leaf-cuttings in spring. Remove

Crassula falcata

entire leaves and insert in a sandy compost. Place in 21°C/21°F. Also, sow seeds in spring in John Innes potting compost, and place in 24-27°C/75-80°F.

The Airplane Propeller Plant is a shrubby evergreen plant with stout and thickened fleshy stems and blue-green, fleshy, pointed leaves. It is the 7.5cm/3in wide, clustered, orange-red flowers during mid and late summer that give the plant its common name. From above they have the appearance of airplane propellers.

When young it can be grown indoors, although to keep it to a manageable size as a houseplant it needs to be trimmed in late spring. It then will grow 30-38cm/12-15in high.

Echeveria agavoides
Moulded Wax

Height 7.5-10cm/3-4in
Spread 13-20cm/5-8in
Native Mexico

Greenfinger Guide

Temperature W 5-7°C/41-45°F – avoid high temperatures in winter. S 10-21°C/50-70°F

Light W Full light S Full light

Watering W Just moist S Water freely, but ensure good drainage.

Feeding From late spring to the onset of late summer feed every week with a weak liquid fertilizer.

Echeveria agavoides

Humidity Mist spraying is not necessary.

Compost Four parts loam-based potting compost, two of moist peat and three of sharp grit. Alternatively, use two parts peat-based compost and one of sharp grit.

Potting In spring, when roots fill the pot – usually every year.

Propagation Take leaf-cuttings in late spring or early summer and insert in sandy compost. Place in

15-18°C/59-64°F.

The Moulded Wax has rosettes formed of 3.6-13cm/1½-5in long, spine-tipped, stiff green leaves with brownish-red tips. It does, as its name suggests, resemble a small agave. Occasionally, large plants develop reddish flowers with yellow tips, rather sparsely and on stems 20cm/8in or more tall. There is an attractive cristate variety – 'Cristata' – which is well-worth growing.

Echeveria agavoides 'Cristata'

Echeveria derenbergii
Painted Lady/Baby Echeveria

Height 5-7.5cm/2-3in
Spread 7.5-13cm/3-5in
Native Mexico

Greenfinger Guide

Temperature **W** 5-7°C/41-45°F – avoid high temperatures in winter. **S** 10-21°C/50-70°F

Light **W** Full light **S** Full light

Watering **W** Barely moist **S** Water freely, but ensure good drainage.

Feeding From late spring to the onset of late summer feed every week with a weak liquid fertilizer.

Humidity Mist spraying is not necessary.

Compost Four parts loam-based potting compost, two of moist peat and three of sharp grit. Alternatively, use two parts peat-based compost and one of sharp grit.

Potting In spring, when roots fill the pot – usually every year.

Propagation Take leaf-cuttings in late spring or early summer and insert in sandy compost. Place in 15-18°C/59-64°F. The freely produced offsets can be removed in spring, the cut-surfaces allowed to dry and then potted into sandy compost. Offsets

Echeveria derenbergii

take two to three weeks to develop roots.

The Painted Lady is ideal for growing on a sunny windowsill, as well as in a sun-roomEcheveria derenber or greenhouse. It creates a small, leafy, stemless rosette of grey-green leaves that are covered with an attractive white bloom. Part of its attraction is that it forms a cushion, with freely-developing offsets. During mid-summer orange-yellow, bell-shaped flowers are borne on stems up to 7.5cm/3in high.

Echeveria gibbiflora

Height 60cm/2ft
Spread 38-45cm/15-18in
Native Mexico

Greenfinger Guide

Temperature **W** 5-7°C/41-45°F – avoid high temperatures in winter. **S** 10-21°C/50-70°F

Light **W** Full light **S** Full light

Watering **W** Just moist **S** Water freely, but ensure good drainage.

Feeding From late spring to the onset of late summer feed every week with a weak liquid fertilizer.

Humidity Mist spraying is not needed. Indeed, keep water away from the leaves.

Compost Four parts loam-based potting compost, two of moist peat and three of sharp grit. Alternatively, use two parts peat-based compost and one of sharp grit.

Potting In spring, when the roots fill the pot – usually every year.

Propagation Take leaf-cuttings in spring, insert in sandy compost and place in 15-18°C/59-64°F. This often ruins the shape of good specimens, although if the plant has already lost many of its lower leaves this is not a problem. If plants have lost most of their lower leaves cut the plant down in spring, and use shoots which develop from the old base as cuttings.

Echeveria gibbiflora is one of the taller-growing echeverias, with a shrubby nature and stems bearing long, fleshy, spoon-shaped, slightly concave, grey-

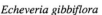

Echeveria gibbiflora

Echeveria harmsii

green leaves up to 25cm/10in long. Red and yellow flowers on tall stems are borne in autumn.

The form 'Carunculata' is widely grown and bears lavender-pink leaves with bluish-green bumps on their upper surfaces. Young plants do not have these protuberances.

Echeveria harmsii
Mexican Snowball/Red Echeveria

Height 25-50cm/10-20in
Spread 25-45cm/10-18in
Native Mexico

Greenfinger Guide

Temperature W 5-7°C/41-45°F – avoid high temperatures in winter. S 10-21°C/50-70°F

Light W Full light S Full light

Watering W Just moist S Water freely, but ensure gooddrainage.

Feeding From late spring to the onset of late summer feed every week with a weak liquid fertilizer.

Humidity Mist spraying is not necessary.

Compost Four parts loam-based potting compost, two of moist peat and three of sharp grit. Alternatively, use two parts peat-based compost and one of sharp grit.

Potting In spring, when roots fill the pot – usually every year.

Propagation Take leaf-cuttings in late spring or early summer and insert in sandy compost. Place in 15-18°C/59-64°F.

The Mexican Snowball is an interesting succulent, forming a branching shrub with lance-shaped, mid-green leaves which form large, loose rosettes. In early summer it produces small clusters of 2.5cm/1in long, slightly bell-shaped, scarlet flowers with yellow tips.

There are many other interesting and colourful echeverias which can be grown as houseplants, including *Echeveria ciliata*, which is illustrated here. Others include *Echeveria hoveyii* with loosely clustered rosettes formed of greyish-green leaves with cream and pink stripes. *Echeveria runyonii*, from Mexico, is

diminutive at 7.5cm/3in high, forming flattened rosettes of spoon-shaped leaves covered with white hairs. It has the bonus of producing white flowers in late summer *Echeveria tolucensis*, often listed as a variety of *Echeveria secunda*, is another variety illustrated here.

Echeveria setosa

Echeveria setosa
Firecracker Plant/Mexican Firecracker

Height 7.5-10cm/3-4in
Spread 10-13cm/4-5in
Native Mexico

Greenfinger Guide

Temperature W 5-7°C/41-45°F – avoid high temperatures in winter. S 10-21°C/50-70°F

Light W Full light S Full light

Watering W Just moist S Water freely, but ensure good drainage.

Feeding From late spring to the onset of late summer feed every week with a weak liquid fertilizer.

Humidity Mist spraying is not necessary.

Compost Four parts loam-based potting compost, two of moist peat and three of sharp grit. Alternatively, use two parts peat-based compost and one of sharp grit.

Potting In spring, when roots fill the pot – usually every year.

Propagation Take leaf-cuttings in late spring or early summer and insert in sandy compost. Place in 15-18°C/59-64°F.

The Firecracker Plant is an easy-to-grow, stemless succulent plant which forms a compact rosette of dark-green leaves densely covered with white hairs. During late spring it develops orange flowers on stems up to 10cm/4in high.

The lower leaves of the rosette are in close contact with the compost. If any show signs of decay or shrivelling they should be removed immediately. If left, they encourage the presence of diseases.

Echinocactus grusonii

Echinocereus cinerascens

Echinocactus grusonii

Golden Barrel Cactus/Barrel Cactus/Golden Ball Cactus/Golden Ball

Height 10-15cm/4-6in – eventually to 90cm/3ft
Spread 13-15cm/5-6in – eventually to 30cm/1ft
Native Mexico

Greenfinger Guide

Temperature W 7-10°C/45-50°F – it survives temperatures down to 5°C/41°F, but keep the compost dry. **S** 10-27°C/50-80°F

Light W Full light **S** Full light

Watering W Keep dry **S** Water freely, but ensure good drainage.

Feeding From late spring to the onset of late summer feed every week with a weak liquid fertilizer.

Humidity Mist spraying is not necessary.

Compost Four parts loam-based potting compost, two of moist peat and three of sharp grit. Alternatively, use two parts peat-based compost and one of sharp grit.

Potting In spring, when the roots fill the pot – usually every year.

Propagation Sow seeds in spring in a sandy compost, and place in 24-27°C/75-80°F.

The Golden Barrel Cactus is grown for its attractive barrel-shape which is covered with pale golden-yellow, awl-shaped spines. Small yellow flowers appear on very large plants in very sunny positions.

It is essential to give it full sunlight, and either a position on a south-facing window-sill or in a conservatory is ideal. Most plants seldom exceed 15cm/6in wide, but in the wild a width of 90cm/3ft is quite common.

Most specimens of this plant when sold are less than 10cm/4in wide, although occasionally specimens 20cm/8in or more wide are available.

Echinocereus pentalophus

Height 10-15cm/4-6in
Spread 2.5cm/1in – but forms a sprawling clump
Native Mexico

Echinocereus pentalophus

Greenfinger Guide

Temperature W 5-7°C/41-45°F – do not allow the temperature to rise above these figures, and preferably keep to the lower end of this range. **S** 13-21°C/55-70°F

Light W Full light **S** Full light

Watering W Keep dry **S** Water freely, but ensure good drainage. Allow the compost to dry out between waterings.

Feeding From late spring to the onset of late summer feed every week with a weak liquid fertilizer.

Humidity Mist spraying is not necessary.

Compost Four parts loam-based potting compost, two of moist peat and three of sharp grit. Alternatively, use two parts peat-based compost and one of sharp grit.

Potting In spring, when the roots fill the pot – usually every two years.

Propagation Sow seeds in early spring in loam-based seed compost, and place in 24-27°C/75-80°F.

Echinocereus pentalophus is a rapid-growing, sprawling cactus with a branching habit to its five-ribbed green stems. Bell-shaped, reddish-purple flowers up to 10cm/4in long are borne in mid-summer.

A warm, sunny, south or west-facing window-sill creates a good place for it.

In addition to this species and the ones described earlier, there are many other echinocereus species widely grown and available. These include

Echinocereus cinerascens with 7.5cm/3in long rose-purple flowers, and E. scheerii with rosy-red flowers.

Echinopsis 'Green Gold'
Echinopsis 'Green Gold'

Height 7.5-15cm/3-6in
Spread 7.5-13cm/3-5in
Native Hybrid

Greenfinger Guide

Temperature W 2-5°C/36-41°F – do not subject the plants to high temperatures, as they need a cool period in winter to ensure they flower well during summer. S 10-21°C/50-70°F

Light W Full light S Full light

Watering W Keep dry S Water freely, but ensure good drainage and allow the compost to become dry between waterings.

Feeding From late spring to late summer feed every week. Use a high potash fertilizer once the flower buds are forming.

Humidity Mist spraying is not necessary.

Compost Four parts loam-based potting compost, two of moist peat and three of sharp grit. Alternatively, use two parts peat-based compost and one of sharp grit.

Potting In spring, when roots fill the pot – usually every one or two years, especially when young.

Propagation This echinopsis is easily increased in spring or early summer by removing offsets, allow the cut surfaces to dry for a few days and then potting them into the usual compost. Take care not to excessively water them during the period in which they are forming roots, as this encourages the onset of decay in the offsets.

This well-known hybrid forms a mid-green, globular body with about twelve ribs. During summer it produces 10cm/4in long, golden-yellow flowers on stems which bear them well above the plant's body.

There are many other bright and colourful hybrids now widely available. These include 'Bridal Pink', 'Fluffy Ruffles', 'Gay Blaze', 'Gay Firecracker', 'Gay

Echinocereus scheerii

Echinopsis 'Green Gold'

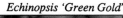

Echinopsis 'Fluffy Ruffles'

Echinopsis 'Gay Stripes'

Echinopsis 'Bridal Pink' and Echinopsis 'Gay Blaze'

Echinopsis 'Gay Firecracker'
Echinopsis 'Gay Morning Mid-pink'

Echinopsis 'Huasha Hybrid'

Morning Mid-pink', 'Gay Stripes' and 'Huasha Hybrid'. All of these are illustrated here.

Ephiphyllum 'Ackermannii'
Orchid Cactus/Pond Lily Cactus

Height 60-75cm/2-2½ft
Spread 30-45cm/1-1½ft
Native Hybrid

Greenfinger Guide

196

Temperature W 10°C/50°F – from early winter to late winter. Take care not to exceed this temperature. From late summer to early winter maintain at 10-13°C/50-55°F, and from late winter to mid-spring also keep at 13°C/55°F. These plants will survive temperatures down to 5°C/41°F, but if this happens they do not flower so well.
S 13-21°C/55-70°F – from mid-spring to late summer.

Light W Bright but diffused sunlight **S** Place on an east-facing windowsill, so that they receive bright but diffused light.

Watering W Lightly moist – never allow the compost to dry out – from early winter to late winter. From late summer to early winter keep the compost moist, watering whenever the compost dries out. From late winter to mid-spring slowly increase the amount of water, thoroughly saturating the compost whenever it dries out. **S** From the mid-spring to late summer keep the compost moist, but never waterlogged. Take care not to allow the compost to dry out when the plants are flowering.

Feeding From when the flower buds start to form to when the last flower fades, feed every week with a weak, high-potash, liquid fertilizer.

Humidity Mist spray the leaves in summer, but avoid splashing the flowers.

Compost Four parts loam-based potting compost, two of moist peat and three of sharp grit. Alternatively, use two parts peat-based compost and one of sharp grit.

Potting Epiphyllums are encouraged to flower by keeping them in the same pot for several years.

However, every two or three years repot them slightly after the last flower fades. Sometimes, stems at the top of the plant may be shrivelled, and these can then be cut back to a leaf-joint. The stems which are cut off can be used as cuttings.

Propagation Many epiphyllums can be raised by sowing seeds in spring and placing them in 24-27°C/75-80°F. Hybrids, however, cannot be raised in this way as the plants they then produce are not like the parents. Therefore, they are invariably raised from cuttings. During mid-summer, take 13-15cm/5-6in long stem cuttings. Allow the surfaces to dry for a few days and then pot them into equal parts loam-based compost and sharp sand. Place in 21°C/70°F. Keep the compost moist, and position the plant in light shade. Do not cover with a plastic bag, as they need fresh air. When rooted – usually after about three weeks – pot up and care for in the same manner as established plants.

Epiphyllums are forest-type cacti, in the wild growing in tropical forests in Central America. They grow attached to trees, in total contrast to desert cacti which grow at ground level in dry and arid conditions. Because the desert cacti grow at ground-level and need protection they are covered with spines. Forest cacti, however, usually grow from trees and do not have spines. The Rat's Tail Cactus (*Aporocactus flagelliformis*) is an exception: it has long, spine-covered stems and is best treated as a desert cactus.

Epiphyllums have long, flattened, strap-like leaves with pronounced central veins and notched or wavy edges. During summer, large, bell-shaped flowers up to 15cm/6in wide are produced at the ends of these

Ephiphyllum 'Ackermannii'

Epiphyllum 'Clarence Wright'

stems. Invariably it is the hybrid epiphyllums which are cultivated, the species being slightly more difficult to grow. Epiphyllum hybrids can be divided into two types. The first is those with red or scarlet flowers, which can be 10-15cm/4-6in wide. The plants have triangular or flattened leaves, with wavy edges. The flowers appear during late spring and early summer, and open during the hours of daylight. *Epiphyllum* 'Ackermannii' – and other hybrids derived from it – belongs to this group.

The other type encompasses the yellow and white-flowered hybrids, which bear 10cm/4in wide flowers during late spring and early summer. They open during the evening, and many of them are sweetly scented. Although this type usually produces larger and more vigorous plants than the red and scarlet type, flowering is not so prolific.

There are many named hybrids representing both of these types, and several are illustrated here.

Euphorbia obesa
Turkish Temple/Living Baseball/Gingham Golf-ball

Height 15-25cm/6-10in
Spread 13-23cm/5-9in
Native Cape Province

Greenfinger Guide

Temperature W 7-10°C/45-50°F – it survives

Epiphyllum 'Moonlight Sonata'

Epiphyllum 'Giant Express'

Epiphyllum 'Queen Anne'

Euphorbia obesa

temperatures down to 5°C/41°F, but is better at the suggested figures. **S** 10-21°C/50-70°F

Light **W** Full light **S** Full light

Watering **W** Keep dry **S** Water freely, but ensure good drainage.

Feeding From late spring to the onset of late summer feed every week with a weak liquid fertilizer.

Humidity Mist spraying is not necessary.

Compost Four parts loam-based potting compost, two of moist peat and three of sharp grit. Alternatively, use two parts peat-based compost and one of sharp grit.

Potting In early spring, when roots fill the pot – usually every year when young. Use a deep pot, as this succulent has a long tap-root.

Propagation It does not produce offsets and therefore is raised from fresh seed sown in loam-based seed compost and placed in 24-27°C/75-80°F.

The Turkish Temple is a distinctive, spineless succulent

Euphorbia valida

Ferocactus acanthodes

with a greyish-green body which reveals a pale purple pattern. At first it is spherical, becoming cylindrical with age. During summer, minute, sweetly-scented, bell-shaped green flowers are borne at the tops of plant.

When young it is an ideal plant for a sunny windowsill, but with age needs a sun-room or greenhouse.

Euphorbia valida

Height 10-13cm/4-5in
Spread 10-15cm/4-6in – with age it broadens
Native Cape Province

Greenfinger Guide

Temperature W 7-10°C/45-50°F – it survives temperatures down to 5°C/41°F, but is better at the suggested figures. S 10-21°C/50-70°F

Light W Full light S Full light

Watering W Keep dry S Water freely, but ensure good drainage.

Feeding From late spring to the onset of late summer feed every weekwith a weak liquid fertilizer.

Humidity Mist spraying is not necessary.

Compost Four parts loam-based potting compost, two of moist peat and three of sharp grit. Alternatively, use two parts peat-based compost and one of sharp grit.

Potting In early spring, when roots fill the pot – usually every year when young.

Gasteria lilliputana

Propagation Sow seeds as soon as they are gathered from growing plants. Place in 24-27°C/75-80°F.

Euphorbia valida grows to about 30cm/1ft high in the wild, but in a pot is less vigorous. Initially it is spherical, but with age broadens. It is rarely branched and forms a neat succulent with a green body bearing eight to ten distinct ribs. Some time between late spring to late summer it develops sweetly-scented green flowers on small, woody stalks which remain for several years after the flowers fade. Some plants have male flowers, others female.

Gasteria verrucosa

summer feed every week with a weak liquid fertilizer.

Humidity Mist spraying is not necessary.

Compost Four parts loam-based potting compost, two of moist peat and three of sharp grit. Alternatively, use two parts peat-based compost and one of sharp grit. A layer of grit over the compost helps to keep the plant's base dry.

Potting In spring, when the roots fill the the pot – usually every year.

Propagation Sow seeds in loam-based seed compost in spring and place in 24-27°C/75-80°F.

California, which forms a blue-green body up to 60cm/2ft high. It seldom produces offsets when cultivated as a houseplant. Clusters of up to nine yellow spines, some 6cm/2½in long, grow from the areoles, and during early and mid-summer the plant bears 5cm/2in long, pale yellow flowers.

The Devil's Tongue (*Ferocactus latispinus*) is well known and produces clusters of sharp, deep yellow spines from the deeply indented bright green body. Eventually, this cactus produces purple-red flowers, about 36mm/1½in wide, that open in autumn.

Ferocactus horridus is a fiercely-armed cactus which does not usually grow more than 10cm/4in wide as a houseplant. It has about twelve ribs which bear reddish spines up to 5cm/2in long. The longest spine in each cluster is flattened and hooked at its tip. The yellow flowers are seldom produced on small plants.

Gasteria lilliputana

Height 5-7.5cm/2-3in
Spread 10-13cm/4-5in
Native Southern Africa

Greenfinger Guide

Temperature W 5-10°C/41-50°F – do not allow the temperature to fall below the lowest figure suggested here. S 10-18°C/50-64°F

Light W Full light S Full light

Watering W Barely moist, but if the temperature rises be prepared to apply more water.

Feeding From late spring to the onset of late summer feed every weekwith a weak liquid fertilizer.

Humidity Mist spraying is not necessary.

Compost Four parts loam-based potting compost, two of moist peat and three of sharp grit. Alternatively, use two parts peat-based compost and

Graptopetalum paraguayensis

Ferocactus acanthodes

Height 30-18cm/12-15in – but occasionally to 90cm/3ft
Spread 10-15cm/4-6in
Native Southern California

Greenfinger Guide

Temperature W 5-7°C/41-45°F S 10-21°C/50-70°F

Light W Full light S Full light

Watering W Keep dry S Water freely, but ensure good drainage and allow the compost to become dry between waterings.

Feeding From late spring to the onset of late

Ferocactus acanthodes is, in its native land, a giant cactus but in a pot is slow-growing and seldom more that 15cm/6in wide. Bright sunlight is essential for success and therefore it usually grows better in a sun-room or greenhouse than on a dull windowsill.

Initially it is spherical, but with age becomes elongated. Up to twenty-three ribs run up the glaucous-green body, with long spines growing from raised, grey and woolly areoles. The centre spine of each group is longer, red and hooked.

The 5cm/2in long, yellow flowers, borne during mid-summer, do not usually appear on young plants.

There are several other fascinating plants in this genus which are frequently grown. These include *Ferocactus melocactiformis*, also from Southern

one of sharp grit.

Potting In spring, when roots fill the pot – usually every year when young.

Propagation Divide large clumps in spring when being repotted.

Gasteria lilliputana is, like its name suggests, a diminutive plant, with 5cm/2in long, dark green leaves shaped like a keel on their undersides. They are borne in a spiral from a short stem, and attractively marked with white flecks.

Gasteria verrucosa
Ox Tongue/Warty Aloe/Wart Gasteria/Rice Gasteria

Height 13-15cm/5-6in
Spread 13-23cm/5-9in
Native South Africa

Greenfinger Guide

Temperature W 5-10°C/41-50°F – do not allow the temperature to fall below the lowest figure suggested here. S 10-18°C/50-64°F

Light W Full light S Full light

Watering W Barely moist, but if the temperature rises be prepared to give the plant more water. S Water freely, but ensure good drainage.

Feeding From late spring to the onset of late summer feed every week with a weak liquid fertilizer.

Humidity Mist spraying is not necessary.

Compost Four parts loam-based potting compost, two of moist peat and three of sharp grit. Alternatively, use two parts peat-based compost and one of sharp grit.

Potting In spring, when roots fill the pot – usually every year when young.

Propagation Divide large clumps in spring when being repotted.

Gasteria verrucosa is very distinctive, with 13-15cm/5-6in long, tapering, dark green leaves covered with white, wart-like blotches. The leaves are borne in pairs set one above another.

It is an ideal succulent plant for growing on a sunny windowsill.

Graptopetalum paraguayensis
Ghost Plant/Mother-of-Pearl Plant

Height 25-30cm/10-12in – stems initially erect, then becoming prostrate.
Spread 20-25cm/8-10in
Native Mexico

Greenfinger Guide

Temperature W 5-10°C/41-50°F S 10-27°C/50-80°F

Light W Full light S Full light

Watering W Just moist – but take care that the compost does not become dry or the plant will shrivel and be damaged. S Water freely, but ensure good drainage. Continual saturation of the compost soon causes this plant to deteriorate.

Feeding From late spring to the onset of late summer feed every week with a weak liquid fertilizer.

Humidity Do not mist spray this plant.

Compost Four parts loam-based potting compost, two of moist peat and three of sharp grit. Alternatively, use two parts peat-based compost and one of sharp grit.

Potting In spring, when roots fill the pot.

Propagation In spring, remove rosettes together with several inches of stem, allow to dry for a couple of days, and insert in the normal potting compost. Do not destroy the remains of the plant, as fresh leaves and shoots will develop from the rootstock if the compost is kept moist.

The Ghost Plant forms a miniature tree, with short stems which bear rosettes of thick, fleshy but brittle, greyish-green leaves with a silvery bloom. The rosettes of leaves first appear on long and upright stems, but later these become prostrate.

Graptopetalum filiferum, again from Mexico, is a stemless, miniature type with light green, rather greyish leaves forming rosettes about 2.5cm/1in across. Each rosette is formed of up to one-hundred leaves.

Haworthia margaritifera
Pearl Plant

Height 7.5-10cm/3-4in
Spread 13-15cm/5-6in
Native South Africa

Greenfinger Guide

Temperature W 5-10°C/41-50°F – do not allow the temperature to fall below the lowest recommended figure. S 10-21°C/50-70°F

Light W Full light S Light shade to full light

Watering W Keep dry if the lower winter temperature is given, or barely moist if slightly higher. S Keep moist, but allow the compost to dry out between waterings.

Feeding From late spring to the onset of late summer feed every week with a weak liquid fertilizer.

Humidity Mist spraying is not necessary.

Compost Four parts loam-based potting compost, two of moist peat and three of sharp grit. Alternatively, use two parts peat-based compost and one of sharp grit.

Potting In early spring, when roots fill the pot – usually every year.

Propagation Remove offsets in early summer, allow to dry and then pot up into the usual compost. Offsets are freely produced, and this is the easiest

Haworthia margaritifera

Haworthia maughanii

Kalanchoe tomentosa

way in which to increase this plant. Alternatively, sow seeds in spring in loam-based seed compost and place in 24-27°C/75-80°F.

The Pearl Plant forms a stemless rosette of curved, dark green, fleshy leaves prominently marked with white, wart-like protrubences. During mid and late summer it bears small, bell-like, greenish-white flowers at the ends of long, wiry stems.

It is an ideal plant for a sunny or slightly shaded windowsill.

Haworthia maughanii

Height 2.5cm/1in
Spread 18-25mm/0.75-1in – but forms a cluster of rosettes
Native South Africa

Greenfinger Guide

Temperature W 5-10°C/45-50°F – do not allow the temperature fall below the lowest recommended figure. **S** 10-21°C/50-70°F

Light W Full light **S** Diffused light

Watering W Keep dry if the lower winter temperature is given, or barely moist if slightly higher. **S** Keep moist, but allow the compost to dry out between waterings.

Feeding From late spring to the onset of late summer feed every week with a weak liquid fertilizer.

Humidity Mist spraying is not necessary.

Compost Four parts loam-based potting compost,

two of moist peat and three of sharp grit. Alternatively, use two parts peat-based compost and one of sharp grit.

Potting In spring, when roots fill the pot – usually every two or three years.

Propagation Sow seeds in spring in loam-based seed compost and place in 24-27°C/75-80°F.

Haworthia maughanii is a slow-growing plant with cylindrical, mid to dark green, succulent leaves that have the appearance of being sliced off. In their native dessert conditions, these sliced-off tops – with the appearance of windows – are level with the surface soil, but when cultivated this plant is best grown with the rosettes above the surface of the compost to prevent them rotting. Small, bell-like white flowers appear in late summer and early winter.

Kalanchoe tomentosa
Panda Plant/Pussy Ears/Panda Bear Plant/Plush Plant

Height 30-45cm/12-18in
Spread 20-25cm/8-10in
Native Madagascar

Greenfinger Guide

Lithops optica

Temperature W 10-13°C/50-55°F S 13-18°C/55-64°F

Light W Bright, indirect light S Bright, indirect light

Watering W Slightly moist S Water thoroughly, but allow the compost to dry out slightly between waterings.

Feeding From late spring to late summer feed every week with a weak liquid fertilizer.

Humidity No mist spraying required.

Compost Four parts loam-based potting compost, two of moist peat and three of sharp grit. Alternatively, use two parts peat-based compost and one of sharp grit.

Potting In spring, when the roots fill the pot – usually every two years.

Propagation Sow seeds in spring in loam-based seed compost with extra sharp sand added. Place in 24-27°C/76-80°F. After germination and when large enough to handle, prick off singly into small pots.

The Panda Plant creates a mass of thick and succulent leaves that, together with the stems, are densely covered with whitish hairs that create the impression of dense felt. The edges of the leaves become brown, especially

towards the rounded tips.

It is a superb plant for growing on a net-curtained windowsill, but take care not to rub the leaves as they then lose some of their attraction.

Lithops optica
Living Stone/Stoneface/Mimicry Plant/Flowering Stone

Height 18mm/0.75in
Spread 2.5-4cm/1-1½in
Native Namaqualand (South-west Africa)

Greenfinger Guide

Temperature W 5-10°C/41-50°F S 10-27°C/50-80°F

Light W Full light S Full light

Watering W Keep dry S Sparingly, but do not give any water until the old leaves have shrivelled, usually in late spring.

Feeding From late spring to the onset of late summer feed every week with a weak liquid fertilizer.

Humidity Mist spraying is not necessary.

Compost Four parts loam-based potting compost, two of moist peat and three of sharp grit.

Alternatively, use two parts peat-based compost and one of sharp grit.

Potting In spring, when roots fill the pot – usually every three years.

Propagation In early summer divide congested clumps. Alternatively, sow seeds in spring in loam-based seed compost and place in 24-27°C/75-80°F.

This Living Stone has a succulent, grey-green body with a distinctive deep cleft at its centre. During late autumn and early winter, white, daisy-like flowers are borne on short stems from the clefts.

The form *L. o. rubra* is frequently grown, and has a purplish-red body.

Lithops pseudotruncatella
Living Stone/Stoneface/Mimicry Plant/Flowering Stone

Height 30mm/1.75in
Spread 30-36mm/1.75-1½in – forms a clump
Native Namaqualand (South-west Africa)

Greenfinger Guide

Temperature W 5-10°C/41-50°F S 10-27°C/50-80°F

Light W Full light S Full light

Watering W Keep dry S Sparingly, but do not give any water until the old leaves have shrivelled, usually in late spring.

Feeding From late spring to the onset of late

Lithops pseudotruncatella

Lobivia jajoiana

summer feed every week with a weak liquid fertilizer.

Humidity Mist spraying is not necessary.

Compost Four parts loam-based potting compost, two of moist peat and three of sharp grit. Alternatively, use two parts peat-based compost and one of sharp grit.

Potting In spring, when roots fill the pot – usually every three years.

Propagation In early summer divide congested clumps. Alternatively, sow seeds during spring in loam-based seed compost and place in 24-27°C/75-80°F.

This Living Stone forms a 25-30mm/1-1¿in high, olive-green and rounded body with brown markings radiating from a central cleft. Several forms of this widely-grown succulent are grown, including *L. p. alpina*. This has a light brown body mottled with a darker brown. It has the bonus of producing yellow flowers in early summer. *L. p. mundtii* is a similar size, with a greyish-brown body marked with brown lines and green dots. It produces yellow flowers in late summer.

There are many other Living Stone plants widely available. *Lithops bella* has a pale grey body with darker markings and white flowers which appear in early autumn.

L. helmutii develops a bright green body marked with grey. It forms large clusters, and in early autumn produces golden yellow flowers. *L. lesliei* forms flat-topped bodies which vary from pinkish-grey to brownish-green. Additionally, the top of the body is attractively covered with reddish-brown markings. During summer it develops daisy-like, 2.5cm/1in wide, bright yellow flowers with pink shading on the undersides of the petals. *L. fulleri* is another popular species, with grey sides to its body and a greyish-green mottle on the top. White flowers appear in autumn.

Lobivia jajoiana
Cob Cactus

Height 10-15cm/4-5in
Spread 3.6-5cm/1½-2in
Native Northern Argentina

Greenfinger Guide

Temperature W 2-5°C/36-41°F S 10-24°F/50-75°F

Light W Full light S Full light

Watering W Keep dry S Water freely, but ensure good drainage.

Feeding From late spring to the onset of late summer feed every week with a weak liquid fertilizer.

Humidity Do not mist spray, as this may cause plants to decay.

Compost Four parts loam-based potting compost, two of moist peat and three of sharp grit. Alternatively, use two parts peat-based compost and one of sharp grit.

Potting In spring, when new growth begins, but only when roots fill the pot. This is usually when plants are young.

Propagation Lobivias are easily raised from seeds. In spring, sow seeds thinly on a well-drained compost and lightly cover with sharp sand. Water and place in 24-27°C/75-80°F. Germination takes three to four weeks. This lobivia sometimes produces offsets – although usually very few – which can be removed from spring to mid-summer and used as cuttings. Allow the cut surfaces to dry for a few days and then pressing into the normal potting compost.

Lobivia jajoiana creates an almost cylindrical green body with short, pale red and black spines.

During summer, 5cm/2in wide claret-coloured, short-lived flowers with black throats are produced.

There are many other lobivias widely offered by specialist nurseries, as well as garden centres. These include *Lobivia winteriana* and *Lobivia miniatiflora* (both illustrated here), as well as *Lobivia saltensis* with bright red, funnel-shaped flowers.

Lobivia winteriana

Lobivia miniatiflora

Mammillaria bocasana multicanata

Mammillaria bocasana
Powder Puff Cactus

Height 10-15cm/4-6in
Spread 5cm/2in – but forms a mound of rounded
cushions up to 15cm/6in wide.
Native Mexico

Greenfinger Guide

Temperature W 5-7°C/41-45°F **S** 10-21°C/
50-70°F

Light W Full sun **S** Full sun

Watering W Keep dry **S** Water freely, but ensure
good drainage and do not let water rest on or around
the cushions.

Feeding From late spring to the onset of late
summer feed every week with a weak liquid
fertilizer.

Humidity Mist spraying is not necessary.

Compost Four parts loam-based potting compost,
two of moist peat and three of sharp grit.
Alternatively, use two parts peat-based compost and
one of sharp grit.

Potting In spring, when roots fill the pot – usually
every year.

Propagation Remove offsets in summer, allow to
dry and pot up into equal parts loam-basedseed
compost and sharp sand. Alternatively, sow seeds in
loam-basedseed compost in spring and place in 24-
27°C/75-80°F.

Mammillaria bocasana

The Powder Puff Cactus is an easily-grown cactus, forming rounded, dark green cushions covered with silky hairs and white spines. During mid-summer it bears 12mm/½in wide, bell-shaped, creamy-yellow flowers, with a brown stripe down the centre of each petal. *Mammillaria bocasana multicanata* is illustrated here, while another attractive one is *M. b. splendens*, covered with fine, white hairs.

This is an undemanding plant, ideal for a sunny windowsill.

The range of mammillaria species is extensive, with specialist nurseries often offering more than twenty-five different species.

Mammillaria densispina

Height 10-15cm/4-6in
Spread 7.5-15cm/3-6in
Native Mexico

Mammillaria densispina is a slow-growing cactus with a rounded, dark green body densely covered with yellow and brown spines. During summer it bears purplish-red flowers which open to a bell-shape.

It is an easily-grown species for displaying on a sunny windowsill.

Mammillaria zeilmanniana
Rose Pincushion Cactus

Height 5cm/2in
Spread 5-6cm/2-2½in – forms a cluster
Native Mexico

Mammillaria zeilmanniana forms a cylindrical, pale green and glossy body which forms a multi-headed clump. The body is covered with tufts of fine, white hairs. During mid-summer, long-lasting, reddish flowers about 18mm/—in wide and freely produced. The form 'Alba' is also attractive, with white flowers.

Mammillaria gracilis

Height 5cm/2in
Spread 5cm/2in – but forming a cluster
Native Mexico

Mammillaria gracilis has a somewhat slender, cylindrical, bright green body with a branching habit at its top. The plant's body is attractively covered with spines, some short and white and other long and tipped in brown. White, bell-shaped flowers appear in summer.

Eventually, this cactus forms a large, rounded clump in the wild and when planted in a cacti garden in a large greenhouse.

Notocactus graessneri
Ball Cactus

Height 10-13cm/4-5in
Spread 10-13cm/4-5in
Native Southern Brazil

209

Mammillaria zeilmanniana

Mammillaria gracilis

Notocactus graessneri

Greenfinger Guide
Temperature W 5-10°C/41-50°F – do not allow the temperature to fall below these recommended figures. **S** 10-24°C/50-75°F

Light W Full light **S** Full light

Watering W Keep dry, but if the temperature is higher than that suggested, light watering may be necessary. **S** Water freely, but ensure good drainage and do not allow water to rest on or around the plant.

Feeding From late spring to late summer feed every week with a weak liquid fertilizer.

Humidity Mist spraying is not necessary.

Compost Four parts loam-based potting compost, two of moist peat and three of sharp grit. Alternatively, use two parts peat-based compost and one of sharp grit.

Potting In spring, when roots fill the pot – usually every year when young.

Propagation Sow seeds in loam-based seed compost in spring and place in 24-27°C/75-80°F.

Notocactus graessneri has a pale green, somewhat globular body with a flattened top. It is covered with yellow spines, and from early to late summer bears 18mm/0.75in wide, greenish-yellow flowers.

Notocactus leninghausii
Golden Ball Cactus

Height 18-25cm/7-10in in a pot, but can reach 90cm/3ft when planted in a border in a conservatory or greenhouse.
Spread 8-13cm/3½-5in
Native Southern Brazil

Greenfinger Guide

Temperature W 5-10°C/41-50°F – do not allow the temperature to fall below the lowest figure recommended here. **S** 10-24°C/50-75°F

Light W Full light **S** Full light

Watering W Keep dry, but if the temperature is higher than that suggested, light watering may be necessary. **S** Water freely, but ensure good drainage.

Feeding From late spring to late summer feed every week with a weak liquid fertilizer.

Humidity Mist spraying is not necessary.

Compost Four parts loam-based potting compost, two of moist peat and three of sharp grit. Alternatively, use two parts peat-based compost and one of sharp grit.

Potting In spring, when roots fill the pot -usually every year when young.

Propagation Sow seeds in loam-based seed compost in spring and place in 24-27°C/75-80°F. Plants that become excessively tall indoors can

Notocactus leninghausii

have their top 10-15cm/4-6in cut off in early summer, the cut surface allowed to dry and then inserted in a sandy compost.

The Golden Ball Cactus is slow-growing, initially globular but after about three years adopts a cylindrical stance to its pale green body, with about thirty ribs which bear a mixture of pale yellow and golden-yellow spines. From early to late summer it produces funnel-shaped, 5cm/2in wide, bright yellow flowers.

It is an ideal cactus for introducing height into a collection of cacti, and when young is superb for growing on a sunny windowsill. With age it is best grown in a sun-room or greenhouse.

Opuntia microdasys
Bunny Ears/Prickly Pear/Rabbit's Ears/Yellow Bunny Ears/Goldplush Plant

Height 25-30cm/10-12in when grown in a pot. Up to 90cm/3ft when planted in a border in a conservatory or greenhouse.

Spread 15-20cm/6-8in when grown in a pot – slightly wider when in a conservatory or greenhouse.

Native Mexico

Greenfinger Guide

Temperature W 7-13°C/45-55°F – do not allow the temperature to fall below the lowest figure suggested here. **S** 13-27°C/55-80°F

Light W Full light **S** Full light

Watering W Slightly moist **S** Water freely, but ensure good drainage

Feeding From late spring to the onset of late summer feed every week with a weak liquid fertilizer.

Humidity Mist spraying is not necessary.

Compost Four parts loam-based potting compost, two of moist peat and three of sharp grit. Alternatively, use two parts peat-based compost and one of sharp grit.

Potting In spring, when the roots fill the pot – usually every year when the plant is young.

Propagation Remove some of the younger pads during mid-summer, allow the cut surfaces to dry and then pot up in a loam-based potting compost No. 2 with extra sharp sand. Alternatively, sow seeds in loam-based seed compost in spring. However, germination is slow because the coat of the seed is hard – prior to sowing, soak the seeds in water for twenty-four hours. Place the sown seeds in 24-27°C/75-80°F.

The Bunny Ears is probably the most popular and widely grown of all opuntias, forming a much-branched plant with many beautiful bright green pads which are really flattened stems. These pads do not have spines, but are dotted with attractive tufts of yellow, barbed bristles. In the wild plants produce yellow flowers, but in cultivation these are seldom seen. Several attractive forms are grown, with reddish or white clusters of

Opuntia microdasys

Opuntia scheerii

bristles.

There are several species and varieties of this cactus. The form 'Albatus', sometimes called 'Angel's Wings', is particularly attractive and does not have a prickly nature. *Opuntia microdasys albispina* has the advantage of being slow-growing, while *O. m. minima* is a naturally small form, with pads about 5cm/2in long. *O. m. rufida* and *O. m. pallida* are two further attractive forms.

Opuntia scheerii
Prickly Pear

Height 60-90cm/2-3ft – but in its native country

has tree-like proportions

Spread 20-38cm/10-15in – but in its native country has a much wider spread

Native Mexico

Greenfinger Guide

Temperature W 7-13°C/45-55°F S 13-27°C/55-80°F

Light W Full light S Full light

Watering W Keep dry S Water freely, but ensure good drainage and do not keep the compost continually wet.

Feeding From late spring to the onset of late

summer feed every week with a weak liquid fertilizer.

Humidity Mist spraying is not necessary.

Compost Four parts loam-based potting compost two of moist peat and three of sharp grit. Alternatively, use two parts peat-based compost and one of sharp grit.

Potting In spring, when roots fill the pot – usually every year when the plant is young.

Propagation Remove pads during mid-summer, allow the cut surfaces to dry and then pot up into loam-based potting compost with extra sand. Alternatively, sow seeds in loam-based seed compost in spring. However, germination is slow because the coat of the seed is hard – prior to sowing, soak the seeds in water for twenty-four hours. Place the sown seeds in 24-27°C/75-80°F.

Opuntia scheerii is a slow-growing species which adapts well to cultivation in a pot. The bluish-green, somewhat oblong and flat pads, about 15cm/6in long and 5cm/2in wide, are covered with golden spines and yellowish-brown barbed bristles.

Pachyphytum oviferum
Sugared Almond Plant/Moonstone Plant

Height 15-20cm/6-8in
Spread 13-15cm/5-6in
Native Mexico

Greenfinger Guide

Temperature **W** 5-10°C/41-50°F **S** 10-27°F/50-80°F

Light **W** Full light **S** Full light – strong light is essential to encourage the attractive, mealy coating on the leaves.

Watering **W** Barely moist, just enough to prevent the compost becoming dry. It is essential that the plant should not shrivel through lack of moisture.

S Water freely, but ensure good drainage.

Feeding From late spring to late summer feed every week with a weak liquid fertilizer.

Humidity Do not mist spray this plant, as water which falls on the leaves will impair their appearance.

Compost Four parts loam-based potting compost, two of moist peat and three of sharp grit. Alternatively, use two parts peat-based compost and one of sharp grit.

Potting In spring, when roots fill the pot.

Propagation Plants usually lose their lower leaves until a cluster remains at the top, forming a rosette. At this stage, the rosette and piece of stem can be cut off in spring, the cut surface allowed to dry for a couple of days and then inserted into the normal potting compost. Do not destroy the leafless base of the plant, as if kept evenly moist – not waterlogged – new rosettes of leaves will develop on it.

The Sugared Almond Plant is a small, shrubby plant with fat and rounded leaves covered with a silvery-white bloom and clustered around a sturdy stem. During winter, progressively the lower leaves shrivel. These are best removed, as if left tend to encourage the presence of diseases. Eventually, a rosette of leaves is left at the top of the plant.

During spring, white, bell-like flowers appear on short stalks above the leaves.

Rebuntia kupperiana
Crown Cactus

Height 3.6-5cm/1½-2in
Spread 3.6-5cm/1½-2in – eventually forms a clump 10-13cm/4-5in wide.
Native Bolivia

Greenfinger Guide

Temperature **W** 5-10°C/41-50°F **S** 10-21°C/50-70°F

Light **W** Full light **S** Full light, but light shade from the strongest sunlight is usually welcome.

Watering **W** Barely moist, just enough water to prevent the compost becoming bone dry. **S** Water freely, but ensure good drainage and allow the compost to dry out slightly between waterings.

Feeding From late spring to the onset of late summer feed everyweek with a weak liquid fertilizer.

Humidity Mist spraying is not necessary.

Compost Four parts loam-based potting compost,

Pachyphytum oviferum

two of moist peat and three of sharp grit. Alternatively, use two parts peat-based compost and one of sharp grit.

Potting In spring, when roots fill the pot – usually every year when young.

Propagation Sow seeds in loam-based seed compost in spring and place in 24-27°C/75-80°F.

Rebuntia kupperiana is formed of a reddish-green body, covered with white spines with copper-coloured tips. During late spring and early summer it produces 2.5-3.6cm/1-1½in wide orange-red flowers.

Feeding From late spring to the onset of late summer feed every week with a weak liquid fertilizer.

Humidity Mist spraying is not necessary.

Compost Four parts loam-based potting compost, two of moist peat and three of sharp grit. Alternatively, use two parts peat-based compost and one of sharp grit.

Potting In spring, when roots fill the pot – usually every year when young.

Propagation Sow seeds in loam-based seed compost in spring and place in 24-27°C/75-80°F.

Greenfinger Guide

Temperature W 13-16°C/55-61°F – it survives temperatures down to 5°C/41°F if the compost is kept dry. **S** 16-24°C/61-75°F

Light W Full light **S** Full light

Watering W Barely moist **S** Water thoroughly, allowing the compost to become dry before giving further applications

Feeding From late spring to late summer feed every week with a weak liquid fertilizer.

Humidity No mist spraying is needed.

Compost Four parts loam-based potting compost,

Rebuntia senilis

Rebuntia senilis
Fire-crown Cactus/Crown Cactus

Height 7.5-10cm/3-4in
Spread 7.5cm/3in – but eventually forms a cushion-like clump 25-30cm/10-12in wide.
Native Argentina

Greenfinger Guide

Temperature W 5-10°C/41-50°F **S** 10-21°C/50-70°F

Light W Full light **S** Full light, but light shade from the strongest sunlight is usually welcome.

Watering W Barely moist, just enough water to prevent the compost becoming bone dry. **S** Water freely, but ensure good drainage and allow the compost to dry out slightly between waterings.

Rebuntia senilis is a superb cactus for a sunny windowsill. The pale green, spherical stem is depressed at its top and densely covered with silvery-white, bristly spines. During spring and mid-summer it displays funnel-shaped, 18mm/0.75in wide, carmine-red flowers with white throats. They appear in a ring around the plant's body, attractively contrasting with the white spines.

Sansevieria trifasciata
Mother-in-law's Tongue/Snake Plant/Devil's-tongue/Bowstring Hemp/Good Luck Plant/Hemp Plant

Height 38-45cm/15-18in
Spread 15-20cm/6-8in
Native West Africa

two of moist peat and three of sharp grit. Alternatively, use two parts peat-based compost and one of sharp grit.

Potting Established plants are best left alone, until the pot is completely packed with roots. Then, repot in spring.

Propagation Divide large and congested plants in spring. This is the best way to increase variegated forms. All-green types can be increased by cutting mature leaves into 5-6cm/2-2½in long pieces in summer. Insert these to half their depth in equal parts moist peat and sharp sand. Place in 21°C/70°F. Variegated forms increased by cuttings do not produced variegated plants.

The Mother-in-law's Tongue is a very distinctive succulent plant, with upright, sword-shaped, sharply-

Feeding From mid-spring to the onset of late summer feed every week with a weak liquid fertilizer.

Humidity Mist spraying is not necessary.

Compost Four parts loam-based potting compost, two of moist peat and three of sharp grit. Alternatively, use two parts peat-based compost and one of sharp grit.

Potting In spring, when roots fill the pot – usually every year when plants are young.

Propagation Sow seeds in spring in a sandy compost and place in 24-27°C/75-80°F. The individual succulent leaves often fall off the plant and root on surrounding compost. These can be potted up into small pots. Individual leaves can also be removed during summer and inserted into sandy compost. Place the whole pot of leaf-cuttings in a plastic bag and when small shoots appear, pot them up in small pots.Congested plants can also be divided in spring when being repotted.

The Donkey's Tail is ideal for growing in an indoor hanging-basket. The thick, trailing stems are clustered with succulent, fleshy, pointed, grey-green leaves, up to 18mm/–in long, which are more dense towards the ends of the stems. The leaves are also covered with a whitish bloom. From mid to late summer, pale pink flowers are borne in clusters at the ends of the stems – but only on large and mature plants.

Sedum sieboldii
October Daphne/October Plant

Height 5-7.5cm/2-3in
Spread 23-38cm/9-15in – then cascading
Native Japan

Greenfinger Guide

Temperature W 7-10°C/45-50°F – it survives temperatures down to 5°C/41°F, but is happier at a few degrees higher. S 10-18°C/50-64°F

Light W Full light S Full light

Watering W Barely moist S Water freely, but

Sansevieria trifasciata

Sedum morganianum

tipped, dark green leaves with mottled, greyish-white bands. A more attractive form is *Sansevieria trifasciata* 'Laurentii', with leaves beautifully edged in creamy-yellow.

The Bird's Nest Sansevieria, *Sansevieria trifasciata* 'Hahnii' creates a nest of 15cm/6in high, triangular and spirally arranged, deep green leaves with lighter cross-banding. This plant is frequently sold under the name *Sansevieria hahnii*. There is a beautiful golden-leaved form of this plant, with broad yellow stripes along the leaves, revealing a green centre.

All of these sansevierias are ideal for brightening a windowsill or a table in bright sunlight.

Sedum morganianum
Donkey's Tail/Beaver-tail/Burro's Tail/Horse's Tail/Lamb's Tail

Height 2.5-5cm/1-2in – then cascading
30-60cm/1-2ft
Spread 15-30cm/6-12in
Native Mexico

Greenfinger Guide

Temperature W 7-10°C/45-50°F – it survives temperatures down to 5°C/41°F, but is happier at a few degrees higher. S 10-18°C/50-64°F

Light W Full light S Full light

Watering W Barely moist S Water freely, but ensure good drainage and allow the compost to become dry between waterings.

Sedum sieboldii 'Medio-variegatum'

ensure good drainage and allow the compost to become slightly dry between waterings.

Feeding From mis-spring to the onset of late summer feed every week with a weak liquid fertilizer.

Humidity Mist spraying is not necessary.

Compost Four parts loam-based potting compost, two of moist peat and three of sharp grit. Alternatively, use two parts peat-based compost and one of sharp grit.

Potting In spring, when roots fill the pot – usually every year when plants are young.

Propagation Sow seeds in spring in a sandy compost and place in 24-27°C/75-80°F. Alternatively, divide congested plants in spring when being repotted.

Sedum sieboldii is an eye-catching succulent plant, with long, spreading stems that bear sparsely-arranged, rounded leaves that almost encircle the stems. These leaves are first grey-blue but slowly change to brownish-green with a tinge of red around the edges. In early autumn, it produces 5-7.5cm/2-3in wide clusters of pink flowers at the ends of the stems.

The variegated form, 'Medio-variegatum', is widely grown, slightly smaller and with greyish leaves splashed with creamy-white.

Both of these plants can be grown in indoor hanging-baskets, but especially the variegated form.

In addition to the three previously mentioned sedum, there are many other fascinating species which are grown as houseplants. These include the Jelly Bean Plant (*Sedum pachyphyllum*), a shrubby plant which grows to about 25cm/10in high and about the same in width. It is also known as Many Fingers, which aptly describes the succulent, club-shaped, 2.5cm/1in long pale green leaves with red tips which cluster around the stiff stems. During early and mid-spring it produces yellow flowers in flat clusters up to 7.5cm/3in wide.

Sedum allantoides from Mexico is a slow-growing succulent, eventually reaching 30cm/12in high and with prostrate stems which bear club-shaped, glaucous-grey leaves. During late spring to early summer it produces greenish-white flowers. The Golden Sedum (*Sedum adolphi*) and *Sedum bellum* are other plants with club-shaped leaves.

Senecio citriformis

Height 7.5-10cm/3-4in
Spread 20-30cm/8-12in
Native Southern Africa

Greenfinger Guide

Temperature W 10-13°C/50-55°F – it survives temperatures down to 5°C/41°F, but is happier at a few degrees higher. S 13-18°C/55-64°F – take care that it does not go higher than 21°C/70°F.

Light W Full light S Full light

Watering W Just moist S Water freely, but ensure good drainage.

Feeding From mid-spring to the onset of late summer feed every week with a weak liquid fertilizer.

Humidity Mist spraying is not necessary.

Compost Four parts loam-based potting compost, two of moist peat and three of sharp grit. Alternatively, use two parts peat-based compost and one of sharp grit.

Propagation During mid-summer take stem cuttings, inserting them in equal parts moist peat and sharp sand.

Senecio citriformis is a shrubby, branching succulent with a tuft of fleshy stems which bear lemon-shaped, bluish-grey leaves covered with whitish, waxy dust. The plant has the bonus of developing yellowish-white flowers in early winter.

Senecio rowleyanus
String-of-Beads

Height 5cm/2in
Spread 15-25cm/6-10in – then trailing for up to 90cm/3ft.

Senecio citriformis

Senecio rowleyanus

Native South-west Africa

Greenfinger Guide

Temperature **W** 10-13°C/50-55°F – it survives temperatures down to 5°C/41°F, but is happier at a few degrees higher. **S** 13-18°C/55-64°F – take care that it does not go higher than 21°C/70°F.

Light **W** Full light **S** Full light

Watering **W** Just moist **S** Water freely, but ensure good drainage.

Feeding From mid-spring to the onset of late summer feed every week with a weak liquid fertilizer.

Humidity Mist spraying is not necessary.

Compost Four parts loam-based potting compost, two of moist peat and three of sharp grit.

Alternatively, use two parts peat-based compost and one of sharp grit.

Potting In spring, when roots fill the pot.

Propagation Divide congested plants in spring, when being repotted.

The String-of-Beads plant is an unusual trailing plant, ideal for growing in an indoor hanging-basket or a pot positioned at the edge of a high shelf. Initially it is mat-forming, creating a wealth of long, slender but fleshy stems freely covered with small, round, glossy green leaves which very much resemble beads.

From late summer to early autumn it bears sweetly-scented white flowers with rich purple stigmas.

picture index

CACTI AND SUCCULENTS

ACKNOWLEDGEMENTS

The publishers would like to express their grateful thanks to all the many individuals and organisations who provided invaluable advice and assistance throughout the preparation of this book. Special thanks are due to the following:

Barnsfold Nurseries, Tismans Common, Sussex

Chessington Nurseries – Des Whitwell, Daphne, Ian and Wayne

Clarke and Spiers, Ripley, Surrey – Keith Francis, Rosalind Reeves,
Felicity Wilcox and Douglas Hammond

Hollygate Cactus Nursery, Ashington, Sussex – Terry Hewitt

Plumpton Horticultural College, Plumpton, Sussex

Secrett Garden Centre, Milford, Surrey – Robert and Gill Secrett, and Jane Barney

Allan Smith Nurseries, Titchfield, Hants – Alland and June Smith

Vesutor Air Plants, Billingshurst, Sussex

S. C. Glass of Horsham, Sussex

Hand modelling by Angela Taylor, Diana Letts and Fiona Sutherland.